The Structure
of
British Industry

The Structure
of
British Industry

Second Edition

Edited by
Peter Johnson

Department of Economics,
University of Durham

London
UNWIN HYMAN
Boston   Sydney   Wellington

Published by the Academic Division of
Unwin Hyman Ltd
15/17 Broadwick Street, London W1V 1FP, UK

Allen & Unwin Inc.,
8 Winchester Place, Winchester, Mass. 01890, USA

Allen & Unwin (Australia) Ltd,
8 Napier Street, North Sydney, NSW 2060, Australia

Allen & Unwin (New Zealand) Ltd in association with the
Port Nicholson Press Ltd,
60 Cambridge Terrace, Wellington, New Zealand

First published in 1988

British Library Cataloguing in Publication Data
The structure of British industry. – 2nd ed.
1. Great Britain – Industries
I. Johnson, P. S.
338.0941   HC256.6
ISBN 0–04–338146–4

Library of Congress Cataloging in Publication Data
The structure of British industry
edited by Peter Johnson. – 2nd ed.
p.   cm.
Includes index.
ISBN 0–04–338146–4 (alk. paper)
1. Great Britain – Industries.   I. Johnson, P. S.
HC256.6.S76 1988
338.0941 – dc 1987–18803 CIP

Set in 10 on 11 point Times by Columns of Reading
and printed in Great Britain by Biddles of Guildford

Contents

Preface to the Second Edition

This edition, like the first, is designed to meet two objectives. First, it provides sixteen chapter-length studies on a wide range of industries. Each chapter is intended as an authoritative source of reference on the main structural, behavioural and performance characteristics of the industry in question, and as a starting point for further study. Secondly, the book offers illustrative material for use in those courses in higher education and elsewhere whose contents relate to industrial activity. Thus, for example, a discussion on pricing in industry would be able to draw on most of the chapters for case-study material.

Two factors determined the coverage of the book. The first was the desire to cover as wide a spectrum of industrial characteristics as possible. Hence declining and expanding, 'traditional' and 'science-based', private and nationalized, capital- and labour-intensive industries are analysed. The production of both goods and services is included. The second consideration was the need to find someone able and willing to write each chapter.

Inevitably the particular selection of industries given in this book will be the subject of criticism. It is a very easy task to suggest other industries that might have been included. However, given the factors mentioned in the previous paragraph, and the constraints imposed by the economics of publishing (as seen by the publisher!) the industries chosen do represent a reasonably balanced and wide-ranging picture of industrial characteristics. Nearly 40 per cent of employees in employment in Great Britain are accounted for by the industries covered in this book. This percentage assumes that employment in information technology, the subject of Chapter 7, is limited to labour utilized in the production of relevant hardware. As that chapter shows, however, nearly 40 per cent of total employment may be classified as being in 'information-related' occupations.

Most of the chapters are listed in the order in which the relevant industries appear in the 1980 Standard Industrial Classification (SIC). The chapter on North Sea oil and gas, however, precedes the chapter on coal because the former also contains some information on the energy sector as a whole. Information technology does of course impinge on the activities of a wide range of industries and is not separately identified in the SIC. It has nevertheless been located in the position occupied by data processing and telecommunications in the SIC as it is these industries that supply a significant proportion of the relevant equipment. It is perhaps appropriate that consideration of information technology is now at the centre of a book on British industries. Tourism, the last chapter in this book, also straddles a number of industries.

There have been so many changes in British industry since the first edition was published in 1980 that most of the chapters have had to be extensively revised or rewritten. In addition the coverage of the book has changed. Brian Hill has contributed a chapter on agriculture, an important omission from the first edition. Paul Stoneman has replaced his chapter on computers with a more wide-ranging one on information technology. I have extended the coverage of transport with a chapter on domestic air transport. There have also been some changes in personnel. Danny Hann has collaborated with Colin Robinson on North Sea oil and gas. Nicholas Wells has revised Duncan Reekie's chapter on pharmaceuticals. (Although Nicholas is Associate Director of the Office of Health Economics, a body financed by the pharmaceutical industry, he has nevertheless written in a personal capacity.) The chapter on synthetic fibres is now the joint work of Richard Shaw and Paul Simpson. Stuart Eliot has substantially rewritten the chapter on retailing. Finally, I found myself – rather late in the day – contributing the tourism chapter.

All contributors were asked to follow, where appropriate, a common structure–conduct–performance (s–c–p) approach for their studies. Despite reservations that a number of writers have expressed about the use of the s–c–p framework for analytical purposes (some of which were discussed in the Introduction to the first edition), this framework nevertheless remains a very useful device for ordering the discussion of key industrial characteristics.

To ensure a consistent level of exposition throughout the book, contributors were asked to assume that the reader's knowledge of economics did not extend beyond that contained in a first-year university 'Elements' course. Contributors were free to express their own views on the industry about which they were writing. No editorial control was exercised in this respect. As a result a variety of views on topics such as nationalization and government intervention in industrial affairs is expressed. The views of individual contributors are not necessarily shared by anyone else.

As editor my first acknowledgement must once again be to the contributors. It has been a pleasure to work with them on this venture. I am also grateful to Julie Bushby and Kathryn Cowton who undertook much of the typing work at the Durham end, and to a number of publishers who have kindly granted permission for material in which they hold the copyright to be reproduced in this book. Full acknowledgement is given in the text. Crown copyright material is used with the permission of the Controller of Her Majesty's Stationery Office.

Peter Johnson
Durham

Chapter One

Agriculture

BRIAN HILL

1.1 INTRODUCTION

According to official estimates for 1985 agriculture contributes about 2 per cent of UK GDP, its share of gross fixed capital formation is 2.1 per cent and it employs 2.6 per cent of 'total civilian manpower engaged in all occupations' (Ministry of Agriculture, Fisheries and Food, 1986a). These figures must be treated with some caution; although the GDP figure values output at market prices, these are artificially raised to levels far above world prices (see Section 1.4), and the employment figure is just over 2.2 per cent if manpower in agriculture is expressed as a percentage of civilian manpower including the unemployed. Even if the official figures exaggerating the importance of agriculture are accepted, this industry is exceptionally small in the UK compared with other industrialized countries: see Table 1.1.

Agriculture has a unique place in economic development. Initially it is the major, indeed almost the only, economic activity occupying the labour force, largely as subsistence producers. (This is still the situation in less developed countries today.) Gradually, due to

Table 1.1 *Agriculture in Industrialized Countries, 1982*

	Share of GDP % (1)	Share of labour % (2)	Relative income $\frac{(1)}{(2)} \times 100$
Belgium	2.3	3.0	77
West Germany	2.2	5.5	40
France	4.2	8.2	51
Italy	5.8	12.4	47
Netherlands	4.3	5.0	86
United Kingdom	1.7	2.7	63
Sweden	2.8	5.6	50
USA	2.6	3.6	72
Japan	3.6	9.7	37

Source: Statistical Office of the European Communities, *Eurostat Review*, 1975–84.

improvements in labour productivity, a decreasing proportion of the population can produce sufficient food to feed the whole population, thus permitting an outflow of labour from agriculture. The surplus of labour in agriculture is reallocated to other sectors by the price mechanism – earnings in agriculture are necessarily lower than elsewhere. Concomitant with increasing labour productivity is increasing land productivity, and the extra output causes the price of food to fall in real terms. Falling relative returns to agricultural resources are a normal consequence of economic development, but in the twentieth century low incomes in agriculture have become regarded as a social evil, and much government intervention has aimed to raise farmers' incomes. The methods currently employed in the UK, and their consequences, are outlined in Section 1.4 below.

In some respects agriculture may be seen as virtually perfectly competitive. In the UK there are 231,000 farms, each of which is extremely small in relation to total output, and each farm product is homogeneous. This atomistic structure means that farmers are price-takers. There is freedom of entry and exit, though many resources – most notably land and labour – are not perfectly mobile. Producers are generally well informed about techniques of production, but lack knowledge in many other areas. Thus, when production costs are incurred it is in ignorance of the actual yields and prices to be obtained in the future. Indeed in production processes which are essentially biological and peculiarly subject to the influence of the weather considerable uncertainty exists.

Characteristically farm firms are family-based with the farmer acting as combined entrepreneur, manager and labour force, and with the farm being both the workplace and dwelling. Only a small minority of farmers hire regular full-time employees. In Great Britain 70 per cent of farms were wholly or mainly owner-occupied in 1985. The remaining 30 per cent were tenanted and these were larger on average since they accounted for 39 per cent of the land area. In Northern Ireland virtually all farms are owner-occupied (MAFF, 1986a, p. 2).

Farms are invariably multi-product firms, for three reasons. First, farm products are always joint products. For example, milk cannot be produced without simultaneously producing beef, hides and manure; similarly grain production necessarily results also in straw. Second, many products are interrelated (for details see Hill and Ingersent, 1982), most notably through crop rotations whereby a variety of different crops follow each other on the same area of land year by year in 'rotation'. These rotations prevent the build-up of pests and diseases affecting a particular crop, harness the beneficial effects of some crops upon the yields of others, largely by improving the soil structure; and ensure that the mix of activities will keep the resources – particularly labour and machinery – fully occupied through the year. The final reason why farms are multi-product firms relates to uncertainty. Farm products are peculiarly subject to output variation due to the effect of pests, diseases and weather; market price variation may also be substantial. So to reduce income variation most farmers avoid 'putting all their eggs in one basket'. There are however some 'specialist' farms, where one particular product dominates revenue. Such farms reflect either limited product opportunities, for example, ·hill sheep farms, or a main product having a low revenue variance. Milk which has a relatively stable yield and an unusually stable price (due to government intervention) is the main example here.

British agriculture is a very capital-intensive industry. In December 1985 the total capital employed was estimated to be £64 billion, of which land represented £45 billion (Pettitt, 1986). Dividing total capital by total agricultural employment (that is, including all farmers and workers whether full or part time) of 616,000 (MAFF, 1986a, p. 14) gives a figure of £73,000 per person. The net product of agriculture in 1985 was £4 billion of which £3.76 billion was the return to labour (taking the opportunity cost of farmers' labour to be the income of general farm labourers). So the return to capital was less than 0.4 per cent.

In 1985 the £12 billion revenue of agriculture included large subsidies and an even larger element of consumer transfer (money transferred to farmers via prices raised above free market levels, see Section 1.4.1 below). Direct public expenditure on the support of agriculture in 1985/6 (April/March financial year) was forecast to be £2,215 million. This contrasts sharply with forecast farming income (that is, 'the return to farmers and spouses for their labour, management skills and own capital invested after providing for depreciation'), for 1985 of £1,154 million (MAFF, 1986a, pp. 39, 47). This is only the second time that public expenditure has exceeded farming income, the previous occasion being 1983, but the growth rate of public expenditure now greatly exceeds that of farming income and these trends seem set to continue. Another indication of economic ills afflicting the industry is the rapid increase in its debt-to-income ratio since 1979; during the 1970s this ratio was at or near to unity, but between 1979 and 1985 it increased to exceed 4 (Craig *et al.*, 1986, p. 43). Also during this period depreciation has generally exceeded gross fixed capital investment, that is, investment has been insufficient to keep the capital stock intact. Land prices have been falling in money terms since 1985, and in real terms since 1979, and as land accounts for more than half of the assets of UK agriculture this has helped to cause a decline in net worth. Between its peak in 1979, and 1985 the net worth of UK agriculture has declined by 40 per cent (MAFF, 1986b, pp. 52–3).

Table 1.2 shows that UK agriculture is dominated by livestock and livestock products, which account for about 60 per cent of total revenue. Cows' milk is the single most important product, closely followed by fat cattle and calves, so altogether cattle contribute more than one-third of total output. England and Wales together produce

Table 1.2 *Structure of Agricultural Output by Value, UK*

	Current prices £ million	
	1984	1985 (forecast)
Farm crops:		
Wheat	1,447.2	1,432.0
Barley	946.8	850.3
Potatoes	578.4	308.2
Sugar beet	243.7	232.6
Oilseed rape	253.8	244.5
Other	154.3	167.6
Total crops	3,624.2	3,235.2
Horticulture:		
Vegetables, fruit, flowers, shrubs	1,251.7	1,240.4
Livestock:		
Fat cattle and calves	1,938.1	1,919.3
Fat sheep and lambs	557.4	589.9
Fat pigs	994.0	978.5
Poultry	673.5	708.0
Other	94.1	104.5
Total livestock	4,257.1	4,300.2
Livestock products:		
Milk	2,297.1	2,351.7
Eggs	553.5	530.4
Other	113.9	123.1
Total livestock products	2,964.5	3,005.2
Total output	12,097.5	11,781.0

Note: output is measured as revenue
Source: MAFF, 1986c, pp. 1, 2.

more than 80 per cent of total UK revenue, livestock and livestock products being about 58 per cent. Scotland contributes some 13 per cent of output of which livestock and livestock products are about 70 per cent. The latter category accounts for well over 90 per cent of revenue in Northern Ireland, but this country's share of UK revenue is less than 4 per cent.

1.2 PRODUCTION

1.2.1 Structure

In the UK the farm unit in official statistics is termed a 'holding'. A full agricultural census has been conducted annually since 1866, and although many of the original holdings have now been amalgamated farmers often continue to fill in separate census forms for two or more holdings long after they have become one farm. Despite Ministry of Agriculture efforts to remove this source of distortion it has been estimated that there are probably about 10 per cent fewer farm businesses than holdings enumerated (Britton *et al.*, 1980). Since the number of farms in the UK is unknown, the number of holdings must be used as a reasonably close proxy.

Measuring holding (farm) size is surprisingly difficult. Traditionally the land area was used as a basis, but this can be very misleading – a hectare of high yielding land in Lincolnshire is a very different unit to a hectare of rough grazing in the Pennines, for example. One way of measuring farm businesses is by labour input. The standard labour inputs for each activity on a farm can be aggregated to give a measure in terms of standard man-days. Some 250 standard man-days (smd) of 8 hours each, are taken to constitute employment for one man for one year. This method of measurement gives the business size in terms of the number of ('standard') men a farm might employ.

Table 1.3(a) indicates that more than half of UK holdings appear to provide less than enough work to occupy one man fully, but it must be remembered that this results from applying 'modern efficient' labour standards to all farms and many may well not use the standard methods. Thus many of these smaller 'part-time' businesses occupy a farmer full time, and sometimes some family or hired assistance also. The table shows that in terms of both size of business and area, there has been a decline in the numbers of holdings of all sizes except the largest, and that the decline is most marked in the smallest holdings. This reflects opportunities for economies of size, discussed below.

Table 1.4 provides further details of holdings having 250 or more smd. These holdings, which are very slowly increasing in both number

Table 1.3 *Number and Size of Holdings in UK, 1975 and 1985*

	(a)			(b)		
Size of business (standard man-days)	No. of holdings ('000)		Crops & grass area (hectares)	No. of holdings ('000)		
	1975	1985*			1975	1985*
Under 250	138.0	127.9	0.1–19.9	119.9	94.7	
250–499	56.4	42.0	20–49.9	73.2	64.3	
500–999	45.8	40.5	50–99.9	41.7	41.4	
1000 and over	28.3	29.8	100 and over	29.3	31.0	
Total	268.6	240.3	Total	264.1	231.4	

*provisional
Note: the 'size of business' measure includes some holdings which have too small an area to be included in the second half of the table.
Sources: MAFF, 1978, 1986a.

Table 1.4   *Holdings of 250 Standard Man-Days and over*

	1975	1985
Average size of business (smd)	857	928
Average total area per holding (hectares)	111.3	124.5
Estimated contribution to production (%)	90.2	90.5

Source: Statistical Office of the European Communities, *Eurostat Review*, 1975–84.

and size, account for fewer than half the total but contribute more than 90 per cent of total output. The corollary is that more than half the holdings supply less than 10 per cent of output. This very great disparity in output is reflected in the similar disparity in incomes discussed later.

As one would expect, the disparity in size of holdings is paralleled by disparities in the full-time employed labour force. Table 1.5 shows that three-quarters of all holdings have no full-time regular employees. Fifty-two per cent of full-time regular employees work in small groups of 1 to 3 persons, whilst the remaining 48 per cent are employed on less than 5 per cent of the holdings.

The regular whole-time labour force discussed so far is only a quarter of the total number of persons engaged in agriculture. Less detailed information is available for most of the remainder, but the numbers and categories and their changes during the past decade are shown in Table 1.6.

Table 1.6 illustrates the continued outflow of labour from agriculture. The greatest reductions in both absolute and relative terms occurred in the number of hired whole-time workers. Whole-time farmers declined numerically far more slowly. It is not clear how the data on part-time farmers, partners and directors should be interpreted. For example, the 'part-time' description can apply to semi-retired farmers whose offspring have become full-time farmers, or to farmers who spend some or most of their time on other business interests, and are really 'hobby farmers'. The importance of seasonal work in agriculture is emphasized by the large number of seasonal and casual workers. During the past ten years this group of workers has expanded 26 per cent – the increasing work capacity of machinery has allowed a declining full-time workforce to cope with work during most of the year, but the reduction in the latter requires extra seasonal labour to deal with the work peaks at harvest times.

Most holdings are farmed by farmers, the alternative being salaried managers. As Table 1.6 shows there are very few such managers. Indeed, the generally small size of labour force on the minority of holdings which employ full-time labour, results in little need for a managerial grade between farmer and workers – consequently there is no career structure in this industry.

Table 1.5 *Distribution of Holdings by Total Regular Whole-Time Family and Hired Workers Size-Groups, Great Britain, 1984*

	0	1	2	Size of workforce 3	4	5–9	10–14	15–19	20+	Totals
No. of holdings	159,454	32,375	15,316	6,926	3,413	4,934	926	305	429	224,078
No. of workers	0	32,375	30,632	20,778	13,652	30,866	10,631	5,078	16,736	160,748

Source: Agricultural Statistics UK 1984, HMSO, pp. 20 and 30.

Table 1.6 *Number of Persons Engaged in UK Agriculture*

	'000 persons	
	1975	1985*
Workers		
Regular whole-time		
Hired: male	157	111
female	15	10
Family: male	37	31
female	13	5
Total	222	157
Regular part-time		
Hired: male	22	19
female	26	22
Family: male	15	13
female	18	7
Total	80	61
Seasonal or casual		
Male	41	59
Female	32	40
Total	73	99
Salaried managers	7	8
Total employed	382	325
Farmers, partners and directors		
Whole-time	212	199
Part-time	68	92
Total	280	291
Total	662	616

*provisional
Source: MAFF, 1978, 1986a.

Farming is male-dominated. Only in the part-time, seasonal and casual elements are women a larger proportion of the workforce. The annual June census does not give a breakdown of farmers by sex, but analysis of the 1981 national census suggests that about 10 per cent of farmers are female (Craig *et al.*, 1986, p. 64).

The use of capital in agriculture has changed dramatically in the period since the Second World War. Before then, most farm inputs were produced within agriculture. Horses, for example, provided horsepower! These have now been replaced by tractors. Mechanization has replaced not only horses but much manpower, and improving the technical efficiency of many farming operations has effected an increase in output. Similarly a chemical revolution has also occurred through the development of fertilizers, pesticides, herbicides, fungicides and veterinary products. To a considerable extent these inputs purchased from outside agriculture mean that much of the reduced labour force inside agriculture is compensated for by extra employment in other industries. Craig *et al.* (1986, p. 98) estimate that for 1981 employment in other industries selling to UK agriculture (that is, excluding agricultural inputs exported) exceeded 200,000 persons. Similarly, it could be argued that the sale, distribution and processing of UK-produced agricultural products was also agriculture-related, and Craig *et al.* estimate that these activities employed a further 252,000 people in 1981.

1.2.2   Economies of Size

In many forms of economic activity it is known that as output increases the unit costs of production at first fall (economies of size) but will eventually begin to increase (diseconomies of size) as further growth occurs. Britton and Hill (1975) examined economies of size in British agriculture, concluding that most economies were achieved by the two-man farm, with generally smaller gains up to four men, and that significant diseconomies appeared to set in above 15 workers (pp. 175–9). They also noted that many American studies showed that a modern two-man farm could use all the available size economies. Table 1.3 shows that in the UK, during the last decade, farms of 1,000 smd and over have been increasing in number whilst all smaller sizes have been declining: this suggests that significant economies exist to at least the four-man size of farm. The fact that more than half of the UK holdings are less than 250 smd suggests that most farms are too small to be wholly efficient.

The importance of diseconomies, though not well documented must be emphasized. In agriculture diseconomies set in at small business sizes compared with many other industries; thus UK agriculture's relatively small firm-size structure will persist despite the continual decline in the number of small holdings.

So far economies of size have been discussed in relation to the whole farm business. Turning to the individual products economies of size are very important, and the scope for further exploitation of such economies is substantial. Table 1.7 shows that in response to the opportunity for economies, the average size of most production units has increased considerably during the past decade. Since the number of holdings has declined only slightly, and the total agricultural area is almost unchanged (land losses to non-agricultural uses have almost been balanced by the 'reclamation' of rough grazings), it follows that an increase in the average size of production unit must result in fewer products per farm. Clearly British farms are becoming more specialized.

1.2.3   The Importance of Fixed Costs

In British agriculture fixed costs are typically 40 to 60 per cent of total costs. In agriculture full-time labour is considered a fixed cost. This is

Table 1.7   *Changing Size of Production Unit in the UK*

		1975	1985	% change
No. of holdings ('000)		264	231	−12.5
Average area:	Cereals (hectares)	30.1	42.1	+39.9
	Potatoes (hectares)	3.6	4.9	+36.1
	Sugar beet (hectares)	12.5	17.8	+42.4
Average nos:	Dairy cows	40	58	+45.0
	Beef cows	19	18	−5.3
	Breeding sheep	167	191	+14.4
	Breeding pigs	23	47	+104.3
	Laying fowls	587	848	+44.5
	Broilers	23,400	30,964	+32.3

Sources: MAFF, 1978, 1986a.

obviously true for those farms – the majority – in which the full-time labour force consists solely of the farmer. It is also likely to be true for farms where the employed full-time labour force is very small because of the close personal relationships which exist and which tend to rule out the shedding of labour. Some farms employ enough men for labour turnover to permit more ready adjustment of numbers, but these are so few as to not upset the general proposition that full-time labour is a fixed cost.

High fixed costs imply significant short-run resource immobility. Land is obviously physically immobile, and although some land is transferred to non-agricultural uses each year such opportunities are principally restricted to the urban fringe. Capital in the form of farm buildings is similarly immobile. Much machinery is specifically designed for agricultural use, and has little use elsewhere. Finally labour is occupationally immobile. Farm employees have many skills, but talents for milking cows, ploughing or harvesting, for example, are not very marketable outside agriculture. This point applies equally to farmers, and is in their case reinforced by their social position as self-employed persons, and, when they are also owner-occupiers, by their ownership of the land – which gives unique status. When agricultural product prices fall, the high proportion of fixed costs means that total output is adjusted downwards very slowly. Even the product mix can change only slowly because of the necessity of maintaining rotations and because some of the capital inputs are highly product-specific. Similarly, total output is slow to adjust to rising prices, the most obvious constraint being the fixed area of land available. Consequently, the short-run price elasticity of supply of agricultural products tends to be low.

1.2.4 Technological Advance

In previous centuries technological advances in agriculture resulted from the inspirations of a few individual farmers. In modern conditions the degree of sophistication of the industry puts further progress beyond the resources of individuals and restricts research to large manufacturers of inputs, principally chemical and mechanical, and to universities, government, and other official bodies such as marketing boards and commodity commissions. Biological (new crop varieties, improved livestock) and chemical (herbicides, pesticides, fertilizers) advances tend to be farm-size-neutral, that is, they can be adopted on small farms as easily as large, but some mechanical advances favour large farms. The combine harvester is a good example. Over a period of fifty years it has replaced the much cheaper reaper–binder. Use of the latter was labour-intensive compared to the combine, but the lower unit costs which can be achieved by a combine require that its fixed costs be spread over the greatest possible area – in a normal British harvest this would be several hundred acres. Consequently only the very large farms can minimize their harvesting costs. Smaller farms must manage by using old second-hand machines or through buying economies of size via the services of machinery contractors. Thus many farms which were once large enough to take full advantage of the technology of past centuries have become too small to utilize efficiently much large modern machinery.

Table 1.8 illustrates the most significant consequences of techno-logical advances by providing data on the rapid increase in yields during the past 20 years. Past years are represented by averages of groups of 3 years because year-to-year fluctuations in yields are substantial, as the differences between 1984 and 1985 demonstrate. Nevertheless the seemingly inexorable upward trend in yields is one of

Table 1.8 *Average Yields of Crops and Livestock Products*

Unit	Average of 1964–6	Average of 1974–6	1984	1985	1986*
Crops, tonnes/hectare					
Wheat	4.05	4.39	7.71	6.33	6.95
Barley	3.65	3.75	5.59	4.95	5.21
Oats	3.00	3.48	4.89	4.59	4.93
Potatoes	24.00	25.16	37.03	35.84	35.76
Sugar beet	—	27.27	45.90	38.28	40.00
Oilseed rape	—	2.03	3.43	3.01	3.12
Hops	1.50	1.41	1.55	1.37	1.38
Livestock products					
Milk litres/cow	3,565	4,113	4,749	4,847	4,952
Eggs number/bird	202.5	232.5	256.5	258.5	258.0

*forecast
Source: MAFF *Annual Review*, various years.

the most significant features of modern agriculture, and its effects will be discussed further in Section 1.4.

1.2.5 Externalities

Discussion of externalities usually focuses on the problem of pollution. Certainly there are pollution problems in agriculture, notably of silage effluent which is many times more destructive of river life than is raw sewage. However, of even more significance is agriculture's production of untraded but desired outputs. Without the intervention of man, the natural vegetation of the British Isles would be principally deciduous forest. The present appearance of the countryside is a product of agriculture. Hedges and hedgerow trees, dry stone walls, ponds, ditches and the patchwork pattern of fields are the results of centuries of agricultural activity.

Modern agricultural methods have in some areas caused rapid changes in the landscape which are deplored by many. For example, large pieces of modern machinery, especially combine harvesters, and other arable equipment are most economically employed in large fields, so many hedgerows and their associated trees have been removed. Not only have farmers changed the rural scenery, their use of modern chemicals has reduced or removed much of the flora and fauna. Herbicides have greatly reduced the number of wild flowers. The loss of the latter as food plants, exacerbated by the widespread use of pesticides, has in turn reduced insect populations. These losses have reduced the number and variety of birds (see Bowers and Cheshire, 1983, for a further discussion). Farmers' activities produce/enhance/destroy our natural environment, but they are not rewarded or penalized for these aspects of their farming. Thus there is a major divergence between private and social costs and benefits; despite a growing recognition of this problem, there is little indication of the development of any effective remedies.

1.3 CONSUMPTION

British agriculture's traded output is mainly food, and the discussion below is confined to this. As one would expect in a country where the population is plentifully fed the price and income elasticities of demand for food in total are low. For an individual food item the elasticities depend upon the degree of luxury associated with the item and the proportion of food expenditure for which it accounts. The single largest element in most consumers' diets is expenditure on meats (see Table 9.2). Therefore individual meats are relatively price-responsive and for luxury items like beefsteak the price and income elasticities are relatively high. Some foods are inferior goods – the income elasticities of demand for bread, potatoes and sugar, for

Table 1.9   *Price and Income Elasticities of Demand, Great Britain, 1984*

	Price elasticity	Income elasticity
Milk	−0.50	0.03
Beef and veal	−2.02	0.25
Mutton and lamb	−1.82	−0.02
Pork	−2.15	0.06
Broiler chicken	−1.51	0.28
Sugar	−0.50	−0.27
Potatoes	−0.11	−0.32
Cabbage	−0.08	−0.26
Apples	−0.17	0.48
Bread	−0.52	−0.13

Source: Household Food Consumption and Expenditure, MAFF, 1985.

example, are negative: see Table 1.9.

The price elasticities quoted are estimated at the retail level after much value has been added by the addition of marketing utilities, such as storage, distribution and processing. Because marketing margins tend to be fixed, the price elasticities tend to be much lower at the farm stage of selling (Hill and Ingersent, 1982, pp. 84–5). For further data on price elasticities, see Section 9.1.3.

There are two major consequences of low demand elasticities. First, as noted earlier many agricultural commodities are subject to major fluctuations in supply and short-run supply elasticities are low. If the price elasticity of demand is also low, such fluctuations cause – in a free market – even more violent changes in market price. Second, increasing output by the industry will not lead to much extra consumption, but will disproportionately reduce prices. Indeed, for a commodity having an absolute value of price elasticity of less than unity, an increase in output will depress the industry's revenue. Of course these comments assume the absence of both market intervention and international trade.

1.4   GOVERNMENT POLICY

In 1846 the UK repealed the Corn Laws and then followed a policy of free trade for agricultural products. Imports of cheap grain from the mid-1870s onwards caused a severe depression in arable areas though many livestock farmers benefited. By the time the First World War began three-quarters of the wheat in British bread was imported. Sea warfare rapidly curtailed such imports and the government began to intervene in agriculture in order to expand output. This strategic reason for supporting agriculture is still relevant but is treated as secondary to the social problem of low incomes, and income support has become the main motive behind increasing government intervention. Prior to accession to the European Community in 1973, British farmers were supported by a mixture of input subsidies and product price guarantees. The latter were known as the deficiency payments system because the government guaranteed minimum prices to farmers for each major product, farmers sold their produce on a free market in competition with imports and received any deficiencies between market prices and the guaranteed minima directly from the Exchequer. Thus consumers enjoyed low prices determined by the world market, whilst farmers received higher prices considered to be 'fair'. The costs of the system were borne by the taxpayers. A simple diagrammatical representation of this system is given in Figure 1.1. Here *S* and *D* represent, respectively, home supply and demand, *MGP* is the minimum guaranteed price set by the government. The market price is determined by the world market where the supply is assumed to be perfectly elastic at *WP*, the world price. Imports are the difference between the home demand at price *WP* and home supply at price *MGP*. The total deficiency payment made to farmers is as shown.

The European Community (EEC) came into being in 1958 as both a customs union and a political organization (for details see Hill, 1984). As each of the member countries – West Germany, France, Italy,

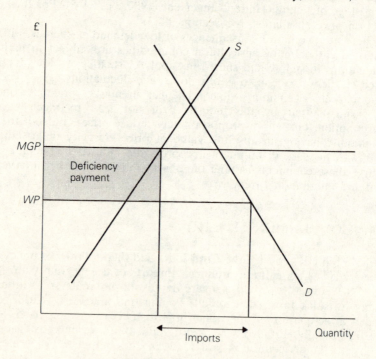

Figure 1.1   *UK deficiency payments scheme 1953–73.*

Netherlands, Belgium, Luxembourg – had pre-existing agricultural policies it was considered essential to replace these with a Community policy. The resulting Common Agricultural Policy (CAP) is a complex and expensive system. Acceding countries have been obliged to adopt the CAP. The UK, Denmark and Ireland joined in 1973 and had completely introduced the CAP by 1978. Greece joined in 1981 and has almost completed the adoption of the CAP. In 1986 Spain and Portugal joined but are permitted to introduce CAP measures slowly, taking 7 to 10 years for most commodities.

1.4.1 Common Agricultural Policy

Price policy

There are two major elements to this policy: guaranteed prices and structural measures. The guaranteed prices policy affecting the major products operates by raising internal market prices to desired levels (target prices) by restricting imports. If internal market prices fall significantly below the target levels intervention agencies purchase 'surpluses' and store them. Some of these stores may be released on to the market in seasons of relative shortage, but the majority must be used as animal feeding stuffs, industrial inputs, food aid, or be sold on world markets. Thus skimmed milk powder may be used in animal feeds, excess wine may be distilled to produce industrial alcohol, surplus wheat may be used in famine relief or for a food aid programme. Each of these uses implies the generous use of subsidies. Similarly, since world market prices are on average about half of EEC prices, surpluses can only be exported if export subsidies are employed. The system is depicted in Figure 1.2, which shows how surpluses are generated and indicates the costs of exporting them and the costs to consumers of raised prices. Here S, D and WP are as defined in Figure 1.1; TP is the EEC's target price. Because TP is above the home equilibrium price, a surplus is generated. The figure shows the extent of the consumer subsidy to farmers, the costs of disposing of the surplus, and the export subsidy per unit of output.

The consequences of the CAP price policy are numerous. Because target prices have been determined in a cost-plus fashion and politicians have been afraid to reduce them, farmers have faced perfectly elastic demand curves, and so have taken advantage of technological advances to expand output. High prices, low income elasticities, and virtually constant population sizes have ensured that consumption has failed to keep pace with output. Table 1.10 details the main elements of expenditure involved in disposing of surpluses. Total expenditure is seen to be very large. It is not, however, the major cost, being exceeded by consumer transfers to farmers. These comprise for each commodity, the EEC market price less the world price times consumption (see Figure 1.2). As the level of the world

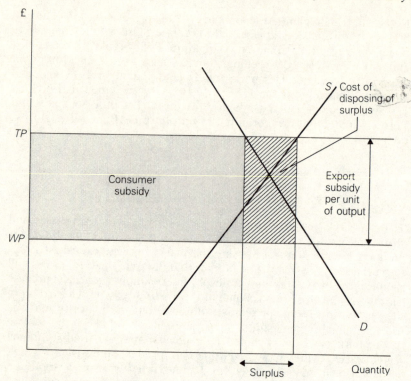

Figure 1.2 *Raising prices for farmers, and to consumers in the EEC*

price in the absence of EEC and other trade distortions is unknown and the subject of much debate, no precise estimate of the consumer transfers can be made.

Expenditure on price support dominates the EEC agricultural support system and the Community budget (Table 1.11). The budget revenue consists of member country receipts of customs duties on all imports, levies on agricultural imports, and exchequer transfers. The latter are a balancing item calculated as the difference between budgetary expenditure and revenue – that is, the import duties and levies. The exchequer transfers are expressed as a notional rate of VAT calculated on a common basis (they are not raised from consumers as a specific tax). Between 1979, when this system of financing was introduced, and 1985, the exchequer transfers were limited to the equivalent of a 1 per cent rate of VAT. When it became obvious in 1984 that agricultural guarantee expenditure was soon going to cause total EEC budget expenditure to exceed its revenues the Community agreed to raise the notional VAT limit to 1.4 per cent from 1 January 1986.

The method of financing the CAP has placed heavy burdens on the UK economy. As a major importer the UK has to contribute

Table 1.10 *EEC-Guarantee Expenditure on Surplus Disposal by Commodity, 1984, million ECU*

	Export subsidies	Market intervention	Totals
Cereals	918	732	1,650
Sugar	1,190	442	1,632
Olive oil	8	1,088	1,096
Fruit and vegetables	59	1,396	1,455
Wine	19	1,204	1,223
Milk and milk products	1,943	3,498	5,442
Beef and veal	1,393	1,154	2,547
Other	674	2,278	2,951
Total	6,204	11,792	17,996

Note: ECU is the European Currency Unit
Source: European Communities Commission, *The Agricultural Situation in the Community 1985*, 1986, pp. 274–5.

substantial import duties and levies to the Community budget, but has relatively low receipts from the budget because these are dominated by expenditures on surplus disposal – mainly produced by other members. Additionally, a significant part of the consumer transfers to farmers are from UK consumers to farmers in other EEC member states. There is thus a major net loss in the UK's dealings with the Community – a much larger loss than budgetary data suggest.

Structural policy
When the Community was formed it was generally believed that farmers had low incomes because their farms were too small. Certainly there is a severe small-farm size problem, with the average holdings

Table 1.11 *European Community Budget 1980–6, million ECU*

	1980	1981	1982	1983	1984	1985*	1986*
Expenditure on agriculture for:							
Price policy	11,283	10,960	12,370	15,788	18,328	19,955	21,012
Structural policy	602	575	646	750	703	632	805
Expenditure on other policies	4,405	6,528	7,407	7,775	8,493	7,846	11,498
Total	16,290	17,793	20,423	24,313	27,524	28,433	33,315
Agriculture's share %	73	65	64	68	69	72	65

*forecast
Note: ECU is the European Currency Unit
Sources: Eurostat Review 1975–84; The Agricultural Situation in the Community 1985; EEC Background Report ISEC/B13/86.

area (of the 12 current members) being less than a quarter of the average area in the UK. The Community's first Commissioner for Agriculture, Dr Mansholt, proposed in 1968 to solve this structural problem by persuading the majority of farmers to leave agriculture. But farmers were outraged, and politicians were embarrassed. Mansholt's plans were not acted upon and structural policy has remained a minor part of the CAP.

Although since 1972 the structural policy has included measures to encourage farmers to retire and allow their vacated land to be amalgamated with that of neighbours, the main thrust of policy has been towards compensating for small farm size and unfavourable environments. Co-operative marketing has been encouraged by measures to aid the launching of 'producer groups', with further subsidies to help with the training of managers and staff and with assistance for investments. In mountain and hill farming, and other 'less favoured' areas there are special subsidies. These are intended to compensate farmers for the permanent natural handicaps of these areas and so to encourage their continuation in business. Without such aids further depopulation of such areas would occur and the infrastructure of many remote areas would disintegrate.

Much expenditure in this section of agricultural policy is aimed at improving marketing and processing facilities for agricultural products. In some of the poorer areas of the Community there are measures to provide public amenities such as clean water, electricity and better roads.

Table 1.11 shows that structural policy expenditure is of far less financial importance than the price policy. The structural consequences of price policy should be noted: by raising prices above their free market levels the policy enables some farmers to survive who would otherwise have to leave the industry. In the economic climate of the 1980s this may be desirable: a policy which resulted in all farms being large enough to benefit from economies of size would necessarily involve the removal of many farmers to dole queues.

1.4.2 Agricultural Incomes

Since the major justification for government intervention is the need to raise farm incomes it is appropriate to consider this topic in the policy section.

The minimum wages payable to farm workers are determined by the Agricultural Wages Board, a statutory body whose decisions are legally enforceable. This situation has existed since the First World War (except for 1921–4), and resulted from the belief that excessively low wages were often paid to these workers, because they were too dispersed to be sufficiently strongly unionized to help themselves. History confirms the latter point since the National Union of Agricultural and Allied Workers never included more than half the farm workers as members, and becoming unable to survive alone, has been swallowed up by the Transport and General Workers' Union. Agricultural workers may have provided the Tolpuddle Martyrs, but they have never achieved a successful strike. Although the minimum wage payable is set by a statutory body it is extremely unusual for this to be the actual wage paid. Most workers receive a significantly higher wage.

In the period since the end of the Second World War, the earnings of full-time hired agricultural workers have remained at approximately two-thirds of the level of other manual workers as shown in Table 1.12. However, agricultural wages data should be interpreted with particular care because the earnings include payments in kind valued at standard rates by the Agricultural Wages Board. The main payment in kind relates to housing – well over half of the full-time workers live in houses belonging to the farm – and this benefit has been valued at a constant £1.50 per week since 1976. Clearly the earnings data are conservative estimates!

The incomes of farmers may be first examined at the aggregate level. A widely used, though crude, method of examining relative farm incomes is to look at the ratio of agriculture's share of GDP to its share of employment. In 1982 this ratio was 0.63 in the UK suggesting that farm incomes were signifiantly lower on average than non-farm incomes. However, this compares very favourably with a ratio of 0.5 in the Community (then of ten nations) as a whole – a ratio which has remained unchanged since the Community (of six) was first formed! Another aggregate measure is public expenditure on UK agriculture. This expenditure (mainly via the CAP) has slightly exceeded farming income in the three years 1983–5.

Table 1.12 *Incomes of Farmers and Farm Workers and Non-Agricultural Manual Workers, 1985*

	Gross annual earnings £	Annual weekly hours worked
General farm workers	6,048	46.9
Stockmen[a]	6,999	49.1
Gardeners and groundsmen	6,198	41.3
General non-farm labourers	6,968	43.9
All non-farm manual	8,507	44.5
Farmers:		
Farming income[b]	5,799	—
Cash flow[b]	8,432	—

Notes: Except for farmers, all earnings are for full-time adult males.
[a] Data for stockmen have high standard errors, see original source.
[b] For definitions of these measures of farm incomes, see the footnote to Table 1.13.
   Source: Farmers' data as for Table 1.13; other data from *New Earnings Survey 1985, Part A*, Table 8, Department of Employment.

Table 1.13   *Average Farm Incomes per Full-Time Farmer 1981–5, at 1985 prices*

	Farming income £	Cash flow £
1981	8,414	10,733
1982	10,344	11,257
1983	8,247	8,810
1984	10,646	11,258
1985	5,849	8,322
1986 (forecast)	6,962	9,212

Notes: Farming income is the return to farmers and spouses for their labour, management and own capital invested after providing for depreciation. Cash flow is the pre-tax revenue of farmers and spouses less cash outlays (i.e. less spending on materials, services and capital items, plus grants).

Sources: Derived from Tables 5 and 23A, *Annual Review of Agriculture 1987* and adjusted by the retail prices index.

Table 1.13 illustrates the variability of farm incomes from year to year and also shows that these incomes have not followed any recognizable trend in recent years. Two alternative measures of farm incomes are used in the table. 'Farming income' is the usual formal measure, but 'cash flow' is probably nearer to the farmers' perceptions of their incomes. Whichever measure is used, the average incomes are remarkably low in relation to the quantities of capital, management and labour for which they are the reward. Indeed, it is generally recognized by agricultural economists that most small farmers would be financially better off if they were employed as farm workers (see Table 1.12) and invested their capital elsewhere.

It was noted earlier that there was a major disparity in the sizes of farm businesses. Table 1.14 indicates a similar disparity in farm incomes. Indeed the disparity is greater than the data show, for they omit the approximately half of all holdings which are classified as 'part-time'. About 40 per cent of 'full-time' farms fall into the 'small' category which Table 1.14 shows to have very low farming incomes. The medium-size group accounts for just over a third of full-time farmers whilst large farms constitute a little over 20 per cent of full-time farmers or 10 per cent of all farmers.

It should be noted that the income data of Table 1.14 relate to incomes from farming only, and by treating all farms as rented exclude income from land ownership. As about 60 per cent of farms are owner-occupied the data obviously substantially underestimate the actual incomes of farmers.

The inadequacies of the income data so far discussed are underlined by surveys of their 'clients' conducted by the Inland Revenue (see MAFF, 1986b, pp. 54–5). Unfortunately the latest available survey related to 1982 but it still throws considerable light upon the situation.

Table 1.14 *Net Farm Income of Full-Time Farms by Size and Type, England, 1983/4 and 1984/5*

		1983/4 £	1984/5 £
Small			
	Dairying	3,903	3,637
	Hill and upland livestock	3,316	3,882
	Specialist cereals	1,613	3,711
	Other cropping	3,395	1,524
Medium			
	Dairying	7,373	7,717
	Hill and upland livestock	10,329	11,051
	Lowland livestock	8,172	6,291
	Pigs and poultry	10,379	34,594
	Specialist cereals	11,414	13,360
	Other cropping	13,603	10,607
Large			
	Dairying	17,058	17,886
	Lowland livestock	13,526	8,374
	Pigs and poultry	30,943	63,747
	Specialist cereals	39,205	48,265
	Other cropping	46,095	41,427

Notes: Net farm income is the return to the farmer and spouse for their labour, management and return on tenants' capital – that is, all farms are treated as though rented. Data refer to accounting years, farmers use a variety of accounting years but on average these results relate to March–February years.

Source: MAFF, 1986b, p. 18.

First, it should be noted that in 1982/3 the Inland Revenue estimated that farming was the main source of income for 250,000 people (thus indicating that the part-time/full-time split used in MAFF classifications is not very appropriate) and that some income from agriculture was important to a further 30,000 people whose main income derived from some other source. In 1982/3 about 61 per cent of farmers' incomes were attributable to their farming activities (including land ownership), 14 per cent from employment, 6 per cent from pensions, and the other 19 per cent from investments outside agriculture. The proportion of income from farming was broadly constant across all income groups.

In conclusion, farmers' incomes are evidently higher than MAFF data suggest, but it is still true that the majority of farmers have incomes that are low relative to those enjoyed by people in other sectors. It is also obvious that a rather small minority of farmers enjoy very large incomes.

1.5 TRADE

Before the UK's trade in agricultural products is discussed two features peculiar to world agricultural trade should be noted. First, the General Agreement on Tariffs and Trade (GATT) by which the free world's trade in other items is ordered, does not effectively apply to agricultural trade. The latter is consequently in a state of chaos, and for virtually all the major commodities world markets are seriously distorted by widespread dumping. Second, for most countries, and certainly for the EEC, agricultural trade policy is determined by domestic support policy. Clearly, if farmers are substantially supported trade in food becomes a balancing item, with net imports if home consumption exceeds home supply, or net exports, using whatever subsidies are necessary, if home supply exceeds consumption.

As the UK's agricultural support policy necessarily consists of the application of the CAP, its agricultural trade policy is similarly predetermined. Within the Community there are (officially) no barriers to trade, but the CAP constitutes a system of Community preference. Consequently, accession to the Community has substantially altered the UK's source of agricultural imports and destination of its exports, with the Commonwealth countries being displaced by the Community.

Trade in 'food, and live animals chiefly for food' in 1985 accounted for 9.5 per cent of UK imports and 4.1 per cent of exports. This trade generated net imports of £4,790 million. In 1985, 60 per cent of the UK food supply was home produced, having increased from 49 per cent in the period immediately preceding accession to the Community (that is, average of 1970–2). Much of the imported foods are from tropical areas. Looking at indigenous foods only, that is, the foods which are normally produced in the UK, the increase over the same period was from 61 per cent to 80 per cent.

Scientific progress and the stimulus of high EEC prices have combined to bring about the large increases in UK agricultural production shown in Table 1.15, which also illustrates some of the trade consequences. Most spectacular is the expansion of cereals. The UK had been a net importer since the late eighteenth century, but increasing yields and high CAP prices mean that the UK now adds to the Community's cereal surpluses, as shown by negative signs in the table. Large increases in output and therefore reductions in imports have also occurred for sugar and the meats. Cereals, sugar and meats are supported by the CAP; potatoes are the only major UK commodity not supported by the CAP. It is notable that trade in potatoes has not undergone any marked change although potato yields were shown in Table 1.8 to have increased substantially. Finally, milk has been the largest single source of CAP expenditure. Growth in output has

Table 1.15   *UK Supplies of Agricultural Commodities*

	Average 1970–2	1983	1984	1985*
Total cereals[a]: '000 tonnes				
Production	14,571	21,307	26,590	22,271
Net trade: with Nine	688	−1,528	−2,645	−1,815
with third countries	4,907	−950	−2,158	−1,262
Potatoes: '000 tonnes				
Output for human consumption	5,106	4,942	6,045	5,513
Net trade: with Nine	345	450	354	357
with third countries	0	250	288	262
Sugar: '000 tonnes, refined basis				
Production	959	1,062	1,314	1,200
Net trade: with Nine	67	159	112	104
with third countries	1,726	820	899	870
Total meat: '000 tonnes				
Production	2,727	3,134	3,191	3,240
Net trade[b]	948	395	364	374
Milk: million litres				
Output for human consumption	12,786	16,590	15,592	15,411
Sales for liquid consumption	7,412	6,977	6,957	6,896
Butter: '000 tonnes				
Production	76	242	206	204
Net trade: with Nine	141	52	55	43
with third countries	239	79	81	74
Cheese: '000 tonnes				
Production	160	245	245	253
Net trade: with Nine	61	104	119	126
with third countries	93	−3	−6	0
Eggs: million dozen				
Production	1,249	1,044	1,022	1,031
Net trade: with Nine	5	10	32	34
with third countries	6	−1	0	−1

Notes: [a] wheat, barley, oats, mixed corn and rye
   [b] breakdown of figures not available.
   * forecast
Throughout this table the 'Nine' refers to both the UK's EC partners in 1983–5 and the same countries in 1970–2 although only six were then EC members.
   Sources: MAFF *Annual Reviews*, various years.

occurred at the same time as a gradual decline in liquid consumption leaving a rapidly increasing quantity for manufacturing into dairy products, mainly butter, its joint product skimmed milk powder, and cheese. As UK butter production has expanded, consumption has been reduced so that the balance of required imports has been greatly curtailed; third country imports now relate entirely to New Zealand, for whom special arrangements were made under the treaty of accession. New Zealand cheese has not been treated in such a favourable manner, and imports from the Nine are in the ascendant. For milk and milk products, the net result of the CAP is that the UK's self-sufficiency has greatly increased, though the introduction of farm milk production quotas by the EEC in 1984 ensures that the UK cannot expand further, regardless of the laws of comparative advantage or its situation as a net importer.

1.6 EFFICIENCY OF UK AGRICULTURE

1.6.1 Pricing Efficiency

Prices should transmit consumer requirements with respect to both quantity and quality, to producers, and conversely should reflect supply changes (such as factor costs or new technology) to consumers.

In a free market, in the short run, uncontrollable supply fluctuations due to weather, pests, or diseases, in conjunction with low price elasticities of demand, can lead to very large price changes. To take an extreme example the drought of 1976 reduced potato yields by about 20 per cent and raised prices to approximately 500 per cent of normal. Very large price changes exaggerate the messages which the price mechanism should be transmitting and so confuse both producers and consumers. The reduction of excessive price fluctuations so that producers can more nearly satisfy consumer requirements is one of the justifications for government intervention in agriculture. Unfortunately in the EEC the potential benefits of a reduction in price instability are largely swallowed up by the excessive stability conferred by the CAP. Excessive stability here refers to the fact that once prices fall to intervention levels no further price falls can occur. Indeed, political decisions have tended to raise intervention prices annually in at least partial compensation for inflation even for products in chronic surplus. From the farmer's point of view, for products in surplus (that is, most major products) the resulting industry demand has been almost perfectly elastic and therefore totally unrelated to consumer requirements: the CAP can thus be said to have severely damaged pricing efficiency.

1.6.2 Technical Efficiency

Technical efficiency means maximizing the output:input ratio. Measures of technical efficiency are usually partial, relating either to land or labour productivity and in either case ignoring capital. However, Rayner *et al.* (1986) have calculated a total factor productivity index for UK agriculture from 1964 to 1979. This indicates that productivity was increasing by approximately 1 per cent per year. Rayner *et al.*

have also produced a value-added *labour* productivity index, which does not take the contribution of land and capital into account. This shows spectacular gains of almost 6 per cent per year for 1964–79. Significantly, they also show that much of the increase in labour productivity is due to a shift of labour out of agriculture upstream to industries supplying agriculture with intermediate inputs, notably agricultural chemicals and machinery.

1.6.3 Economic Efficiency

Economic efficiency is achieved when no reallocation of resources within a farm, between farms, or between agriculture and industry will result in a net addition to economic welfare. At the individual farm level it means maximizing profits, which in the context of perfect competition also implies minimizing unit costs. As indicated earlier, most UK farms are too small to exploit fully the available economies of size, suggesting that structural reform involving the amalgamation of small farms would increase efficiency. It would almost certainly improve technical efficiency and probably the total profits of the industry. Paradoxically it could reduce total economic welfare. This is because welfare includes externalities ignored by calculations of profits, and small farms, with their small fields may well contribute more positively to society's rural environment than the large farms produced by amalgamations.

The very existence of large public expenditures to support agriculture suggests that this industry is inefficient. Clearly government intervention, largely in the form of raised agricultural prices, results in the use of resources by agriculture which would otherwise be available to other industries. To the extent that the other industries which would use the resources are unsubsidized this represents a misallocation of resources. The direct economic cost to the UK of agricultural support, that is, taxpayer plus consumer costs, was estimated by Howarth (1985) to be more than £3.5 billion in 1980. It has certainly increased since then, probably exceeding £5 billion annually by 1986. The indirect costs through misallocation of resources, loss of export markets (because food is grown in the UK which would without support be imported), and associated expanded unemployment are extremely difficult to estimate.

Whatever the true figures for the cost of agricultural support are, it is clear that with current policies this industry is a serious burden to the UK economy. Yet the policy fails signally to achieve its income objectives, instead it benefits the richer farmers rather than the poor whom it is supposed to sustain.

REFERENCES

Bowers, D. K., and Cheshire, P. (1983), *Agriculture, the Countryside and Land Use* (London: Methuen).

Britton, D. K., Burrell, A. M., Hill, B., and Ray, D. (1980), *Statistical Handbook of UK Agriculture*, Wye College, University of London.

Britton, D. K., and Hill, B. (1975), *Size and Efficiency in Farming* (Farnborough, Hants: Saxon House; and Lexington, Mass.: Lexington Books).

Craig, G. M., Jollans, J. L., and Korbey, A. (eds) (1986), *The Case for Agriculture: An Independent Assessment*, Centre for Agricultural Strategy, University of Reading.

Hill, B. E. (1984), *The Common Agricultural Policy, Past, Present and Future* (London: Methuen).

Hill, B. E., and Ingersent, K. A. (1982), *An Economic Analysis of Agriculture* (London: Heinemann).

Howarth, R. W. (1985), *Farming for Farmers?* (London: Institute of Economic Affairs).

Ministry of Agriculture, Fisheries and Food (1978), *Annual Review of Agriculture 1976* (HMSO).

Ministry of Agriculture, Fisheries and Food (1986a), *Annual Review of Agriculture 1986* (HMSO).

Ministry of Agriculture, Fisheries and Food (1986b), *Farm Incomes in the UK* (HMSO).

Ministry of Agriculture, Fisheries and Food (1986c), *Departmental Net Income Calculation, Annual Review 1986* (HMSO).

Pettitt, C. H. (1986), *Agriculture – the Current Financial Scene*, synopsis of a paper presented at the Sixth Agricola Conference, Wye College, quoted in Craig *et al.* (1986), p. 43.

Rayner, A. J., Whittaker, J. M., and Ingersent, K. A. (1986), 'Productivity growth in agriculture (revisited): a measurement framework and some empirical results', *Journal of Agricultural Economics*, XXXVII, 2, 127–50.

FURTHER READING

Harris, S., Swinbank, A., and Wilkinson, G. (1983), *The Food and Farm Policies of the European Community* (London: Wiley). A detailed analysis of the CAP as it affects the food industry and trade as well as agriculture.

Hill, B. E., (1984), *The Common Agricultural Policy, Past, Present and Future* (London: Methuen). An introduction to the development and operation of the CAP.

Hill, B. E., and Ingersent, K. A. (1982), *An Economic Analysis of Agriculture* (London: Heinemann). Undergraduate textbook.

Howarth, R. W. (1985), *Farming for Farmers?* (London: Institute of Economic Affairs). A critique of UK agricultural policy since the Second World War.

Peters, G. H., and Clark, K. R. (1987), *Agriculture: Reviews of UK Statistical Sources*, no. 41 (London: Economic and Social Research Council, and the Royal Statistical Society).

Chapter Two

North Sea Oil and Gas

COLIN ROBINSON and DANNY HANN

2.1 INTRODUCTION

This chapter is concerned with UK oil and gas production; that is, oil and gas are treated as primary industries, engaged in extracting non-renewable natural resources from the earth. However, we begin with some essential background on the worldwide development of oil and gas, and on the economic characteristics of the two fuels.

2.1.1 Oil and Gas Worldwide

Since its beginnings in the late 1850s the oil industry has expanded at remarkable speed. First in the United States and then in other areas, the falling relative price of oil coupled with technological changes allowed oil to increase its share of fuel markets worldwide. Originally, oil was a lubricant and lamp fuel, but it became a source of energy for transport, for electricity generation and for industry; more recently it has provided the feedstock for a fast-growing petrochemical industry. Natural gas, which at one time had been regarded as rather a useless by-product of oil which could only be burned off (flared) at the wellhead, also came into increasing use, being extracted both from oil reservoirs as 'associated gas' and from gas fields.

During most of the period since the Second World War, oil and gas consumption expanded rapidly; as their prices fell relative to the price of coal (OECD, 1973) their shares of the world energy market rose sharply at the expense of coal. By 1973 the combined share of oil and natural gas in the world energy market was about 65 per cent. However, by 1985, after the price increases of the 1970s and early 1980s, it was down to 58 per cent. Oil's share of world energy fell sharply, as its relative price rose, from 47 per cent in 1973 to 38 per cent in 1985.

World trade in oil was also much reduced, following the oil 'shocks' in 1973–4 and 1979–80. Between 1973 and 1985, it fell by about one-third (British Petroleum, 1986a). Natural gas is more costly to transport over long distances than oil; nevertheless, gas trade has increased considerably in recent years as techniques of liquefying gas for tanker transportation have been developed and long-distance pipelines have been laid (British Petroleum, 1986b).

2.1.2 Economic Characteristics

Both crude oil and gas are characterized by relatively low price elasticities of demand. A recent study (Myhr and Raaholt, 1986) suggests price elasticity of demand for oil is between -0.05 and -0.2 in the short run and between -0.3 and -1.0 in the long run.

For all fuels, long-run price elasticities are likely to be significantly greater than short-run elasticities. Since the demand for fuel is derived from the ownership of complementary fuel-using equipment such as a car, a central heating appliance, or an industrial boiler, it takes a period of years after a change in prices for consumers' price expectations to change and for the investment decisions to be made which will alter stocks of appliances. Thus the impact of a sharp change in oil prices, such as the increase of 1973–4, takes many years to work through the system as consumers shift gradually away from oil-burning equipment.

Occasionally, crude oil is burned in power stations, but more generally it is refined into a variety of products which sell into submarkets with different characteristics. For example, motor gasoline and jet fuel are products in highly inelastic demand because they have virtual monopolies in the motor car and aviation markets. The market demand for heavy fuel oil is, however, very elastic with respect to price because coal, natural gas and nuclear power (for electricity generation) are close substitutes. Fuel oil demand proved very responsive both to the oil price increases of the 1970s and to the oil price decline of 1985–6. Natural gas requires relatively little treatment before sale to the final consumer. In many uses it can sell at a premium over oil because it is on tap and therefore requires no storage; moreover, it frequently has characteristics (such as comparatively low sulphur content) which are desirable environmentally and reduce equipment maintenance costs.

2.2   OIL AND GAS IN THE UK

The UK has only a short history as an oil and gas producer. In common with other European countries, the rising demand for energy was (until the late 1970s) met principally by imported oil. There was a radical change in the structure of energy consumption between 1950 and 1973 as coal prices rose relative to oil prices: in 1950 the energy market was still dominated by coal, but in the early 1970s oil overtook coal as the largest single fuel source and the ratio of energy production to energy consumption consequently fell from over 0.9 in 1950 to about 0.5 in 1973 (Table 2.1). Import-dependence would have increased even more had it not been for the significant quantities of natural gas which by the early 1970s were being produced from the southern North Sea: in 1973 the share of natural gas in the energy

Table 2.1 *UK Fuel Production and Consumption, 1950–85*

	1950 mtce	% of total	1960 mtce	% of total	1973 mtce	% of total	1985 mtce	% of total
Fuel production								
Coal	219	100	198	99	132	70	94	24
Oil	—	—	—	—	1	1	217	54
Hydro	1	—	2	1	2	1	2	1
Nuclear	—	—	1	—	10	5	22	5
Natural Gas	—	—	—	—	43	23	63	16
Total	220	100	201	100	188	100	398	100
Fuel consumption								
Energy uses:								
Coal	204	90	199	74	133	38	105	32
Oil	23	10	68	25	164	46	115	35
Hydro	1	—	2	1	2	1	2	1
Nuclear	—	—	1	—	10	3	22	7
Natural Gas	—	—	—	—	44	12	82	25
Total energy uses	228	100	270	100	353	100	326	100
Non-energy uses of oil	3		7		20		14	
Marine bunkers:								
Coal	4		—		—		—	
Oil	4		9		9		4	
Total consumption	239		286		382		344	
Self-sufficiency ratio	0.92		0.70		0.49		1.16	

Note: mtce = million tonnes of coal equivalent
Source: Department of Energy, *Digest of UK Energy Statistics* (various issues); *Energy Trends* (various issues).

market was over 12 per cent. In the late 1970s and 1980s increasing offshore oil production meant that the UK became energy self-sufficient (net) around 1980–1 and in 1985 the ratio of UK production to consumption was about 1.15.

Small quantities of oil have for many years been extracted from onshore fields in the UK, but it was not until the early 1960s that hopes of substantial finds emerged. At that time exploration began in the southern basin of the North Sea stimulated by the very large Groningen natural gas find in Holland and some small gas discoveries in Yorkshire. A pre-condition for exploration was that international agreement should be reached on how rights to exploit the North Sea were to be apportioned among countries bordering the North Sea. Particularly important was the division between Britain and Norway because they are the two countries with the longest North Sea coastlines. After this division was concluded by the median-line principle for the area south of 62°N, UK law was extended to the North Sea by the Continental Shelf Act 1964, an enabling Act subsequently amplified by successive Petroleum Production Regulations.

Success came quickly. In October 1965, BP made the first natural gas discovery in the West Sole field and a series of larger finds in 1966 and 1967 showed the North Sea southern basin to be a significant gas-bearing region. On the basis of these discoveries, the British gas distribution network was converted from manufactured gas to carry natural gas of about twice the calorific value per unit, and the nationalized gas industry became one of the fastest growing industries in Britain. Subsequent exploration in the 1970s resulted in one major find of non-associated gas in the UK northern North Sea (the Frigg field which is about 60 per cent in the Norwegian sector), and the discovery of – and later production from – the Esmond, Forbes and Victor gas fields in the southern basin. At the end of 1985 some twelve gas fields were producing in the British sector, one of which (Morecambe) is to the west of Britain to the Irish Sea. Discoveries of gas associated with oil have been made in the Brent, Piper, and several smaller oilfields.

At the end of 1985 remaining recoverable natural gas reserves in British offshore waters were officially estimated to be between 860 and 2,850 billion cubic metres. This is roughly equivalent to 720 and 2,400 million tonnes of oil, or 1,200 and 4,000 million tonnes of coal.

North Sea oil finds turned out to be even more significant than the gas discoveries. By the late 1960s attention had switched to the deeper, northern areas of the North Sea off mainland Scotland, Orkney and Shetland. The oil companies were disappointed at the prices paid for natural gas by the Gas Council (now British Gas) which the government had decided should be virtually sole buyer of offshore gas, and they also believed the larger gas reservoirs in the southern North Sea had already been found. Consequently, they moved north to search for oil. Success again came rapidly. The first big North Sea oil discovery was Ekofisk in the Norwegian sector in 1969 and during the next six years there were numerous oil finds – mainly in the UK sector, although one more large·field (Statfjord) was found lying mainly on the Norwegian side of the median line.

Remaining UK recoverable oil reserves at the end of 1985 were estimated at between 1,050 and 4,100 million tonnes – considerably greater than estimated remaining recoverable gas reserves (Department of Energy, 1986).

British North Sea oil production started in 1975 and increased rapidly up to the mid-1980s when its probable peak was reached. As Table 2.1 shows, it is primarily because of sharply rising crude oil production that UK energy import-dependence has dropped so much in recent years. How long into the future Britain remains more than self-sufficient in oil and energy will depend mainly on future crude oil price trends. If prices are expected to remain around the late-1986 level ($14–15 per barrel), then very few oilfield projects will be started in the foreseeable future. In such circumstances, UK oil output would show a steep decline as production from existing fields declined (see Section 2.3.5 below) and UK oil self-sufficiency would be unlikely to last much past the early 1990s.

North Sea oil is of relatively high quality (light and low in sulphur) so that it commands a higher price than many other crude oils. Thus there is an advantage in exporting some North Sea oil, provided transport costs do not exceed the quality premium. Moreover, there are technical advantages in refining some heavier imported crude oils as well as lighter North Sea oil in meeting the UK pattern of demand for oil products. In 1985 the UK exported about 79 million tonnes of crude oil out of 122 million tonnes produced and imported some 35 million tonnes. The UK is an importer of natural gas – chiefly from the Frigg field in the Norwegian sector which has supplied about 25 per cent of UK natural gas consumption in recent years. Governments have not permitted exports of natural gas and in 1985 the government vetoed British Gas Corporation's plans to purchase Norwegian gas from the Sleipner field.

2.3   THE NORTH SEA INDUSTRY

There are two features of the North Sea environment particularly relevant to an analysis of industrial structure. Since the early 1960s successive governments have shown a keen interest in offshore matters. They not only allocate rights to explore for and extract any hydrocarbon deposits found in British waters, but are also eager to be involved in and legislate for most areas of the industry. The market structure that has emerged in the 1970s and 1980s has evolved alongside an array of public policies (see Section 2.4 below).

Second, British oil and gas production is only a small segment of an internationally well-developed industry; proven oil reserves in the whole of Western Europe at the end of 1985 (mainly in the North Sea) only amounted to some 3.7 per cent of the world total (Institute of Petroleum, 1986). The international industry consists of many thousands of organizations exploring for and developing oil and gas, but it is dominated by some of the largest multinational companies in the world.

2.3.1 Involvement of UK Firms

Because of the international nature of the oil industry, one can hardly expect the majority of North Sea extraction rights to be held by British firms. The large multinational oil companies were encouraged to explore the UK continental shelf (UKCS) during the 1960s and the British share of the licensed area was thus relatively low: 30 per cent after the first licensing round in 1964. During the 1970s the government implemented its policy of preferential treatment for British companies – particularly the British National Oil Corporation (BNOC) and British Gas Corporation (BGC); hence the British share increased to around 70 per cent by the end of the 1970s. By 1986, however, much acreage from early licensing rounds had been handed back to the government and the British share had fallen to under 50 per cent.

The offshore supplies industry providing the exploration rigs, the production platforms, the supply boats, the services and the pipe lines and tankers to transport the oil and gas also has international roots. Although companies engaged on the continental shelf at first imported many of these items, the establishment of a British offshore supplies industry has increased the UK share of the North Sea supplies market from under 30 per cent in the early 1970s to around 80 per cent – worth £2.7 billion – in 1985 (Department of Energy, 1986). It should be noted, however, that because of the problem of classifying firms and earnings as British or foreign, this 80 per cent figure may overstate the UK share. Refining and marketing North Sea output also involves the international oil companies long established in the UK.

2.3.2 Economic Characteristics of North Sea Production

North Sea oil and gas projects are far from homogeneous (Robinson and Morgan, 1978; Robinson, 1979). With respect to oilfields, apart from physical and geological differences between reservoirs, the crude itself varies in its make-up, for instance, in sulphur content and API gravity (Mabro *et al.*, 1986). There are, nevertheless, common characteristics of producing oil and gas from the North Sea which make this industry conducive to certain types of enterprises. The geographical environment is a serious deterrent to companies not already involved in offshore oil and gas exploration, with water depths of around 200 metres in the northern North Sea, local winds of up to 100 miles per hour, waves as high as a five-storey building and reserves typically located a couple of miles under the sea-bed. More important, certain economic features of North Sea production restrict entry into the industry. For example, the return on investment in the North Sea is highly uncertain, and project costs are massive. The importance of these factors varies according to the stage of the exploration and production cycle: the greatest unknowns must be faced during 'wildcat' drilling in the exploration phase, but costs are highest and the potential for cost variation greatest during the subsequent development of any discovery.

Although a company has access to seismic information about the geology of the continental shelf, it can only be sure of the presence of oil or gas if it sinks a well through the sea-bed. In 1976 the average cost of an exploration well was £3.5 million, in 1980 it was £7 million, and in 1985 it was over £9 million though there was some decline in drilling costs in 1986 as falling exploration activity produced surplus drilling capacity. Well costs vary according to specific geographical and geological circumstances.

Unlike exploration risks, some development risks can be offset by insurance, but the size of development expenditure generally dwarfs exploration spending. Capital cost estimates of North Sea oilfields currently in production range from under £25 million for a very small project such as Innes or Deveron, to over £3,500 million for Brent, so that nearly all North Sea fields are very large investment projects – some of them 'giant projects' similar in size to major hydroelectric schemes or long-distance pipelines. In the early 1970s, initial cost estimates had to be revised upwards very sharply as material prices soared and unforeseen technical and managerial problems arose (Department of Energy, 1976). In the mid-1980s with greater experience, much lower cost inflation and technical innovation such as greater computerization and the use of remote observation vessels, the tendency for cost overruns has been much reduced.

Another important characteristic of North Sea projects is the long pre-production period. From discovery to first output for a typical offshore project is likely to be around five years (except for small satellite fields), during which time investment costs accumulate with no offsetting revenues. Thus the time profile of costs is heavily 'front-end loaded', especially when costs are expressed in discounted terms. Once the field is onstream there may be another three to five years to wait before peak production is achieved, which may be maintained for two or three years before output steadily declines. A North Sea investor must therefore be able to commit large-scale funds for a period of several years without suffering short-term financial stress.

There are other barriers to and incentives for entry into this industry – notably the government's licensing regime discussed in Section 2.4 below – but the economic characteristics discussed above tend to determine the types of companies which will undertake the great part of North Sea activities. Larger companies, with diversified and integrated operations, appear better equipped to deal with the risks and high costs which are involved. Exploration risks can be spread and the companies can cope with the high and uncertain costs of development. Although there is a fringe of smaller firms (see Section 2.3.3 below), these economic considerations tend to restrict their activities in the North Sea.

2.3.3 Concentration

Consequently, the major multinational oil companies are prominent in the British North Sea. As is often the case in oil exploration and production, both the oil majors and the smaller companies have formed partnerships and consortia so that risks and costs to any one firm are scaled down to a manageable level. Even the two largest oil companies (Exxon and Shell) conduct most of their North Sea activities in partnerships. Licences are issued to groups of up to fifteen companies with each member committed to a specified proportion of the costs incurred in the licensed area and in return entitled to the same proportion of the revenues from any discovery, although there are a few cases of sole licences.

Joint licensee opportunities have opened up the North Sea to a wide variety of companies ranging from the oil majors, through slightly smaller oil companies such as Phillips and Conoco, state-owned companies such as Deminex, institutional investors such as LASMO, to companies which wished to diversify (such as RTZ, Thomson and Volvo). However, the six oil majors have a relatively high proportion (almost one-third) of the area licensed. Although 169 companies are licensed, many of them own only a very small proportion of one block.

Since not all the companies with licences have made discoveries and brought them into production, there is a greater concentration of output than of licensed area (Table 2.2). Only 75 companies have producing fields – 15 with both oil and gas production, 5 with gas only and 55 with only oil. Companies with shares of 2 per cent or more of output are listed in Table 2.2. Concentration within the group of successful companies is notable in the production of both gas and oil. The largest four North Sea gas supplying companies accounted for about 50 per cent of the estimated 30 million tonnes of oil equivalent of natural gas produced from the North Sea in 1986 (Table 2.2). The degree of concentration in oil supplies is rather more marked. BP, Exxon and Shell accounted for nearly half of the 122 million tonnes of crude oil extracted in 1986. This dominance reflects the nature of the North Sea oil industry whereby the profitable 'giant' fields such as BP's Forties and Exxon and Shell's Brent have been developed first. These fields are now in decline; hence the degree of concentration is likely to be reduced as North Sea output increasingly comprises many fields owned by many companies.

The degree of concentration of remaining reserves is somewhat less than the degree of concentration of output shown in Table 2.2. Nevertheless, the three companies with the largest shares·are world majors and the six majors operating in the North Sea account for over 50 per cent of remaining reserves in fields given development approval by the Department of Energy.

However if a further 26 oilfields that have been discovered but which do not as yet have any firm development plans ('potentially commercial' fields) are included, a rather lower level of concentration is implied.

To give some idea of the degree of concentration in the offshore industry, the Herfindahl (H) Index (which equals one in the case of a monopoly) may be used. For remaining established oil reserves the H-index is 0.07 and falls to 0.05 when potentially commercial reserves are included. When calculated for output of oil and gas (Table 2.2), the H-index is also relatively low, below 0.1, because of the large number of companies with North Sea interests.

2.3.4 Market Behaviour and Conduct

Although neither in terms of production nor of reserves ownership do individual companies have dominant market portions, the degree of

Table 2.2 *Shares of North Sea Output by Company, 1986*

Oil		Gas (% of total output)		Oil and gas combined	
BP	20	Exxon	17	BP	17
Exxon	14	Shell	17	Exxon	15
Shell	14	Elf	9	Shell	15
Britoil	7	BGC	8	Britoil	7
Texaco	5	Britoil	6	Texaco	4
Occidental	3	Conoco	6	Conoco	3
Conoco	3	Amoco	5	Mobil	2
Gulf	2	Total	5	Occidental	2
Mobil	2	BP	5	Elf	2
ICI	2	Amerada Hess	4		
Thomson	2	Arco	3		
Union Texas	2	Texas Eastern	2		
Chevron	2	Hamilton	2		
Deminex	2	Mobil	2		
Total output (million tonnes oil equivalent)	122		30		152

Source: Authors' estimates.

concentration might lead one to expect oligopolistic pricing strategies and marketing policies. However, conditions are different in the North Sea. In the gas market the producers face a monopsonist, with considerable power to set prices, in the form of British Gas (see Section 2.4.2 below). In the oil market, although the North Sea is only a small segment of world oil trade, rapidly rising output in the late 1970s and early 1980s probably had some depressing effect on world oil prices. Nevertheless, each individual North Sea producer probably sees itself as a price-taker competing with a large number of other crude oil producers and faced by a very elastic demand curve. North Sea oil prices are usually some 5 to 10 per cent above the average world crude oil price because of the higher than average quality of North Sea crude (relatively low gravity and sulphur content) and the transport cost saving (compared with OPEC oil) of moving oil from the North Sea to European consumers (in 1985 over 80 per cent of British crude exports were destined for Europe).

So, despite the degree of concentration, North Sea companies tend to act competitively, extracting oil until the costs (including taxes and royalty) of the marginal unit of output are equal to the exogenously set price of that output. Similarly, the companies will adjust planned annual output until the expected discounted marginal profit from a barrel produced in one year is approximately the same as the expected discounted marginal profit of producing that barrel in any other year. The analysis of market behaviour of North Sea companies, is thus of less economic interest than is the case with many of the other industries discussed in this volume – although there is a great deal of interest in the behaviour of companies in the world oil market as a whole.

There is some 'merger' activity within the industry in the form of 'farm-out' deals, in which a company which has discovered an oil or gas reservoir 'farms out' all or part of its interest to another company in exchange for the other company's meeting all or part of the development costs. Although large corporations tend to take over parts of discoveries made by smaller companies, the prospect of farm-out deals reduces perceived risks for smaller enterprises and gives them an incentive to explore the North Sea.

2.3.5 Performance

British gas production in 1986 is close to the yearly output plateau of around 45 billion cubic metres (bcm) which is generally expected to continue to the early 1990s. Although there is a broad consensus on UK gas demand up to 2000 (Brierley, 1986), forecasts of the demand and supply balance after 1990 are highly speculative, ranging between self-sufficiency achieved sometime in the 1990s and maintained to 2020 and imports increasing from 10 bcm in 1990 to 25 bcm in 2020 (Stern, 1986).

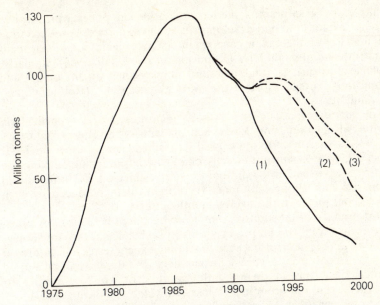

Figure 2.1 *North Sea oil output, 1975–2000*
(1) Output from established commercial fields.
(2) Additional output from potentially commercial reserves.
(3) Additional output from assumed discoveries.
Source: Authors' estimates

Oil output probably reached its peak in 1985 after its rapid expansion during the previous ten years. Figure 2.1 shows a somewhat speculative profile for British North Sea oil production up to the end of the century based on the aggregation of individual field depletion profiles. The lowest line in the figure, peaking at just under 130 million tonnes in the mid-1980s, represents a scenario comprising only 38 established commercial fields which are already producing or likely to begin production in the near future. Virtually regardless of foreseeable events, the plans for these fields are likely to go ahead, so this path represents a minimum for North Sea oil supplies. The middle curve includes a further 26 'potentially commercial' discoveries already made which may be developed in the 1990s. Lastly the highest curve assumes that future exploration activity reveals more fields – although of much smaller size and in more remote waters. The main effect of developing these prospects would be to reduce the rate of production decline towards the end of the century. In the last four years UK oil consumption has been between 70 and 80 million tonnes a year; if it continues at about that rate, then Figure 2.1 suggests that oil self-sufficiency is unlikely to be sustained to 2000. Indeed, it may be that Britain will again be a net oil importer by the early 1990s. However, there are some very considerable uncertainties. There might, for example, be a substantial increase in crude oil prices which would increase exploration and development activity and boost production in the mid-1990s; the tax regime might change again; or government policy in general might alter (Robinson and Marshall, 1984); similarly, geological surprises (pleasant and unpleasant) might occur and significantly affect North Sea output prospects (Robinson and Rowland, 1978).

The standard labour productivity measures are not particularly helpful when comparing North Sea oil with other energy industries because of sharply differing capital intensities. For example, in 1985, under 30,000 people were directly employed in producing oil from the UKCS; this yielded an output per person of almost 4,500 tonnes of oil compared with about 340 tonnes of oil equivalent produced by each British coal miner in the twelve months after 1 April 1985.

Performance of the industry may to some extent be gauged by after-tax returns on individual projects though such calculations are subject to wide margins of error because remaining expenditures and future oil outputs are only known very approximately, and the price of oil will be dictated by events in the oil industry at large which is subject to political, social and economic shocks (Rowland and Hann, 1987).

In comparing North Sea profitability with that available in other sectors of the UK, one must remember the economic features of offshore production. Companies operating in the North Sea face substantial risks and long lead times for their investments, and consequently tend to look for returns that would seem high in other industries. In addition, the project costs only include expenditures specifically attributable to each discovery: abortive exploration costs and company overheads that must be accounted for somewhere are not incorporated.

2.4 GOVERNMENT POLICY TOWARDS THE NORTH SEA

Almost everywhere political forces have a significant impact on the activities of the oil industry. In most countries with oil and gas reserves there is either direct state involvement in the exploitation of those reserves or government 'regulation' of the oil industry. In the UK, there appear to have been three phases of government policy since 1964. First, the so-called 'rapid exploitation' policy designed to encourage companies to explore in the North Sea and bring any discoveries into production quickly; then a tightening of the fiscal regime and an increase in direct government control and involvement in the 1970s; finally, since 1979, there has been a policy of privatization and less intervention. Here the extent of government intervention that is desirable is not the issue; the concern here is to decribe what has happened in Britain rather than to pass judgement on it.

There are many ways in which government exerts influence on company activities in the North Sea. The tax system is one of the principal means. In Britain, as in other countries, special taxes on oil have been devised; the tax regime and its effects are discussed in Section 2.5 below. First, however, the ways in which the Department of Energy regulates North Sea operations, the role played by the British Gas Corporation (now British Gas plc) and the establishment and break-up of the British National Oil Corporation (BNOC) are examined.

2.4.1   Licence Allocation

Because petroleum resources are the property of the state, once the Continental Shelf Act 1964 had been passed (see Section 2.2), the government had then to determine how licences to exploit oil and gas resources were to be allocated to private sector companies. Essentially there are two possible methods of licence allocation (Dam, 1976; Hann, 1986a). One is to hold an auction in which potential licensees bid in competition with each other. Competitive bidding has been used in the United States and also on three occasions in the UK (as part of normal licensing rounds). Generally though, in Britain, as in Norway and most other countries, licences have been issued by 'administrative discretion' with the only payments being relatively small rental fees. Briefly, the system is that politicians lay down certain guidelines for licence issues and civil servants in the Department of Energy are supposed to decide, within those guidelines, which companies shall be allocated which areas. The British sector of the North Sea is divided into blocks, mostly of about 250 square kilometres, and production licences cover one or more blocks or part-blocks.

The initial guidelines for operating the discretionary allocation system, laid down by a Conservative government for the First Licensing Round in 1964, set the pattern for subsequent rounds. The criteria were rather vague. Rapid exploitation was to be encouraged and applicants should be making some 'contribution towards the development of resources of our Continental Shelf and . . . of our fuel economy generally' (HMSO, 1973). Undoubtedly a considerable amount of discretion was left to civil servants.

Further licensing rounds retained essentially the same system of awards (apart from the limited auctions of 1971/2, 1982/3 and 1984/5), but increasingly preference was given to British interests in general and, until the Seventh Round in 1980/1, to nationalized industries in particular. By the 1977 Fifth Round 51 per cent participation by BNOC or BGC was required and applicants were expected to agree participation terms for finds made under previously issued licences. The 1978 Sixth Round was intended to strengthen further the positions of BNOC and BGC. This trend was reversed by the 1979 Conservative administration, although control was still exercised through licence awards. In the Seventh Round preferential treatment was no longer given to BNOC and BGC and in the Eighth and Ninth Rounds the government attempted to direct companies to less attractive 'frontier' acreage. In the Ninth Round preferential treatment was given to small independent companies, again showing the importance of political criteria in the discretionary system. The Tenth Round, announced in 1986, relaxed many conditions in order to maintain activity during a period of low oil price expectations.

The decision to issue licences by Civil Service discretion, rather than by auctioning, had certain consequences. An auction, provided there is competition among bidders, is in theory capable of extracting the rent associated with natural resources as well as allocating licences. Companies will bid what they believe the areas on offer are worth (in a competitive situation they will not underbid because of fear of not gaining licences) and in this way the state will collect much of the surplus which arises from resource exploitation. A discretionary award regime, however, only allocates licences – it does not collect rent – so some other means of revenue collection becomes necessary.

2.4.2 A Monopsony for North Sea Gas

In the case of oil a special rent collection mechanism was eventually established in the Oil Taxation Act 1975 (see Section 2.5 below). For gas, which was discovered much earlier than oil, a different method was used. Because production licences had been awarded almost free of charge, oil companies which were successful in finding gas might have made substantial profits had they been able to sell gas at market prices. However, a countervailing power had been established by the state's granting to the nationalized gas industry – which already had a monopoly of piped gas distribution in Britain – virtual monopsony rights over North Sea gas. With a few minor exceptions, companies with gas to sell were required to offer it to the (then) Gas Council which was constrained only to pay a 'reasonable price'. Companies were in an inherently weak bargaining position since they had little alternative to selling to the Gas Council.

Partly as a result of the council's strong negotiating position and partly because of government pressure, the price fixed for natural gas from the large offshore fields in negotiations between 1966 and 1969 was low relative to then existing energy prices. One would normally expect gas to be priced higher than crude oil because the former is generally regarded as a superior product and it needs little processing in comparison with crude oil. In fact the gas price (1.2p/therm) was only about two-thirds of the imported crude price. Subsequently, the oil price rose sharply whilst the natural gas price increased only gradually under limited escalation provisions in the gas contracts, and the relative price of gas at the UK coast declined to only about 15 per cent of the crude price in 1977.

The economic rent from gas production was therefore extracted by rather unusual means – via a corporation granted sole buying rights by the state. Whether such a method can be regarded as satisfactory depends on what happened to the economic rent which was initially transferred to the Gas Council and Area Boards (later to become the BGC and then British Gas plc). If the rent remained in (then) BGC – in the form of organizational slack, for example – the initial method of removal would be difficult to justify, for the surplus would simply have been transferred from large private corporations to a large nationalized corporation rather than being used for the public benefit (Robinson, 1978). By the end of the 1970s it became apparent that the hiatus in drilling activity caused by the low gas price might result in a gas shortage sometime in the late 1980s and 1990s. In addition, the Oil and Gas (Enterprise) Act of 1982 gave oil companies possible opportunities to sell gas to large consumers in Britain, bypassing the BGC. These factors seem to have led BGC to offer higher prices for gas in the early 1980s, thus stimulating gas exploration activity.

The privatization of BGC at the end of 1986 is expected to free the gas industry from a degree of political intervention and control, though its monopoly and monopsony power seem likely to be undiminished and it will be able to diversify its activities. The new corporation will again be able to search for and develop oilfields (its oil interests had been split from BGC in 1983 in the form of 'Enterprise Oil'), and will be able to operate overseas. There was considerable criticism of the privatization plans (Institute for Fiscal Studies, 1985; Robinson 1985; Robinson and Marshall, 1985, 1986; Price, 1986) as they went through Parliament. One potentially important policy change came when the Secretary of State for Energy announced in March 1986 that the government may be willing to permit gas exports.

2.4.3 Output Controls

Until the magnitude of Britain's offshore oil reserves began to emerge in the early 1970s, there had been no explicit controls on production from North Sea fields except to the extent that output was governed by the BGC's ability to absorb gas. As first oil production neared, the two major political parties agreed that regulation of oil depletion rates might be necessary by the 1980s, although they differed on the way this control should be exercised (Robinson and Morgan, 1978).

The Labour government elected in 1974 passed the Petroleum and Submarine Pipelines Act 1975 which, *inter alia*, contained powers to control output from North Sea fields. These powers were intended to regulate depletion rates from the early 1980s onwards – either by delaying the development of oil which had been discovered or by reducing output rates for fields already in production. Companies were reassured as to the use of these powers in a Commons statement by Mr Eric Varley – then Secretary of State for Energy – in 1974. These

'Varley Guidelines' were reaffirmed by one of his successors, Mr Nigel Lawson, in 1982. Under the legislation, companies with North Sea finds had to seek Department of Energy approval for their investment programmes and production rates. Plans initially approved could be subsequently modified within specified limits and with given periods of notice. The general intention was clearly to give scope for reduction of company output programmes, although a limited power to make companies increase production is also contained in the 1975 Act.

The Energy Department has changed its method of approval of company programmes since depletion control was first instituted: Instead of approval being given for the full life of a field, it is now only given in stages, the first stage being the period during which production builds up to its maximum. Formal production cut-backs have yet to be imposed by a government and the only example of a development delay is the Clyde field, postponed for two years in 1982. Although all the apparatus for detailed control of depletion rates exists (Robinson, 1982), governments have not been keen on using it.

However, there are other, less direct, ways in which production can be controlled. For instance, the Energy Act of 1976 allows the Secretary of State for Energy to control oil output if deemed necessary in the interests of energy conservation. Another obvious way of slowing North Sea development and reducing production is through the size and timing of licensing rounds. There was a gap of five years between the Second and Third Rounds and also between the Fourth and Fifth Rounds. Although since the Fifth Round in 1976–7 the rounds have been at more regular intervals, they have varied considerably in size. A very indirect way of influencing depletion rates in the North Sea is by the use of the tax system. Incentives and concessions may be used to encourage certain types of investment, or indeed the tax system may act as a disincentive to North Sea activity (whether intentionally or not).

2.4.4 Participation

As explained in Section 2.4.1 above, under the discretionary licence allocation system, the preference given to British nationalized industries increased during the first four licensing rounds. However, the Labour government decided that, in addition, there should be a state oil company which would participate in North Sea licences. The British National Oil Corporation (BNOC) was set up in January 1976, under the Petroleum and Submarine Pipelines Act 1975. The main reasons put forward for its creation were that it would promote the security of oil supplies, it would permit control over the disposal of North Sea oil and it would be an effective instrument by which a national oil policy could be implemented (Hann, 1986b). By the end of 1979 the volume of oil traded by BNOC had reached some 1 million barrels per day (equivalent to about 60 per cent of British oil production at that time).

The 1979 Conservative administration had committed itself to dismantling BNOC and immediately withdrew some of the privileges BNOC had enjoyed under the Labour government. The Oil and Gas (Enterprise) Act 1982 provided powers for the government to split off BNOC's 'upstream' (exploration and production) activities into a subsidiary company, Britoil, which would then be sold to the general public. In December 1982 Britoil became a private sector oil company with a government shareholding of 49 per cent; this minority share was sold off in May 1985. BNOC remained solely as an oil trading company until it was abolished in 1985, to be replaced by the Government Oil and Pipelines Agency (OPA), a small organization required to carry out residual functions other than oil trading. The rise and fall of BNOC illustrates well how the offshore sector is subject to political control and intervention: a future Labour government may decide to resurrect a state oil company in the 'national interest'.

2.5 OIL TAXATION

Tax regimes exert significant influences on oil company activities in all countries. The rather complex North Sea taxation system, which has assumed a very important place in government North Sea policy, is explained very briefly below.

2.5.1 Objectives and Means

In the early years of North Sea activity the government's 'rapid exploitation' policy was facilitated largely by a benign fiscal regime which attracted multinational oil companies to British waters. Royalties (which are a common form of tax in oil producing areas) were to be levied at a fixed 12½ per cent of the gross wellhead value of oil, and corporation tax was to be charged on profits as defined by standard UK corporation taxation rules.

By the early 1970s, as the extent of recoverable oil and gas reserves became apparent, the government's objectives began to change. Exploration activity was no longer the prime concern, depletion became an issue (see Section 2.4.3 above) and there was a consensus in favour of changing the tax laws. It was argued that corporation tax rules would allow companies to deduct from North Sea profits large onshore and overseas losses. Hence, to raise its North Sea tax take, the government proposed a corporation tax 'ring fence', effectively isolating company North Sea profits from relief resulting from losses in other areas of a company's business.

By 1975 the escalation in world oil prices pushed prospective North Sea returns higher, despite a considerable inflation of costs. Claims that companies operating offshore would make massive 'windfall' profits were made and the government clearly felt it should increase its income from the North Sea. But whilst receipts from both corporation tax and royalties would rise automatically with higher oil prices, the additional receipts were thought to be insufficient given the anticipated sharp rise in oil company profitability. In preference to a competitive bidding system for licence allocation (see Section 2.4.1) for collecting this rent the government chose to restructure the fiscal environment by introducing Petroleum Revenue Tax (PRT) in the Oil Taxation Act 1975. PRT is the only British tax specific to an industry and it is levied on each field, not on the customary corporate basis.

Although the rent collection objective for PRT was clear, operationally it posed many problems. What are 'excess' profits? Can they be defined *ex ante*? Will marginal projects be made unprofitable by the tax system? These difficulties were compounded by the great differences among North Sea fields which were explained in Section 2.3.2, and by the unpredictable dramatic changes which have characterized the oil industry in the 1970s and 1980s. It is extremely hard to design a fiscal regime which will discriminate between the highly profitable and the less profitable oilfields, whilst also being sensitive to unanticipated changes in oil affairs.

The offshore fiscal environment was made increasingly onerous until, in 1982, the government decided the tax system was having an adverse impact on North Sea activity. Major concessions were introduced in 1983 in order to encourage exploration and development in the North Sea. However, because the tax system responds imperfectly and slowly to the changing economics of oil projects, lobbying for tax changes has been a continuous process (Hann, 1986c). By the mid-1980s, with low oil price expectations prevailing, companies were arguing for further tax concessions to assist marginal projects and promote incremental investments (United Kingdom Offshore Operators' Association, 1985).

Features of the offshore tax system have been its instability and its complexity (Rowland and Hann, 1987). Originally PRT was a 45 per cent charge on net annual profits after allowing for three items – carried-forward losses, an 'uplift' depreciation provision, and an oil allowance of 1 million tonnes a year – but restricted by a 'tapering' limit. PRT payments in any one year can neither reduce returns to less than 30 per cent of accumulated capital costs nor collect more than four-fifths of the net revenue above this 30 per cent figure. Since 1975 the rate of PRT has been increased to 60 per cent, to 70 per cent and again to 75 per cent. A Supplementary Petroleum Duty (SPD) was introduced in 1981 and subsequently abolished in 1982. Advance PRT (APRT) was introduced in 1983 and at the time of writing (July 1987) is being phased out though the 1986 budget provided for early repayment of some APRT. As a result of a slowdown in exploration activity, the 1983 budget introduced a dual tax system for the North Sea specifically to encourage new activity. For fields granted development consent after 1 April 1982 royalty payments were abolished and the PRT oil allowances, after being halved in 1978, were restored to their initial level.

2.5.2 Implications and Problems

The government 'take' – the total of royalties, corporation tax and PRT expressed as a percentage of net revenues – from all North Sea ventures now under way is likely to be around 70 per cent. Among individual projects, however, there will be considerable differences in tax take. Some fields such as Piper, Forties and Dunlin pay over 80 per cent whilst for some projects such as Deveron and Duncan the take will be much lower, probably with no PRT at all paid. The variation of tax takes between fields is only loosely related to expected oilfield profitability. Instead of a progressive tax regime (where, as profits rise the tax take, as a proportion of profits, increases), Britain has a complex and frequently changed tax structure with uncertain effects. The progressive element in PRT is supposedly provided by the tax-free oil allowance. Since it is calculated purely in terms of a fixed quantity of oil, the oil allowance is of greater benefit to small fields than to large fields. However, it is a serious mistake to equate the size of a field with its profitability.

A second distorting effect of the oil tax system occurs because it depresses the normal return on capital. In tax systems which do not have full allowance for long lead times and heavy front-end loading of capital expenditure, capital will be diverted away from sectors with such characteristics. The uplift provision in PRT fails to alleviate this distortion and because Corporation Tax is calculated using historic costs (not including any normal return on capital) it also has a distorting impact on oilfield economics.

Companies investing on the scale necessary to develop an offshore oilfield must consider events that could undermine their expected returns. Initial appraisals of field economics must incorporate expected profits sufficient to compensate for risk bearing. These risk-related profits will be most crucial on the less profitable developments: the more promising reserves are likely to be worthwhile even under pessimistic forecasts of oil prices and costs. The provision in PRT which appears to protect risk profits is the tapering and safeguard clause. However, it does not seem to prevent PRT deterring some marginal projects and, indeed, sometimes assists projects not needing protection. Because of the restricted time period for its use, the tapering and safeguard provision only operates when other allowances are clearly shielding revenues from PRT (Rowland and Hann, 1987).

A further problem associated with the offshore tax system is that over time as oil prices have increased (in nominal terms) governments have increased tax takes. However, a rising oil price is a signal both to reduce demand and to increase supply. By interfering with the incentive to increase supply (by harsher taxation), the government jeopardizes the desirable supply response – or at least confuses the economic signals to producer and consumer. Moreover, because altering the *rate* of PRT has a relatively small impact on government tax receipts (because of the complex PRT allowances) structural changes to the system are usually necessary when government wishes to respond to changes in the oil industry. A particular problem in the mid-1980s is the tax system's failure to deal adequately with oilfield abandonment – a problem requiring specific attention (Kemp and Rose, 1985).

In spite of the curious characteristics of the offshore tax system, it is clear that the North Sea is going to be a significant (though probably declining) source of government revenue into the 1990s. The size of tax receipts from offshore oil operations will depend on the future course of world oil prices, on the extent of North Sea oil reserves, on the nature of new oilfield discoveries and on the tax regime itself.

2.6 CONCLUSION

The North Sea oil and gas industry is now a well-established sector of the British economy accounting for about 5 per cent of GNP. Whether another generation of fields will maintain offshore activity on a substantial scale beyond 2000 is uncertain. The lowest-cost reserves may well already have been brought into production, so that future developments are likely to be inherently higher cost projects which, on average, are smaller. Nevertheless, progress in extraction technology may continue to limit the rise in costs so that some new fields will come into production: just possibly, some further low-cost discoveries may be made. However, oil prices in the mid-1980s have had an immediate depressing impact on offshore exploration and development. The future scale of North Sea activity will depend crucially on the course of crude oil prices, though the energy and fiscal policies adopted by British governments will also be very important.

REFERENCES

Brierley, C. (1986), 'UK gas prospects', in P. Stevens, (ed.), *International Gas, Prospects and Trends* (London: Macmillan).
British Petroleum (1986a), *Statistical Review of World Energy* (London: BP).
British Petroleum (1986b), *Review of World Gas* (London: BP).
Dam, K. W. (1976), *Oil Resources: Who Gets What How?* (Chicago: University of Chicago Press).
Department of Energy (1976), *Development of the Oil and Gas Resources of the UK* (London: HMSO).
Department of Energy (1986), *Development of the Oil and Gas Resources of the UK* (London: HMSO).

Hann, D. (1986a), *Government and North Sea Oil* (London: Macmillan).

Hann, D. (1986b), 'The process of government and UK oil participation policy', *Energy Policy*, 14, 253–61.

Hann, D. (1986c), 'Political and bureaucratic pressures on UK oil taxation policy', *Scottish Journal of Political Economy*, 32, 278–95.

HMSO (1973), First Report from the Committee on Public Accounts, North Sea Oil and Gas, Session 1972–73 (London).

Institute for Fiscal Studies (1985), *Regulation of the Gas Industry*, Memoranda of Evidence, House of Commons Energy Committee, Session 1985–86: November.

Institute of Petroleum (1986), *Petroleum Statistics* (London: Institute of Petroleum).

Kemp, A. G., and Rose, D. (1985), *Fiscal Aspects of Field Abandonment in the UKCS*, University of Aberdeen, North Sea Study Occasional Paper no. 22.

Mabro, R., Bacon, R., Chadwick, M., Halliwell, M., and Long, D. (1986), *The Market for North Sea Crude Oil* (Oxford: Oxford University Press).

Myhr, G., and Raaholt, M. H. (1986), 'Oil prices, less than $15 to the year 2000 – is it possible?', International Association of Energy Economists Conference, Bergen.

Organization for Economic Co-operation and Development (1973), *Oil – The Present Situation and Future Prospects* (Paris: OECD).

Price, C. (1986) 'Privatising British Gas', *Public Money*, 2, 1, 13–19.

Robinson, C. (1978), 'A review of North Sea oil policy', *Zeitschrift für Energie Wirtschaft* (4/1978).

Robinson, C. (1979), 'North Sea investment and profitability', *Oil Now*, Den Norske Creditbank.

Robinson, C. (1982), 'Oil depletion policy in the United Kingdom', *Three Banks Review*, 135, 3–16.

Robinson, C. (1985), 'Gas depletion and policy towards the nationalised gas industry', in *United Kingdom Gas Depletion Policy*, Memoranda (Second Volume), House of Commons Energy Committee, Session 1984–85, March.

Robinson, C., and Marshall, E. (1984), *Oil's Contribution to UK Self-Sufficiency*, British Institutes' Joint Energy Policy Programme, Energy Papers No. 12 (London: Heinemann).

Robinson, C., and Marshall, E. (1985), *Regulation of the Gas Industry*, Memoranda of Evidence, House of Commons Energy Committee, Session 1985–86, November.

Robinson, C., and Marshall, E. (1986), *The Privatisation of British Gas*, Additional Memorandum, Memoranda of Evidence, House of Commons Energy Committee, Session 1985–86, January.

Robinson, C., and Morgan, J. (1978), *North Sea Oil in the Future: Economic Analysis and Government Policy* (London: Macmillan).

Robinson, C., and Rowland, C. (1978), 'An economic analysis of British North Sea oil supplies', *OECD Workshop on Energy Supply and Demand*, Paris.

Rowland, C., and Hann, D. (1987), *The Economics of North Sea Oil Taxation* (London: Macmillan).

Stern, J. P. (1986), *Natural Gas in the UK: Options to 2000*, British Institutes' Joint Energy Policy Programme, Energy Papers No. 18 (Aldershot, Hants: Gower).

United Kingdom Offshore Operators' Association (1985), *Getting the Most out of the North Sea* (January) (London: UKOOA).

FURTHER READING

A comprehensive text on the economics of the offshore industry is provided by C. Robinson and J. Morgan (1978), *North Sea Oil in the Future: Economic Analysis and Government Policy* (London: Macmillan). The development of BNOC is analysed in G. Corti and F. Frazer (1983), *The Nation's Oil: A Story of Control* (London: Graham & Trotman), whilst S. G. Hall and F. Atkinson (1983), *Oil and the British Economy* (London: Croom Helm) discusses the macro-economic impact of North Sea oil. There are several books focusing on specific issues associated with the oil extraction sector: R. Mabro *et al.* (1986), *The Market for North Sea Crude Oil* (Oxford: Oxford University Press) analyses the trade in Brent Blend; C. Robinson and E. Marshall (1984), *Oil's Contribution to UK Self-Sufficiency* (London: Heinemann) assesses the merits of oil self-sufficiency; H. Motamen (1983), *Macroeconomics of North Sea Oil in the United Kingdom* (London: Heinemann) looks at oil depletion in a quantitative model. A detailed criticism of the oil tax system is presented in C. Rowland and D. Hann (1987), *The Economics of North Sea Oil Taxation* (London: Macmillan) and in D. Hann (1986), *Government and North Sea Oil* (London: Macmillan) the government oil policy process is examined. A series of issues are confronted in the British Institutes' Joint Energy Policy Programme Energy Papers series – for instance J. P. Stern (1986), *Natural Gas in the UK: Options to 2000*, Energy Papers no. 18. Evidence presented to the Energy Select Committee by C. Robinson and E. Marshall, P. Odell and J. Stern is of interest, as are the papers issued by industry lobby organizations such as the United Kingdom Offshore Operators' Association and the Association of British Independent Oil Exploration Companies. Energy-related journals such as *Noroil, Energy Economics, Energy Policy* and the *Petroleum Economist* often deal with offshore oil and gas issues. The Department of Energy publishes an annual record (*Development of the Oil and Gas Resources of the UK*, (HMSO)) providing useful statistical information on various North Sea matters.

Chapter Three

Coal

BARRY THOMAS

3.1 INTRODUCTION

The coal industry has a prominent place in the economic and social history of Britain. Its dominance of the energy sector during the last two hundred years of industrialization, its unmistakable imprint on the landscape, and the distinctive characteristics of mining communities and organizations have been the hallmarks of a great industry. But times change and in postwar years there has been a spectacular decline in the size of the industry.

Since nationalization in 1947 British Coal (formerly called the National Coal Board) has been responsible for about 99 per cent of UK production, so the firm and the industry may be treated synonymously. The UK industry is the largest in Europe. In 1987, 110 collieries produced 88 million tonnes of coal and employed 125,000 workers. On average each pit employed about 1,200 men, produced about 0.87 million tonnes and had a productivity level measured in terms of output per manshift (OMS) of 3.29 tonnes. In addition to the colliery output a further 14 million tonnes were produced from opencast sites.

World output of coal is expanding, though most of the older industrial nations reached their production peak in the early years of this century. In the UK, as Figure 3.1 shows, the most rapid period of contraction in postwar years was in the 1960s when there was increasing use of oil and natural gas. Since the energy crisis in 1973 the rate of decline has slowed and there has been a substantial investment programme.

Coal is a sedimentary rock, of vegetable origin, which varies greatly in its physical and chemical properties. Access to the coal seams is normally by the sinking of a shaft, though sometimes a drift mine, with direct tunnelling, is possible. The present general method of extraction in UK mines is longwall face mining in which a machine is moved back and forth along a coal face. As it moves it cuts a web of coal and loads it on to a conveyor. In some cases instead of advancing the face, complete access roads may be driven before cutting, which then begins at the most distant point, and the face retreats.

Production in this mature extractive industry is quite different from

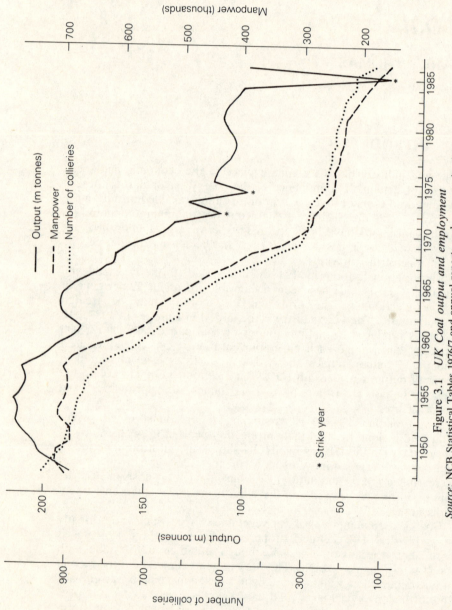

Figure 3.1 *UK Coal output and employment*

Source: NCB Statistical Tables 1976/7 and annual reports and accounts (various years).

that in manufacturing industry. It is as if 'a large part of the factory has to be uprooted and moved on every working day' (Berkovitch, 1977, p. 96). This means that costs of production are constantly tending to rise (leaving aside the offsetting effects of technical progress) as operations have to go deeper and further from the shaft. Working faces may be five miles or more from the shaft so supervision is often difficult. Geological conditions are such that the raw material sometimes disappears or becomes so difficult to work that part or all of the 'factory' has to close. These risks can be more easily pooled in large-scale multi-plant organizations and this is one argument in favour of single ownership. Apart from this there is no economic rationale for single ownership. Each year substantial replacement investment is required to make good the loss in capacity, which can be up to 3 per cent of output per annum. Pit closures are usually irreversible because of flooding and choking-up with underground waste.

Opencast (surface mining) has become increasingly significant; in 1987, 85 per cent of output was from deep-mines, 14 per cent from opencast and about 2 per cent from private mines licensed from British Coal. Davison (1977) has shown that it is now possible to undertake opencast working at considerable depths so that for the first time a choice of technique, between surface and underground mining, is sometimes feasible. The quality of some deep-mined coal has deteriorated, because machines smash the coal and may mix dirt and coal. However, opencast coal is of sufficient quality to offset this deterioration and it has helped to preserve a mix of coals, without which some markets might have been lost. A major external diseconomy of opencast working is environmental despoliation, but there is at present no adequate machinery for calculating these social costs and weighing them against social benefits.

The main coalfields in the UK are in South Wales, Scotland, the North-East, the central regions of Yorkshire, Derbyshire and Nottinghamshire, and the South and West Midlands. The present distribution of output and employment is shown in Table 3.1. The geographical concentration of mining means that it has been a dominant activity in certain localities, some of which owe their development entirely to coal. When the coal was exhausted many mining communities proved to be very vulnerable and regional economic policy has therefore been closely associated with the coal industry. The pit closure programme has been most intense in regions with poor alternative employment prospects and this has meant that regional employment considerations have had a major impact on decision-making in the industry.

The coal industry has a wider range of duties and obligations than private industry but it has been less subject to financial discipline in that the ultimate sanction of liquidation has been absent and the government has underwritten its finance. British Coal is subject to continuous political pressures arising from social, regional and other

Table 3.1 *Area Statistics, 1986*

	Saleable output of deep-mined coal		Colliery average manpower		Colliery output per manshift		Costs of production		Operating profits
	m tonnes	% of total	thousands	% of total	tonnes	% of mean	£ per gigajoule	% of mean	£ per tonne
Scottish	4.3	4.9	8.8	5.7	2.21	81.3	2.29	127	−10.70
North-East	9.5	10.8	19.8	12.8	2.23	82.0	1.96	108	−3.58
North Yorkshire	13.9	15.8	22.8	14.7	3.04	111.8	1.86	103	−4.39
South Yorkshire	12.5	14.2	22.0	14.2	2.90	106.6	1.67	92	0.88
North Derbyshire	6.2	7.1	9.7	6.3	3.04	111.8	1.82	101	−4.19
Nottinghamshire	18.7	21.3	27.2	17.6	3.21	118.0	1.50	83	5.19
South Midlands	6.2	7.1	9.7	6.3	3.01	110.7	1.82	101	−2.74
Western	9.4	10.7	16.3	10.5	2.74	100.7	1.88	104	2.87
South Wales	6.6	7.5	16.7	10.8	1.87	68.8	2.15	119	−9.85
Kent	0.5	0.6	1.7	1.1	1.66	61.0	2.10	116	−6.00
Total	87.8	100.0	154.7	100.0	2.72	100.0	1.81	100.0	−1.95

Source: British Coal, *Report and Accounts, 1985/6.*

issues, and its relationship with government, which should be characterized by trust, continuity and accountability has been ill-defined for most of the postwar period. There is now, however, agreement that British Coal should give full weight to commercial objectives.[1]

3.2 THE STRUCTURE OF PRODUCTION AND DEMAND

3.2.1 The Structure of Production

The production of coal is characterized by inflexibility. Output responses to changes in demand are slow because there is little 'spare capacity' and lead times are long. The industry has become more concentrated with the fall in the number of pits but the most significant feature of the industry's structure is that there is still great variation across pits in output, employment and productivity. Average figures mask an enormous dispersion in these variables.

There is a distinct and persistent geographical pattern to these differences, so some areas perform much better than others (see Table 3.1). Inter-Area variation in earnings is less than that in productivity, thus costs vary substantially across areas.[2] Furthermore, since inter-area differences in prices are less than those in costs, the profits per tonne vary considerably across areas. On short-term efficiency grounds the case for more concentration in profitable areas, and more particularly in profitable pits, is obvious, though other considerations such as local employment cannot be dismissed.

At pit level there are economies of scale. Bigger pits tend to have lower costs[3]: there is a highly significant positive correlation between pit size (measured by output) and OMS, and a highly significant negative one between OMS and costs per gigajoule.

Some crude idea of the cost structure for the industry as a whole in 1984 can be obtained from Figure 3.2 which shows the cumulative ranking of pits according to their productivity.[4] The inverted productivity scale can be regarded as a rough proxy for costs per tonne, and the *AB* curve is akin to a system marginal cost curve because it shows the 'cost' at which any increment in output (below the total output level *OD*) can be obtained. *AC* shows the 'average cost' of producing different levels of output. It is clear that a substantial proportion of total output (*ED*) is produced at a 'cost' (shown by the inverted productivity scale) higher than the industry average.

Figure 3.2 is drawn on the assumption that British Coal operates a merit order of pits and that any cost-minimizing multi-plant operator runs the lowest-cost pits first. However, as Bates and Fraser (1974) have noted, if social constraints mean that high-cost pits have to be run at some minimum output level then some of the low-cost pits would run at less than full capacity until the constraint is met. Thereafter low-

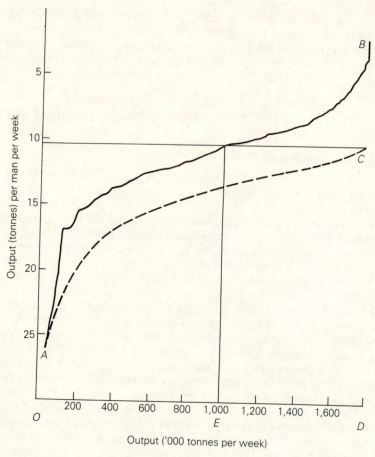

Figure 3.2 *'Cost' curves*

Source: See note 4.

cost pits would provide the additional output and the system marginal cost curve may therefore fall.

British Coal is attempting to improve its competitive position by using a long-term strategy of further concentration on low-cost pits (which will flatten the curves shown in Figure 3.2) and also by using a short-term strategy of increasing the productivity of all pits by an' incentive payments scheme (which will shift the curves downwards).

3.2.2 Demand

The demand for energy has a low positive income elasticity, thus the energy market has been growing slightly faster than incomes. But coal's share of this market has fallen. Indeed, there has been a long-term absolute decline in the demand for coal. Over the two centuries to 1955 *primary* fuel consumption was virtually all coal but there has been a marked fall since then to about 36 per cent of the market. Oil, gas and nuclear power have become more important. Among *final* users of energy solid fuel's market share has fallen from 74 per cent in 1950 to 13 per cent by 1985. The fall in coal consumption has been accompanied by a pronounced change in the structure of coal markets. In the 1950s and 1960s two major markets, railways and gas production, were entirely eliminated. The power stations have increased steadily in importance. In 1948 they took 14 per cent of coal sales but by 1986 the figure was 76 per cent. Thus about three-quarters of sales are to a single buyer, the Central Electricity Generating Board (CEGB).

Relative fuel prices are the most important factor determining the demand for coal and the pronounced rises and falls in the price of oil have been of especial relevance. The price of coal (in pence per therm) has generally been much less than that of other fuels[5] but its non-price attributes such as handling costs, cleanliness and variability in quality compare unfavourably with other fuels. Also confidence in the reliability of supply from British Coal has been dented by major industrial disputes, and imports of substitute fuels have become more attractive.

The price elasticity of demand is determined by the existence of substitutes and, where coal is a derived demand, by product market elasticities, by the ratio of fuel costs to total costs, and by the elasticity of the supply of co-operating factors of production. This last point is highly significant. The demand for coal is complementary to the demand for coal-fired equipment which cannot be changed quickly. Indeed the high capital cost of coal-fired equipment and the very short pay-back periods used by industrialists[6] (2–3 years) have been major factors in the decline and limited expected growth of coal demand. In the long run the estimated own-price elasticities are high, for example, -4.6 for industrial users and -2.96 for domestic users.[7]

Another factor affecting the demand for coal is government intervention. Legislation which was chosen as the method of combating the external diseconomies of coal burning (for example, the Clean Air Acts of 1957 and 1968 and subsequent regulations) caused a decline in demand, especially in the house-coal market, which has not been fully offset by the consequent development and production of smokeless fuel. On the other hand, the government has, at various times, boosted the demand for coal. It has used a mixture of direct controls (for example, controls on imports), taxes (on fuel oil), subsidies (to induce the electricity-generating and steel industries to stock more coal and to induce consumers to install coal-fired equipment), exhortation (to the electricity industry and to government establishments), and financial aid to make coal more competitive.

These influences almost certainly moderated the long-run fall in demand.

Finally, the demand for coal is determined by the demand for the products of industrial users and increased efficiency in fuel burning. For example, in 1979–83 the recession and energy conservation measures caused industrial users to reduce demand by about 40 million tonnes. As far as the future is concerned the massive dependence of British Coal on the CEGB is of the greatest importance. The CEGB's dependence on coal has lessened[8] and although its current consumption of coal is largely fixed by existing installations, there can be some switching in the merit order of power stations. The future demand for coal is uncertain. There is a growing move to nuclear power stations,[9] more reliance on imports (and the tendency to locate power stations near the south coast), and great uncertainty about the growth in the demand for electricity and the movement of oil prices.

3.3   PRICING AND INVESTMENT

3.3.1   Pricing

Different consumers value differently the various physical and chemical properties of coal and in any general discussion of pricing it must be remembered that coal is not homogenous.[10]

In principle the efficient price of coal is the short-run marginal cost, assuming that labour and other factors of production are correctly priced. This view has been espoused by the government on a number of occasions.[11] It has argued that prices set in this way are one of the most important instruments for giving both producers and consumers accurate signals about the costs of energy supply. Marginal cost pricing would imply that prices will vary from pit to pit but in fact there has been a degree of price uniformity across pits. Area rather than pit costs have been used as a basis for pricing which implies some cross-subsidizing across pits, but there has also been some inter-Area cross-subsidizing because costs per tonne have varied more than prices per tonne. Prices are certainly not completely uniform but there has been a tendency for the price dispersion to narrow.[12] Any such movement away from pricing according to local costs would have significant implications for the CEGB: Newbery (in Belgrave and Cornell, 1985) has argued that locationally specific coal prices could alter the merit order of CEGB operations with consequent cost savings. Any uniformity in prices means that weaker high-cost peripheral regions are subsidized by stronger low-cost central regions.

Recently British Coal has rejected a simple cost-plus approach to pricing and has said that prices should be based competitively, taking account of substitute fuels and of internationally traded coal. 'Competitive prices will determine acceptable costs of production, not the other way round' (NCB Memorandum in HMSO, 1986, p. 17). These pricing rules would then be used as a basis for capacity planning. For example, any additional output should have a marginal cost of not more than £1 per gigajoule (at 1985 prices).

The basis of pricing to the CEGB, the largest customer, has already begun to reflect some of these considerations, and recent deals have specified that initial tranches of supply would be priced to reflect average costs and the price of further tranches would be aligned to the price of oil and to overseas coal delivered at London. It is interesting to note that there are also quantity clauses in the deals with the CEGB. The CEGB has agreed to a 7-year commitment to take 95 per cent of its coal from British Coal, but such restrictions on imports which are sometimes advocated in terms of self-sufficiency and security, may not be desirable given the uncertainty of domestic labour problems.

3.3.2 Investment

The major determinant of the level of investment in the coal industry has been long-run expected demand. This produced a pattern of moderate fixed investment in the 1950s, followed by disinvestment in the 1960s, and a sizeable investment programme in the 1970s and to a lesser extent the 1980s. Since the change of government in 1979 the emphasis has swung from long-term expansion, as a basis for investment, to short-term viability, but since the driving force for the most postwar years has been long-run demand it is instructive to comment briefly on the experience of the 1960s and 1970s.

The substantial disinvestment of the 1960s raises the question of the optimality of the size and speed of the contraction. Posner (1973) has argued that the optimal rate of contraction of the coal industry requires the production in each year of that quantity of coal which minimizes total resource costs of fuel subject to social and distributional constraints, but it is clearly difficult to assess how nearly such a rate was achieved. In an industry where future demand is uncertain, where fixed investment has long lead times and where pit closures are often irreversible, slow output responses are to be expected. But even in a world of certain demand and zero gestation lags, it would not be optimal to adjust output instantaneously if there were increasing marginal costs of adjustment. The more steeply these costs rise, the slower the optimal adjustment should be.

Labour is the main cost of production so it is labour adjustment costs which are the most relevant. The total financial costs of redundancy and early retirement will be linearly related to the size of layoffs and so the optimal rate of contraction would thus be instantaneous. Other labour costs, however, probably increase with the size of adjustment. 'Morale effects' show up in recruitment difficulties, increased absenteeism, and increased wastage of the younger and more skilled workers that the industry wishes to retain. This last effect reduces the average quality of employees. The impact of these 'morale effects' is to reduce OMS and raise average costs. The possibility of redeployment within the industry also becomes increasingly difficult as the more obvious possibilities for transfer and early retirement are used up. Thus the cost of closure rises as the rate of closure increases. It is difficult to quantify these adjustment costs but they do appear to be significant in the coal industry. Social costs of unemployed miners and equity factors relating to regional distribution of employment also have to be considered.

The scale of contraction in the 1960s was massive compared with other reallocations of resources in the economy. The workforce fell by well over 30,000 men each year. Some critics have argued that the rate of rundown should have been faster, but the various efficiency and social criteria suggest that the optimal rate of rundown was much less than instantaneous and it is therefore quite possible that no serious misallocation occurred through sub-optimal rates of contraction.

In the 1970s a much more optimistic view was taken and in 1974 a major ten-year investment programme was launched as part of a 'Plan for Coal' which aimed to expand output to 135 million tonnes by 1985. This was followed in 1977 by a further plan, *Coal for the Future*, which set a target of 170 million tonnes by the year 2000. The government of the day endorsed these plans, but they proved to be seriously unrealistic and by 1986 deep-mined output was in fact only 88 million tonnes. Part of the problem was the assumption that the long-term demand for coal was assured.

Long-term demand forecasting, however, has been full of hazards. First, guesses have been required about political factors that affect coal. It is difficult to exaggerate their significance, and it is interesting to note (Sheriff, 1978) that British Coal has found political factors to be so important in some cases that econometric techniques are counter-productive as an aid to planning decisions. Secondly, the relative price has changed dramatically. In 1974, for example, the ratio of coal to oil prices halved, and this gave a massive boost to coal. More recently, in 1986, the price of oil fell from over $30 per barrel to $10–15; if such low prices were to persist a substantial number of pits would become commercially non-viable.

Thirdly, long-term developments in the oil, gas, steel and other industries have had to be forecast, but the most important industry to forecast is electricity. The problems with the latter can be illustrated by the fact that, from the standpoint of 1986, a deviation of only 1 per cent in the central forecast in European electricity demand would mean that the European power station coal-burn could range from 178 to 254 million tonnes in 1995, and from 181 to 358 million tonnes in 2005. Furthermore, assumptions have been required about the future scarcity of supplies of oil and natural gas, about the role of nuclear power, and about technological developments, especially in steelmaking.

It is hardly surprising therefore that the record of forecasting long-term demand for coal has been poor. But in any case the planning of capacity only on the basis of expected demand has been strongly criticized by the Monopolies and Mergers Commission (HMSO, 1983a, para. 5.71) because such planning does not generate specific *performance* targets which lend themselves to monitoring. Very much more emphasis is now placed on shorter-term performance criteria as discussed in Section 3.4.

3.4 PERFORMANCE EVALUATION

It is remarkable that for most of the postwar period there has been no effective framework for measuring performance. This has been the result of successive governments failing to specify an objective function in operational terms and to assign weights to the equity and efficiency arguments. The Monopolies and Mergers Commission noted that 'in the past undue emphasis has been placed on production targets' (HMSO, 1983a, para. 19.24) but substantial changes have now occurred, and the practice of setting physical output targets is giving way to the setting of financial targets so that the market determines production levels.

3.4.1 Financial Performance

Financial criteria for assessing performance are only possible if financial objectives are clear. Throughout the 1960s and 1970s various financial criteria were set and subsequently waived or abandoned, but now the broad aim of British Coal is to break-even after paying interest on capital and receiving social grants (though the date by which it should do this has continuously been put back during the 1980s). More specifically, the government requires British Coal 'to earn a satisfactory return on its assets in real terms, after payment of social grants [and] to maximise its long-term profitability' (HMSO, 1986, p. 2). Thus it now seems unequivocal that British Coal is required to be market-driven. The government has not specified what is a satisfactory rate of return in the case of coal, though it requires a real rate of return of 5 per cent on new investment programmes (before payment of interest and tax).[13] This latter rate reflects the opportunity cost of capital and thus indicates a central concern with allocative efficiency.

Table 3.2 shows that opencast coal, most of which is produced by private contractors for British Coal, is highly profitable whereas losses are made on deep-mined coal. (Table 3.1 showed, however, a large variation between Areas.) This position is typical of recent years though improvements in profitability seem likely.

The financial results shown are calculated after taking account of

Table 3.2   *British Coal's Mining Profits, 1986/87*

	Output m tonnes	Total profit £	Profit per tonne £
Deep-mined coal	87.2	41	0.47
Opencast coal	13.3	244	18.39
Total	100.5	285	2.84

Source: British Coal, *Report and Accounts,* 1986/7.

substantial government aid (though this aid is small compared with that given in other European coal producing industries). The aid has been of several kinds. First, there has been aid with the social costs of pit closures, such as redundancy payments, aid to pension funds, and mobility and housing allowances to transferees. Secondly, in the past various capital reconstructions have allowed the writing-off of some debts. Thirdly, there have been some direct subsidies to coal buyers, especially the CEGB, and grants for the conversion to coal-burning equipment. Fourthly, there have been deficit grants to cover losses. These have been large (particularly in the strike year of 1985 when the grant reached £2.2 billion) but will probably lessen in the later 1980s with tighter financial discipline.

This aid has been piecemeal and not obviously based on some criteria for optimal subsidies. In effect there has been some *ex post* compensation. More stringent financial controls are now imposed on the industry by the government, particularly in the form of the amount of external finance which British Coal may raise.

3.4.2   Productivity

Some discussion of labour productivity is appropriate because this has been British Coal's principal measure of performance even though, as the Monopolies and Mergers Commission (HMSO, 1983a, para. 6.58) pointed out, it does not achieve a balanced monitoring of *all* resources and their unit costs linked to commercially oriented measures.

Figure 3.3 shows that productivity has increased substantially but at a very uneven pace, and comparisons with other countries and other industries indicate that performance has been modest in relative terms.

Productivity has grown, first, because of a redistribution of output in favour of pits with higher OMS. The move to fewer but larger pits[14] has brought economies of scale by spreading overheads and allowing greater use of machinery. In 1986 the average size of colliery (by output) was 40 per cent larger than a decade earlier and 240 per cent larger than in 1947.

Secondly, there has been capital investment in face and surface machinery. The percentage of total output from faces with power-loaders jumped from 5 per cent in 1953 to almost 100 per cent by the

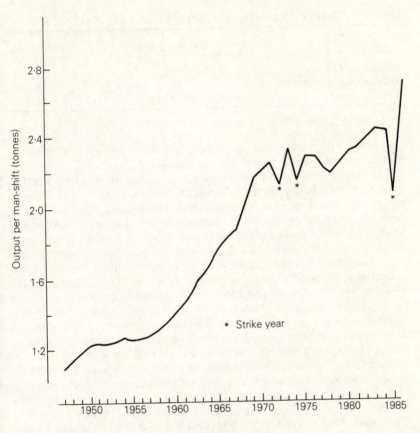

Figure 3.3 *Productivity*

Source: as for Figure 3.1

end of the 1960s. More recently there is growing use of heavy-duty technology at the coal face, such as the installation of shield supports. Table 3.3 shows that on these faces OMS is over 80 per cent more than on conventional faces. This development is especially significant because it heralds the switch from a labour-intensive to a capital-intensive industry, and this is likely to have major repercussions for labour. Not all technological progress has been embodied in new equipment. Changes in pit layout and roof-control techniques can raise productivity. There is, for example, growing use of retreat faces rather than advancing faces. (In 1985 the average daily output per face was 1,104 tonnes on retreat faces, compared with 878 tonnes on advancing faces.) Mines differ greatly in their operating conditions and the best-practice technique of production comprises pit-specific combinations of general machines. It is as if each plant in the industry adopts a unique technology.

Table 3.3 *Productivity on Different Types of Coal Face, 1985*

	Shield supports	Conventional
Number of faces	72	358
Daily output/face (tonnes)	1481	824
OMS (tonnes)	33.8	18.7

Source: HMSO, 1986, p. 224.

A third factor contributing to productivity increases has been the greater use of pit-based incentive schemes.

The forces leading to productivity growth have been constrained in various ways. The mechanization and the concentration of the industry by pit closures (for reasons other than exhaustion) have sometimes been attended by industrial relations problems. The increasing use of heavy-duty faces makes good industrial relations an imperative, as in other capital-intensive industries such as electricity supply and petrochemicals. On the question of pit closures, union resistance can sometimes impede the process, though it should be noted that in the 1960s when the closure programme was greatest, union co-operation was quite exceptional. However, British Coal's view (*Report and Accounts*, 1983/4, p. 4) is that there has been substantial investment in new capacity and the reconstruction of existing mines, but the pace at which old capacity has been retired has not kept up with the new and replacement capacity, consequently 'the industry has been burdened by the retention of high-cost capacity that has reduced competitiveness'.

A quite different constraint on productivity growth is that which arises from the peculiar nature of the production function in mining. The usual short-run diminishing returns to labour apply, assuming that the level of technical knowledge and quantity of capital are fixed, and also each further tonne of coal produced is won from more remote or difficult faces so that productivity in terms of coal at the pithead must fall. Even if the rate of output were to fall this would be so, which means that some part of the increase in mechanization is merely offsetting the inevitable fall in productivity. Moreover the putty-clay nature of the production function means that when the number of pits is falling there is less scope for building new 'factories' embodying current best-practice with respect to mine layouts. The industry is committed to previous layouts which often involve excessive distances or complex patterns of underground workings which require greater manning and maintenance.

Finally, the state of the product market may determine the vigour with which higher productivity is pursued, though this should not be relevant if there were wholehearted commitment to cost minimization. From 1947 to 1957, when the demand for coal exceeded supply, there was little serious drive for concentration or mechanization. This only came with the unfavourable change in the product market in the late

1950s. In the 1970s with the oil price rises, productivity growth again slowed, though there is now a strong move to increase productivity.

3.4.3 Innovation

British Coal has had an impressive innovation record. It has been a leader in the development of new machines and techniques to a surprisingly large degree, given its size in the world coal industry. It has generally been quick to adopt best-practice techniques from abroad, where these are appropriate to the difficult UK conditions, and many machines, such as the early cutter–loaders and powered roof supports, have been developed. There have been substantial sales of equipment to the USA and other countries where the longwall face system of mining is used. The Mining Research and Development Establishment (MRDE) has also developed hydraulic transport of coal in pipes and pneumatic transport, where fine coal is pumped to the surface to increase the throughput of the main shaft. Computerized control systems for underground coal transport are also being developed successfully, though more comprehensive automation, involving remote control of a complete integrated system of underground operations, remains at the experimental stage.

Product innovations, which have largely been responses to deteriorating market conditions, have been of two sorts: first, fuel processing to provide smokeless fuels, and improved blending techniques to allow the use of poorer quality coals; secondly, the development of more efficient combustion systems and techniques for handling coal and ash. These innovations reduce both the price per therm and the unfavourable non-price attributes such as dirt and inconvenience.

In some longer-term developments such as the conversion of coal into substitute natural gas (SNG), liquid transport fuels, and chemical feedstocks, British Coal is a leader. An interesting feature of these developments is the high degree of collaboration in R & D with other EC countries (for which the European Coal and Steel Community (ECSC) gives grants) and with other industries such as equipment manufacturers, British Gas and chemical companies.

At present the conversion of coal to petrol or SNG is not economic and will not be so until the production of North Sea oil and gas eventually declines and alters relative prices in favour of coal-based stocks. This is not likely to happen until the 1990s so coal conversion will probably first become economic in countries such as Australia, the USA and South Africa where coal can be mined cheaply. These countries are therefore likely to have fully developed technologies before UK needs arise. Whether it will be better for the UK to pursue its own R & D or buy in technology from abroad will depend on the expected relative costs of each. British Coal has chosen the former because the estimated cost is small in relation to potential licence fees. Such a strategy also enables the industry to keep its options open as many of the processes will be specific to UK conditions, so the lengthy induction period necessary if British Coal were to become an informed buyer and a successful adaptor of foreign technology, would be shortened by involvement in pilot plant work.

3.4.4 Labour

The demand curve for labour, which according to Carruth and Oswald (1985) has a wage elasticity of -1.0 to -1.4, has shifted leftwards because of the fall in the demand for coal and the growing substitution of capital. The management of employment reduction has been a major concern for the industry for the last thirty years and will continue to be important in the near future. In the first half of the 1980s, 80,000 jobs were lost. This was achieved almost entirely by miners leaving voluntarily in response to strong financial incentives – notably the Redundant Mineworkers' Payment Scheme (RMPS) – which are supported by the UK government and the ECSC. The leavers have mainly been older workers so the average age of the workforce has fallen from 43.2 years to 34.7 years in the decade to 1987. Further redundancies will now be harder to achieve because early retirement possibilities have been exhausted. The RMPS payments have been exceptionally generous compared with other industries and this raises important questions about the use of such selective subsidies for shaking out and reallocating labour.

Miners in the UK, as in other countries, have always played a notable part in labour conflict. There were major national disputes, over pay, in 1972 and 1974 which played a part in the introduction of a 3-day working week for much of the economy and in the change of government. The 1984/5 dispute in the industry was the most momentous in the entire history of labour in Britain. There are many views about the causes, ranging from a set-piece confrontation between a right-wing government and a Marxist union leader (for which encounter, preparations had been made well in advance), to a series of industrial relations accidents and mistakes. The putative issue was pit closures. British Coal (*Report and Accounts*, 1984/5) estimates that the dispute cost it about £1.7 billion; about £3.3 billion in lost output less £1.6 billion in cost savings. The Treasury estimates that the cost to the economy was £2 billion to £3 billion including £1.25 billion for the extra oil-burn at power stations, £0.75 billion in damage to mines, and £0.25 billion in peace-keeping.

The longer-term economic costs are difficult to assess. Consumers have again been led to doubt the reliability of supply and not all of the increased imports of coal have been won back by British Coal. The industrial relations consequences have been profound. The workforce was split on the question of support for the strike and a break-away union was formed so that British Coal now finds labour management awkward at a time when there is a drive to higher productivity and the greater use of heavy-duty technology.

3.5 PUBLIC POLICY

Where perfectly competitive conditions prevail and ignorance, uncertainty and externalities are absent, the price mechanism will produce allocative efficiency and the government may concentrate on producing an equitable distribution of real income. But such conditions do not apply in the coal industry. The case for intervention has been justified on several grounds. The first is the high degree of interdependence between the fuel industries and the importance of the energy sector for the rest of the economy which make issues such as security of supply relevant.[15] This is especially important where there are long lead times. Secondly, there are externalities such as environmental despoliation (though modern pits are no more unsightly than any other factory). Thirdly, there are special employment considerations such as safety[16] and the preservation of jobs in areas of very high unemployment. This last matter has meant that the issue of pit closures has been of central importance, especially in recent years.

Where pits are physically exhausted there is nothing to debate, but in practice 'exhaustion' is often defined in economic terms, given the prevailing technology, and the more general issue is whether 'uneconomic' pits should be closed.[17] If pits were always to be worked to exhaustion this would merely entail a subsidy from coal users to miners (see Bending and Eden, 1984, p. 237). There is considerable difficulty in defining 'uneconomic' pits: there is general agreement that the relevant data are future costs that would not be incurred and future revenues that would be lost if a pit closed, but much less agreement on what should be included in these categories and whether the shadow wage of miners is near zero if there is no alternative employment available.

There have been a number of policy responses to these issues. In practice there has been intervention in the market to affect both price and quantity. Price has been influenced by taxes (for example, on substitutes such as fuel oil) and subsidies (for example, grants for converting oil-burning appliances to coal), and quantity has been influenced by the government's setting or endorsing production targets and by issuing directives (for example, on the type of new power stations).

Any discussion of policy requires consideration of the institutional framework. Who are the appropriate decision-makers and do they have the relevant knowledge, responsibility and authority? In the case of coal this is in effect asking about the relative merits of decision-making by governments on the one hand and through markets on the other, or perhaps by some combination of the two. In the postwar years many strategic decisions in the coal industry have been decided on a political basis. Some observers such as Littlechild and Vaidya (1982, p. 17) have argued that the choice of policy in coal must ultimately be political, but in recent years (as described in Section

3.4.1) market tests have become more prominent. Obviously the use of commercial criteria means that non-commercial matters have to be handled separately and the government accepts that British Coal 'cannot . . . be expected to bear responsibility for the wider social costs associated with pit closures' (HMSO, 1986, p. 4). Some attempt to counter the physical and social deterioration that besets pit-based communities when mines close is being made through British Coal (Enterprise), which is a government-funded agency whose function is to stimulate the creation of jobs in such areas.[18]

The growing use of market tests in decision-making has implications for the structure of the industry. Robinson and Marshall (1985, p. 31) have argued that British Coal is 'a very unnatural monopoly created by government', so if market pressures were to be increased not only would it be desirable to allow freedom to import coal but also competition between pits should be encouraged. This would provide 'every incentive to produce at least cost and to appraise investments judiciously' (Newbery, in Belgrave and Cornell, 1985, p. 89). Proposals for a more competitive structure do not necessarily entail a move to private ownership of mines but in practice privatization has been seen as an obvious route to greater competition and the alleged consequent efficiency gains.

Two of the more important concerns with this type of argument are social considerations and the monopsonistic power of the CEGB. Where private decisions favour pit closures the case for keeping pits open would depend on a social cost–benefit analysis. The dominance of the CEGB as a customer raises the issue of whether, on welfare grounds, mergers of particular pits and power stations is the appropriate organizational form. If the socially relevant objective function were some joint maximand for the two industries this would be the case.

3.6 CONCLUSION

The output of the coal industry has been on a downward trend for over 70 years, but the long-term prospects are that output levels might stabilize or even rise as North Sea output is eventually reduced. There is no shortage of coal. At current rates of production using current mining technology, Moses (1981) has estimated that recoverable coal resources in the UK will last more than 400 years, compared with less than the 25 years estimated for UK oil and gas. How far coal recovers will depend *inter alia* on the pace of the nuclear programme in electricity generation and the extent to which the UK coal market is opened to imports.

A significant feature of the industry in the 1980s has been the government's greater insistence on the use of financial performance measures and the requirement to break even. Such an approach has thrown up the important issue of the definition of 'uneconomic' pits and the case for their closure. British Coal's continuing desire to concentrate production on low-cost high-productivity capital-intensive pits is part of the move towards greater efficiency, in terms of market criteria, but the social consequences of pit closures remain a major problem. The debate on the (de)politicization of decision-making in the coal industry is not yet fully resolved. This is hardly surprising in an area where both market failure and government failure are evident.

NOTES TO CHAPTER 3

1 National Coal Board, *Report and Accounts 1983–4*, p. 8.
2 Costs are now usually measured in pounds sterling per gigajoule rather than pounds per tonne. These two measures do not correspond exactly because coal varies in its quality.
3 It is difficult to be exact about this because the cross-sectional data used implicitly assume that all observations lie on the same cost function. This is unlikely because pits have unique geological and other operating conditions, employ different levels and types of technology, and do not therefore have the same production function.
4 In order to construct these proxies for 'cost' curves data on output (tonnes per week) and manpower for each pit were taken from Glynn (1984).
5 In 1985 for instance the relative price (in pence per therm) to large industrial customers, excluding iron and steel, was: coal 100 (20.32p); heavy fuel oil 184; gas oil 251; gas 140; electricity 433.
6 See the Science Policy Research Unit's survey (reported in HMSO, 1986, p. 306) which showed that among large-sized industrial customers 63 per cent of respondents mentioned the short length of the pay-back period as an obstacle to fuel switching.
7 These estimates are by the Department of Energy (HMSO, 1983b). For other estimates see Weyman-Jones (1986). Earlier estimates can be found in Wigley (1968) and Deaton (1975). It should be noted that the long-run elasticities are not constant and depend on market shares. Cross-price elasticities are positive because other fuels are coal substitutes.
8 In 1960, 82 per cent of the fuel input to power stations was coal compared with 67 per cent in 1975 and 63 per cent in 1986.
9 Some politicians appear to have been influenced by the Chernobyl nuclear accident in the USSR and may show more favour to coal-fired power stations in future.
10 Coals are evaluated according to their category of primary use, that is, industrial or domestic. The analysis here relates to industrial pricing. The pithead price of an industrial coal is based on its calorific value and then multiplied by an Area money value. Adjustments are then made for such factors as ash and sulphur content.
11 See HMSO (1967, 1978a, 1978b).
12 The cross-Area coefficient of variation (that is, the ratio of the standard deviation to the mean) fell from 0.195 in 1974 to 0.072 in 1985.
13 This was set in HMSO (1978b).
14 There has also been growing concentration of faces.

15 The need for government intervention on the grounds of preserving security of supply has been challenged by Robinson (1985).
16 Safety in mines has improved considerably, but there are still fears that due attention will not be given to safety as heavier technology is used in drives for higher productivity. Also the *present* industry has to bear costs of *past* failure in the form of compensation to pneumoconiosis sufferers.
17 See Glynn (1984) and Robinson and Marshall (1985) for opposing views.
18 In practice it operates on a very small scale and much more substantial spending on retraining, infrastructure, environmental improvement and so on has been advocated (see, for example, *The Economist*, 22 November 1986).

REFERENCES

Belgrave, R., and Cornell, M. (eds) (1985), *Energy Self-Sufficiency for the UK?* Joint Studies in Public Policy, 10 (Aldershot, Hants.: Gower).
Bending, R., and Eden, R. (1984), *UK Energy Structure Prospects and Policies* (Cambridge: Cambridge University Press).
Berkovitch, I. (1977) *Coal on the Switchback* (London: Allen & Unwin).
Carruth, A. A., and Oswald, A. J. (1985), 'Miners' wages in post-war Britain: an application of a model of trade union behaviour', *Economic Journal*, 95, 1003–20.
Davison, D. J. (1977), 'Opencast coal mining in the UK and its role in the mining industry'. *The Mining Engineer,* November, 215–21.
Deaton, A. S. (1975), 'The measurement of income and price elasticities', *European Economic Review*, 6, 261–73.
Glynn, A. (1984), *The Economic Case against Pit Closures* (Sheffield: National Union of Mineworkers).
HMSO (1967), *Nationalised Industries: A Review of Economic and Financial Objectives*, Cmnd 3437 (London).
HMSO (1978a), *Energy Policy: A Consultative Document*, Cmnd 7101 (London).
HMSO (1978b), *The Nationalised Industries*, Cmnd 7181 (London).
HMSO (1983a), *National Coal Board*, Monopolies and Mergers Commission Report, Cmnd 8920 (London).
HMSO (1983b), Department of Energy, Wigley, K., and Vernon, K. 'Methods for projecting UK energy demands used in the Department of Energy', in P. Tempest (ed.) *Energy Economics in Britain* (London: Graham & Trotman).
HMSO (1986), *The Coal Industry*, Volume I 29/1/86 and Volume II 18/6/86, House of Commons Energy Committee, Session 1985–86 (London).
Littlechild, S. C., and Vaidya, K. G. (1982), *Energy Strategies for the UK* (London: Allen & Unwin).
Moses, K. (1981) 'Britain's coal resources and reserves: the current position', in *Assessment of Energy Resources*, Report 9 (London: Watt Committee on Energy Ltd).
Posner, M. (1973), *Fuel Policy* (London: Macmillan).
Robinson, C. (1985), 'Coal policy in Britain', *Economic Review*, March, 2–6.
Robinson, C., and Marshall, E. (1985), *Can Coal Be Saved?* Hobart Paper 105 (London: Institute of Economic Affairs).

Sheriff, T. D. (1978), 'Medium term planning in UK nationalised industries', *National Institute Economic Review*, 84, 57–64.
Weyman-Jones, T. (1986), *The Economics of Energy Policy* (Aldershot, Hants: Gower).
Wigley, K. (1968), *The Demand for Fuel 1948–75*, Chapman & Hall for the Department of Applied Economics, University of Cambridge.

FURTHER READING

The most accessible sources of data are British Coal's annual *Report and Accounts* and the Department of Energy's *UK Digest of Energy Statistics*. A review of earlier statistics can be found in D. J. Harris's contribution to W. F. Maunder (ed.) (1980), *Review of UK Statistical Sources*, vol. XI, ESRC/RSS. Useful additional references are:

Bates, R., and Fraser, N. (1974), *Investment Decisions in the Nationalised Fuel Industries* (London: Cambridge University Press).
James, P. (1982), *The Future of Coal* (London: Macmillan).
Manners, G. (1981), *Coal in Britain* (London: Allen & Unwin).

Chapter Four

Steel

ANTHONY COCKERILL

4.1 THE ECONOMIC BACKGROUND

The steel industry, once the mainspring of economic activity, has been in decline in most advanced nations since the first oil shock of 1973. In that year, world steel output was almost 700 million tonnes[1] of which the European Community (EC), the USA and Japan accounted for 410 million tonnes, or 59 per cent. World output was at a similar level (711 million tonnes) in 1984, but the production of the three regions had fallen to 279 million tonnes (43 per cent). The decline in output was particularly apparent in the UK, where production fell from almost 27 million tonnes at the start of the period to less than 14 million tonnes at the end.[2] Figure 4.1 shows the movements in steel output and consumption in the UK, beginning in 1970 when both were at their highest-ever levels. There have been cyclical variations in demand and output as short-run changes in economic activity have occurred, but plainly the trend has been downward. Production exceeded consumption by a considerable margin at the start of the period, but this has been reduced as imports have risen in relation to exports.

Before the oil shock, steel was regarded in general as a mature industry, in which output could be expected to grow more or less in line with economic activity as measured by GNP, the scope for major product innovations was limited, and competition was between large-scale enterprises manufacturing products that were, in the main, hard to differentiate. Several factors can be identified that caused the industry to change from maturity to decline. In the first place, GNP in the industrialized countries grew more slowly after 1973 as a result of the sharp rise in oil prices that depressed incomes in the advanced countries while generating large financial surpluses for the oil-rich nations which they could not readily spend on capital goods or consumer durables. Secondly, the composition of the industrialized countries' GNP was changing, as services became more important at the expense of manufacturing and as manufacturing itself began to emphasize the production of higher value-added goods that contained less steel in relation to their value. Other influences also affected the demand for steel by the manufacturing sector: technological advances

70

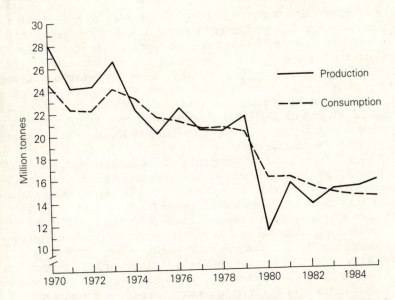

Figure 4.1   *UK steel and consumption 1970–85. (Crude steel equivalent)*
Source: Iron and Steel Statistics Bureau, *Annual Statistics 1982*

meant that thinner gauges of steel could be used in manufacture, thus reducing the tonnage required for any given output of final product, and in the motor vehicle sector, an important source of steel demand, purchasers switched to smaller, more fuel-efficient cars. Thirdly, the international competitiveness of the steel industry in most of the industrialized countries was reduced by the rise of production in newly industrializing countries (for example, South Korea and Brazil), which had the benefits of natural resources, low production costs and strong domestic demand. The result of this was that the industrialized countries' exports weakened while their domestic markets were penetrated by imports. The major producing regions took steps to protect their internal markets from destabilization by imports.

In spite of the downturn in demand, the steel industry remains a significant part of most industrialized economies. In the EC as a whole, it represents about 2 per cent of value added and 3 per cent of employment in the production industries.[3] Its output is an important intermediate product within the manufacturing sector. Steel is used mainly in the motor vehicle manufacturing, wire, cans and metal boxes and industrial plant sectors. About a third of all steel deliveries in the UK passes through stockholders, which cut or treat steel as necessary to meet customers' specific needs. Approximately one-half of total steel supplies is in the form of flat products – sheet, plate, strip and coil – while the other part consists of a variety of bars, angles, shapes, rods and wire. Flat products are generally derived from large oblong shapes called slabs, while other products are made from long narrow shapes known as billets. The greater part of steel products are made from carbon steel, which is suitable for a wide range of general uses and has most of the impurities removed during melting. About 10 per cent of output tonnage is of special steel. This is further refined during the manufacturing process to remove almost all impurities, and other metals such as chromium, tungsten and vanadium are added to produce alloys with particular characteristics such as rust resistance (stainless steels), cutting power (high-speed steels) or heat resistance (in steels for aerospace use).

Although there are many different kinds of finished steel, which sell to a variety of consuming sectors, it is difficult within each group for manufacturers of carbon steel products to differentiate their output from that of their competitors. Competitive advantage therefore depends upon having some command over the channels of distribution, on maintaining close relationships with customers, and in ensuring consistent quality and reliability of supply. Price competition is a distinctive feature of the steel market in the short run. As the demand for steel is derived from that for finished goods, steel consumption is mainly a function of the level and rate of growth of national income, reflecting and amplifying cyclical movements in activity. Demand is income inelastic, as shown by the tendency for consumption to increase more slowly than GNP in the long run. Price elasticity in the market as a whole is also low: a general reduction in steel prices will do little to raise demand in a recession. However, the cross-price elasticity of demand between suppliers of similar products is very high. Given the undifferentiated nature of the good, a unilateral price cut by one supplier will lead to a sharp increase in demand as market share is taken from competitors. But this action will itself induce retaliatory price cuts intended to defend market share. This is one cause of price instability in the steel market at times of weak demand.

There is rather more opportunity for manufacturers to differentiate their products in the special steels sector of the market, where quality and particular use characteristics are important, but even here, technical improvements have meant that quality differences between suppliers have been reduced and international competition has become fierce.

Short-run supply conditions in the steel industry are characterized by high fixed costs on account of the capital intensity of the bulk carbon steel production process. Large-scale steel mills are highly vertically integrated, incorporating mineral preparation, ironmaking, steel melting, casting, rolling and finishing, on the same site. Depreciation, financial charges, indirect labour, energy and other overhead charges represent about a third of total costs in most mills of this type. At times of weak markets, the pressures are strong to cut prices until only variable costs are covered, so as to fill the available capacity. In the long run, economies of scale are important, emphasizing the need for the principal suppliers to concentrate most of their production capacity into a few, large plants that represent, in most cases, a significant fraction of total industry output. The development in the late 1950s of the basic oxygen steelmaking (BOS) system, in which oxygen is blown through liquid metal to speed up the refining process, increased the importance of both scale economies and vertical integration. BOS converters can process batches of metal of 300 tonnes and more and are generally used in sets of three vessels, so that annual production capacities of 6 or 8 million tonnes from a single complex can be reached.

As large quantities of hot metal must be supplied to the converters and then subsequently processed, introduction of the BOS process also made it necessary for improved large-scale ironmaking, casting, rolling and finishing plant to be developed and installed on the same site. Estimates of the economies of scale that are possible in integrated steelworks suggest that reductions in costs per tonne of output can be obtained as annual capacity is increased to about 8 million tonnes a year for mills producing flat products; for long products, the scope for scale economies continues up to about 5 million tonnes (Cockerill, 1974).

The development of the BOS system, which reduced the time for converting iron to liquid steel from 8 hours using the earlier open hearth process to about 60 minutes, obliged most major steelmakers to become involved in expensive reinvestment to take advantage of the lower operating costs and higher labour and capital productivity that the new system offered. They were encouraged by the view generally held that steel demand would continue to grow and would make possible the profitable change from the old system to the new at the same time as overall capacity was increased to capture the economies of scale. In the event, the downturn in demand meant that the investment schemes of most suppliers were too ambitious and had to be cut short, leaving unfinished plant, excess capacity and a residue of old, high-cost equipment. Trading losses and capital expenditures obliged many firms within Western Europe to seek finance from outside, often from their governments.

Meanwhile, another aspect of technical change in the industry was increasing still more the financial and operating difficulties of large, integrated steel producers. Special steel had been made for many years in electric arc furnaces, small vessels (by comparison with the BOS) in which cold metal is melted by passing a strong electric current between two electrodes. The process is well suited to the special steel market because it is small in scale, flexible and produces metal of high quality. Its use in producing carbon steels was limited, however, mainly on account of the high cost of electricity in relation to other forms of energy. But during the 1970s, several factors combined to make the electric arc process competitive with the BOS over a significant part of the output of several major steel-producing countries. First, the real (that is, inflation-adjusted) price of electricity fell as the efficiency of the supply industry was improved. Secondly, the rate of replacement of physical assets increased, giving rise to a growth in the supply, and fall in the price of, steel scrap, from which new steel could be made in electric arc furnaces. Thirdly, industrial expansion meant that the demand for steel rose, often in the same regions in which the supply of scrap was rising. Lastly, improvements in continuous casting techniques, in which molten steel is run through long channels and allowed to solidify, meant that the large scale and high fixed costs associated with ingot casting was no longer essential for carbon steel manufacture. As a result of these factors, steel mills based on scrap, using electric arc furnaces and continuous casting, and producing billets and billet-derived products for sale mainly into adjacent industrial markets became potentially profitable, and a number of such so-called 'mini-mills' were built in North America, Western Europe and Japan. At first it was expected that they would complement the output of the integrated producers, specializing in those long products for which quality was not important and giving the industry flexibility in adjusting to demand variations, but their low overhead costs, widening product ranges and improvements in quality enabled mini-mills to take market share from their larger competitors as the effects of the recession were felt. Technical change and falling demand posed the major suppliers a severe dilemma: to what extent should they press ahead with investment in large-scale BOS plants, close redundant capacity, and themselves become involved in mini-mills? The uncertainties and the concern of governments with employment meant, almost inevitably, that none would resolve the dilemma satisfactorily.

4.2 THE STRUCTURE OF THE INDUSTRY

4.2.1 The Size of the Industry

In spite of its recent decline, the UK steel industry remains an important component of the economy, accounting for about 2 per cent of manufacturing output and employment and 3 per cent of investment.[4] In 1983 there were 269 enterprises in the industry as defined in the Standard Industrial Classification. These operated 343 establishments. However, the number of actual steelmaking units is very small. In 1984 only 26 produced crude steel, of which 5 were fully integrated from the ironmaking to the finishing stages.[5] Operations are typically on a large scale: the average employment sizes of establishments and enterprises are more than four-and-a-half times those for all manufacturing. About 80 per cent of sales, net output and employment are concentrated in the 5 largest enterprises.[6]

The most important enterprise in the industry is the British Steel Corporation (BSC), formed in 1967 by the nationalization of the 13 largest steel producers. BSC produces virtually all the nation's iron (99 per cent) and an overwhelming proportion of crude steel (86 per cent). Its share of the supply of finished steel products from UK mills is about 60 per cent, as it is a main supplier of semi-finished steel to independent re-rollers and finishers. There are about 130 enterprises in the industry in addition to BSC, of which about 30 produce and process crude steel. These steel producers account for about 14 per cent of crude steel output; about three-quarters of this is non-alloy grades, the rest being alloy steels. This sector of the industry has recently undergone extensive rationalization, involving closure of capacity, the withdrawal of firms from the sector and the setting-up of joint-venture companies in association with BSC. Through their rolling and finishing operations, the independents account for about one-third of finished steel deliveries from UK mills.

Steel imports represent about one-quarter of the supplies of finished products to the UK market, a share that has risen steadily from less than 6 per cent in 1970. Rather more than one-half of all imports comes from elsewhere in the EC. Of the remainder, the greater part comes from other Western European countries, particularly Sweden. Less than 5 per cent of imports come from Japan. Increasing import penetration has been the result of the ending of import protection upon the UK's entry into the EC, the greater competitiveness of some other European producers and, from time to time, the inability of UK producers to meet the needs of the market. Foreign competition has been particularly severe in the markets for sheet steel (where imports accounted for almost 40 per cent of supplies in 1985), plate (20 per cent), tubes and pipes (21 per cent), and reinforcing rods and bars (19 per cent).

Although imports have risen sharply, their market share in the UK is not high by comparison with most of the other nations of the EC. Imports represent more than one-quarter of the market in France and West Germany, and more than two-thirds in the Netherlands, Denmark, the Irish Republic and Belgium and Luxembourg. The UK's experience may reflect the influence of relative advantage in moving the market towards an equilibrium. Indeed, while import volumes have risen, the trend in exports has been flat. Western Europe is the most important market, taking more than one-half of UK steel exports; the North American market absorbs a further 14 per cent. After some years of deficits in the 1970s and early 1980s, the balance of trade has moved back into surplus.

4.2.2 The British Steel Corporation

The intentions of the 1964–70 Labour government to renationalize the iron and steel industry were set out in a White Paper published in April 1965 (HMSO, 1965). This proposed the transfer of the relevant assets of the companies that produced more than 475,000 gross tons

(483,000 tonnes) of crude steel in the period July 1963 to June 1964 to a National Steel Corporation. Compensation was to be paid at a rate determined by the average value of shares over the five-year period before 1964. The ensuing Act of 1967 provided for the establishment of the British Steel Corporation, which was to absorb the 14 largest companies.[7] At its formation, BSC's crude steelmaking capacity was about 24 million tonnes a year, making it then second only to the United States Steel Corporation.

Such a large-scale amalgamation of steelmaking activities gave rise inevitably to major problems of co-ordination and rationalization. The first step was to concentrate production on those mills that were the largest in capacity, had the most up-to-date equipment, and could be expanded to take account both of rising demand and production transferred from other works that were to be closed. It was some time before the new management was able to give thought to BSC's longer-term strategy. Proposals were drawn up for a major increase in capacity to meet the expected growth of demand, at home and abroad, to yield economies of scale and to enable new technology to be introduced. The scheme's approval and implementation were delayed by the initial scepticism of the Conservative government elected in 1970, but in 1973 a development plan was announced to raise BSC's steel producing capacity from 25 to between 36 and 38 million tonnes by the middle of the 1980s. Production was to be concentrated on five major sites – Port Talbot and Llanwern in South Wales, Scunthorpe and Lackenby in England, and Ravenscraig in Scotland. The first four of these are situated on or near the coast, allowing ease of movement of imports of raw materials and exports of finished steel.

No sooner had work begun on the expansion scheme, however, than steel demand began to fall in the wake of the first oil crisis, beginning a trend that was to continue throughout the 1970s. The return of a Labour government in 1974 meant that priorities changed from modernization and raising efficiency to protecting jobs; the pace of investment slowed down and the closure of old, high-cost, mills was halted. Falling demand and intense competition from foreign producers drove prices down, whilst costs were pushed up by the increase in excess capacity and the need to keep jobs. BSC's losses and its claims on government finance increased. Matters came to a head in 1978 when the government, anxious to cut public spending, announced both that the planned expansion was to be deferred and that necessary mill closures could go ahead.

There would still be a need for external finance, to meet the costs of essential capital expenditure, operating losses and redundancy and rationalization costs. This would be provided as 'new capital', under the terms of Section 18(2) of the 1975 Iron and Steel Act, which empowers the Secretary of State to subscribe to the corporation 'such sums as he sees fit', subject to the borrowing limits set by Parliament. These funds, which totalled almost £5 billion between 1978 and 1986 are non-repayable, non-interest-bearing equity; they impose no charges on the profit and loss account and amount, in effect, to capital subsidies from the Treasury.

The new policy was intended to reduce the claims of the steel industry on public expenditure and to bring capacity into line with the lower level of demand that had become apparent since 1973. Unfortunately, it was insufficient to cope with the continued reduction in demand that took consumption in 1983 to below 15 million tonnes for the first time. Output was affected more severely, chiefly as a result of a 13-week strike within BSC in the first quarter of 1980, which reduced production for the whole of that year to almost 11 million tonnes. The gap between consumption and production of almost 5 million tonnes (or almost a third of total demand) was met by imports. Production recovered to reach 14 million tonnes in 1981 and has ranged between that level and 12 million tonnes a year subsequently, a rate of output well below that throughout most of the 1970s.

The election in May 1979 of a Conservative government pledged to cut public expenditure and reduce the size of the public sector through privatization increased the pressures on BSC to improve productivity and cut costs. The 1980 strike was brought about in part by the corporation's refusal to negotiate a national pay deal with the steelworkers' union on account of a sharp reduction in external financing by government, and in part also by employees' fears that schemes would be brought in to raise productivity by reducing job opportunities, and to cut capacity.

In June 1980, the government appointed Mr (now Sir) Ian McGregor to be chairman of BSC. He described the corporate plan submitted in December of that year as a 'survival strategy'. The plan aimed, over the course of 1981/2, to regain the share of the home market for finished steel products of 54 per cent that BSC had held before the strike; to reduce manned annual capacity to just above 14 million tonnes; to increase exports, and to raise productivity by further reductions in employment. At the same time, the government asked BSC to plan to keep the five major steelmaking sites, including Ravenscraig, in operation at least until 1985, and agreed to a reconstruction of the corporation's finances. This wrote off more than £4.5 billion of equity and debt and provided for the remaining debt to be replaced progressively by equity capital.

Although steel demand remained below the projections of the plan, it was in general successful in its aims. Domestic market share and exports increased as the cost competitiveness of the business improved. This was achieved by raising labour productivity through reductions in overmanning and improved working practices; by increasing the utilization of manned capacity; by relating earnings increases to productivity gains; by concentrating capital expenditure on schemes that would improve operating efficiency, and by competitive pricing, within the terms specified by the European Commission, which the reduction in costs made possible. The fall in the sterling exchange rate after 1981 also aided cost competitiveness. External financing requirements have been reduced progressively from more than £1 billion in 1980/1 to less than £500 million in 1985/6. BSC returned to profit after depreciation and interest in 1985/86 and achieved a surplus of £178 million in 1986/87.

In addition to rationalizing its mainstream steelmaking operations, BSC has also disposed of most of its peripheral interests in the construction and chemicals sectors and has taken an active part in the reorganization of the independent sector of the steel industry. This has been done in two stages. First, with government approval, financial interests were taken in steelmaking companies which were experiencing trading difficulties as a result of the recession and the strength of foreign competition, and some capacity has been closed. Next, a number of joint ventures has been arranged with private-sector firms to provide modern and efficient facilities for the production of engineering steels and a range of special steel products, including stainless steels.

The government announced in December 1987 that it intended to privatize BSC in 1988 or 1989. The chief uncertainties for the business are the future level of steel demand and government's attitude to the continuing excess of capacity, particularly in flat products, that threatens the future of one of the major integrated works.

4.2.3 The Independent Sector

The output threshold laid down in the nationalization Act of 1967 was designed to capture the principal producers: enterprises with small outputs or which were ironmakers or steel re-rollers and finishers only were excluded from public ownership. The independent sector was formed as a residual, virtually by legislative accident. Since that time, the sector has undergone two periods of major change. The first, running from 1967 to 1978, was one of expansion, in terms both of volume and market share, as the sector's output became more diversified and its competitiveness in relation to BSC and imports improved. The second period, from 1978 to the present time, has been characterized by declining international competitiveness, excess capacity and extensive restructuring, assisted by government, the European Commission and – not least – by BSC.

There are now three parts that can be defined within the independent sector, which overlap to a greater or lesser extent with each other and with BSC. These are: the special steelmakers, the mini-mills and the joint-venture companies, operated as subsidiaries of BSC and private-sector enterprises. There are now about ten independent steelmakers manufacturing special steels, chiefly in Sheffield, and supplying about two-thirds of the output of these grades. Rationalization during the 1970s concentrated production on three companies, but the subsequent fall in demand and increase in competition from abroad brought severe financial difficulties to the producers. The result was that two of the leading manufacturers, Johnson Firth Brown and Aurora, closed their capacity and concentrated on other activities.

The second group, the mini-mill producers, developed after nationalization to take advantage of the opportunities offered by rising demand for common grades of steel (especially in the construction industry), lower production costs that the new technology made possible, and the supply difficulties that BSC encountered from time to time. Several new suppliers came into the industry, the largest of which were Sheerness Steel (a subsidiary of a Canadian company), Manchester Steel (owned by a Norwegian engineering company) and Alpha Steel (Greek-owned). The producers concentrated on billet and reinforcing bar manufacture, some for export. The second recession after 1978 caused financial difficulties for most of the firms in this part of the industry. Incentives were offered by the government and the European Commission for producers to leave the industry and BSC acquired some of the capacity with a view to closing it. The remaining major mini-mill is Sheerness Steel, with an annual capacity of about 1.5 million tonnes.

Joint-venture companies, the third group, have been formed to rationalize steel production in those parts of the industry in which the activities of BSC and the independent producers overlap. The aims are to avoid wasteful competition, to remove surplus capacity and to concentrate production on the larger and more modern facilities (whether initially in the public or the private sector of the industry) so as to improve efficiency and profitability and to withstand competition from imports. In some cases BSC has an equal share in the equity of the business with its private-sector partners; in others, the corporation has a minority interest. The major ventures have been schemes to reorganize the production of rods, bars and wire; forgings; engineering steels, and stainless steels.

Negotiations have often been difficult, because of the conflicting interests of the parties involved, but the effects of the schemes are now starting to be seen. Rod, bar and wire manufacture, undertaken by Allied Steel and Wire, has so far been profitable, but Sheffield Forgemasters, formed to operate the heavy castings and forging interests of BSC and Johnson Firth Brown, had financial difficulties for some time. The performance of the engineering and stainless steels enterprises is not yet clear, as they were not formed until 1985. As was intended, the joint ventures have made the boundary between the nationalized and independent sectors of the industry indistinct.

Privatization will remove it altogether and once more change fundamentally the ownership and production structures of the steel industry.

4.3   CONDUCT

The main feature of inter-firm behaviour in the steel industry is price competition in a generally undifferentiated market, with limited opportunities to achieve a competitive advantage by means of market segmentation and by emphasizing the non-price aspects of product quality and speed and reliability of supply.

Figure 4.2 plots the movement in the index of prices in real terms (that is, adjusted for inflation) in the UK in relation to steel consumption, from 1974 to 1985. The connection between consumption and prices is apparent: prices have fallen with declining demand.

Demand has been subject to fairly regular cyclical movements, and from the mid-1970s these have been superimposed on a declining trend in consumption. The amount of capacity available is, in contrast, not flexible in the short run and capital charges (interest and depreciation) and other costs that are invariant with output form a significant part of total production expenses. The lack in general of product differentiation opportunities means that suppliers typically face an individual demand curve that is (nearly) perfectly elastic (dd_1 in Figure 4.3). As consumption and price fall in the market, each supplier's individual demand curve moves downwards (dd_2). As fixed charges are unavoidable in the short run, suppliers will continue to produce at any price level that is in excess of short-run average variable costs (AVC), shown in the figure to be constant at each level of output until full capacity is reached, at output q_1 at which point the function becomes perfectly

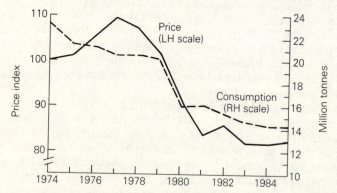

Figure 4.2   *Real price[a] and consumption of steel, UK, 1974–85*
Note: [a] Nominal prices reduced by GDP deflator.
Source: Iron and Steel Statistics Bureau, *Annual Statistics* (various years)

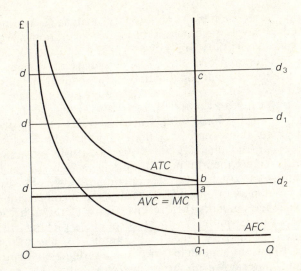

Figure 4.3 *Short-run demand and costs for a steelmaking firm*

inelastic. The constancy of average variable costs assumed in the example means that average variable and marginal costs (MC) are equal in the short run. As price falls below average total costs (ATC) financial losses will be incurred by the enterprise, shown per unit of output by the distance *ab*, but for so long as price is greater than average variable costs the firm will be minimizing its losses by continuing to produce, because each unit sold is making some contribution to fixed charges.

These conditions mean that prices are likely to vary closely with movements in demand. The higher the proportion of fixed charges in total costs, the greater will be the extent to which prices can be cut at times of low demand. This effect is also apparent if there are differences in the average variable cost levels of firms competing in the same market, for example, because some producers have fully depreciated equipment or higher operating levels of efficiency. Firms with high fixed costs will try to maintain or increase their short-run output in order to spread their unavoidable costs over as large a volume as possible. This may contribute to even larger surpluses of supply over demand and depress prices still more. In contrast, in times of buoyant demand prices will be driven upwards since supply is inelastic in the short run. If steps are not taken to control prices or to allow imports, high profits can be made by the suppliers. With demand at dd_3 in Figure 4.3, unit profits will be *bc*.

Severe fluctuations in prices and the likelihood of losses at times of poor demand have at various times encouraged steel producers in most industrialized markets to attempt to control the market, either by means of a formal cartel or through more informal arrangements. The intention is in this way to regulate the outputs of the participants so that supply and demand are broadly matched and prices are maintained at levels that permit profitable operations. Agreements that achieve these aims are however very difficult to devise and maintain in operation. The high cross-elasticity of demand for steel gives an incentive to individual members to 'shade' their prices below the agreed level in order to increase output and market share. This can be done by secret discounts or rebates. Output quotas are most commonly set on the basis of past market shares and producers with maximum limits below those they think appropriate will have a strong incentive to break them. Cost differences will encourage some suppliers to increase their output if they believe their marginal revenue exceeds marginal cost in the relevant output range. Finally, cartels require a system of profit sharing and some members may not be satisfied with the amounts they receive. Each of these factors makes steel cartels very unstable. In the face of the structural crisis in the European steel industry, the EC Commission has attempted to establish systems of minimum prices and production quotas, while encouraging the removal of surplus capacity, but it has proved very difficult.

In the absence of an effective cartel, the recognition of interdependence between steel producers may result in one of them emerging temporarily or for a longer period as a price leader. This is most likely in a market such as the UK in which one supplier accounts for the greater part of supplies. Small suppliers will make their output and pricing decisions against the background of the anticipated actions of the major supplier which in turn, will base its strategy on the share of the market it is prepared to yield to its smaller competitors. At times of general increases in costs, the leader can point the way for the phased increase of prices throughout the industry without severe disruption to historic market shares. But if the shares of the smaller competitors increase at the expense of the major supplier or if there are uncertainties about the future growth of demand, the leader may make aggressive pricing moves in order to increase its share of the market.

Firms may increase their degree of control over prices by segmenting their markets in order to develop some competitive advantage over their rivals. There is some scope for emphasizing product quality, especially in supplies to the engineering and motor vehicle markets. The demand for special steels is less price-sensitive than that for ordinary grades, but the scope for profits for the major steelmakers is limited by the relatively small size of the market. Close contacts can be built up with important customers and new products developed such as coated steels or pipes for submarine oil production. The ability to meet customers' orders at short notice from stock can be an important aspect of competitive advantage which can lead suppliers to purchase or develop stockholding networks. For producers in some countries, however, the greatest scope for price discrimination has been through the separation of the home and export markets. It is customarily asserted that Japanese steelmakers have achieved this to the greatest extent, benefiting from a large and rapidly expanding home market effectively protected from imports and the opportunity to sell abroad at prices related to marginal rather than full costs. Such practices can lead to allegations of 'dumping' or selling in the export market at prices below the full cost of production in the home market, but these can be very difficult to prove because of the problem of obtaining unambiguous cost information.

The characteristic patterns of competitive behaviour in the industry are thus those of an undifferentiated oligopoly – large enterprises dominate the market and compete strongly with each other and with the smaller suppliers mainly on the basis of price. The scope for obtaining competitive advantage by means of sales promotion or enhanced customer loyalty as a consequence of service or product quality are limited to individual, and typically small, segments of the market.

4.4 PERFORMANCE

In this section the performance of the UK steel industry is gauged in terms of five indicators: its sectoral importance, profitability, investment, productivity and competitive ability. This discussion is mainly in terms of BSC, as comparative data for the independent sector are not easily available. Nevertheless, given the importance of BSC in the whole industry, its experience and achievements provide a reliable guide to the performance of the overall sector.

4.4.1 Sectoral Importance

The share of the iron and steel industry in manufacturing net output fell persistently during the 1970s, from 6 per cent at the start of the decade to less than 2 per cent in 1983. This decline was associated with a trend fall in annual output. These movements were the result of two main influences: the fall in demand from the UK metal-using industries and steel's loss of international competitiveness.

The main steel-using industries each declined in the face of increasing international competition during the period. Moreover, technical progress, together with changes in the pattern of consumer demand and in the proportions of materials used, led to less steel being used in final products. Cars provide an eloquent example. They are now typically smaller than before the first energy crisis, are built of thinner steel thanks to advances in metallurgical technology, and use more plastic in place of heavier steel. These developments brought an inevitable fall in the demand for steel from within the UK but their impact was made worse by the declining international competitive position of the steel industry itself. Imports, in the main from other EC countries, rose in volume and as a proportion of the market, whilst exports grew more slowly (see Section 4.2.1). UK suppliers failed to compete effectively on the grounds of price, quality, or delivery. Measured in terms of the change in its sectoral importance, it is clear that the performance of the steel industry has been poor.

4.4.2 Profitability

By March 1986 the accumulated net losses of BSC since its formation amounted to more than £5 billion. Table 4.1 gives the annual record of BSC's profits and losses from 1975. Profits were made only in the first year, and in the two years from 1986. Although the size of the combined losses is plainly enormous, they are not so large as those incurred by some other large steelmakers in other European countries. The fall in the volume of output and depressed prices have been important factors in the losses but their effect has been made worse by the high cost base of BSC and of some other UK steelmakers in relation to their European competitors. These cost disadvantages have been associated with higher energy costs (in part as a result of government policy), low labour and capital productivity and higher rates of increases in the prices of raw materials, energy, labour and capital than elsewhere. Less flexibility and a higher proportion of fixed charges in total costs as compared to competitors have also contributed to the upward pressure on costs. BSC's operating losses have been covered by loans and subscriptions of interest-free finance from government. Independent producers, who came under severe com-

Table 4.1   *British Steel Corporation: Annual Profits and Losses, 1975–87*

Year ended March	Profit/(Loss)[a] £m
1975	70
1976	(268)
1977	(117)
1978	(513)
1979	(357)
1980	(1,784)
1981	(1,020)
1982	(504)
1983	(869)
1984	(256)
1985	(383)
1986	38
1987	178

Note: [a]After depreciation, tax, interest and exceptional items.
Source: British Steel Corporation, *Annual Reports and Accounts.*

petitive pressure after the 1978 oil crisis, have not had access to comparable levels of assistance although rationalization measures, usually involving co-operation between the public and independent sectors, have been encouraged.

4.4.3 Investment

The fast rate at which steelmaking technology has developed obliged BSC to undertake an extensive programme of modernization and, at first, capacity expansion. Investment in the independent sector was encouraged by the growth prospects for mini-mills as well as by the modernization of special-steel production units.

Table 4.2 shows capital expenditures at 1980 prices in the metals sector from 1972 to 1985. BSC accounts for the greater part of this by far. The two periods of intense investment from 1970 to 1972 and again from 1974 to 1979 are clearly shown. It was intended that the rate of investment should be sustained through the 1970s but this was prevented by market and financial conditions. Most of the investment was met from government expenditure by means of loans or other forms of finance.

The main aims of the investment programmes were to increase the scale of operations, introduce basic oxygen steelmaking, and modernize casting and rolling facilities. The UK was rather slow in introducing new technology in comparison with its main competitors; the delays meant that the period of intensive investment coincided with the

Table 4.2 *Capital Expenditure at 1980 Prices^a, Metals Sector, 1972–82*

Year	Capital expenditure £m
1972	966
1973	718
1974	878
1975	1076
1976	1193
1977	1008
1978	701
1979	520
1980	388
1981	271
1982	225
1983	207
1984	302
1985	295

Note: [a] Gross domestic fixed capital formation deflator.
Source: Central Statistical Office, *National Income and Expenditure* 1983 edition; *UK National Accounts*, 1986 edition.

Table 4.3 *Productivity and Labour Costs per Tonne in the Steel Industry, UK and West Germany, 1973–84*

Year	Man-hours per tonne UK	W. Germany	Labour costs per tonne UK	W. Germany at current exchange rates	at 1973 exchange rates
	hours	hours	£	£	£
1973	13.76	7.73	18.02	20.16	20.16
1974	15.94	7.28	24.38	24.10	22.38
1975	17.35	8.50	37.82	34.30	28.70
1976	14.71	8.09	37.06	42.30	29.33
1977	16.04	8.34	46.19	51.35	31.96
1978	15.00	7.60	50.10	50.87	30.03
1979	13.63	6.90	52.30	48.96	29.31
1980	23.63	6.94	104.90	49.33	32.03
1981	11.00	6.90	59.40	48.61	32.90
1982	10.35	7.22	62.10	55.97	36.53
1983[a]	7.99	6.72	54.90	61.38	36.51
1984[a]	6.28	5.76	n/a	n/a	n/a

Notes: [a]estimates.
Source: Cockerill, 1986, revised.

collapse of the market. This seriously impaired the effectiveness of the modernization schemes.

4.4.4 Productivity and Unit Labour Costs

In common with most UK manufacturing industries, labour productivity in the steel industry has been low in relation to the levels in other advanced economies. The cost disadvantage that this implies has been modified, however, by the low hourly earnings that are another characteristic of the UK economy, and by exchange rate movements.

Table 4.3 compares productivity and labour costs per tonne of steel in the UK and West Germany between 1973 (a year of high output) and 1984. In terms of labour productivity at least, the West German industry is the most efficient in Europe and is thus an appropriate standard for comparison.

Labour productivity is measured in the table by the number of man-hours per tonne required in a year to produce a tonne of steel: it is thus the reciprocal of output per man-hour, the more common measure, and productivity increases are shown by a reduction in man-hours. It is apparent that there has been a substantial improvement in labour productivity in the UK recently: by 1984 less than 7 man-hours per tonne were required. These gains have been made by shutting excess capacity, by reducing overmanning, by selective investment in modern equipment, and by improved working methods that have increased flexibility. There is still room for improvement, however, as productivity in West Germany has also increased.

The competitiveness of the two industries, in terms of unit labour costs, is compared in columns 4 to 6 of the table. The first shows that UK costs rose persistently until 1982. (The high figure for 1980 is an aberration, resulting from the strike.) Column 5 gives West German costs, expressed in sterling at the average exchange rate for each year. The UK had a slight cost advantage in 1973 and competitiveness was maintained in broad terms until 1979, when high inflation and a rising sterling exchange rate increased costs sharply in relation to those in West Germany. The fall in the exchange rate after 1981 has improved the UK's competitiveness. Column 6 re-expresses West German costs in terms of the 1973 exchange rate. On this basis, costs in West Germany were significantly lower than in the UK over most of the period emphasizing the importance of exchange rate movements in maintaining the UK's competitiveness in the 1970s.

4.4.5 Competitive Ability

One aspect of the decline in the UK industry's competitive ability is shown by the changes in the market shares of BSC, the independent producers, and imports (Table 4.4). BSC suffered a substantial fall in market share from more than 70 per cent at the start of the period to about 50 per cent in 1980. For most of the period this erosion was the result in the main of the rise in the share of imports from 5 to 25 per cent of the market. The independents' share remained fairly steady until after 1980, although their output fell with the recession, but the composition of production changed as ordinary grades of steel made in mini-mills became more important. The recent rise in the independent's share is chiefly the result of the transfer of some of BSC's activities to joint-venture enterprises.

That some fall in BSC's share of the market should have taken place during this period is not surprising, as it was very high initially compared to those of other large steel firms in other countries. This was directly the result of the structure of the industry established by nationalization and the protection given to home producers by trade

Table 4.4 *Share of Supplies of Finished Steel to UK Consumers (percentages)*

	1970	1980	1985
BSC	70	50	45
Independent Steel companies[a]	24	22	30
Imports	6	28	25

Note: [a] including joint ventures.
Sources: Cockerill and Cole, 1985; industry estimates.

quotas and tariffs before accession to the EC. Exposure to increased international competition would have led inevitably to an increase in the importance of imports. Nevertheless, a significant part of BSC's decline has been due to an inability to meet the demands of the market. Low productivity leading to a cost advantage for competitors played a part in this, as did the rise in the sterling exchange rate after 1978 which made imports cheaper. On some occasions, BSC has tried to lead prices upwards only to find that foreign producers have seized the opportunity to hold their prices and increase their share of the market. It is also true that BSC, as the most important and publicly visible UK producer, has felt it necessary to follow carefully EC directives on minimum prices and output quotas whilst other suppliers have taken advantage of weak markets to undercut official prices and increase sales.

But on occasions too, BSC has simply been unable to supply. This has occurred both when demand has been high and when it has been depressed. Technical difficulties during the first stages of the capital development programme reduced available capacity, particularly for iron production, at a time when demand was rising strongly. Later in the 1970s, when demand generally was poor, the growth of North Sea oil exploration and production gave rise to a demand for large-diameter high-quality pipe, but owing to lack of the appropriate equipment, the British industry was unable to meet this need.

Special steelmakers in the independent sector in the early 1970s benefited from strong demand and their concentration on a market segment in which price elasticity was relatively low. But the recessions and the associated increase in competition from foreign producers meant that their competitive position was steadily eroded and far-reaching restructuring, in association with BSC and with help from government, has been necessary. The experience of the mini-mills, which were new entrants to the industry at the start of the period, has been similar. Buoyant demand, low overheads, greater flexibility and BSC's supply difficulties gave ample scope for market penetration. But falling demand, rising costs and weak prices turned the profits to losses in the second half of the 1970s and some enterprises left the industry. Exports of steel from the UK have shown annual fluctuations in line with movements in demand among the industrialized countries, but the general tendency has been for export sales to increase. This has not been at the same rate as the rise in imports, however, and the balance of trade has deteriorated.

The factors in the increased market penetration of imports are in essence the counterpart of the declining competitiveness of the UK suppliers. Foreign producers have had the benefits of a low initial market share from which to expand, lower costs, favourable exchange rate movements, and the ability to practise price discrimination between their home and export markets. State financial assistance has sometimes been influential.

It is apparent that the economic and financial performance of the UK steel industry since 1970 has been poor. The decline has been due in part to changes in the wider economic environment, over which firms have little control, but due also to efficiency and managerial deficiencies which it is essential should be rectified. Steady economic growth will help to raise the demand for steel but if the industry is to regain part of its market share it must continue to improve productivity and the quality of its output.

4.5 PUBLIC POLICY

The main dimensions of public policy towards the UK steel industry have been nationalization, subsidies and – in conjunction with the European Commission – the formation of a cartel and protection against imports from outside the Community. In micro-economic terms, the purpose of such policies is to override the effects of the market mechanism, in the belief that a smoother adjustment to changing demand and supply conditions can be brought about. There are, of course, political, social, and wider macro-economic considerations that are taken into account when such policies are considered and applied.

When proposals were drawn up in 1966 to nationalize most of the steel industry, the presumed failure of the product and capital markets was an important economic argument used to justify the political action. It was alleged that capital expenditure under private ownership had been inadequate for the modernization of the industry that was necessary in the face of rapid technological change and that the structure of the industry, because it was fragmented, was unsuitable for the attainment of economies of scale. Moreover, the low rate of return was said to have discouraged investors from providing additional funds. Public ownership would permit the creation of a single enterprise capable of rationalizing and expanding steel production.

Once BSC was formed, the chief function of government in regard to the steel industry was the supply of finance for re-equipment and expansion of capacity. The needs were clearly beyond the amounts BSC could hope to generate from revenue, but it was expected that future sales would allow interest and dividends, at the market rate, to be paid on the additional capital that was provided. In the event, of course, the hopes proved false. The capacity expansion plans were too ambitious and were begun too late. The capital was lost and financial support for the industry was necessary because of operating losses, continuing (but reduced) capital expenditures and – eventually – the costs of rationalization and redundancy. Subsidies, it can be seen, have been given both for the expansion and the contraction of the industry.

The costs of supporting BSC through these difficult times were due in part to the change in the demand for steel that was generally unforeseen, but in part also to government interventions. These included limits on price increases at times of strong demand, delays in approving expansion schemes, restrictions on capital spending on part-completed projects, and obligations placed on BSC to maintain employment levels and to keep outdated or redundant plant in operation. There can be little doubt that these actions increased by a considerable amount the claims on public expenditure for supporting BSC.

Since 1973, government policy towards the steel industry has had to be formed within the framework of the European Community, as set out in the Treaties of Paris (covering most steel products) and Rome (which contains provisions relating to certain finished products). Outright revenue subsidies are in general prohibited, which is most likely a major reason why the government has chosen to support BSC by capital subscriptions. Not until most steel producers in the Community were in severe financial trouble towards the end of the 1970s did the European Commission find it possible to take steps to co-ordinate the output, pricing and investment plans of enterprises within the industry. The initial scheme, introduced in 1978 under Article 58 of the Treaty of Paris, covered a narrow range of commodity products – mainly reinforcing bar and wire rod. It sought to place output quotas on producers and to put in place a system of minimum prices, in an attempt to stabilize the market. Output, capacity utilization and profitability continued to worsen, however, and in 1981 a more comprehensive and mandatory scheme was introduced that set minimum prices for a wide range of products, allocated to producers output quotas based upon their market shares in the recent past, and tied direct subsidies to rationalization and capacity reductions. As with most cartels for commodity products, it has been fairly easy for producers to undercut the published minimum prices and to exceed their output quotas, so weakening the effectiveness of the scheme, but there have been signs recently that the second, tougher, regime has had some effects in reducing the amount of excess capacity, in encouraging rationalization and efficiency increases, in improving the profitability of most of the major producers, and in laying the basis for subsidy payments to be reduced, if not eliminated entirely.

Such benefits for producers that the cartel will realize have to be set against some considerable costs. Steel purchasers have been most directly affected, as the cartel, coupled with controls on imports from outside the Community, has raised the price of many types of steel above the world level. The purchasers themselves in many cases face strong international competition, which the price rises have intensified. The cartel has also delayed the adjustment process to lower demand by emphasizing historic market shares, preventing new entry into the industry (in particular by mini-mills), and discouraging major changes in ownership.

If interventionist policies such as state ownership, subsidies and cartels are to bring about effective adjustment to changing demand and supply conditions, they must work with the market rather than against it. From the standpoint of industrial economics, therefore, the critical issue is whether public policy has aided or hindered adaptation in the steel sector. One way to approach this question is to consider the counter-factual: what would have happened in the absence of the kinds of policy instruments that have been applied? This must be conjecture, of course, but it is possible to describe a likely pattern of events. Had nationalization not taken place, financial losses would have forced some firms out of business and encouraged others to merge. Surplus capacity eventually would have been eliminated and the burden of the lost financial capital would have fallen on shareholders. Undoubtedly, demands would have been made to government by the industry for financial and other assistance. New investment would have been limited mainly to schemes that would reduce costs or improve quality. Some firms might have been acquired by businesses from outside the steel sector or may have entered new areas of activity. The decision at the time of nationalization to incorporate most of the iron and steel industry within one enterprise reflected both the general approach to public ownership in the UK since 1945 and a belief in the importance of economies of scale and planning. It also inevitably brought problems of rationalization and flexibility, and limited the opportunities for diversification. The UK's membership of the European Community would have obliged steel producers to participate in the crisis cartel, but they may have been able to achieve more flexibility in output and pricing decisions than has been possible for BSC. As a result of the process, by the mid-1980s there may have been more than one major integrated steel firm, but the size of the industry and the organization of production, based upon four or five large sites, most probably would not have been very different from the pattern that is emerging from BSC's extensive rationalization. What is likely, however, is that the adjustment would have occurred sooner, more smoothly, and at much less cost to the public purse.

While this suggests that the market mechanism would have operated with more effect than the policies that were actually applied, it does not mean that an interventionist strategy towards the steel industry was necessarily ill-conceived. The problems in the UK's case arose mainly from prevarication by successive governments and the inclusion of policy goals (such as employment protection) that conflicted with the improvement of efficiency and competitiveness. Had there been a sustained commitment first to modernization and then to tailoring the size of the industry to fit demand, steel could have achieved a stronger and more profitable position within the European Community than is at present the case. It is hard to resist the conclusion that any policy stance other than that actually adopted would have given better economic results.

NOTES TO CHAPTER 4

1 Here and throughout the unit of steel output is the tonne (metric ton) (0.9842 standard tons).
2 Eurostat (1985), *Iron and Steel Yearbook* (Luxembourg: Statistical Office of the European Communities).
3 Ibid., Table 1.4.
4 Business Monitor (1986), *Report on the Census of Production 1983*, Business Statistics Office (London: HMSO).
5 Iron and Steel Statistics Bureau (1986), *Annual Statistics 1985* (Croydon, Surrey: ISSB).
6 Ibid.
7 As the result of an agreement effective from vesting day, one of the companies, Round Oak Steelworks, was jointly owned by BSC and Tube Investments Ltd, the former owner.

REFERENCES

Cockerill, A. (1974), *The Steel Industry*, University of Cambridge Department of Applied Economics Occasional Paper no. 42 (Cambridge: Cambridge University Press).
Cockerill, A. (1986), 'Downward adjustment in the steel industry: the case of the UK', in G. C. Hufbauer and H. Rosen (eds), *Domestic Adjustment and International Trade* (Washington, DC: Institute for International Economics).
Cockerill, A., and Cole, S. (1985), 'The British Steel Corporation's corporate plan', *Proceedings and Papers of the Sesquicentennial Conference of the Manchester Statistical Society* (Manchester: Manchester Statistical Society).
HMSO (1965) *Steel Nationalisation*, Cmnd 2651 (London).
HMSO (1973) *British Steel Corporation: Ten-Year Development Plan*, Cmnd 5226 (London).
HMSO (1978) *British Steel Corporation: The Road to Viability*, Cmnd 7149 (London).

FURTHER READING

The process of adjustment to reduced demand in the UK steel industry is traced in the author's paper 'Downward adjustment in the steel industry: the case of the UK', in G. C. Hafbauer and H. Rosen (eds) (1986), *Domestic Adjustment and International Trade* (Washington, DC: Institute for International Economics). Details of BSC's restructuring plan are given in the 1981 report of the House of Commons Industry and Trade Committee, *Effects of BSC's Corporate Plan*, HC(1980/81)336, HMSO. The development of the British steel industry up to nationalization is described in J. Vaizey (1974), *The History of British Steel* (London: Weidenfeld & Nicolson). The international structure of the industry during a period of intense technological change and the onset of recession is analysed in the present author's 1974 book, *The Steel Industry* (Cambridge: Cambridge University Press). A fascinating study of the politics of steel nationalization is contained in K. Ovenden (1978), *The Politics of Steel* (London: Macmillan). The problems of the US steel industry are reviewed in R. W. Crandall (1981), *The US Steel Industry in Recurrent Crisis* (Washington, DC: Brookings Institution). The global nature of the difficulties facing the industry is considered in W. Goldberg (ed.) (1986), *Ailing Steel* (Aldershot, Hants: Gower). Basic production, consumption and trade statistics of the UK industry are in *Annual Statistics*, Iron and Steel Statistics Bureau (the 'Brown Book'). Data for the European Community are in the *Iron and Steel Yearbook* (Luxembourg: Eurostat).

Chapter Five

Pharmaceuticals

DUNCAN REEKIE and NICHOLAS WELLS

5.1 INTRODUCTION

5.1.1 The Nature of the Industry

There is considerable diversity between the firms that comprise the modern pharmaceutical industry. Companies may specialize in the manufacture of a small number of medicines used in the treatment of just a few disease entities (although the markets concerned may of course be substantial), or they may have product portfolios extending over an extremely wide range of therapeutic categories. Of the major manufacturers, some have UK origins but most are subsidiaries of overseas parents, notably from the United States, Germany, Switzerland, France, Italy and the Netherlands. The significance of pharmaceuticals in the overall pattern of corporate activity also shows substantial variation between manufacturers: for example, pharmaceuticals generate most of Glaxo's income but less than 10 per cent of that for ICI where other manufacturing interests include paints, plastics, fibres, industrial chemicals and fertilizers.

A precise definition of the pharmaceutical industry is therefore necessary in order to isolate it conceptually from the wide variety of company types that participate in it. From the viewpoint of the consumer, the industry consists of firms that manufacture medicines in finished forms such as tablets, capsules, ointments and syrups. As seen by the producer, it is engaged in the production of medicines which involves, first, the preparation of physiologically active ingredients and second, the conversion of these substances into the forms in which they are consumed. With regard to the former, active compounds may be obtained by a number of processes:

(1) bulk manufacture of synthetic organic chemicals such as vitamins, antihistamines and diuretics;
(2) bulk manufacture by fermentation, synthesis, or both, of antibiotics;
(3) preparation of sera and vaccines by micro-organism culture; and
(4) production from naturally occurring animal or vegetable sources of drugs such as insulin and hormones.

Following this stage, the active substances are combined with other ingredients to facilitate ultimate administration, converted into tablets and other forms, and then packed for distribution.

The products of the pharmaceutical industry can also be viewed from the perspective of their 'technological' content. At one end of the spectrum, there are medicines which are advertised and sold directly to the public without the need for a doctor's prescription. Innovation in this range of 'over the counter' products usually involves reformulation or new packaging of established brands rather than genuinely novel entities.

At the other end of this spectrum of medicines for human use are the products which are available only with a doctor's prescription, the so-called ethical preparations. In developed countries, the largest share of the prescription-bound medicines market is occupied by products which still have patent protection. These products have generally evolved as a result of substantial investments in research and development (R & D) and as innovative new means of treating ill health they are able to command a price premium. The firms producing these medicines represent the driving force of the industry as it is understood today (Organization for Economic Co-operation and Development, 1985).

The remainder of the prescription market consists of generic or multi-source medicines. These are products whose patents have expired and, in consequence, may be manufactured by companies other than the original patent holder. The medicines may be marketed under their generic name or as a branded generic. The manufacturers supplying this part of the prescription market, in which price competition takes place to a greater extent than in the innovative sector, include the large multinational research-based companies as well as the small non-innovating firms.

5.1.2 History

The beginnings of chemotherapy are associated with Paul Ehrlich (1854–1915) who built on Robert Koch's observations that certain aniline dyes could kill bacteria. Ehrlich realized the potential implications if these dyes could attach themselves to diseased bacteria without harming whole body tissues and began his search for a 'magic bullet', a drug that would seek out its own target. However, it was not until 1904, after more than 600 substances had been screened, that his efforts were rewarded with the discovery of arsphenamine (Salvarsan) which kills the organisms connected with syphilis without harming the host.

The search for other chemotherapeutic magic bullets continued but it was not until the 1930s that the take-off into the modern era of sustained progress occurred. The initial landmark was the discovery by Gerhard Domagk of the antimicrobial properties of the dye Prontosil.

In 1935, sulphanilamide was identified as the active ingredient. Subsequent research led to the development of a number of related compounds, known collectively as the sulphonamides. One of the early major successes in this therapeutic area was sulphapyridine. Developed by May & Baker in their UK laboratories, this compound became pre-eminent in the treatment of pneumonia.

Over the following decades, a wide range of effective new medicines became available. Penicillin was initially discovered by Alexander Fleming in 1928. Ten years later, Howard Florey and Ernst Chain isolated and purified the active substance and commercial production began in 1942. The following year saw the discovery of streptomycin, a drug effective against tuberculosis. And chloramphenicol, the first broad spectrum antibiotic, became available in 1949.

By 1950, the 'first therapeutic revolution' was therefore well under way. In the late 1950s and 1960s antihypertensive preparations facilitating control of high blood pressure and effective psychotherapeutic medicines, including the major tranquillizers, were becoming available. The 1960s also brought oral contraceptives, anti-inflammatory medicines for rheumatism and arthritis and beta blockers for heart disease. More recently, medicines to treat ulcers and new generation antibiotics, among others, have been introduced, thereby sustaining the progress that began to be achieved just over fifty years ago.

The extent of therapeutic advance that has been gained in this relatively short period of time can be gauged from the fact that 95 per cent of the medicines available today were unknown in 1950. In the 1920s, six drugs, singly or in combination, accounted for over 60 per cent of prescriptions. Most innovations have been made in the laboratories of pharmaceutical companies. The latter have developed along different routes but in broad terms the European pharmaceutical multinationals tended to diversify from dyestuffs and fine chemicals into medicines whereas most of the United States manufacturers started in pharmaceuticals, grew and diversified domestically prior to the Second World War and thereafter expanded internationally (Rigoni *et al.*, 1985).

5.1.3 Current Supply and Demand Patterns

In 1984 the output of the pharmaceutical industry in the UK was valued at £3,577 million. This sum derives from a broad range of products although a few therapeutic groups predominate. Thus cardio-vascular, alimentary tract, respiratory and central nervous system preparations together accounted for almost £1 in every £3 of output in 1984.

The pharmaceutical industry's total output is the result of production by a large number of companies. According to the 1985 Census of Production there are 358 enterprises operating in the UK pharmaceutical industry. The size of these operations, however, varies considerably. Over half of the enterprises employ just 10 people or less. More than three-quarters have fewer than 50 employees. Less than one-fifth of the enterprises employed 200 or more people in 1985. (Total employment in the UK industry stood at 81,400 in 1984. In addition it has been estimated (Association of the British Pharmaceutical Industry, 1985) that the industry's activities generate a further 150,000–200,000 jobs in other related sectors of the economy.)

Returning to output values, available data indicate that the pharmaceutical industry's output amounts to less than 2 per cent of that of UK industry as a whole. However, the industry is one of the fastest growing sectors of the economy. Over the period 1974–84, output increased fourfold in cash terms and by 32 per cent in constant prices. Growth measured in the latter terms was more than twice that achieved by the chemical industry and the economy as a whole. British manufacturing industry's output fell by about 10 per cent between 1974 and 1984.

The principal markets for the UK pharmaceutical industry's output are shown in Figure 5.1. In 1984, the largest share – almost half – went to the National Health Service. Thirty-four per cent was exported. Export values have increased rapidly in recent years and have outpaced the growth of imports. As a result the UK industry's trade

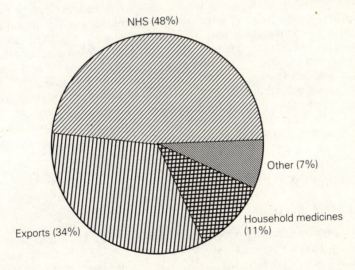

Gross output in 1984: £3,577 million.

Figure 5.1 *The UK pharmaceutical industry's principal markets in 1984, percentage of Gross Output.*
Sources: Census of Production, Customs and Excise, and Office of Health Economics.

balance increased to £680 million by 1984 (from £107 million in 1970). At this level, the pharmaceutical industry's visible trade surplus ranked fourth in the league table of industry trade surpluses in 1984. A similar position obtains when visible trade balances in pharmaceuticals are viewed from an international perspective. The UK emerges as one of four nations with a particularly successful pharmaceutical industry in terms of balance of payments contribution and innovative success (Chew *et al.*, 1985).

The demand for pharmaceuticals is characterized by a number of special features. Since the industry's products are employed to restore or maintain health, it is generally considered that demand is inelastic. It might further be argued that this inelasticity is reinforced in the ethical (prescription-bound) market by the fact that the patient (or consumer) does not select the product. The doctor chooses but does not pay and as a consequence will be relatively price-indifferent. Finally, few patients in the UK are required to make any direct financial contribution to the cost of the medicines prescribed for them by their doctors. In 1985, 81 per cent of the 393 million prescriptions dispensed by chemists were exempt from charge because the patients concerned were elderly, children under 16 years, expectant mothers, women with a child under 1 year old, suffering from a specified illness, low income earners, or had purchased pre-payment certificates. This factor too will decrease demand elasticity.

The converse of these arguments is that consumers rarely choose intermediate goods in any industry. Thus the separation of consumer choice from consumption in health care delivery will have no more unique an effect on elasticity than for any good whose demand is derived. In addition, the domestic industry faces a monopsonistic buyer (the NHS) which exerts downward pressures on prices. In export markets either similar monopsonistic situations exist or patients pay direct, cost-related prices to dispensing pharmacists. Thus the separation of consumption, choice and payment may not have such a unique effect on demand in this industry as is sometimes suggested.

5.2 MARKET STRUCTURE

5.2.1 Concentration

The significance of the different companies in the UK pharmaceutical industry inevitably varies considerably, as can be seen from data on the distribution of sales to the NHS of medicines prescribed by general practitioners and dispensed by pharmacists. At one end of the distribution, the data show that just 5 companies accounted for 17 per cent of total sales in 1984. On average, each of these leading 5 companies therefore had sales valued at almost £49 million. At the opposite end of the spectrum, 10 per cent of this particular market was

Pharmaceuticals

supplied by 144 manufacturers, each with average sales valued at just £998,000.

Inevitably, a more marked degree of concentration becomes apparent if the analysis shifts from company to corporate entity. Table 5.1 shows, for example, that the top 5 corporate groupings accounted for almost 29 per cent of pharmaceutical sales through retail pharmacies in 1984 compared with a figure of 17 per cent for the leading 5 companies. Nevertheless, it is clear that a large number of small producers are able to exist side by side with large or medium-scale firms. In part this is explained by the absence of any obvious benefits deriving from economies of scale. Only a small minimum size is required for efficient operation of manufacturing processes. Moreover, the wide variety of medicines manufactured by the industry permits a small plant concentrating on only a few products to compete efficiently with a larger factory turning out a wider range.

The ethical market may be divided into a series of submarkets and within these groupings further subdivision is possible. Thus the alimentary system submarket comprises medicines for the treatment of ulcers as well as laxatives. The medicines produced to satisfy the demand in any one submarket are of little or no value as a means of satisfying demand in others. Between the submarkets there is generally a very low cross-elasticity of demand although cross-elasticity of supply may well be quite high if the same producers can supply a variety of submarkets. This is not a contradictory concept because the same manufacturing techniques can frequently be used to produce drugs with entirely different pharmacological functions. Consequently, there is much scope for competition within the various submarkets although the patterns of competition show substantial variation, for example, in terms of numbers of competing products and market share.

Table 5.2 summarizes the market pattern for the leading eight companies (by value of non-hospital prescription medicine sales to the NHS) in 1986. In contrast to the overall levels of concentration described above, these data show that at the level of the submarket industrial structure is highly concentrated. Thus the leading products

Table 5.1 *Percentage Share of UK Market by Leading Corporations (Pharmaceutical Sales to Chemists), 1984*

Corporations	% share
Top 5	28.5
10	44.4
15	55.1
20	63.8
25	69.7

Source: Office of Health Economics based on Intercontinental Medical Statistics UK data.

Table 5.2   *Top Eight Companies: Number of Products, Main Products Share of Company Sales and of Submarkets, 1986*

Company	No. of products		% of total company sales	% of submarket
A	15	1	49	30
		2	22	14
		3	15	9
		others	14	
B	33	1	73	56
		2	8	36
		3	7	28
		others	12	
C	14	1	63	49
		2	23	41
		3	7	12
		others	7	
D	17	1	77	54
		2	9	65
		3	6	44
		others	8	
E	23	1	59	17
		2	16	9
		3	10	30
		others	15	
F	34	1	32	50
		2	18	79
		3	16	20
		others	34	
G	33	1	81	39
		2	9	13
		3	2	10
		others	8	
H	16	1	88	65
		2	7	9
		3	2	36
		others	3	

Source: Intercontinental Medical Statistics.

Table 5.3 *Percentage of Total Sales Value of Leading 100 Products Attributable to those Products still in Patent*

	1973	1978	1983	1985
Per cent of top 100's sales value attributable to patented products	73	43	36	49
Value of top 100 products as % of total market value	58	58	58	60

Source: Industry estimates.

of five of the eight companies account for half or more of the sales in the various submarkets in which they compete. At the same time, it is also clear that most firms are heavily dependent on only a few leading products.

5.2.2 Barriers to Entry

The principal absolute cost advantage of existing firms is the ability to preclude competition with identical products unless royalties are paid to the patentee. In 1965, some 72 per cent by value of all prescription sales was of patented products. This proportion has, however, fallen over time. Table 5.3 shows the percentage of the combined total sales value of the leading 100 products prescribed by general practitioners that was under patent coverage in selected years between 1973 and 1985. Over this period, the leading 100 products (according to sales value) have consistently accounted for about 60 per cent of the total market but the sales value of this group covered by patent protection has fallen from 73 per cent in 1973 to 49 per cent in 1985. Furthermore, the latter figure would be even smaller if those products among the leading 100 subject to the licence of right provision[1] were excluded on the grounds that they do not enjoy full patent protection. Consequently, there are growing opportunities for entry to the non-patent protected market.

Economies of scale appear to be largely unimportant as an inhibitor of entry. In promotion there are no evident economies of large-scale advertising. The most effective method of pharmaceutical promotion is the medical representative. At a local level there is no case to assert that the small firm's representative force need have less impact on a doctor's prescribing habits than a large firm with a detail force covering the country. Similarly direct mail advertising can be carried out on a restricted scale geographically. Journal advertising, however, may require to be carried out nationally. Even so this form of promotion is relatively unimportant, accounting for only around 10 per cent of all pharmaceutical promotional expenditure, and the absolute cost is not prohibitive. (In 1986, a full-page colour advertisement in the *British Medical Journal* which is circulated to 75,000 doctors in the UK cost between £1,500 and £2,500.)

Product differentiation advantages of existing firms are the most obvious entry barriers. Focusing on prescribable medicines, in 1984 there were 1,100 active ingredients giving rise to 2,100 branded products which in turn generated 3,900 formulations in the UK (Walker *et al.*, 1985). The extent of product differentiation is vast. The entry-deterrent effect of the latter is measured by the extent of the financial sacrifice an entrant firm must incur to sway prescribers bound by loyalty away from existing brands towards the entrant's products. Existing firms will, of course, attempt to strengthen this loyalty. They can do this by emphasizing product differences through advertising and/or by creating new ones to produce new or improved therapies through conducting research and development (R & D).

Entrant firms can only hope to revoke this loyalty if they incur some financial sacrifice not currently incurred by existing firms. This implies, for example, selling at a cheaper price, promoting more effectively, producing products which are different from those already on the market – for example, by initiating successful R & D – or some combination of these or other sacrifices. If existing firms are attempting meanwhile to strengthen the loyalty of prescribers to their own brands, then a spiral commences. Entrants must cut prices still further, shout still louder through the promotional media, or make even greater technical advances through R & D if their products are going to have the marginal attractiveness to cause customers to shed existing loyalties. What form this 'spiral' takes, and its net effects, are contentious issues in the economic debate over the industry's behaviour and performance.

5.3   MARKET BEHAVIOUR

5.3.1   Innovation

The R & D efforts of pharmaceutical manufacturers underpin the development of new medicines enabling them to engage in innovatory competition. Over the period 1970–84, the number of new chemical entities marketed for the first time in the UK averaged around twenty per year.

The demand for pharmaceuticals is sensitive to quality differences resulting from R & D. The market is therefore characterized by a high degree of product competition and often only short-lived domination of submarkets. This phenomenon has been recognized for some time. In the mid-1960s, Cooper (1966), for example, illustrated the necessity of product innovation if company domination of the submarket is to continue. Such innovation must have clear advantages over the new products almost certain to appear from rivals' R & D laboratories. Table 5.4 indicates however that this does not always occur, and that sometimes when it does, it is frequently too belated to prevent a loss of

Table 5.4   *Therapeutic Submarket Competition: Changes in Market Leadership between January 1962 and June 1965*

Submarkets		Number	%
Firms:		90	100
	Change in leadership	29	32
	More than one change	10	11
Products:	Change in leadership	33	37
	More than one change	8	9

Source: Cooper, 1966, p. 60.

market position. Of the submarkets 37 per cent had product leadership (as determined by sales value) changes in the three-and-one-half year period covered by Table 5.4. In 32 per cent of the submarkets leadership was lost by the original leading firms, while in 11 per cent of the markets studied, more than one change in class leadership occurred. Thus while the submarkets are oligopolistic in structure there is little chance, from a dynamic point of view, for long- or even medium-term oligopolistic domination to occur.

A more recent illustration of the impact of innovation may be drawn from the anti-peptic ulcer submarket. This submarket was effectively created in 1976 with the launch of a new histamine H_2-receptor antagonist preparation. Sales of this medicine grew 55-fold between 1976 and 1982 but thereafter, instead of continued growth, sales were barely maintained at their 1982 level. The explanation for this abrupt change in fortunes was the launch in 1981 of a direct competitor product. By 1984, sales of this new product almost matched those of the original medicine which had seen its share of the submarket fall from 98 per cent in 1981 to 52 per cent in 1984.

Even at the level of the total market the vigour of this 'competition in creativity' is apparent. Table 5.5 shows that only two of the leading ten products (by NHS sales value) in 1984 had been in the top ten in 1973. And of the ten leading companies in 1973 only three remained among this 'elite' grouping in 1984. The second ranked company in 1973 fared especially badly over the subsequent decade, falling to twenty-third position in 1984.

Research underpins new product development and is the key to maintaining or improving market share. It is therefore not surprising that the industry invests heavily in R & D. According to estimates produced by the UK industry's trade association, the Association of the British Pharmaceutical Industry (ABPI), expenditure by the industry amounted to £490 million in 1984. This sum was 16 times the figure reported for 1970 and even in constant-price terms still represents expenditure growth of almost three-and-a-half-fold over the period. ABPI data also indicates that about 15 per cent of the 81,400

Table 5.5 *(A) Position of 1984's Leading Ten Products in 1973; (B) Position of 1973's Leading Ten Companies in 1984*

| | (A) Products | | (B) Companies | |
1973	1984	1973		1984
8	1	1		5
42	2	2		23
–	3	3		18
–	4	4		14
–	5	5		16
–	6	6		2
35	7	7		11
–	8	8		7
–	9	9		17
3	10	10		13

Note: – Indicates products not then available.
Source: Intercontinental Medical Statistics, UK.

employees in the pharmaceutical industry are engaged in R & D activities. In British industry as a whole, this proportion is second only to the aerospace sector.

5.3.2 Price

The emphasis on competition by innovation has traditionally been assumed to have arisen from two sources: the supply of new technology arising from the therapeutic revolution and the rising demand for ever-improving levels of health care. The latter has been encouraged by the growth of health care insurance schemes throughout the world (either private or, as in Britain, state-sponsored). These factors, coupled with the nature of the product (a 'necessity') and the structures of the therapeutic submarkets if observed at any one point in time (highly concentrated) have led most observers to believe that the level of consumption will be determined by disease incidence and not by price. Moreover, the relative levels of these factors imply that the low price and high quality elasticities of demand will be further exaggerated by the fact that the market is 'over-insured'. Insurance is generally a service provided to guard against situations which are likely to involve an individual in exceptionally high expense relative to his total income or wealth and/or one whose occurrence is improbable. (The average cost of a prescription to the NHS in 1984 including the retailer's margin, was £4.41.) Except for the chronically sick and the indigent it is difficult to see why insurance (private or state-initiated) is required in the pharmaceutical market. Nevertheless, as a consequence of this 'over-insurance' neither doctor not patient will be price-sensitive and price competition, it is argued, has little if any role to play in the drug industry. Recent studies (see Reekie and Weber, 1978, and Section 5.5 below), however, have cast considerable doubts on the view that price competition is absent in pharmaceuticals or that demand is wholly inelastic.

5.3.3 Promotion

Promotion is essential for driving market change in any competitive commercial system. For pharmaceutical manufacturers, it is particularly important because of both the natural conservatism of prescribers and the relatively short period of patent-protected time that research-based companies have to establish new medicines before they become subject to low-cost, non-innovative competition. Furthermore, pharmaceutical promotion costs tend to be higher as a proportion of total revenue than those in many other industries because, *inter alia*, of the pace of innovative activity and because prescribers, who number many tens of thousands, cannot adequately be contacted by relatively low-cost 'omnibus' media.

Pharmaceutical promotion expenditure as a proportion of the industry's NHS turnover has however fallen over time. During the decade following the 1967 Sainsbury Report, spending remained constant at 14 per cent of NHS revenue. By 1983/4, this figure had fallen to 12 per cent and under the newly negotiated Pharmaceutical Price Regulation Scheme (see Section 5.5.1 below) which became effective from October 1986 there has been a further reduction to 9 per cent. This means that the industry as a whole is now spending about £150 million per annum on promotion.

Despite these developments, the pattern of promotion expenditure has shown little tendency to change over the last 10–15 years. Approximately 45 per cent of total spending goes on medical representatives who facilitate two-way communication between manufacturers and prescribing doctors – that is, in addition to their principal role in sales promotion, representatives are a conduit for the reporting of adverse reactions and other related information by doctors to manufacturers. The remaining half of the promotion expenditure is divided between advertising in medical journals, direct mailing, meetings and other forms.

Recent innovations are regarded as the products requiring the greatest intensity of marketing back-up but promotion expenditure is by no means confined to new or relatively new medicines. Once a product has gained acceptance, there is still a need for some advertising of the reminder type. Doctors, like any other human 'buyers', 'do not have perfect memories; nor are they a static body: there are continually new potential recruits to be drawn from the newly employed . . . familiar products are from time to time improved or adapted to different purposes, and the manufacturer must make known their new look' (Harris and Seldon, 1962, p. 75).

5.4 PERFORMANCE

The benefits generated by the activities of the pharmaceutical industry embrace health and related improvements as well as economic gains. However, the measurement of these benefits is rarely straightforward and a detailed discussion of the issues involved is beyond the scope of the present chapter.

In the context of health gains, there has been much debate about the contribution from medicines. It is clear that a precise quantification of that part of the improvement in society's health attributable to the industry's operations is not possible. Improved health is also a consequence of higher standards of nutrition, hygiene and housing, progress in understanding the functioning of different bodily systems, and advances in surgery.

Improved health is usually measured by comparative mortality and/or morbidity statistics. Unfortunately such statistics are not easily convertible into meaningful economic measures. In a few disease areas, however, it is possible to obtain a picture of the welfare contribution of the industry to society. This occurs where the incidence or killing power of the disease has abruptly declined after a relevant pharmaceutical breakthrough. The decline in mortality from tuberculosis since the introduction of streptomycin, para-aminosalicylic acid and isoniazid has been one of the most dramatic developments of the century. In 1984, there were only 375 deaths from pulmonary tuberculosis compared with 19,008 in 1946.

More generally, the development of antibiotics has contributed along with environmental improvements to significant reductions in mortality from infectious diseases. Indeed, without the improvements achieved since the mid-1940s, it may be calculated that in 1984 in England and Wales there would have been 1,220 more deaths each week among people aged 1–44 years than was actually the case.

The discovery of the first tranquillizers in 1952 and of the antidepressants in 1960 signalled the beginning of psycho-pharmacology. The use of psychotherapeutic drugs was one of the major causes, in 1956, of the first-ever annual decrease in the number of hospital beds occupied due to mental illness. From 151,000 in-patients in 1956, the mental-illness hospital population fell to 125,000 in 1966, 92,000 in 1975 and to under 70,000 in 1984. Decreased use of mental hospital beds has also been paralleled in other diseases. Despite the dramatic benefits which the advent of chemotherapy has provided, the proportion of total NHS expenditure on pharmaceutical services has remained virtually static over the years: the nation's drug

bill (at manufacturers' prices) has consistently accounted for less than
10 per cent of the total cost of the NHS.

Profitability is of course conventionally employed as one of the
principal indicators of performance. It is, however, extremely difficult
to obtain reliable and meaningful figures for profits and profitability in
the pharmaceutical industry. To some extent this difficulty stems from
the fact that the pharmaceutical business of a company frequently
forms only a part of a larger organization engaged in a variety of non-
pharmaceutical activities as well. Available data must also be treated
with caution if comparisons are drawn with other industries. For
example, higher than average return on capital might be a consequence of substantial assets such as research know-how, patents and
trade marks being excluded from pharmaceutical companies' capital
value.

Some guide to profitability may however be gained from the
aggregate returns submitted by the main pharmaceutical companies to
the Department of Health under the Pharmaceutical Price Regulation
Scheme in connection with their sales to the NHS. The data contained
in Table 5.6 show that in 1983 the rate of return on historical capital
employed was 14.6 per cent. If comparison is drawn with the rates
prevailing during the second half of the 1960s the pattern that appears
to emerge is generally one of long-term decline. However, employing
the early 1970s as the reference point in time suggests a picture of
regular cyclical fluctuation between approximate limits of 14 and

Table 5.6   *Rates of Return on Historic Capital Employed for the
Pharmaceutical Industry (based on sales to the NHS), 1967–83*

Year	% return on capital
1967	27.2
1968	23.0
1969	21.2
1970	18.1
1971	18.5
1972	18.0
1973	16.8
1974	14.7
1975	15.4
1976	16.9
1977	19.5
1978	21.0
1979	14.9
1980	16.3
1981	19.7
1982	18.2
1983	14.6

Source: DHSS.

20 per cent. In 1983, the pharmaceutical industry's rate of return on historic capital was approximately three percentage points below that for all manufacturing industry in the UK.

Profitability figures for the industry as a whole disguise the extent of variation that exists on an individual company basis. At one extreme, almost one company in eight recorded a loss on its NHS business in 1982. At the other end of the range, one company in five achieved a return on capital of 30 per cent or more. This spectrum of success is to be expected in an industry in which innovation and risk are predominant characteristics.

Two main questions are raised by profitability figures. First, are they fair and reasonable? Second, to what extent does the continued performance of R & D depend on profitability? These closely related issues are central to public policy and are considered below.

5.5   PUBLIC POLICY

5.5.1   Prices and Profits

Pharmaceutical manufacturers supplying the National Health Service are subject to the Pharmaceutical Price Regulation Scheme (PPRS) which is a non-statutory agreement between the industry and the Department of Health. Despite its name, the scheme aims to control profits rather than prices. A company is assigned a rate of profit which takes account of its particular circumstances especially its economic contribution, realized and potential, in terms of capital investment, research expenditure, employment and foreign earnings. The scheme, the origins of which may be traced back to 1957, has recently been renegotiated and a revised version came into effect on 1 October 1986. The purposes of the scheme are officially stated to be:

- to secure the provision of safe and effective medicines for the NHS at reasonable prices,
- to promote a strong and profitable pharmaceutical industry in the UK capable of such sustained research and development expenditure as should lead to the future availability of new and improved medicines, and
- to encourage in the UK the efficient and competitive development and supply of medicines to pharmaceutical markets in this and other countries.

'Reasonableness' is a concept with no generally accepted meaning. Consequently, the reasonableness of the return on capital earned by companies on home sales of NHS medicines is a matter for negotiation within a published range between the companies and the DHSS. Under the revised scheme this range increased 1½ percentage points to

16–18½ per cent. A further increase was granted from 1 October 1987. For 1988/9 and each subsequent financial year changes in the target range will take account of

> any relevant and significant alterations since the last PPRS rate change in the underlying average return on capital of British Industry as brought out for example in relevant changes in the FT 500 index or of any relevant policies that may be generally in force on the appropriate levels of profitability on public sector business.

In addition, companies may in certain circumstances be permitted to retain profit above their target range. This discretionary allowance is known as the 'grey area' and will at a maximum be equivalent to 50 per cent of target profit. Retention of such profits will be allowed where they arise from

> the launch of a new product, improved efficiency or other factors clearly arising from the company's own efforts: retention of profits in the grey area will not be allowed following a price increase in the year in question (except where the above factors can be demonstrated to have played a part) nor where they arise from factors external to the company, for example, from favourable movements in exchange rates or general movements in input costs.

The rationale for a price control scheme is the belief that unregulated market forces fail to bring about price levels that would result in reasonable profits in drugs. This belief may exist because on the demand side of the market doctors and patients do not pay directly for the medicines they prescribe and consume and are therefore indifferent to the prices paid by the NHS; or it may be because on the supply side firms are believed to have the ability persistently to price their products above reasonable levels because competitive market rivalry is absent, for whatever reason.

The difficulty for policy-makers in innovative industries is, of course, the confusion caused by the words 'perfect competition'. These suggest that the phenomenon (and its associated condition of price equal to marginal cost) is an *ideal*. In fact, the concept is a *predictor*. And in an innovative industry, where unit variable costs are near to zero (as in drugs) but fixed costs such as R & D expenditure are relatively very high, the problem of correctly defining marginal cost is wellnigh insuperable. Unless this is understood, we are in the hypothetical area of homogeneous products, where no improvement or innovation can bring extra profits exclusively to the supplier. If he cannot reap the rewards there is no incentive to make improvements. Hence 'perfect' price competition (or price equal to short-run marginal cost) is a prescription for the non-existence of innovation.

It is worth noting that many new drugs are priced at levels lower than leading substitutes (Reekie, 1978). Those priced at high levels relative to competitors tend to be innovations providing important therapeutic gains. This complies with the behaviour pattern one would expect from simple price theory. Firms *can* charge a higher price in those cases where consumers are willing to pay that price. Consumers *will* pay if the innovation is relatively more productive than alternative products. Minor variants, conversely, can only penetrate a market if their price is below that of existing rivals. Given the Sylos postulate, their demand curve is that part of the market demand curve to the right of the ruling price.

Moreover, the evidence suggests that new drug prices tend to fall over time; that existing products tend to be cut in price in the face of innovations as firms attempt to gain a price advantage where a quality advantage has been lost; and that price elasticity of demand increases as products mature (and so are subject to competition from later drugs) and/or is lower initially the more important is the therapeutic gain represented by the innovation.

'Price' for the consumer should not be equated solely with the monetary payment he or she pays for the pharmaceutical product itself. Like any other good or service, a pharmaceutical's real price is measured by the amount of other goods and services the customer must forego in order to purchase the characteristics of the drug. For example, if an existing drug requires four pills per day to be consumed for one week at 10p per pill, with the additional requirement of confinement to bed then the real price of that drug to the consumer is £2.80 (that is, $7 \times 4 \times 10p$) *plus* the week's wages he has forgone by being confined to bed. (Alternatively, if the total cost is borne by society through socialized medicine and health insurance, the social cost is the same, namely £2.80 plus the value of goods and services the patient could have produced had he been at work.) On the other hand, if an alternative drug becomes available at £2.00 per pill, to be consumed at a rate of one pill per day for three days with only a three-day home confinement, then the real price to the consumer is £6 plus only the proportion of one week's wages represented by three days' loss of work.

The new drug costs £6 for a full treatment, the first £2.80. But the second drug is by far the more competitive in terms of real price. For a five-day week for a patient normally earning £20 per day the second drug's real price is £6 plus three days' wages – £66; the first drug's price is £102.80. The second drug has lowered the price of treatment by £36.80. That is price competition in the real meaning of the phrase.

In the simple example just described, the new drug lowered the real price of treatment. If competition works it would be expected that the price of the existing drug would fall to combat the price advantage of the innovation. Because the quality of the existing product cannot be changed, the alteration must occur in its cash price. The evidence suggests that this is precisely what happens (Reekie, 1978). As new products are introduced into the market, the cash prices of existing products are pushed down by competitive forces, and the elasticity of demand for existing products increases. Doctors continue prescribing older products only if they are reduced in cash price and their real price disadvantage relative to better quality products is minimized.

Similarly, the empirical evidence (Reekie, 1978) indicates that new drugs that do not reduce the real price of treatment via improved therapeutic quality must, in order to enter the market, reduce the real price of treatment by offering a lower cash price. There is little or no evidence on the demand side of the drug market to suggest that doctors are unaware of real price differentials. Little support is provided for the apparently obvious Sainsbury view that drug prices need to be regulated by government because demand is highly inelastic.

The Sainsbury committee (1967, p. 16) explicitly concluded that they 'did not gain the impression that there was any significant degree of price competition in medical speciality products'. This conclusion was arrived at after the committee had surveyed firms and asked how prices were determined. Some said they considered the prices of alternatives, others that they aimed to obtain a required rate of return on investment and others that they tried to recover cost in a given period. These objectives, of course, need not be incompatible, but the latter two in particular could appear to depart from perfect competition as an *ideal* (although not necessarily as a *predictor*; that is an empirical question). It is on just this point that the qualitative evidence of Sainsbury seems to depart from the actual behaviour patterns of drug industry prices both over time and among products. Price competition is present and *works* as predicted. Perfect competition is, however, absent.

5.5.2 Advertising

Sainsbury suggested two advantages to be expected if brand names were prohibited: more effective price competition would result and a source of confusion arising from multiplicity of names for the same drug would be removed.

Confusion due to a proliferation of different brand names for the same product is more illusory than real, however. In 1984, a total of 2,100 branded products involved 1,100 different active ingredients, an average of 1.9 brand names per active ingredient. The emergence, *ceteris paribus*, of a greater degree of price competition if branding were to disappear is, of course, indisputable. Other things are not equal, however. Innovation occurs and entry barriers to the industry may be increased. Because the average life of a drug is short, the average length of brand-name-induced monopoly is also relatively short. When the drug disappears from the market, so too does any monopoly position it may have provided. If, however, doctors prescribed by manufacturer, then promotional stress might well shift from product to company names. In such a situation, any monopoly position or market preference created by unique name advertising would not wither away with the demise of a product but would last for as long as the firm. An innovating company previously unknown in the market would be at a marked disadvantage.

There are other dangers existing from regulation of promotion. Qualitative control may be misleading whilst quantitative control of promotion may inhibit both market entry and the rapid spread of the benefits of innovation. Even if expenditure is high, it may be better in an innovative industry to bear some waste than to suffer the costs of low diffusion. In the Soviet Union, promotion of new drugs is undertaken by the Health Ministry, not by the industry. Information about new drugs is usually restricted to mailed literature or journal articles. It is frequently overlooked, forgotten or ignored. It is not prompt enough, voluminous enough, nor sufficiently persuasive to encourage the doctor to use new advances. The result is a substantial lag between the introduction of a new medicine and receipt of incremental benefits by the patient.

Peltzman (1975) attempted to measure the benefits that might have accrued to society (in the USA) had diffusion been more rapid in the case of two major drug innovations, TB drugs and tranquillizers. He suggests that if one considers only the added earnings of potential TB victims in present value terms of, say, $50,000 per life, then the present value, in the year of innovation, of more rapid diffusion of TB drugs would have been $3 billion. For the tranquillizers Peltzman obtains estimated savings of $9 billion by calculating savings in hospitalization costs alone (ignoring productivity increases from shorter patient confinements). He concludes: 'By way of comparison, gains of this order once per decade could easily pay for a doubling of current drug promotion expenses, if that is what it takes to realize them.'

5.5.3 Research and Development

The debate surrounding the topic of market structure is intimately connected with the relationship between R & D and size of firm. Two issues are of particular importance. First, whether or not larger firms perform proportionately more R & D than smaller ones. Second, whether or not larger R & D efforts produce proportionately more innovations.

Research and development is absolutely expensive. It is presumed firms must be of some minimum size in order to undertake a meaningful effort. Those who argue that larger firms conduct proportionately more R & D usually do so on the basis that larger firms (1) have greater resources and (2) have a greater degree of market power that can be used to generate an absolutely higher level of profits from any resulting innovation. Disagreement arises not over the need to have some degree of size and market power to encourage R & D activity, but over whether or not an increase in market power and size above such a threshold would result in a relatively complacent large firm whose urge to engage in the risks of innovative activity would be relatively less.

The second facet of the controversy, whether larger R & D efforts are more productive, is, of course, merely a restatement, in the R & D context, of the question as to when, if at all, scale economies are exhausted. No definitive case for or against a higher level of concentration in the industry can be made. Economic theory is too imprecise to predict with certainty the strength of any relationship between market structure and innovation. Indeed it is too imprecise to predict even the direction of the relationship.

A number of earlier empirical studies about pharmaceutical R & D (for example, Comanor, 1965) arrived at broadly the same conclusion: the largest pharmaceutical firms, while possibly the biggest absolute performers of R & D, are not the most research-intensive firms. A large number of studies have provided evidence that diseconomies of scale exist in R & D irrespective of which index of input is used. Later investigations have, however, challenged this picture (for example, Schwartzman, 1975). This may reflect changing circumstances in pharmaceutical R & D. The real costs of R & D are rising. This is attributable to two factors. First, the areas of unconquered disease remaining provide relatively difficult technological problems. Second, the costs of meeting the requirements for new drug registration, both in the UK and overseas, are rising dramatically. Both phenomena originally appeared in the 1960s and may be responsible for the apparent contradictions. Confirmation for the view that the relationship between firm size and innovative output has altered in recent years is provided by Grabowski and Vernon (1977) who explicitly compared different time periods. The findings indicate that the four largest firms in the US ethical drugs industry accounted for a share of innovational output from 1957 to 1966 not dissimilar to their share of sales. By 1967–71, however, their share of innovational output was much greater (at 48.7 per cent) than their share of total sales.

In an attempt to ascertain why the change depicted has occurred the US results were compared with those from another country (the UK) where the regulatory climate was less stringent. The authors suggested that the depletion of R & D opportunities would affect the productivity of R & D in all countries in a similar manner. However, any negative effects of regulation would show up as an additional influence in a country with a stiffer regulatory framework. They found, in a comparison between the UK and the USA, that in the USA, R & D productivity declined about sixfold between 1960–1 and 1966–70. The corresponding decrease in the UK was only half as great.

They argued as a consequence that the 1962 Amendments to the Food, Drug and Cosmetic Act, by themselves, roughly doubled the cost of producing and introducing a new drug in the USA.

Wardell and Lasagna (1975, p. 122) found that from 1962 to 1971 nearly four times as many new drugs became available in the UK as in the USA. For those drugs marketed in both countries twice as many were introduced first in Britain as in the USA. Specialist physicians in the USA were often unaware of the drug lag but when informed of the existence of new, effective drugs abroad wished they were available in America. Britain exercised a more permissive policy towards new drugs but a stricter post-marketing surveillance of innovations. Wardell and Lasagna thus recommended that surveillance of new drugs after marketing be intensified in the USA.

Finally, there is the issue of state support of R & D. Government subvention of R & D in an industry (by subsidy or actual performance) is generally justified on one or more of the following grounds:

(1) the size of project requires more resources than the industrial unit has available;
(2) project risks are too great for the industry to assume them; and/or
(3) the market mechanism fails to reflect adequately the social benefits.

State aid to R & D, or its actual performance by a nationalized unit, cannot be justified on the first two grounds. There is no evidence that R & D projects are of a size beyond the resource pool of firms. Most, in fact, conduct several projects simultaneously. Equally there is no information to indicate that firms are risk-averters to the extent that R & D is not being conducted. With a 1 in 10,000 success rate, the evidence rather points in the reverse direction.

The third category, however, is more likely to provide grounds for government support of industrial R & D in commercially unattractive disease areas in which the benefits recoupable through the market are less than the cost incurred, and both, in turn, are less than the social benefits. Clearly, in such circumstances a profit maximizing business-man will allocate his R & D effort towards the more common disease areas where the surplus of commercial benefits over costs is greatest. This is an attractive argument. The opportunity cost of such interference would, however, be far greater than any benefits. Because of a fixity in resources for pharmaceutical R & D, any increase in the research effort directed towards finding cures for less common diseases implies, of necessity, a reduction of R & D activity in the areas of high disease incidence. (This is not an unrealistic assumption: the main R & D resource is trained manpower which is a fixed pool. An increase in the number of chemists, pharmacologists and the like cannot be obtained at a stroke.) Consequently government inter-ference of this type might help the few, but it would harm the many.

5.6 CONCLUSION

The research-based pharmaceutical industry in the UK is a relatively young industry that has already given rise to substantial economic and social benefits. In 1984, 11 of the leading 20 medicines by sales value in the UK had originated in laboratories in the UK as had 5 of the top 12 pharmaceutical products on the worldwide market. Innovative success on this scale – beta blockers for hypertension and angina, non-steroidal anti-inflammatories for arthritic pain, sodium cromoglycate for asthma and histamine H_2-receptor antagonists for stomach ulcers, for example, are all UK innovations – has generated obvious health benefits for patients as well as gains for the national economy in the form of employment opportunities and balance of payments surpluses.

Looking to the future, there is little doubt about the need for further innovation if treatments are to become available for diseases such as senile dementia, multiple sclerosis and the acquired immune deficiency syndrome (AIDS). There is of course also scope for further improvements in practically all of the therapies that are employed today. Yet some degree of uncertainty surrounds the prospects for future innovation. In particular, there is concern that fundamental medical research conducted in academic settings, which provides the knowledge base from which new therapies may eventually be developed by the pharmaceutical industry, is underfunded at the present time. The financing of such investigations is the responsibility of government, but the money it makes available to the Medical Research Council for this purpose has fallen in real terms in the first half of the 1980s (Wells, 1986). As a result many top-rated research grant applications have either gone unfunded or have been supported at lower levels than requested.

From the perspective of the pharmaceutical industry, a major barrier to future innovation lies in the expense of undertaking the necessary research and development. Although it is impossible to isolate the development costs attributable to a specific new medicine, current estimates put the figure at between £50 million and £100 million. This sum compares with £2–3 million during the first half of the 1960s. This cost escalation derives from a combination of factors including the need to employ increasingly sophisticated and correspondingly expensive research equipment. In addition, as the relatively more straightforward chemotherapeutic needs have been met, attention has transferred to problems of greater complexity that are considerably more costly to resolve. However, the most significant cause of the increasing expense of developing a new medicine is the lengthening period of time between initial discovery in the laboratory and eventual release on to the market. In the early 1960s, it was not unusual for this transition to be completed within about 3 years; today this phase may last for around 12 years.

In addition to the increase in direct costs caused by lengthening development times (which themselves are linked, *inter alia*, to the extension of regulations governing the testing of prospective new medicines) this trend has inevitably resulted in a commensurate reduction in the duration of patent protection available to new medicines entering the market. Walker and Prentis (1985) have shown that medicines first introduced in 1960 had an average of over 13 years of their patent lives still to run but that by the early 1980s this had fallen to about 8 years including the 4-year licence of right provision. With this reduction in the period during which marketing can take place without the presence of price-lowering generic competition, manufacturers are finding it increasingly difficult to obtain the volume of sales receipts required to cover research and development costs (Reekie and Allen, 1985; Joglekar and Patterson, 1986; Prentis *et al.*, 1987).

Pharmaceutical research and development is therefore becoming increasingly expensive and the commercial and other risks of the innovative process are escalating. Further disincentives to long-term investment in R & D have stemmed during the first half of the 1980s from a series of government measures to contain the cost of the NHS drug bill. Short-term expedients such as price freezes, reductions in the level of allowable profit and the introduction of a limited list prohibiting the prescribing of certain medicines at NHS expense have had a deleterious effect on the confidence necessary for long-term investment and a number of companies are reported to have cancelled research and capital construction projects as a result (*Scrip* 19 February 1986 p. 7). The newly negotiated PPRS does however attempt to address this concern – the proposal that the scheme should operate for 6 years, with an opportunity for review after 3 years, is designed to provide the industry with an assurance of stability.

Against this background, predictions about the future structure of the industry are highly uncertain. Nevertheless, it might be speculated that a combination of rising research costs and increasing limitations on the capacity to fund such activities will mean that fewer manufacturers will be able to remain among the ranks of the major innovators. (And for companies that do, there may develop an increasing tendency to risk-aversion so that efforts become increasingly focused on 'safer' areas of research, that is, on diseases and therapies where knowledge is well advanced and the market is of sufficient size to offer reasonable prospects of recouping investment costs.) Concomitant with this trend towards concentration of innovative activity there may be an increase in the number of generic manufacturers competing in out-of-patent products, essentially on the basis of price. Entrants to this subgroup of manufacturers will include companies no longer able to sustain a viable R & D programme as well as companies newly entering or diversifying into pharmaceuticals.

NOTE TO CHAPTER 5

1 In June 1978, the UK followed the ruling of the European Patent Convention and raised patent terms to 20 years (previously 16 years) from the date of filing. Existing patents at this time were not granted an extension of their terms with the exception of those filed after 1967 (the 'new' existing patents). Instead, the latter had imposed upon them a licence-of-right endorsement which means that other companies can apply as of right to manufacture and/or sell the product concerned after the first 16 years of patent life. New legislation is now going through Parliament, however, to abolish the licence of right provision.

REFERENCES

Association of the British Pharmaceutical Industry (1985), *The Pharmaceutical Industry and the Nation's Health* (London).

Chew, R., Teeling Smith, G., and Wells, N. E. J. (1985), *Pharmaceuticals in Seven Nations* (London: Office of Health Economics).

Comanor, W. S. (1965), 'Research and technical change in the pharmaceutical industry', *Review of Economics and Statistics*, 47, 182–90.

Cooper, M. H. (1966), *Prices and Profits in the Pharmaceutical Industry* (Oxford: Pergamon).

Grabowski, H. G., and Vernon, J. M. (1977), 'Consumer protection regulation in ethical drugs', *American Economic Review*, 67 (Papers and Proceedings), 359–69.

Harris, R., and Seldon, A. (1962), *Advertising and the Public* (London: Deutsch).

Joglekar, P., and Paterson, M. L. (1986), 'A closer look at the returns and risks of pharmaceutical R and D', *Journal of Health Economics*, 5, 153–77.

Organization for Economic Co-operation and Development (1985), *The Pharmaceutical Industry, Trade Related Issues* (Paris: OECD).

Peltzman, S. (1975), 'The diffusion of pharmaceutical innovation', in Helms, R. B., *Drug Development and Marketing* (Washington, DC: American Enterprise Institute).

Prentis, R. A., Walker, S. R., Heard, D. D., and Tucker, A. M. (1987), *Pharmaceutical Innovation and R and D Investment in the UK*, in press.

Reekie, W. D. (1978), 'Price and quality competition in the US drug industry', *Journal of Industrial Economics*, 26, 223–37.

Reekie, W. D., and Allen, D. E. (1985), 'Generic substitution in the UK pharmaceutical industry: a Markovian analysis', *Managerial and Decision Economics*, 6, 2, 93–101.

Reekie, W. D., and Weber, M. H. (1978), *Profits, Politics and Drugs* (London: Macmillan).

Rigoni, R., Griffiths, A. and Laing, W. (1985) *Pharmaceutical Multinationals, Polemics, Perceptions and Paradoxes*, Institute for Research and Information (IRM) Report No. 3 (Chichester: Wiley).

Sainsbury Report (1967), *Report of the Committee of Enquiry into the*

Relationship of the Pharmaceutical Industry with the National Health Service, Cmnd 3410 (London: HMSO).

Schwartzman, D. (1975), *The Expected Return from Pharmaceutical Research* (Washington, DC: American Enterprise Institute).

Walker, S. R., Girling L., and Prentis, R. A. (1985), 'Innovation and the availability of medicines', *Pharmaceutical Journal*, 2 March, 264–6.

Walker, S. R., and Prentis, R. A. (1985), 'Drug research and pharmaceutical patents', *Pharmaceutical Journal*, 5 January, 11–13.

Wardell, W. M., and Lasagna, L. (1975), *Regulation and Drug Development* (Washington, DC: American Enterprise Institute).

Wells, N. E. J. (1986), *Crisis in Research* (London: Office of Health Economics).

FURTHER READING

Association of the British Pharmaceutical Industry 1985, *The Pharmaceutical Industry and the Nation's Health* (London).

Cooper, M. H. (1966), *Prices and Profits in the Pharmaceutical Industry* (Oxford: Pergamon).

National Economic Development Office (NEDO) (1986), *A New Focus on Pharmaceuticals* (London: HMSO).

Reekie, W. D. (1975), *The Economics of the Pharmaceutical Industry* (London: Macmillan).

Reekie, W. D., and Weber, M. H. (1978), *Profits, Politics and Drugs* (London: Macmillan).

Sainsbury Report (1967) *Report of the Committee of Enquiry into the Relationship of the Pharmaceutical Industry with the National Health Service*, Cmnd 3410 (London: HMSO).

Schwartzman, D. (1975) *The Expected Return from Pharmaceutical Research* (Washington, DC: American Enterprise Institute).

Chapter Six

Synthetic Fibres

RICHARD SHAW and PAUL SIMPSON

6.1 INTRODUCTION

6.1.1 Early History

Synthetic fibres were introduced to the UK market on a small scale during the Second World War. Nylon (a polyamide fibre) was first produced in the UK in 1941 by British Nylon Spinners (BNS), a jointly owned ICI and Courtaulds subsidiary, though substantial commercial development was delayed until after the war. The two other major synthetic fibres, polyester and acrylic, were introduced in the 1950s. Polyester fibre was first produced commercially in the UK by ICI in 1954. Acrylic fibre was first produced in the UK by Courtaulds and Monsanto (an American-owned firm) between 1957 and 1959. Synthetic fibres today are used in a wide range of clothing, household and industrial textile products.

Nylon was originally developed in two main forms: nylon 66 and nylon 6. The former was discovered and developed by the American company Du Pont in the 1930s and was protected by patents. British involvement began when ICI received an exclusive UK manufacturing licence for nylon 66 from Du Pont in 1939. Manufacturing licences were also granted to some other European firms. Although ICI's chemical base provided know-how for ongoing technical developments the firm lacked experience of the textile industry. Thus, in 1940 ICI formed a joint manufacturing company with Courtaulds who were able to draw on their knowledge of the textile industry. The jointly owned company was named British Nylon Spinners (BNS) and was owned 50 per cent by ICI and 50 per cent by Courtaulds. BNS enjoyed a patent-protected monopoly for nylon 66 yarn production in the UK at least until 1961, although a second major patent concerning the manufacturing process (steam spinning) did not expire until 1964. However, competition was still possible from both domestically produced nylon 6 and imported nylon fabrics as well as other textile products.

Nylon 6 was developed by I. G. Farben in Germany again in the 1930s. However, it was not introduced to the UK until the 1950s. The company concerned, British Celanese, was acquired by Courtaulds in 1957 giving the latter a stake in both nylon 6 and nylon 66.

119

Polyester fibre was discovered and initially developed in the UK by J. R. Whinfield and J. T. Dickson at the Calico Printers Association (CPA) in 1940. However, as CPA's interests were mainly in the specialized area of the printing and finishing of fabrics the commercial development of polyester fibre was carried out by ICI, which was given an exclusive licence in the UK and the rest of the world except the USA, and by Du Pont which was given an exclusive licence in the USA. ICI subsequently gave sublicences to producers in France, Germany, Holland and Italy; these gave the firms concerned exclusive rights in their own countries and non-exclusive rights elsewhere. Du Pont began commercial production in the USA in 1953; ICI followed in the UK in 1954. The basic UK patents expired in 1963, although a considerable degree of protection continued in Europe under the sublicensing agreements until the end of 1966.

Acrylic fibre was first discovered and developed by Du Pont in the USA in the early 1940s, though commercial-scale production did not begin until 1950. A variety of acrylic and the related modacrylic fibres developed by other firms in the USA and Europe were introduced in the 1950s: Courtaulds and Monsanto being the first to produce in the UK in about 1959.. Unlike nylon and polyester fibres a competitive situation thus existed from the beginning.

6.1.2   Growth of the Industry in the UK and Western Europe.

Starting from an almost negligible usage in the immediate postwar period, by 1969 synthetic fibres had captured a 30 per cent share of the

Table 6.1   *United Kingdom Synthetic Fibre Production, Imports, Exports and Net Available Supply (thousand tonnes)[a,b]*

Year	Production	Imports	Exports	Available supply
1962	84.0	11.4	22.7	72.7
1966	174.7	25.7	44.7	155.7
1970	336.8	53.8	120.2	270.4
1973	453.9	122.5	175.7	400.7
1975	361.1	119.8	145.9	335.0
1980	287.6	151.4	192.6	246.4
1982	204.3	176.9	135.2	246.0
1984	237.5	196.9[c]	159.2	275.2
1985	239.5	209.6[c]	159.2	289.9

Notes: [a] Production includes polypropylene and other minor synthetic fibres as well as the three main fibres.
 [b] Imports and exports exclude spun yarn.
 [c] Excludes high-tenacity polyamide.
Sources: Textile Organon; CIRFS (International Rayon and Synthetic Fibres Committee).

Western European market for all textile fibres. By the end of the 1970s synthetic fibres' share of mill consumption had first grown to and then stabilized at approximately 50 per cent. Cellulosic fibres were responsible for about 15 per cent with natural fibres (predominantly cotton and wool) accounting for the remaining 35 per cent (Man-Made Fibre Production EDC, 1983).

Details of the growth of the UK industry from the early 1960s are given in Table 6.1. As is readily apparent, UK industry production grew extremely rapidly in the 1960s – at an average annual rate of 19 per cent. The rapid growth continued up to 1973 but then production fell sharply from the mid-1970s before a modest recovery began in 1982. In addition it is clear that both imports and exports became much more significant in the 1970s and 1980s compared with the early and mid-1960s. Thus imports were over 87 per cent of UK production in 1985 compared with only 15 per cent in 1966. Similarly 66 per cent of UK production was exported in 1985 compared with only 26 per cent in 1966. Whereas the trade balance had been in the UK's favour up to 1980, from then onwards imports exceeded exports. It is worth noting also that over the whole period the significance of imports is understated since the trade statistics refer only to trade in staple fibre and filament yarn and omit trade in fabrics and finished textile goods (such as shirts).

The early growth and rapid market penetration by synthetic fibres reflected their superior performance in some respects (for example, easy care of clothes) compared with traditional fibres such as cotton and wool, sustained promotional expenditure, quality improvements, and a broadening range of products. In addition the synthetic fibres became more price-competitive as a result of both cost reductions arising from technical improvements and economies of scale, and increased price competition among synthetic fibres producers. The subsequent decline from the mid-1970s reflected both the cessation of growth in the overall fibres market in Western Europe and increased competition from the Far East and elsewhere in the world.

6.2   THE CHANGING MARKET STRUCTURE

The discussion of market structure–conduct–performance relationships is dominated by the evolution of the industry in the postwar period. The latter includes the market introduction, early penetration, rapid growth and maturity phases of the synthetic fibres product life cycle. In line with these stages the market structures for particular fibres, and to a lesser extent for synthetic fibres generally, changed from monopoly, or near monopoly, protected by patent rights to oligopoly and unprotected by patent rights. Further, the essentially isolated national markets, protected by patents, licensing agreements and tariffs, developed into a much more closely integrated Western European market as patent protection ended and tariff barriers were removed. These changes coincided with increasing buyer knowledge of the particular physical properties of the different fibres, and also of the generic similarities of the competing products of a single fibre type made by rival firms.

This development, together with increasing competition from outside Western Europe, is reflected in the increased importance of imports and exports reported above for the UK. From the mid-1970s onwards both the UK and the wider Western European industry has been adjusting to substantial excess capacity. This has led to significant changes in market structure, conduct and performance in the 1970s and 1980s.

6.2.1 Seller Concentration

The early history of the synthetic fibres industry has already been summarized in the introduction. As the innovators in the UK, ICI and BNS initially had a monopoly in polyester and nylon respectively. In acrylics, where UK production started somewhat later, Monsanto, Courtaulds and Du Pont (with imports) were in early competition.

During the 1960s the UK nylon market was transformed: first, by Courtaulds' sale of its share in BNS to ICI in 1963, and the subsequent independent development of Courtaulds and ICI in this fibre; secondly, by the entry in the mid-1960s as domestic producers of Monsanto (US parent firm) and British Enkalon (Dutch/West German parent firm); and thirdly, by imports notably from Du Pont. In the UK polyester market ICI was joined as a domestic producer by British Enkalon (1966), Hoechst (West German parent firm) (1969) and

Table 6.2 *Estimated Market Shares of Total Domestic Consumption of Synthetic Fibres in the UK, 1969, (%)*

Producer	Polyester	Acrylic	Nylon
ICI	75	–	56
Courtaulds	–[a]	46	15
Monsanto	–	29	8
Du Pont	7[b]	21	3[b]
British Enkalon	7	–	13
Hoechst	9	*[c]	–
Bayer	–	2[b]	–
Others	2[b]	2[b]	5[b]

Notes: [a] Courtaulds announced its intention to enter the polyester market in 1969 and production began in 1971.
[b] Based on imports only.
[c] Less than 1 per cent.
Source: O'Neill, 1970.

Courtaulds (1971), and by Du Pont as an importer from its manufacturing plant in West Germany. Finally in the UK acrylics market Courtaulds and Monsanto were joined as domestic producers by Du Pont – a major importer for many years – at the end of the 1960s. Dow (US firm) and Bayer (West German firm) were also active importers. The estimated UK market shares including imports for the three fibres at the end of the 1960s are shown in Table 6.2.

The penetration of the UK market by Western European and American synthetic fibre manufacturers was to a large extent paralleled in other markets. For instance, ICI began manufacturing nylon and polyester fibres in West Germany for the EC market in 1965 and 1967 respectively. Similarly Courtaulds began manufacturing acrylic fibre in France, also in the 1960s. With local ownership participation in subsidiaries ICI also began both nylon and polyester production in Spain in the early 1970s.

As already indicated the ending of patent and tariff protection within the EC, together with the increasing knowledge of buyers, substantially removed the significance of national boundaries in the 1970s. Indeed the severe and persistent excess capacity which first emerged in 1974 led to a co-ordinated Western European, or at least EC producer response, rather than a series of separate national responses. Production capacity market shares of leading firms in the wider Western European market at the beginning of the excess capacity phase and ten years later in 1985 are summarized in Tables 6.3 and 6.4.

Table 6.3   *Estimated Western European Production Capacity Shares, 1975, (%)*

Producer	Country of parent company	Acrylic	Polyester	Nylon
ANIC	Italy	5.5	3.0	1.5
Bayer	W. Germany	14.5	4.5	6.0
Courtaulds	UK	20.0	1.5	5.5
Du Pont	USA	7.5	6.5	6.0
Enka	Holland/W. Germany	4.5	22.0	18.0
Fabelta	Belgium	3.0	–	0.5
Hoechst	W. Germany	9.5	22.0	0.5
ICI	UK	–	14.0	19.0
Monsanto	USA	8.0	–	4.0
Montefibre	Italy	12.5	6.0	5.5
Rhône Poulenc	France	6.5	13.5	16.5
SIR	Italy	1.0	2.0	–
Snia Viscosa	Italy	5.0	2.5	9.5
Others		2.5	2.5	7.5

Source: Shaw and Shaw, 1983.

Table 6.4 *Estimated Western European Production Capacity Shares, 1985, (%)*

Producer	Acrylic	Polyester	Nylon
ANIC	14.4	5.0	2.0
Bayer	19.4	withdrawn	1.0
Courtaulds	27.3	withdrawn	withdrawn
Du Pont	withdrawn	5.0	7.0
Enka	withdrawn	20.0	12.0
Fabelta	withdrawn	–	1.0
Hoechst	7.7	20.0	withdrawn
ICI	–	10.0	28.0
Monsanto	withdrawn	–	withdrawn
Montefibre	16.8	10.0	withdrawn
Rhône Poulenc	withdrawn	13.0	15.0
SIR	withdrawn	withdrawn	–
Snia Viscosa	7.4	1.0	10.0
Others	7.0	16.0	24.0

Sources: Textile Outlook International, 1986; De Zoete Bevan, 1986; industry sources and trade press.

At a Western European level the 1985 data shows that several firms had withdrawn from particular fibre markets while some of the leading firms had strengthened their positions. While some weaker firms such as SIR (acrylic and polyester) and Fabelta (acrylic) were eliminated or like Fabelta (nylon) taken over, others had decided to withdraw from part of the synthetic fibres market in order to concentrate on another segment. Examples of the latter include Courtaulds' withdrawal from nylon and polyester segments while strengthening its position as a leader in acrylics; and Enka and Rhône Poulenc's withdrawal from acrylics while retaining other synthetic fibre interests. Monsanto, an American firm, chose to withdraw totally from the Western European markets by the early 1980s.

At a UK level the effect of the rationalization was that by 1986 British Enkalon had ceased to be a domestic producer of polyester and Courtaulds had withdrawn from this sector. Only ICI and Hoechst remained as major domestic producers of polyester. In the nylon market Courtaulds, Monsanto and British Enkalon had closed their UK plants leaving ICI as the sole major UK producer. In the nylon and polyester markets there were respectively two and three minor UK producers, though these were of negligible importance at least on a Western European scale. Finally in the acrylic market Du Pont, Hoechst and Monsanto closed their UK plants, this time leaving Courtaulds as the sole UK producer. However, these changes did not re-create the earlier particular fibre monopolies since imports now constituted a very large part of the available supply.

Table 6.5 *Production Costs Structure, 1985, (%)*

	Acrylic	Polyester
Purchased materials	56.8	47.0
Research and development costs	1.0	1.0
Production and distribution costs	29.2	33.5
Marketing costs	2.5	1.5
Gross operating margin	10.5	17.0
Depreciation	4.5	8.0
Operating profit margin	6.0	9.0

Source: Savory Milln.

6.2.2 Economies of Scale and Cost Structure

There are variations in production costs between different types of fibre but there is broad similarity so that any figures quoted in this section can be regarded as generally representative of all fibres.

Short-run costs

Table 6.5 gives a breakdown of production costs in Western Europe for acrylic and polyester staple fibre. The average cost per kilo of filament yarn is estimated to be some 40 per cent higher due to larger conversion costs.

Historically, substantial fixed costs have meant that operations below full capacity have resulted in significant unit cost increases. Since the 1970s a combination of rising material costs and an industry-wide attempt to reduce overheads has meant that the fixed-cost element has declined in importance. However, this reduction has yet to eliminate the problem that capacity utilization is an important element determining profitability. A recent estimate claimed that to be economic, capacity had to be operated at 85 per cent (Official Journal of the European Communities, 1984). In addition, problems of quality control arise when output falls below 70 per cent of capacity, whilst problems of restarting operations rule out the possibility of complete shutdown.

Long-run costs: economies of scale

Economies of scale in production are significant in relation to total market size, largely because of the reduction in capital costs per unit as plant size is increased.

The estimates in Table 6.6 are for the production of staple fibre for plant sizes up to 100,000 tonnes per year (the largest built). The figures relate to the late 1970s since when the problem of excess capacity has

Table 6.6   *Production Economies of Scale in Polyester Staple Fibre*

| Annual capacity (tonnes) | Capital cost (£m) | Cost indices | | Per cent of Western European polyester staple capacity 1986 |
		Production cost excluding materials	Production cost including materials	
10,000	12	100	100	1.7
20,000	20	92	96	3.3
100,000	75	81	90	17.0

Source: Industry.

put an end to new plant building. The advantage of large size is, however, often nullified by an increase in the number of product lines as plant size increases (Pratten, 1971).

6.2.3   Research and Development Expenditure

Research and development costs have been and remain very important both because of the scale of expenditure and because capital may be tied up for long periods. In the case of nylon and polyester ten years elapsed between initial research and commercial production. In recent years few completely new fibre types of any significance have been introduced. Instead research has been devoted to developing new varieties of existing fibres through chemical or physical modification. For instance, ICI spent $62 million in developing its Mitrelle brand of polyester yarn which has silk-like properties (*Chemical Week*, 15 July 1981). In addition to product innovation funds have also been devoted to the improvement of production technology, for example, Courtaulds' Neochrome process.

As Table 6.5 shows R & D expenditure on average accounts for approximately 1 per cent of European manufacturers' turnover. This represents a considerable reduction from the 3–5 per cent estimated for the 1970s and reflects both the reduction in overheads in the face of continuing losses and possibly also diminishing research possibilities.

6.2.4   Selling Costs and Product Differentiation

During the 1950s and 1960s considerable emphasis was placed by manufacturers on branding their product and promoting through advertising. Advertising sales ratios for the mid-1960s were approximately 1.5 per cent (HMSO, 1969, 1974) indicating high advertising intensity for an intermediate product. Such promotion was intended to establish the manufacturers' brand names and to promote demand for synthetic fibres by final consumers, thus putting pressure on textile and clothing firms to adopt synthetic fibres in preference to natural or cellulosic fibres.

The 1970s witnessed a notable decline in both advertising and branding. The generic names (such as polyester) replaced brand names on fabric and garment labels and retailers emphasized generic rather than brand names in their promotional activities. Increasing knowledge of fibre properties along with competition from imported unbranded fibres reduced the power of the manufacturers' brand name and hence the value of actively promoting it. Fibre manufacturers now emphasize new fibre variants for specific purposes in their promotion, for example, ICI's Tactel for sportswear. Furthermore they now tend to target textile producers as their customers rather than final consumers.

6.2.5 Diversification and Vertical Integration

Diversification in this context can be considered in three ways. First, there is the extent to which the range of synthetic fibres is covered. Rationalization in the early 1980s has resulted in a move away from producers offering a full range to a policy of specialization. Hence Courtaulds specialize in acrylic and ICI have begun to concentrate on nylon. Secondly, there is the degree to which related products are manufactured. Courtaulds, for instance, produces cellulosic fibres and is heavily involved in the textile industry. ICI on the other hand has no interests in either of these areas. Finally, all of the companies listed in Table 6.3 with the exception of Courtaulds are major diversified chemical companies. In 1985, for instance, fibres accounted for only 6.3 per cent of ICI's turnover. The degree and direction of vertical integration is related to this pattern of diversification. Thus ICI manufactures chemical intermediates for its synthetic fibre production but has sought to avoid forward integration into the fibre-using industries. Courtaulds, in contrast, does not manufacture chemical intermediates for fibre production although it does have a subsidiary supplying woodpulp for its cellulosic fibre operation. Through its 1960s take-over activity Courtaulds has major interests in the UK textile industry (Knight, 1974). Recent estimates put Courtaulds' share of cotton system spinning capacity at 50 per cent. It also controls 10 per cent of UK apparel fabrics produced on the cotton system, 10 per cent of the home furnishing market, and it is the UK's largest clothing manufacturer with 5 per cent of production (Buck and Adams, 1985).

6.2.6 Barriers to Entry

Initially patent rights, at least in nylon and polyester, proved effective barriers to new entry but their expiry resulted in some limited entry. Since then high capital costs, sizeable R & D expenditure, significant economies of scale and product differentiation advantages have made entry unattractive to all but the large chemical and man-made fibre firms. For the 1970s and early 1980s excess capacity problems resulting in losses or low profitability have served to diminish further the attractiveness of entry.

6.2.7 Buyer Concentration

The overall level of buyer concentration is on the surface extremely low as synthetics find outlets in several fibre-using industries, some of them containing large numbers of firms. For instance, in 1983 there were 669 enterprises in the woollen and worsted industry, 900 in the hosiery and knitted goods industry, and 356 enterprises in the cotton and allied textile industry (HMSO, 1986). However, this picture is misleading. First, specialized fibre products will only have access to a small proportion of total outlets. Secondly, a combination of moderate levels of concentration, which have risen as a result of recent merger activity in textiles, together with vertical integration by Courtaulds makes the market for synthetic fibres oligopsonistic (see Section 6.3.2).

6.3 MARKET BEHAVIOUR

In order to analyse the relationships between market structure and behaviour the discussion is divided into three sections. The first section concerns the monopoly phase for nylon and polyester. The second and third concern the oligopoly phase for all three synthetic fibres with the second covering the rapid growth period up to 1973, and the third covering the subsequent depressed market period from 1974 until the mid-1980s.

6.3.1 The Monopoly Phase: Nylon and Polyester

Initially BNS and ICI were patent-protected monopolists in the UK for nylon and polyester respectively. Competition was only possible from two sources: alternative fibres, and imported fabric and finished goods made from nylon or polyester. In practice prices were at first set in the UK at a high level to recover the large initial R & D costs and as a reflection of the monopolists' uncertainty as to demand elasticities (Hague, 1957, p. 126). Although synthetic fibre prices were competitive with each other, they were high compared with natural and other man-made fibres. For instance, polyester staple, suitable for the cotton system, was four to five times as expensive as the comparable competitive alternatives, cotton and rayon. In general, apart from some list price reductions in the mid-1950s, probably caused by competition from foreign fabric and other fibres (Hague, 1957, p. 111), prices remained stable until the early 1960s. Throughout this period market penetration was achieved by promotion on the basis of synthetic fibres' superior properties and not by overt price competition. Further, the association of these superior properties with particular brand names – BNS's Bri-Nylon (nylon) and ICI's Terylene and Crimplene (polyester) – was an important feature of the promotion activity.

From 1961 UK prices for both nylon and polyester were progressively reduced. Although it is possible that BNS and ICI were motivated partly by entry deterrence this was probably a minor factor compared with cost reductions, the desire to extend the market, and countering the threat from imports. Indeed in the case of polyester a comparison of the timing and size of the UK list price reductions against movements in USA selling prices suggests that the import threat was a major factor (Shaw and Shaw, 1977).

Other competitive strategies employed, such as the widening of product ranges to cover specialized end-uses and promoting brand names, were consistent with both market extension and enhancing entry barriers. One illustration concerns ICI's development of a textured (bulked) polyester filament yarn at the beginning of the 1960s suitable for the fast, cheap knitting process, which was ultimately used in the production of jersey fabrics, children's clothes and men's suits. In its attack on the market ICI created the Crimplene Club, named after ICI's brand name for the fibre. Only the member firms of this club were licensed to bulk Crimplene yarn, and in return these firms agreed to buy exclusively from ICI. Further, jersey manufacturers were only allowed to sell fabric under the Crimplene name when it had passed ICI quality tests. By creating an element of vertical control ICI was able at the same time both to develop the market rapidly and to establish entry barriers.

6.3.2 The Oligopoly Phase: the Period of Rapid Growth up to 1973

In the acrylic fibre sector an oligopolistic market existed throughout the 1960s; for nylon the oligopoly phase did not begin until about 1964–5; and for polyester this phase only began in 1967. Despite these differences a common feature of all these markets was a pronounced downward trend in prices in the 1960s and early 1970s. Several factors contributed to this development: among them were the threat of imports, the achievement of economies of scale, technical progress, and the desire to widen markets. However, competitive rivalry among the UK and Western European producers seems to have been an important feature of this oligopoly phase.

This rivalry was apparent in the pattern of both investment and pricing announcements which on occasion suggested an apparently aggressive reaction by established firms to the entry and expansion of smaller rivals. For instance, in 1964 when Courtaulds announced plans to become a major producer of nylon, and again in 1969 when it announced its entry into the polyester sector, ICI the dominant producer on both occasions quickly announced its own expansion plans. Similarly in April 1965 ICI reduced its UK nylon prices following Courtaulds' introduction of its nylon 6, Celon, earlier in the year. Indeed the chairman of Courtaulds, referring to Celon's introduction stated at a press conference: 'it is being produced during an increasingly cut-throat price war' (*European Chemical News*, 18 June 1965). In West Germany in December 1966 Hoechst, the established firm, announced its intention to reduce polyester list prices by 25 per cent in the face of entry by ICI and Du Pont. ICI immediately lowered its prices which forced Hoechst to bring forward its own price cuts. The result was that all producers' list prices moved substantially downwards. Similarly in the summer of 1967, under pressure of imports from Du Pont, Hoechst and British Enkalon, ICI, now the established firm, reduced its UK list prices again by about 25 per cent. Du Pont, Hoechst and British Enkalon followed suit.

Although it is clear that the market leaders conceded market share only grudgingly, it would be incorrect to suggest that they were solely responsible for the emerging price competition in the 1960s and early 1970s. A major factor was the often short-term, but rapid, build-up of imports of a particular type of fibre leading to competitive price-cutting and the disregard for official list prices. For instance, due to excess capacity in the USA import restrictions were imposed on fibre entering the United States in 1971. The effect on Western Europe was immediate. Japanese and other Far Eastern supplies of polyester filament were directed to Europe at the same time as demand for textured filament for the knitting industry was cut back. Prices tumbled as firms tried to protect their markets. From their high point at the beginning of 1971, prices fell by 50 per cent by July 1972 (*European Chemical News*, 9 March 1973). When demand improved in the second half of 1972, however, and the pressure from imports eased, there was a sharp recovery in prices in Europe generally.

Similarly excess capacity in Western Europe, even in the period of rapid growth, led to bouts of severe price competition. Between 1965 and 1967 when nylon filament capacity utilization in Western Europe was below 75 per cent, actual (as opposed to list) prices fell by about 40 per cent. A similar reduction in acrylic staple prices occurred in roughly the same period (Berrini, 1973), again in the context of severe excess capacity.

While price competition particularly in the context of new entry, import threats and periodic excess capacity was a clear feature of market behaviour it is important to recognize the role of other competitive strategies. One such strategy involved the continuing search for high-performance speciality fibres by firms seeking outlets unaffected by the increasing price competition in the main sectors. The major firms also continued to seek premium prices for their branded fibres wherever possible.

Another important aspect of market behaviour was the development of vertical control. Courtaulds in the 1960s was actively changing market structure by its vertical integration policy based upon both internal growth and mergers. The initial moves were intended to protect Courtaulds' market for rayon. However, other moves were directly related to the development of Courtaulds' synthetic fibre business (Cowling *et al.*, 1980). Sir Arthur Knight, later to become chairman of Courtaulds, listed 'the inadequacies of the existing market for dealing with a rapidly growing fibre on an adequate scale', Courtaulds' vulnerability to a switch of customers to US fibre competitors, and inadequate quality standards of some independent firms as reasons for vertical integration in acrylic fibres (Knight, 1974, pp. 46–7). Vertical integration into the knitting industry was explained by the need to be close to buyers and because 'it is easier to promote the sale of Courtaulds fibre against US competitors, especially through the rapid translation of new development ideas into commercial products'. Finally, regarding Courtaulds' belated entry into the nylon sector, he commented that 'it was obvious that at that late stage it would be expensive to break into the market held by competitors, and a vertical attack would have more chance of success' (pp. 47–8).

For ICI forward vertical integration into the textile industry was much less important than it was for Courtaulds. Indeed, despite giving some financial assistance to the textile industry through loans and minority shareholdings, ICI avoided direct involvement in the industry until the end of the 1960s. However, as already indicated, ICI did establish a degree of vertical control through its licensing arrangements with the Crimplene Club. Despite the reluctance to become involved ICI eventually acquired control of some textile firms such as Viyella International and Carrington & Dewhurst, though the reasons seem to have been primarily defensive as the viability of these major customers was threatened in the increasingly competitive environment. Finally, ICI used acquisition as a means of achieving vertical integration into the texturizing industry. Here the major reason seems to have been the achievement of technical economies as integration offered the possibility of combining two stages in the production process (Gardner, 1972). However there was probably also a directly competitive reason as two of ICI's competitors – Courtaulds and British Enkalon – had already integrated forward into texturizing and other firms such as Hoechst were threatening ICI's dominance in the UK polyester textured filament fibre market.

6.3.3 The Oligopoly Phase: the Years of Excess Capacity 1974–85

From 1974 onwards market growth was replaced by decline or at best stagnation with consequent severe and persistent excess capacity and financial losses. In the ten years from 1974 until 1983 capacity utilization for all synthetic fibres combined averaged only about 70 per cent in Western Europe. Only in 1984 for the first time since 1973 did capacity utilization exceed 80 per cent. As a consequence of this and depressed prices the Western European industry made heavy losses: according to one producer these amounted to $4,300 million for all man-made fibre producers between mid-1974 and 1979 (United Nations Conference on Trade and Development, 1981). The key feature of market behaviour in this period was how the industry reacted to the very difficult market environment.

One major problem was that new capacity was continuing to be created in the mid-1970s both in the anticipation of continued market growth and through individual firms' attempts to increase market share. Indeed, between 1973 and 1978 Western European synthetic fibre capacity increased by approximately one-third. The industry's problem was also seriously aggravated by increased imports from elsewhere in the world including finished goods containing synthetic fibres. As the 1970s progressed it became clear that restraint in new capacity creation was not enough to solve the problem and that capacity reductions were necessary.

Within the Western European industry there seems initially to have been some difference of opinion with some firms advocating a competitive solution without any government interference or support, while other firms, recognizing the reality of government intervention in some countries, advocated a co-ordinated response to the industry crisis. However, both the persistence of the crisis and the determination of some governments to protect their industries eventually convinced most leading EEC firms that some co-ordination was necessary.

After prolonged negotiations the 'D'Avignon Agreement' was signed in 1978 by eleven major EEC producers including the two UK firms Courtaulds and ICI. All the firms shown in Table 6.3 were participants apart from the two American firms, Du Pont and Monsanto. Non-EEC producers in Austria, Portugal, Spain and Switzerland were also not parties to the agreement. The agreement, named after the EC Commissioner for Industry, Viscount D'Avignon, involved reductions in capacity for six major synthetic fibre types: acrylic staple; polyester staple and polyester textile yarn; nylon staple, nylon textile yarn, and nylon carpet yarn. The seven participating non-Italian producers agreed to reduce their combined capacity of the six fibre types by 16.5 per cent between 1977 and mid-1979, and not to increase their capacity until 1981. The four major Italian producers, whose modernization plans had proved a major difficulty for any collective scheme, agreed to reduce their capacity by 16 per cent by the end of 1978 prior to being allowed to increase capacity again. The agreement also involved market-sharing with producers being expected to maintain their 1976 supply patterns, although the Italian producers were to be allowed to increase their market share from 17 to 21 per cent by 1981 (Shaw and Shaw, 1983).

In November 1978 the EC Commission objected to the market-sharing part of the agreement as being in contravention of the competition policy provisions in Article 85 of the Treaty of Rome. Nevertheless the companies appear to have proceeded to implement the agreement while negotiating on its amendment (Commission of the European Communities, 1979, 1982). The market-sharing problem was circumvented by individual non-Italian producers agreeing to make certain purchases from the Italian signatories. Despite its ambiguous legal status the cartel agreement was successful in achieving a reduction in capacity of around 400,000 tonnes/year, or around 20 per cent of the 1977 level, by the end of 1981.

While the rate of capacity reduction varied between countries with the UK and West Germany being prominent in early plant closures the capacity shares of individual companies in 1980 were extremely close to those reported for 1975 in Table 6.3. Of the 35 company production capacity shares reported for the three synthetic fibres in 1975 only 5 involved changes in capacity share of more than two percentage points by 1980. Two of these involved the American firms, Du Pont and Monsanto, which were not parties to the agreement; and in two other cases it appeared that the firms were planning to withdraw from the sector concerned. Only in the case of ANIC, an Italian firm, did a substantial increase in capacity share occur in any sector by 1980 (Shaw and Shaw, 1983).

A further deterioration in demand in 1980 seems to have convinced the major firms that a more fundamental reappraisal was necessary. Whereas in the period from 1975 to 1980 the number of plants was only reduced from 111 to 98, by 1986 the number of plants had fallen sharply to 68 (each fibre produced at a single geographic location counts as one plant). Similarly whereas up to 1980 only two companies, Monsanto and Hoechst, had withdrawn from any synthetic fibre sector, by 1986 a further eleven sector withdrawals had occurred (Shaw and Simpson, 1986).

Both competitive attrition and collaborative rationalization played a part in this process. SIR and Fabelta were eliminated as a result of financial collapse though Fabelta's nylon facilities were acquired by the Belgian textile firm Beaulieu. Monsanto had withdrawn from the unprofitable Western European synthetic fibre market. Du Pont had rationalized its European activities and withdrawn from the acrylics sector, in the process closing its UK plant. The remaining nine companies listed in Table 6.3 both concluded a new rationalization agreement in 1982 and carried out either separately or collaboratively a series of further rationalization moves.

The new agreement between the nine major EC producers, again including Courtaulds and ICI, provided for further capacity reductions of around 350,000 tonnes/year by the end of 1985. The agreement formula allowed for any reductions in capacity made by a company in excess of the 1978 agreement and also provided for penalties for non-compliance. After some amendments the EC Commission gave its approval to the new agreement in July 1984. However, by that stage most of the planned capacity reductions had already been achieved (Official Journal of the European Communities, 1984).

Apart from the capacity reductions the Western European firms also engaged in a process of rationalization in which most firms withdrew from their weakest fibre sector to concentrate on their strongest areas. Courtaulds, as previously indicated, withdrew from the polyester and nylon sectors, both of which it had been relatively late to enter on any significant scale. On the other hand it strengthened its position in the acrylic sector by acquiring Enka's remaining plant in 1984. ICI which had earlier begun to withdraw from parts of the polyester market announced in 1986 that it was to allow Enka to take over its West German and UK polyester staple business which it was phasing out. In return ICI was to take over the marketing of Enka's remaining nylon output whilst the latter company exits from the market.

In addition to these 'sector rationalizations' the Western European firms, again including Courtaulds and ICI, largely withdrew from bulk commodity production and instead concentrated on the development of specialist fibres.

Finally, a combination of stricter government attitudes to forward integration into textiles along with changes in Courtaulds' company strategy led to little further merger activity after the early 1970s. In addition ICI divested itself of its holdings in Carrington–Viyella in 1982–3.

6.4 PERFORMANCE

Comments on the performance of the UK synthetic fibres industry must be prefaced by the cautionary note that available data generally refers to broader aggregates than desirable. The limited profitability data for Courtaulds concerns its Western European activities and includes cellulosic as well as synthetic fibres. The ICI profitability data although confined to synthetic fibres concerns the firm's worldwide fibre activities. Similarly, comparative national employment and productivity data refer to all man-made fibres and not to synthetics alone.

Turning initially to comparative employment and productivity assessments for man-made fibres it is clear that all major EC fibre producing countries have experienced very substantial increases in

Table 6.7 *Employment in Man-Made Fibres, 1975–85 (thousands)*

	1975	1977	1979	1981	1983	1985	Decline 1975–85
Benelux	n/a	n/a	10.4	9.0	7.7	8.1	n/a
France	20.4	16.5	13.1	9.1	7.6	6.9	13.5
W. Germany	43.1	36.0	30.7	29.1	26.3	26.2	16.9
Italy	41.8	33.7	30.8	24.0	21.8	18.7	23.1
UK	37.0	33.0	27.4	12.7	10.1	8.7	28.4
Spain	12.7	11.0	11.0	9.7	9.2	9.0	3.7

Source: CIRFS (International Rayon and Synthetic Fibres Committee).

Table 6.8   *Output per Employee in Man-Made Fibres, 1975–85 (tonnes)*

	1975	1977	1979	1981	1983	1985	% increase 1975–85
Benelux	n/a	n/a	19.1	17.7	16.9	17.7	n/a
France	14.1	19.7	23.0	27.9	31.1	29.8	111
W. Germany	16.7	22.2	28.3	29.8	32.2	33.6	101
Italy	8.7	13.0	14.2	20.6	22.2	31.5	262
UK	14.9	16.2	21.1	29.8	36.3	36.6	146
Spain	13.5	19.8	24.6	30.0	29.5	34.8	158

Sources: CIRFS (International Rayon and Synthetic Fibres Committee), Textile Organon.

productivity in the 11-year period 1975–85 while reducing their labour forces: see Tables 6.7 and 6.8. In terms of labour productivity the UK had the highest output per employee in 1985 having made the largest percentage gains in the 11-year period of the major fibre-producing countries shown in Table 6.8 with the exception of Italy and Spain. Unfortunately, the UK's success was achieved with the largest decline in labour force for the six countries. It is perhaps also worth noting that while the UK achieved an output per employee of 36.6 tonnes in 1985 the USA achieved an output per employee of 49.8 tonnes.

As indicated earlier the period from the mid-1970s has seen large losses by the Western European man-made fibres industry: an estimated $4.3 billion loss by all producers between mid-1974 and 1979 (UNCTAD, 1981).

Details of Courtaulds' performance in this period are unavailable, but for all ICI's world fibre business losses from 1975–9 amounted to £104 million on sales for the same period of £2,035 million. Profitability data from 1979 are shown in Table 6.9. Close comparison of the performance of the two major UK-based companies is impossible since Courtaulds' data, unlike ICI's, include results for cellulosic fibres. The latter were more profitable than synthetic fibres in this period. More importantly, the results show at least for ICI's synthetic fibres business both the continuing difficulties of the industry in the early 1980s and the subsequent improvement in the mid-1980s. Indeed, by 1984 virtually all the Western European man-made fibres firms had returned to profitability.

While acknowledging the improvements in productivity and profitability the adjustment to Western European excess capacity led to UK plant closures, the loss of over 27,000 jobs and one-third of output between 1975 and 1985. While other European countries also experienced job losses they were generally much less severe and in some cases such as Italy and Spain were accompanied by increased output. (Italian output doubled; Spanish output more than doubled from a lower base.)

Table 6.9 *Courtaulds Western European Man-Made Fibres Profitability 1981–6; ICI Worldwide Synthetic Fibres Profitability, 1979–86*

Year	Courtaulds		ICI	
	Trading profit (loss) £m	*Profit (loss) as percentage of sales*	*Trading profit (loss) £m*	*Profit (loss) as percentage of sales*
1979	n/a	n/a	(38)	(8.1)
1980	n/a	n/a	(86)	(19.9)
1981	(8.3)	(1.7)	(36)	(8.1)
1982	7.2	1.5	(25)	(5.4)
1983	8.1	1.6	(7)	(1.2)
1984	38.9	6.7	22	3.4
1985	36.7	5.5	16	2.3
1986	50.8	7.9	58	8.2

Sources: Company reports and industry sources.

6.5   THE ROLE OF GOVERNMENTS AND COMPETITION POLICIES OF THE EC

In the years of industrial prosperity there was little direct government involvement in the synthetic fibres industry in the UK. However, it should be apparent from the earlier discussion that UK and other governments' patent laws were a key feature in sustaining the monopoly positions of the pioneering firms. Further protection was also afforded by tariff barriers. Finally, within this protected environment the government's usual investment incentives were available for the synthetic fibres industry as for others, though in return the government exercised influence over some of the early plant location decisions to direct investment towards the development areas.

In the 1970s patent and tariff protection largely disappeared. The resulting new entry and import competition were superimposed on the dramatic change in industry growth rate – from nearly 20 per cent per year in the 1960s and early 1970s to stagnation and decline from 1973 onwards. As a result synthetic fibres became one of the 'problem industries' of the 1970s and early 1980s with the emergence of persistent excess capacity.

The two main issues in the changed circumstances concern the support given by governments to firms located in their countries, and the implications for competition policy of co-operative rationalization schemes.

With regard to government support it became clear during the 1970s that some countries were most unwilling to permit plant closures and the resulting redundancies. For instance the Italian government gave continued support in the 1970s for the development of new large-scale synthetic fibre plants as part of its regional policy, while resisting closure of some older plants in the north of the country; in Belgium the state rescued Fabelta, a fibres subsidiary of Enka, by taking majority control in 1976. Despite continuing financial difficulties and protests by the European Commission the Belgian government continued its support into the early 1980s. Similarly, in France rationalization by Rhône Poulenc was delayed as a result of government pressure. In effect governments raised exit barriers and perhaps contributed to the delay in industry adjustment to excess capacity and widespread losses.

The second issue concerns the role of the two synthetic fibre rationalization cartels. These were intended to reduce capacity in an orderly manner and hence indirectly to improve profitability. As indicated earlier the European Commission was unwilling to accept the proposed market-sharing aspects of the 1978 cartel because they seemed to contravene the competition policy provisions in Article 85 of the Treaty of Rome. Nevertheless, the production capacity reductions achieved by the cartel up to 1980 are consistent with the careful maintenance of existing relative market positions. It is possible that while the first cartel may have succeeded in achieving overall capacity reductions it did so by protecting relatively weak competitors. However the second cartel combined capacity reductions with substantial changes in market positions. It seems at the least not to have prevented product rationalization and may have helped create conditions favourable to a significant restructuring of the Western European industry.

NOTE TO CHAPTER 6

This chapter draws heavily on that in the first edition by R. W. and S. A. Shaw for the period prior to 1978.

REFERENCES

Berrini, G. L. (1973), 'The prospects for man-made fibres in Western Europe', Paper delivered at the October 1973 Congress, European Chemical Marketing Research Association.

Buck, D., and Adams, T. (1985), 'A profile of Courtaulds plc', *Textile Outlook International*, no. 2 (November), 77.

Commission of the European Communities (1979), *Eighth Report on Competition Policy* (Luxembourg: Office for Official Publications of the European Communities).

Commission of the European Communities (1982), *Eleventh Report on Competition Policy* (Luxembourg: Office for Official Publications of the European Communities).

Cowling, K., et al. (1980) *Mergers and Economic Performance* (Cambridge: Cambridge University Press).

De Zoete Bevan (1986), *Focus on Fibres: a Study of the Fibres Activities of Courtaulds plc* (London: De Zoete Bevan).

Gardner, K. (1972), 'ICI's links with the textile industry', in 'European fibres survey', *Financial Times*, 1 February.

Hague, D. C. (1957), *The Economics of Man-Made Fibres* (London: Duckworth).

HMSO (1969; 1974; 1986) *Report on the Census of Production*, 1963; 1968; 1981. (London).

Knight, A. (1974), *Private Enterprise and Public Intervention, the Courtaulds Experience* (London: Allen & Unwin).

Man-Made Fibre Production EDC (1983), *Man-Made Fibre Production: Prospects to 1990* (London: National Economic Development Council).

Official Journal of the European Communities (1984), Commission Decision of 4 July 1984 relating to a proceeding under Article 85 of the EEC Treaty (IV/30.810-Synthetic Fibres, no. L 207/16).

O'Neill, H. (1970), 'Synthetic fibres – what it will take to sustain profit?', *Financial Times*, 2 September.

Pratten, C. F. (1971), *Economies of Scale in Manufacturing Industry* (Cambridge: Cambridge University Press).

Savory Milln (1986), *Montefibre* (London: Savory Milln).

Shaw, R. W., and Shaw, S. A. (1977), 'Patent expiry and competition in polyester fibres', *Scottish Journal of Political Economy*, 24 (2), 117–32.

Shaw R. W., and Shaw, S. A. (1983), 'Excess capacity and rationalization in the West European Synthetic Fibres Industry', *Journal of Industrial Economics*, 32 (2), 149–66.

Shaw, R. W., and Simpson, P. (1986), 'Rationalisation within an international oligopoly: the case of the West European synthetic fibres industry', Paper delivered at the Conference on Excess Capacity, December, London Business School.

Textile Outlook International (1986), 'A market and financial profile of Courtaulds fibres', no. 8 (November), (London: Economist Intelligence Unit).

UNCTAD Secretariat (1981), *Fibres and Textiles: Dimensions of Corporate Marketing Structures* (New York: United Nations).

FURTHER READING

Business Monitor, *Production of Man-Made Fibres*, Business Statistics Office, (London: HMSO).

Casson, M. (1986), *Multinationals and World Trade* (London: Allen & Unwin), Chapter 6, on synthetic fibres.

Keynote (1985), *Fibres: an Industry Overview* (London: Keynote Publications).

Monopolies Commission (1968), *Man-Made Cellulosic Fibres*, HC130 1967/68 (London: HMSO).

O'Brien, D. P. (1964), 'Patent protection and competition in polyamide and polyester fibre manufacture', *Journal of Industrial Economics*, 12(3), 224–35.

Robson, R. (1958), *The Man-Made Fibres Industry* (London: Macmillan).

Shaw, R. W., and Shaw, S. A. (1984), 'Late entry, market shares and competitive survival: the case of synthetic fibres', *Managerial and Decision Economics*, 5(2), 72–9.

Textile Organon, *World Man-Made Fibre Survey* (annually in the June issue).

Chapter Seven

Information Technology

PAUL STONEMAN

7.1 INTRODUCTION

7.1.1 Some Definitions

Although information technology is a term that has entered common usage over the last ten years it is rarely defined precisely. The following definitions adapted from Porat (1977) are used here: information is data that have been organized and communicated; the information economy is that part of economic activity that involves the production, processing and distribution of information goods and services and the provision of inputs thereto. Thus, for example, within the firm it includes such activities as research and development, managerial decision-making, market research, filing invoices, data processing and telephone communication. In the wider context such activities as telecommunications, education, the arts and the media may also be included. The sorts of products involved in the information economy include not only computers, but also television, radio, hi-fi systems, telecommunications systems, word processors, videos and many related goods. Information technology is the pattern of products produced by and processes used in the information economy. The media conception of information technology as related to recent advances in, and the convergence of the interrelated fields of, micro-electronics, fibre optics, software engineering, communications, and computer technology, is encompassed within this definition.

It is useful to split the information economy into two separate parts, the primary information sector (PIS) and the secondary information sector (SIS). The definitions of these sectors is taken from Organization for Economic Co-operation and Development (1986). The PIS (p. 16) includes

goods and services which intrinsically convey information (such as books), or which are directly useful in its production, processing or distribution (such as computers). These goods should normally be transacted on established markets for inclusion in the PIS. The PIS is therefore the productive locus of an information based economy, providing the technical infrastructure for a variety of information processing and transmission activities (as with telecommunications networks), as well as offering information goods and services for sale directly as a commodity (as with video recorders and software consultancies).

The SIS (p. 26) includes

information activities used in producing non-information goods and services. In other words this sector incorporates information services produced for internal consumption within that part of the public sector and private enterprise which does *not* belong to PIS.

The information economy thus produces goods, such as cameras, and services, such as insurance services, that satisfy final demands. It also produces intermediate goods (for example, measuring instruments) and intermediate services (for example, computer services) for use in the production of information and non-information goods and services. It uses both information and non-information inputs (for example, electronic components and plastics) in its production processes. The pattern of inputs and outputs in the PIS and the use of information goods and services in the SIS constitutes what is here defined as 'information technology'. Recent changes in these patterns may be called 'new information technology'.

7.1.2 Information as a Product

Pure information (as opposed to information-related goods such as videos or computers) has a number of peculiar characteristics that distinguish it from other goods and services produced in an economy. A piece of information may be considered as a message relating to what is known of the state of the world. Two of the distinguishing features of this piece of knowledge are its accuracy and its timeliness. Some of the peculiar characteristics of the product are as follows:

(1) Once produced, a piece of information has an almost zero reproduction cost.
(2) A piece of information need only be acquired once by any particular individual, and once acquired a repeated message has zero value to that individual.
(3) It is difficult to evaluate the quality of a piece of information until received, and once received by an individual he will demand it no more.
(4) A continually changing environment generates a continuous demand for new (and thus different) information.

The sorts of problems that arise as a result of these characteristics can be illustrated with a few examples. First, (1) can lead to a conflict

Table 7.1   *Percentage Share of PIS in GDP at Factor Cost*

Year	UK	USA	West Germany
1958	n/a	19.6	n/a
1963	16.0	n/a	n/a
1967	n/a	23.8	n/a
1970	n/a	n/a	16.5
1972	22.0	24.8	n/a
1980	25.9	n/a	19.8

Source: OECD, 1986, p. 15.

Table 7.2   *Information Occupations as Percentage of All Economically Active*

UK		USA		West Germany	
Year	%	Year	%	Year	%
1951	27.6	1950	30.7	1950	18.3
1971	35.6	1970	41.1	1970	29.3
1981	41.0	1980	45.8	1981	33.5
				1982	34.8

Source: OECD, 1986, p. 8.

Table 7.3   *Components of Primary Information Sector: Percentage of GDP at Factor Cost, UK, 1980*

Sector	% of GDP
Knowledge production industries	5.0
Search, co-ordination and risk management industries	8.7
Information distribution and co-ordination industries	8.5
Consumption and intermediate goods	1.1
Investment goods	2.6
Total	25.9

Source: OECD, 1986, p. 18.

between the optimal use of information and the provision of sufficient incentives to encourage its production. For example, a software package can be copied at almost zero cost and pricing at this cost would imply optimal use of that package; but if it is so copied and priced then the programmer is unlikely to obtain sufficient reward to encourage the production of the package in the first place. (The taping of records and recording of TV programmes falls into the same category.) For this reason there are copyright laws. Characteristic (3) implies that it is very difficult to establish a perfect market in information. Characteristics (2) and (4) imply jointly that the nature of the product traded will be changing continuously over time and it is thus not possible to consider markets as involving trade in a homogeneous product. Finally, the peculiar characteristics of the product allied with its use as an intermediate input, suggest that it is extremely difficult to value output, particularly that of the SIS. There are of course other implications but these are the major ones of relevance in the current context.

7.1.3 Industry Size

Because of the already noted problems of measuring output in the SIS, estimates of the size of the information sector in terms of output are restricted to the PIS. Such measurement problems can be avoided if the size of the sector (PIS plus SIS) is measured by employment and thus such data are also presented. In Table 7.1 some data relating to the size of the PIS in the United States, the United Kingdom and West Germany are presented. In Table 7.2 employment in information occupations is detailed.

These tables illustrate not only the size of the information sector in the UK both in terms of output and employment but also its growth. With a current employed total labour force of approximately 24 million, the data in Table 7.2 suggest that nearly 10 million persons are employed in information occupations in the UK. Some further details on the industrial pattern of the information sector are presented in Table 7.3.

7.1.4 Technological Change in the Information Economy

There can be no disputing the fact that information technology (IT) has illustrated more rapid technological improvement than any other part of the productive process in the last 25 years. These technological advances have affected both the PIS and the SIS. It is possible to produce extensive detailed lists of major advances in IT. To some degree, however, such lists obscure general trends that are of more importance. These general trends have been detailed by Freeman and Soete (1985) and it is on their work that the following list of the major characteristics of the changes in technology is based.

(1) A very high and continuing rate of technological change in both the PIS and the SIS is apparent. To a considerable degree this is based on continuing dramatic improvements in the large-scale integration of electronic circuits and the resulting reduction in costs. Thus, for example, memory prices have fallen from around 1 US cent per bit in 1971 to about 0.005 US cent per bit in 1986. With these and parallel advances in opto-electronics, communications technology, and computer design and development, there is a

high rate of product obsolescence, with further 'generations' making earlier technology obsolete. The various advances have made and continue to make cheaper and faster the communication, processing and storing of information.

(2) The advances in IT enable the integration of several activities such as design, manufacture, procurement and sales. They have led to the advent of computer-aided design (CAD) and CADCAM (CAD with computer-aided manufacture) and the vision of the all-electronic office based on, for example, networked word processors and facsimile transmission.

(3) The quality of products, processes and services can be improved by the use of recent advances. On-line monitoring control can save capital, labour, materials and energy, and has already shown the ability to do so in industries as diverse as colour TV manufacture and motor car assembly.

(4) Recent advances can provide inter-firm or intra-firm linkages between, for example, sales from stock and stock reordering that may be inventory saving, or, for example, allow production without back-up stocks ('just in time' systems).

(5) It is further argued that recent advances allow smaller production runs to be economic, thus promoting greater flexibility and more frequent changes in models and designs.

(6) Advances in electronics have led and continue to lead to the replacement of electro-mechanical technology by electronic technology with a consequent reduction in the assembly task.

(7) On the basis of the advances in electronics, computer and communications technology, more new products and processes are being introduced. The new products may be goods, such as compact discs and video-recorders, or services such as home banking. The new processes will include such technologies as robotics.

(8) The improvements in communications technology and other changes may result in a greater international integration of industries, services and markets.

Despite the above list the speed of change should not be overemphasized. There is no doubt that significant technological advances are under way, but, as a general rule, the introduction of new technology takes time. The process of diffusion (the spread of new technology) is a lengthy process: for some technologies diffusion can take between 25 and 50 years. This should not be taken to imply that all new IT will have such lengthy diffusion patterns, only that such time scales should be borne in mind when considering technological change. The implication of this is that the impact of new technology on an economy is likely to be evolutionary rather than revolutionary.

7.1.5 The Major Issues

There are at least four issues relating to the information economy that are currently of major concern. The first, given the recent privatization of British Telecom, concerns the whole issue of ownership, regulation and economic performance. The second issue centres upon the relationship between new technology and employment. The third concerns the success or failure of the UK economy, and the fourth and related issue questions the role of government defence expenditures and their impact on the UK information economy. These four issues are examined below.

7.2 OWNERSHIP, REGULATION AND ECONOMIC PERFORMANCE

The transmission of information is a major part of the activities of the information economy. The two most important channels for private transmission are telecommunications and postal services. In the UK from 1912 until 1981 both these services were supplied almost exclusively by the Post Office, but in 1981 British Telecom (BT) was established with responsibility for telecommunications services, the responsibility for postal services being retained by the Post Office. Although this separation has obvious implications for competition, and merits investigation on this account, it is the later changes in the telecommunications sector that are the focus of interest here. In particular, within the context of the British telecommunications sector three particular issues are explored: privatization, that is, the transfer of a firm from public to private ownership; liberalization, that is, the opening up of a market to competition; and regulation, the placing of constraints on firm behaviour through statutory (and/or other) instruments.

The telecommunications industry has three basic elements: the supply of equipment, the running of networks and the supply of services. It is argued (see Vickers and Yarrow, 1985) that the running of networks is likely to be a natural monopoly (an industry in which production by one firm is more efficient than production by several). A person's demand for the services of a telecommunications network depends on who else subscribes to that network, and thus who else that person can contact or be contacted by. The complete duplication of networks would be inefficient and so natural monopoly is likely. However, although these arguments apply strongly to local networks, the supply of long-distance services, that is, linkages between local networks, is unlikely to be a natural monopoly if there is freedom to connect into local networks. Nor is it the case that the supply of equipment and the supply of services are natural monopolies. There seems to be no reason why it should be more efficient to have only one supplier of telephones, nor given the existence of a telecommunications network, why it should be more efficient for only one firm to retail the services of that network. Thus, although some parts of telecommunications may have the characteristics of a natural monopoly, by no means all parts have.

Reference was made above to the extent of recent advances in information technology. Telecommunications is no exception in terms of experiencing technological advance. Perhaps the main long-term trend has been the apparent fusing together of computer and telecommunications technology, but more specific examples are apparent. On the terminal side, a wide variety of equipment can now be linked to the network: for example, computers, word processors, facsimile machines, telex machines and so on. In the networks the use of electronics is advancing at the expense of electro-mechanical methods. In transmission, technologies based on optical fibres, microwaves, satellites and cellular radio are being introduced. It is unlikely that this technological revolution will be slowing down in the near future.

Social welfare maximization requires that an industry should be efficient in production, allocation and technology. The recent reorganization of the industry should thus be evaluated in terms of its impact on these criteria. To do this the nature of the reorganization must first be detailed.

Prior to privatization BT had the exclusive right to run public networks and to regulate the industry. It was a wholly publicly owned (nationalized) industry. Its management and objectives were conditioned by the statutes setting up the public corporations and guidelines established in various White Papers on the nationalized industries. In the period immediately prior to privatization the most important constraints on the behaviour of BT arising from these regulations were: (1) a series of financial targets; (2) external financing limits on net indebtedness to the government; and (3) a real rate of return target of 5 per cent on new investment programmes as a whole.

In August 1984 BT plc took over the business of the public corporation and just over half the company was sold to the public at the end of November 1984. The government retained one 'golden share' to prevent take-over by another company. The 1984 Telecommunications Act enabling this had the following further provisions;

(1) It abolished BT's statutory involvement in regulation.
(2) It required all operators of telecommunications systems to be licensed, and BT's exclusive privilege to run telecommunications systems was abolished.
(3) A post of Director General of Telecommunications (DGT) in charge of an Office of Telecommunications (OFTEL) was created to enforce licensing conditions and to monitor competition in the industry.

Under the Act, licences for public networks have been granted to BT, Mercury and the Kingston-upon-Hull City Council (to which no further reference is made here). The government has announced that it will not grant any further licences of this kind until November 1990. The licence to BT is for a period of 25 years. It requires BT to provide telecommunications services throughout the UK, including some of a 'public service' nature. It also contains a number of measures designed to prevent certain 'anti-competitive' practices. It further constrains BT pricing by the RPI-x formula whereby BT prices for a 'basket' of telecommunications services must reduce by x per cent per annum in real terms (where x has been set at 3). The licence granted to Mercury under the 1984 Act is similar to that of BT but without price regulation or public service obligations.

In the market for terminal operations BT, although dominant, no longer has a statutory monopoly. Part of the safeguards in the BT licence are to ensure that BT provides 'fair' terms for the attachment of terminal equipment to the rest of the system. In the supply of services, the government has allowed competition in the supply of data services (an example of a 'value added network' service (VAN)) but restricted competition in the supply of voice services (no new licences until 1990) and prohibited the buying and reselling of BT capacity by others.

The first question to answer concerns the benefits that may be expected from privatization. Kay and Thompson (1986) argue that privatization may have several objectives including the improvement of industrial performance, the raising of government revenue, the curbing of trade union power, and the promotion of wider share-ownership. It is the first of these objectives that is of most concern here. It is argued, in support of privatization, that the change from public to private ownership removes the industry from the unsatisfactory regime that has previously regulated its activity and provides through the threat of take-over a stimulus to productive efficiency. It is also argued that privatization provides clear objectives to management through an observable measure of performance (share price) and changes the 'atmosphere' in the industry with less emphasis on a public service ethos and more emphasis on profitability. It is clear however that privatization is not necessary to change an unsatisfactory regulatory regime. Furthermore the 'golden share' means that BT is not subject to any threat of take-over. It must also be remembered that share prices depend on profitability and that profitability may derive from monopoly pricing practices as well as efficiency. Finally, changing the 'ethos' of the company may not necessarily be in the public interest. For example, one of the first policy changes of BT after privatization was to source some of its equipment from overseas suppliers rather than continue to rely on UK suppliers (GEC and Plessey). Although such action may be in the public interest it is possible to argue that the detrimental impact on UK output and employment might imply the reverse.

Kay and Thompson (1986), after reviewing the evidence on the performance of private and public sector companies, argue (p. 25) that privatization *per se* is unlikely to improve company performance:

> no simple generalisation about superiority of private sector perform-ance can be sustained. But there is support for the view that the efficiency of all firms – public or private – is improved by a competitive environment . . . under competition private firms are likely to do better, but if there is little competition regulated private firms do not perform better than public firms and may do worse. . . . Privatisation will tend to improve performance in a company only if supported by liberalisation.

The privatized British Telecom is still a dominant enterprise enjoying substantial, although reduced, protection from competition through entry. Kay and Thompson (1986) suggest that the limited liberalization that actually occurred was the result of the time schedule accepted for privatization forcing concessions to the desires of BT management. Whatever the cause, however, one must ask whether the liberalization went far enough. It has been suggested above that in certain areas telecommunications is a natural monopoly – in such a situation it is not efficient to have competition and even with liberalization competition is unlikely to emerge. The theory of contestable markets might however suggest that even with natural monopoly, liberalization making potential entry easier or even possible may constrain the conduct of the incumbent firm. Such liberalization has been limited, with no new licences for issue until at least November 1990. It might be argued that at least Mercury has been licensed – but compared to BT, Mercury is a minnow: while the planned spending of Mercury on its network is £200 million in total, BT has an asset valuation in excess of £10 billion. Mercury may however provide a measure against which the performance of BT can be judged.

There has been greater liberalization outside of the running of networks, that is, in the supply of equipment and the supply of services, although in the latter especially it is limited. (The resale of BT capacity is restricted to non-voice transmission.) It is generally argued, however, that the dominant position of BT in the network can significantly reduce the degree of competition in these other services. It is worth noting that at the time that BT was being privatized with only limited liberalization, AT & T in the United States was being broken up to promote greater competition.

As BT retains a dominant market position with protection from entry (and even new technologies are unlikely under the present regime to generate significant competition to BT) and take-over, the possibility of BT being policed by competitive forces is limited. Thus a regulatory regime has been imposed on the industry. One element of this is the pricing formula, RPI-x, the other is the regulatory body, OFTEL. The problem with the former is that, as an attempt to prevent the abuse of market power it has four limitations: (1) goods and services not in the basket are not regulated; (2) the basket approach still allows price discrimination and cross-subsidy; (3) the fact that the formula is to be reviewed in 1989 may give BT an incentive to underperform prior to that date so that an 'easier' target is set for later years; and (4) the size of x (3 per cent) was set in joint consultation with BT management whose incentives were to make x as low as possible.

OFTEL, with the responsibility to enforce licensing conditions and to monitor competition, is perhaps, therefore, the key to the regulation of the industry. In particular it has a crucial role to play in ensuring access to the BT network on fair terms to other licence holders (Mercury). As yet it is difficult to evaluate the success of OFTEL. The problem with such agencies is that they may be 'captured' by the dominant firm, becoming sponsors rather than regulators. There is, however, no evidence to date that this has happened. Vickers and Yarrow (1985) argue that the impact and effectiveness of regulation are highly sensitive to the delegated powers and procedures of the responsible agency. Whether OFTEL is able to regulate so as to obtain the objectives of productive, allocative and technological efficiency has yet to be seen.

At the time of writing, it is two years since the major upheaval in the UK telecommunications industry. It is too early to evaluate the impact of this. In Table 7.4, the turnover, profit and profit : turnover ratio for BT since 1983 are presented. The growth in the profit : turnover ratio could be interpreted as reflecting increased efficiency, but it may also be considered to contain a large element of monopoly rent.

The discussion above suggests that with the privatization of BT an opportunity for liberalization was missed. In terms of the objectives stated earlier, privatization is a bit of a red herring and the new regulatory environment has yet to be fully tested. However, other information industries may be treated in a similar way in the future, the Post Office being an obvious candidate. The BT experience may have some lessons in this and other contexts. The three issues of privatization, liberalization and regulation are therefore important areas and merit further and continuous study.

Table 7.4 *British Telecom, Performance Figures 1983–6*

	1983	1984	1985	1986
Turnover (£m)	6,414	6,879	7,653	8,387
Profits before tax (£m)	1,031	990	1,480	1,810
Profit/turnover ratio (%)	16.1	14.4	19.3	21.6

Source: British Telecom annual reports.

7.3 NEW INFORMATION TECHNOLOGY AND EMPLOYMENT

It was argued earlier that nearly 40 per cent of employment in the UK may be classified as being in information-related occupations. Moreover it has been shown that extensive technological change is occurring in the information sector. It is therefore no surprise that there should be considerable concern over the impact of these technological changes on employment in this sector. Despite the fact that early forecasts predicted extensive reductions in labour demand as the new technologies appeared, the data above – see Tables 7.1–7.3 – do not illustrate any obvious signs of reductions in information sector employment. In this section the relation between technological change and employment is explored more fully.

To predict the impact of technological change on employment it is necessary to consider its effect on both productivity and output. For a given output level, an increase in labour productivity will lead to reduced employment and for a given labour productivity an increase in output will lead to increased employment. Technological change need not affect labour productivity. It may save energy or raw materials or be of the product innovation type, in which case the impact on employment depends solely on the impact on output. If it does affect labour productivity then the impact on employment will depend on the relative sizes of the changes in output and productivity. With this as a guideline it is possible to consider theoretically how technology might affect employment at the firm, industry and economy levels.

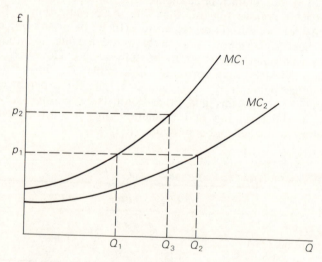

Figure 7.1   *Output and innovation: the competitive firm*

In Figure 7.1 a price-taking firm in a competitive industry with a marginal cost (MC) curve MC_1 is shown. Let the industry price be p_1. At this price the firm will profit-maximize with output Q_1. Let the technological innovation be of the process type (for example, the introduction of a robot) which reduces marginal costs to MC_2. With this new marginal cost curve the firm has a higher desired output level, Q_2. Alternatively let the innovation be of the product type whereby the firm produces (at marginal cost MC_1) a product that has a higher price p_2, and again output will be higher at Q_3. Both exercises illustrate that the general impact of a product or process innovation will be to yield increased output.

Now consider a monopoly in which output is determined where marginal revenue (MR) equals marginal cost; see Figure 7.2. There is an initial demand curve D_1D_1, with initial marginal cost MC_1 and marginal revenue MR_1. A process innovation could shift marginal cost from MC_1 to MC_2. A product innovation, say the production of an improved computer type, could shift the demand and MR curves to D_2D_2 and MR_2 respectively. In the first case output would increase to Q_2, in the second to Q_3. Again there would be an increase in output as the new technology is introduced. This particular example illustrates particularly well that with process innovation the extent of any increase in output depends on the slope of the demand curve (and thus the elasticity of demand) and the extent of the shift in the MC curve (and thus the extent of the innovation). With product innovation the shift of DD (the extent of the innovation) and the slope of the MC curve (which will roughly depend on economies of scale) matter.

To translate these output increases into the impact on labour

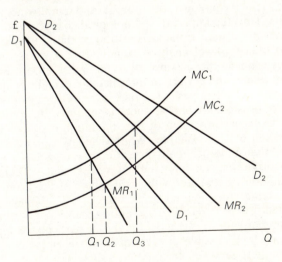

Figure 7.2 *Output and innovation: monopoly*

demand. it is necessary also to know the extent of the bias in technological change, that is, the degree to which inputs are saved in different proportions, and the elasticity of substitution (see Stoneman, 1983). It should be no surprise therefore that, given the complexity of the issues, simple predictions of the impact of new technology on employment cannot be made.

At the industry level, Waterson and Stoneman (1985) have considered what happens to employment as the diffusion of a new technology proceeds. Within the context of a simple model of symmetric Cournot oligopoly they illustrate that in reaction to a process innovation which reduces marginal cost (equals average cost), industry output increases and industry price falls as the number of users of the technology increases. Upon adoption of the new technology a firm's output increases, but as more firms adopt the new technology the output of both users and non-users of the new technology falls. The impact on employment is complicated. As more firms use the new technology the employment of a non-user reduces. The employment in a firm may increase or decrease as it switches to new technology (depending on the size of its productivity increase relative to its output expansion), but as more firms take on new technology the employment of both using and non-using firms falls as their output falls. Industry employment may rise or fall as the new technology is more widely used. Waterson and Stoneman show in a wide variety of circumstances that even if industry employment eventually rises, there may well be a period of employment reduction before this rise is achieved. Perhaps of equal relevance, however, is the observation that when a firm adopts a new technology, this impacts on the output and employment of other firms. In particular, as other firms adopt new technology, the output and employment of non-adopters falls. Thus the impact of technological change on employment may be somewhat distant from the location of the innovation.

Of course industry-level analysis cannot tell the whole story. One industry may gain at the expense of another, or innovation in one industry may change the pattern of intermediate demands expressed to other industries. Such sorts of issues require a macro-economic analysis. It is possible to pursue such an enquiry theoretically, but probably of more use are some of the simulation exercises that have been undertaken by, for example, Whitley and Wilson (1987).

The model that underlies their simulation exercises has a Keynesian structure incorporating an input–output system and concentrates on the determination of changes in the real sector of the economy. The model is a large one and comprises over 1,400 behavioural and technical relationships (excluding accounting identities). The endogeneity of certain variables in the model makes it particularly appropriate for considering how possible direct reductions in employment due to higher productivity may be offset by the following:

(1) increased domestic demand resulting from higher real incomes;
(2) increased foreign demand resulting from improved price and non-price competitiveness;
(3) increased demand for investment goods in order to implement the new technology;
(4) dynamic effects such as the multiplier effects on real incomes following increases in autonomous expenditures;
(5) equilibrating effects in the labour market.

The authors' initial step was to generate a 'most likely' path for employment in the UK given all the knowledge available on the likely effect of technology on production processes in different industries. Although this 'most likely' projection contained a considerable margin for error, the results indicated that even with the introduction of new IT-based technologies into the economy, the projected path of economic aggregates differed little from their past trends. Output and productivity at the macro level were projected to maintain growth at about 2 per cent per annum to 1995, and unemployment was expected to stay around the 3 million mark. Thus at the macro level, the most likely path was not one that seems to indicate any revolutionary impact on the UK macro-economy.

Also at the sectoral level of aggregation past trends were predicted to continue. Primary and manufacturing shares of employment were forecast to continue their decline whereas the transport, communication and services sectors were seen as continuing an expansion in shares. At the individual industry level, some industries were predicted to gain, others to lose.

The authors also undertook a simulation exercise that investigated the impact of an increase in the speed at which new technology is introduced into the economy – an increase in the diffusion speed. The initial results, looking at the faster introduction of new technology in manufacturing stimulating, for example, investment and trade performance, suggested the existence of a 'virtuous circle'. The faster take-up in manufacturing generated higher productivity, faster growth in exports, output and consumption, and higher employment. The results of a related simulation exercise whereby new technology was introduced more quickly into the service sector yielded quite an opposite result, with substantial job losses in both the service and manufacturing sectors. As the authors state, this result arises from several factors. First, the number of jobs at risk is large; secondly, there are only modest compensation effects in capital equipment supply; thirdly, much of the impact falls on non-traded goods and thus no offset is derived from gains in international competitiveness; and finally the simulation is unable to account for product innovation in the sector. This latter point is perhaps one that ought to be stressed, for product innovation may be particularly important in some sectors.

Table 7.5   *The UK IT Industry*

	1970	1980	1983
Output (£m)	563	2,685	4,050
Exports (£m)	140	1,053	1,800
Imports (£m)	168	1,142	2,600

Source: NEDO, 1984, p. 6.

This work by Whitley and Wilson provides a good bridge into other empirical work on technology and employment. More direct evidence is provided by Northcott and Rogers (1984). They have surveyed users of micro-electronics in British industry, investigating the extent of use and impacts on the employment of users. It should be noted that this approach does not take any account of the impact outside the using establishment, but does give a reasonable measure of its local impact. They found that over the period 1981–3 about 69 per cent of the UK factories using micro-electronics reported no change in employment in consequence, 17 per cent reported decreases totalling 54,000 jobs, 13 per cent reported increases totalling 20,000 jobs. Thus the net local effects were a decrease of about 34,000 jobs. This represented about 0.6 per cent of total employment in manufacturing and less than 5 per cent of the total decrease in employment in manufacturing in the period. It is worth noting that it was process applications of micro-electronics that led to the job losses; factories applying micro-electronics in products experienced net increases in jobs.

The survey by Northcott and Rogers (1984) further indicated that the job losses were concentrated amongst the unskilled. There was an excess demand for engineers and others with micro-electronics related skills. This excess demand may in fact have slowed the use of the new technology.

It may be concluded from this work that the impact of new information technology on the aggregate demand for labour may be quite limited. That impact may well differ as diffusion speeds vary and as other factors change but a most likely forecast is a continuation of past trends. At the firm or industry level employment is likely to grow in some industries and decline in others. The impact may also differ by type and area of application. The use of the new technology is likely to affect the skill composition of labour demand as well as its geographical and gender composition. Overall, however, the evidence to date indicates that the effects are unlikely to be particularly large. Perhaps of more concern ought to be the question of what will be the impact of a failure to adopt new technology in the UK economy. For this reason the 'crisis' in the UK IT industry is now considered.

Table 7.6   *The UK IT Industry: International Comparisons*

		UK	West Germany	France	Japan	USA
Output	1970	676	784	444	1,049	4,237
(£m)	1980	2,176	3,866	3,236	7,357	19,341
	1982	2,570	4,332	3,591	n/a	30,404
% Share	1970	9	11	6	15	59
	1980	6	9	7	23	56

Source: NEDO, 1984, p. 6

7.4   THE UK IT INDUSTRY – SUCCESS OR FAILURE?

In National Economic Development Office (1984) it is argued that the UK IT industry has performed less effectively than the industries of competitor nations and as a result may not be able to survive as a serious independent industry. Given the importance of IT to the economy as a whole the implications of this were considered disastrous. To illustrate the argument some of their figures are presented in Tables 7.5 and 7.6.

The main observations made on these figures were that the UK industry has grown rapidly but less fast than international competitors. This is reflected in the dramatic deterioration in the balance of trade, running at a deficit of £800 million in 1983. Furthermore, it is pointed out, employment in the UK industry has been falling.

The NEDO figures relate to two sectors covering electronic data processing (EDP) equipment and telegraph and telephone equipment. Thus the definition of IT as used by NEDO is a restricted one. Output figures for these two industries for more recent years are shown in Table 7.7.

In Table 7.8 figures on employment and the balance of trade are shown for the EDP equipment and telephone and telegraph industries as well as for four other IT sectors covering final products and electronic components. The figures do not match exactly with those of NEDO but it is the trends that are important. The first point to note is that the fall in employment noted by NEDO between 1981 and 1983 is to a considerable degree confined to the telephone and telegraph sector. In this sector employment continued to fall after 1983, but in the other sectors detailed in Table 7.8, the picture is much more one reflecting increased employment rather than decline.

The second point to note is that in the two sectors studied by NEDO there had been by 1985 a considerable turn-round in the trade balance, largely due to improvements in the EDP industry. Of the other sectors detailed, radio and electronic capital goods and electronic consumer goods had balances in 1985 better than in 1983. It may be worth noting that in consumer goods in 1985 nearly half the deficit was due to the

Table 7.7   *The UK IT Industry, Output, 1981–6*

| | Output 1980 = 100 | |
	EDP equipment	Telephone & telegraph equipment
1981	86	102.6
1982	95	103.1
1983	149.1	103.8
1984	217.8	103.8
1985	287.0	114.8
1986 I	250.7	127.9
1986 II	251.4	114.6

Note: I, II refer to quarters 1 and 2.
Source: Business Monitor, PQ 3302, PQ 3441.

importation of video-recorders. The electronic capital goods sector has been running in surplus for each of the years. In electronic components an improvement was registered between 1984 and 1985.

In the light of the trends in these figures and the limited sectoral coverage of the NEDO figures, it may be suggested that the crisis is not quite as bad as made out by NEDO in 1984. There is, however, another side to the issue of crisis. Is the UK ahead or behind competitors in the *use* of IT (as opposed to the supply of IT equipment)? Northcott *et al.* (1985) survey the use of micro-electronics in the UK, France and West Germany with the conclusion (p. 1) that

Britain is slightly behind Germany in the percentage of factories using microelectronics in their production processes, and further behind in the percentage with applications in the products themselves, but ahead of France in both. Compared with Germany, Britain makes less use of CNC machine tools and robots, appears to have fewer professional engineers with microelectronic expertise and sends fewer people on training courses. However, Britain appears to be relatively strong in some areas, such as the electrical engineering and food industries and in the use of semi-custom chips, and to have fewer difficulties with trade unions than the other countries, but British industry has greater problems than the others in raising finance for development and in the general background economic situation.

With respect to other countries, Northcott *et al.* (1985) obtained the results shown in Table 7.9. These figures do not appear to suggest a dramatic falling behind other countries although the general superiority of the Far East, particularly Japan, and also the USA is recognized.

The above, admittedly limited, observations on the UK situation suggest that, if there is a crisis in the UK IT·industry, then that crisis is

Table 7.8 *Employment and Trade Balance, 1981–6*

Year	EDP equipment[a]		Telephone & telegraph equipment		Radio & electronic capital goods		Electronic consumer goods & miscellaneous equipment		Components other than active components mainly for electronic equipment		Electronic sub assemblies & active components	
	Employment ('000)	Balance of trade (£m)	Employment ('000)	Balance of trade (£m)	Employment ('000)	Balance of trade (£m)	Employment ('000)	Balance of trade (£m)	Employment ('000)	Balance of trade (£m)	Employment ('000)	Balance of trade (£m)
1981	75.6	n/a	58.6	35	88.8	n/a	n/a	n/a	29.8	−55	n/a	−89
1982	75.2	−553	57.0	19	86.2	224	n/a	−722	29.7	−96	n/a	−85
1983	74.3	−872	55.1	−43	87.1	317	n/a	−1055	31.0	−132	n/a	−286
1984	73.1	−962	50.8	−51	91.3	285	n/a	−764	33.3	−210	n/a	−466
1985	75.3	−606	47.1	−85	94.7	346	n/a	−845	33.0	−209	n/a	−373
1986 I	75.1	−204	43.7	−9	96.2	77	n/a	−162	32.3	−50	n/a	−61
1986 II	n/a	−144	n/a	−21	n/a	126	n/a	−157	n/a	−50	n/a	−61

Note: [a] Including the supply of office equipment
Source: Business Monitor, PQ 3302, 3441, 3443, 3444, 3454, 3453 in column order.

The Structure of British Industry

Table 7.9 *Position Relative to Competitors, Percentage of User Establishments in Samples*

Competitors in:	Product applications			Process applications		
	Britain	West Germany	France	Britain	West Germany	France
Own country	+36	+9	+20	+19	+3	+21
Europe	+5	+18	+1	−14	+9	−5
N. America	+1	−15	−15	−5	−12	−16
Far East	+4	−20	−8	+8	−15	−11

Notes: + excess percentage thinking they are ahead of competitors over percentage thinking they are behind.

− excess of percentage thinking they are behind competitors over percentage thinking they are ahead.

Source: Northcott *et al.*, 1985.

to a large degree centred upon the EDP industry, that is, the computer supply industry, and the real reflection of this is the large negative trade balance in EDP. Having said this however, the trade balance in electronic consumer goods is also a matter of great concern.

It is not possible to detail cause and effect in the poor performance of the UK EDP industry here. It must however be realized that the EDP industry is dominated by large multinational companies such as IBM, Unisys and Honeywell, and to some degree the trading performance of any one country must reflect the production location decision of these companies. It is also worth pointing out that the main UK computer company, ICL, uses Japanese technology to a considerable degree, and has sold Japanese products under its own name. Thus market-share data may be a misleading indicator of a company's 'strength'.

However, even if the cause of the problem cannot be precisely identified some of the suggested remedies may be discussed. The NEDO report offered many, including the establishment of common UK standards for interfacing to produce a united UK front; more R & D collaboration; integration and merging of UK companies; greater government involvement to stimulate education and training, R & D and inward investment; and preferential procurement.

Each of these issues could be discussed at length. However, only the question of government support for IT is examined here. Such support comes mainly from the Department of Trade and Industry and the Ministry of Defence. The latter is considered in Section 7.5 below. The support from the DTI comes under three individual programmes:

(1) *The Alvey Programme.* The objective of this programme is to help UK firms to capture the maximum possible share of the world IT market by securing competitive levels of achievement in certain

fundamental enabling technologies. The means is a co-operative research programme between and across industry and academia. It is aimed to result in the doubling of research effort in the areas it covers.

(2) *The Electronics Support Programme* has three objectives: to accelerate the take-up of micro-electronics technology, to improve export performance and to strengthen the electronic components industry. The objective is to eliminate the UK trade deficit by 1990.

(3) *The Information Technology Programme* is designed to encourage innovation to match overseas competitors, in order to reduce the UK trade deficit in telecommunications equipment, computer equipment, consumer and capital goods electronics, and computer software. A parallel objective is to stimulate the use of IT technology.

In 1985/6 DTI-funded R & D in these three areas amounted to £102.2 million. This was within an overall R & D support budget for the DTI of £370 million. In addition to the UK programmes, the European Community also has support schemes such as ESPRIT (focusing on pre-commercial generic research in information technology) which are designed to stimulate European success in IT.

Although currently there is a greater emphasis on IT in the government funding of research, support for the electronics and computer industry in the UK has existed for a considerable period of time. The author is unaware of any detailed evaluation of the success of these programmes. Although it might be argued that the position of the UK today would have been worse if those programmes had not existed, the current position of the UK industry as detailed above nevertheless gives considerable cause for concern. It must be hoped that current programmes will achieve their objective. However, if past experience is a reasonable guide to the future, the prospects are not good (see Nelson, 1984).

7.5 THE MILITARY CONNECTION

Finance for R & D in information technology through the DTI is not the only route by which information technology gets government support. There are two other main routes: the first is R & D support through the defence budget, the second is military procurement. Table 7.10 presents some figures from 1984/5 on the relative size of defence and civil R & D expenditure of government as they apply to the major electronics sectors. The dominance of the military support is clear. Moreover in 1984/5, the support for civil aerospace was £107.9 million, and for defence aerospace it was £678.8 million. As electronics and aerospace have become very closely intertwined this just further

Table 7.10   *Government Funding for R & D in the IT Sector, Civil or Military,*
1984/5

Product group	Civil R & D expenditures for improvement of technology or in support of public purchasing £m	Defence R & D expenditures £m	Industrial R & D expenditures £m
Electronic data processing equipment	29.8	24.8	350.9
Basic electrical equipment	3.7	8.4	55.0
Telegraph & telephone apparatus	3.9		393.8
Electrical instruments & control systems	28.6	309.7	252.9
Radio & electronic capital goods	2.1		528.4
Components other than active components	2.5		40.8
Active components and electronic subassemblies	3.5	38.1	159.9
Other electronic equipment	7.8		61.4
Total	81.9	381	1883.9

Source: Cabinet Office (1986), *British Business* (1987), vol. 26, no. 5, pp. 28–29.

emphasizes the stress on the support of military R & D in the UK electronics sector. The third column in Table 7.10 details industrial R & D in these sectors. This includes a considerable amount of R & D financed by government, and thus is not a measure of R & D *financed by industry*. However, in 1981/2, approximately 64 per cent of defence R & D was carried out in private industry. Even if it is assumed that none of the government-financed civil R & D was carried out in industry and that industry-financed R & D was all civil, this would suggest that in the sectors in Table 7.10 20 per cent of all R & D was defence oriented. This is a strong emphasis on military R & D. Moreover, the ratio of defence equipment procurement (net of imports) to manufacturing GDP in 1984 stood at 12.3 per cent, and half of these procurement expenditures went to electronics (21.6 per cent) and aerospace (29.2 per cent), the two sectors with the strongest IT orientation. Thus not only is there a particular emphasis on military R & D in the UK IT sector, but there is a strong emphasis on satisfying military demands for output.

Such a military-based orientation of R & D need not necessarily be harmful. The emphasis on military R & D may generate significant defence exports, it may through spin-offs, economies of scale and risk reduction, stimulate the development of civil technologies, and will of course contribute to the defence of the realm. Kaldor *et al.* (1986) provide a very accessible summary of the evidence on these issues. They illustrate how the UK share of the world market for arms declined from 7.5 per cent to 4.3 per cent between 1963 and 1983 and how the UK share of high-technology exports fell from 12 per cent in 1965 to 8.5 per cent in 1984. Both experiences suggest that two of the expected benefits have not been realized. Whether the defence of the realm has been best served by the past pattern of spending was highlighted by the controversy over the airborne early warning Nimrod aircraft in 1986. Whether it would have been better to have bought the American AWACS aircraft initially and then used the £900 million spent on Nimrod development on civil R & D to generate export revenue to pay for the AWACS plane is an open question.

Kaldor *et al.* consider that the heavy defence commitments of the UK economy have in fact been harmful. They provide three reasons for this. First, the opportunity cost in terms of civil technological and industrial activities are significant especially in the light of the limited availability of highly qualified and skilled manpower in the UK. They suggest that the military sector uses more than 30 per cent of such manpower. Secondly, there are very few civil spin-offs from military R & D. Finally, defence procurement has influenced management styles and priorities, reducing the willingness of firms to take risks. It has also discouraged entrepreneurial and innovative behaviour and as a result eroded management ability to compete in the increasingly competitive international markets of civilian high technology.

It is difficult not to agree with the conclusion of Kaldor *et al.* (1986, p. 48):

> We believe that part of the reason for Britain's poor performance in the information technology sectors derives from defence commitments. At a time when Britain should have been concentrating resources on meeting the challenges and opportunities presented by these new technologies, which involved both developing new industries and updating the design and performance of equipment in older industries, we have seen an increasing proportion of our manufacturing resources, and particularly our highly trained manpower, pulled into the defence sectors. With their protected markets and guaranteed profit margins, the defence sectors inevitably attract all the resources they need. At the same time, in the civilian sectors of the engineering industry, firms have been under severe cost pressures and have skimped on R & D, training and retraining, running down rather than strengthening Britain's capacity to

innovate. As a consequence, Britain today is less capable of competing in the civilian high technology sectors than it was five or ten years ago.

7.6 CONCLUSIONS

The information economy, as defined in Section 7.1 employs almost 40 per cent of the UK labour force. It is a sector experiencing both rapid technological change and significant structural adjustment. Part of the change in structure is due to privatization policies, and these have been discussed. The major instrument of change is, however, the new technologies based on recent advances in micro-electronics and related areas.

The potential impact of the new technologies on employment is a major issue of concern. It was illustrated that although there may be changes in its skill composition the new technology is unlikely to have a dramatic effect on aggregate labour demand. Parts of the information economy in the UK, especially those most closely related to the new electronic technologies have not performed as well as in competitor nations. There is a suspicion that this failure, to some degree, may be due to the heavy emphasis on military spending in the UK information sector, even though there is still considerable support for civil technology through UK government and European programmes. However, past experience has not shown such civil support expenditures to be particularly successful. Given the size of the information economy and the importance of the new technologies as a basis for an internationally competitive economy, past failures do not bode well for the future.

REFERENCES

Cabinet Office (1986), *Annual Review of Government Funded R & D, 1986,* (London: HMSO).

Freeman, C., and Soete, L. (1985), *Information Technology and Employment,* Science Policy Research Unit, Sussex University, Brighton.

Kaldor, M., Sharp, M., and Walker, W. (1986) 'Industrial competitiveness and Britain's defence', *Lloyds Bank Review,* 162, 31–49.

Kay, J., and Thompson, D. J. (1986), 'Privatisation: a policy in search of a rationale', *Economic Journal,* 96, 18–32.

National Economic Development Office (1984), *Crisis Facing UK Information Technology* (London: NEDO).

Nelson, R. R. (1984), *High Technology Policies, A Five Nation Comparison* (Washington, DC: American Enterprise Institute).

Northcott, J., and Rogers, P. (1984), *Microelectronics in British Industry* (London: Policy Studies Institute).

Northcott, J., Rogers, P., Knetsch, W., and de Lestapis, B. (1985), *Microelectronics in Industry* (London: Policy Studies Institute).

Organization for Economic Co-operation and Development (1986), *Trends in the Information Economy*, ICCP no. 11 (Paris).

Porat, M. U. (1977), *The Information Economy, Definition and Measurement*, US Department of Commerce, Office of Telecommunications, OT Special Publication, 77–12(1), Washington, DC.

Stoneman, P. (1983), *The Economic Analysis of Technological Change* (Oxford: Oxford University Press).

Vickers, J., and Yarrow, G. (1985), *Privatisation and the Natural Monopolies* (London: Public Policy Centre).

Waterson, M., and Stoneman, P. (1985), 'Employment, technological diffusion and oligopoly', *International Journal of Industrial Organisation*, 3, 3, 327–44.

Whitley, J., and Wilson, R. (1987), 'Quantifying the impact of information technology on employment using a macroeconomic model', forthcoming in OECD (1987), *Information Technology and Economic Prospects* (Paris: ICCP, no. 12, Organization for Economic Co-operation and Development).

FURTHER READING

Cabinet Office (1986), *Annual Review of Government Funded R & D 1986*, (London: HMSO).

Marstrand, P., (ed.) (1986), *New Technology and The Future of Work and Skills* (London: Frances Pinter).

Nelson, R. R. (1982), *Government and Technical Progress* (New York: Pergamon).

Organization for Economic Co-operation and Development (1982), *Micro-Electronics, Robotics and Jobs*, ICCP no. 7 (Paris).

Stoneman, P. (1987), *The Economic Analysis of Technology Policy*, (Oxford: Oxford University Press).

Chapter Eight

Motor Vehicles

GAREL RHYS

The UK motor industry is an integral part of the European motor industry, in terms of the products made, the policy of the vehicle makers and the markets served. Nevertheless, the production of the British motor industry is a significant feature of the British economy and society, and is likely to remain so for the foreseeable future, notwithstanding any adverse effects of future increases in energy costs on the economics of the internal combustion engine. The car and the bus allow a virtually unprecedented freedom of travel, and for better or worse, the country's internal freight transport industry is wedded to road haulage. Significant social costs emanating from accidents, congestion and pollution do of course arise from the use of road vehicles. However, these factors do mainly emanate from the *use* of road vehicles rather than from their manufacture. Obviously vehicle demand is directly related to vehicle usage but here the concern is mainly with the structure, behaviour and performance of the motor manufacturing industry rather than with matters that belong to the study of transport economics.

8.1 POSTWAR DEVELOPMENTS IN THE INDUSTRY

8.1.1 The Car Industry

Because of the effects of the Second World War on Continental firms, US and UK firms dominated the world's car markets until the mid-1950s. However, by then the West German industry was beginning to compete in overseas markets and was followed by the French and Italian makers at the end of the decade. Britain's overseas marketing position was successfully challenged by this competition. At home successive UK governments used the motor industry and its market as an economic regulator. Both factors hampered the car sector's growth and prosperity in the 1950s and 1960s, so much so that Japanese firms in the early 1970s identified the UK market as the first major European market to attack because of the relative weakness of the domestic car industry.

By 1945 the car industry had already become fairly concentrated.

164

Table 8.1   *Share of Car Production (%)*

	Austin	Nuffield	Standard	Ford	Vauxhall	Rootes	Others	Total ('000)
1946	23	20	11	14	9	11	12	219
1947	17	27	9	18	10	10	9	287
1950	17	22	11	19	9	14	8	523
	BMC							
1955	39		10	27	9	11	4	898
1960	38		9	28	11	11	3	1,353
1964	37		7	28	13	12	3	1,868
		BLMC				Chrysler UK		
1970		48		27	11	13.5	0.5	1,641
1974		48		25	9.5	17.4	0.1	1,534
1975		48		26	8	17.9	0.1	1,268
						Peugeot		
1980		48		37	13.5	7	0.5	924
1985		45		30.5	14.5	6	4.0	1,048
		Rover Group						
1986		39.7		34.0	15.9	5.7	4.7	1,019

Notes: 'Others' covers the output of some twenty firms. In 1986 the largest were Jaguar, Rolls-Royce, Lotus (GM), Reliant and Nissan. The remaining firms were makers of either luxury cars such as Aston Martin and Bristol, or workshop built high performance cars such as Caterham and TVR. From 1985 'others' included Jaguar and from 1986 it included Nissan and Honda. From 1979 Peugeot made its UK-built cars under the Talbot name. In 1986 the Peugeot name itself was used.

Source: From data obtained from the Society of Motor Manufacturers and Traders (SMMT).

However, the unstable economic environment of the postwar period led to further significant increases in concentration, and mergers saw the total disappearance of smaller firms. (In 1986 General Motors (GM) took control of Lotus whilst a take-over of Austin Rover by Ford was briefly considered.) However, in the mid-1980s new firms either appeared or reappeared in the UK industry. For instance, in 1984 the government's privatization policy saw Jaguar being sold off by British Leyland (BL) in a successful stock exchange flotation. In 1986 Austin Rover started making cars for Honda on a contractual basis, and Nissan Motor Manufacturing (UK) began operations in the UK. By 1991 it was expected that the latter would make 120,000 vehicles a year. The distribution of UK car production is shown in Table 8.1.

Unlike many car industries overseas, which had enjoyed strongly growing domestic markets over most of the 1946–87 period, the UK market experienced much more erratic progress. Indeed, although car demand was strong in 1983–7, it had stagnated over the period 1964–82 partly as a result of macro-economic controls on car demand, but

Table 8.2   *Trends in UK Car Production and Exports, and Total UK New Car Registrations per Year (thousands)*

Year	Total production	Total registrations	Exports
1946	219	122	84
1950	523	134	398
1955	898	511	389
1960	1,353	820	570
1964	1,868	1,216	680
1970	1,641	1,127	679
1972	1,921	1,702	690
1976	1,333	1,308	496
1978	1,223	1,618	466
1980	924	1,485	359
1982	888	1,555	313
1985	1,048	1,832	240
1986	1,019	1,882	201

Source: *The Motor Industry of Great Britain*, SMMT, London.

mainly because of a relatively low growth in per capita income levels. In terms of production the situation was worse, for whereas foreign car industries showed almost continuous growth, the UK industry stagnated between 1964 and 1972, and then went into sharp decline (see Table 8.2) until 1980. From that time output stabilized around the 1 million cars a year mark. However, about 250,000 of those were partly assembled from imported kits.

8.1.2   The Commercial Vehicle Industry

In the postwar period, the main UK commercial vehicle producers were the four mass producers: Ford, Bedford (GM), Rootes (now Renault Industrial Vehicles) and British Leyland. The last mentioned combined the quantity production facilities of what was the British Motor Corporation with the specialist vehicle making plants of the Jaguar Group and Leyland Motors. Unfortunately the creation of the British Leyland Motor Corporation (now the Rover Group) in 1968 meant the cross-subsidization of car investment from commercial vehicle (CV) profits with the ultimate result that the CV side suffered from underinvestment in new plant and models. In consequence it fell back in the European league to a position in the 1980s where, despite regaining leadership of the UK market in 1986, Leyland Vehicles was a heavy loss maker. In terms of the European market Leyland had become a small-medium firm with under 5 per cent of the heavy truck market compared with over 25 per cent for Daimler Benz. The mid-1980s saw considerable upheaval in the UK truck industry. In 1986 a failed attempt to merge Leyland-Land Rover with Bedford to stem the heavy losses in both saw General Motors announcing the virtual closure of Bedford trucks. (In 1987 the plant was sold to a British company and vehicle making continued.) Also in 1986 Ford UK in effect sold its loss-making heavy truck activities to Iveco (Fiat) of Italy. Ostensibly a joint venture, the Italian company had managerial control. Both the US firms suffered heavy loss-making in a market characterized by excess capacity and saw little chance of improvement. As a result both effectively left the European heavy truck industry. The UK still had a number of small specialist truck makers such as ERF and Dennis who made up to 2,000 units a year each. However, the largest specialist maker, Seddon Atkinson was a subsidiary of the Spanish ENASA company, whilst Foden was owned by PACCAR of the USA. In 1987 Leyland Trucks was effectively sold by the Rover Group to DAF of Holland. Hence, over a relatively short period between 1974 and 1987 the UK heavy commercial vehicle industry went from a position of strength to the verge of near extinction.

Although CV production in the UK reached a record 465,000 units in 1964 the industry still maintained an output in excess of 400,000 until 1974. Output by 1986 had slipped to under 230,000 units. Since the post-1974 fall in UK output the French industry has been Europe's largest producer of all sorts of CVs, especially light vans. However, West Germany has long had Europe's strongest and largest *heavy* CV industry.

8.1.3 The Economic Significance of the Motor Industry as a Whole

Despite its decline as a world force the UK motor industry is still a major part of the economy. In 1987 the motor industry as defined by the Standard Industrial Classification (Class 35) accounted for about 1.5 per cent of total employment. However, the inclusion of employment in raw materials, component supplies in other industries directly dependent on the motor industry, and other jobs created throughout the economy more than doubled this to 3.4 per cent. Indeed, a recent study (PEIDA, 1984) puts employment in the motor and associated industries at over 600,000 people, with knock-on effects creating another 400,000 jobs. About 5 per cent of gross domestic product (GDP), 11 per cent of manufactured exports and 7 per cent of visible exports are accounted for by the motor industry. In 1985 the motor industry earned £5,046 million overseas despite an adverse balance of £2,758 million. During its last major growth period in 1954–63 about 27 per cent of the 'above-trend' growth of the economy was due to the growth of the motor industry. The economic importance of the industry was always fully understood by the Japanese, West German and French authorities who used their motor industries as the main engines of economic growth and who, unlike their UK counterparts, avoided using them as short-term weapons of demand management in case their growth potential, and hence their effects on the economy overall, were harmed. Consequently, these authorities tried to maintain a steady growth of vehicle production. In the UK, however, the picture was, as we have seen, very different.

8.2   SUPPLY AND DEMAND CHARACTERISTICS

The short-run elasticity of supply depends upon both the degree of capacity utilization and the efficiency with which particular manufacturers can change output levels. The boom in demand in 1972–3 found the industry wanting and various production difficulties lost about one-fifth of achievable output. In the longer term the industry has traditionally responded to the growing vehicle market by new net investment. This was so in 1946–7, 1955–7 and 1962–5. However, the strong demand in the early 1970s did not produce increases in capacity. Indeed, because of the financial difficulties of companies and the commitment of multinationals to export in kit form from the UK, final assembly capacity fell from 2.5 million units in 1973 to 2.3 million in 1978. By 1986 the figure was down to 1.7 million units with much reduced facilities at Austin Rover and Peugeot. However by 1991 Nissan and Jaguar will add about 150,000 units of assembly capacity, with increased productivity and investment at Lotus, Vauxhall and Ford in the late 1980s generating another 200,000 units of capacity.

8.2.1   The Nature of Technology and Optimum Size

The manufacture of motor vehicles mainly involves mass production assembly with the 'job' passing automatically from one piece of equipment to another. Hand-building and even bespoke methods, however, are used in the production of some premium heavy trucks and luxury cars. The *techniques* of mass production require large-scale production for the achievement of least unit-cost operation. Indeed, increased use of automation – involving, for example, the use of robots – has increased the optimum scale in assembly plants from 200,000 units a year to 300,000 on a two-shift basis. However, more flexible equipment has at the same time reduced the model-specific assembly optimum. Another development has been the attempt to enrich the car worker's lot by introducing team assembly where either a team or a single individual can build an entire car or an engine or gearbox. However, such techniques have proved expensive in terms of unit costs and the substitution of labour by capital has so far been seen as a better answer to the needs of mass producers in capital-intensive but high-wage economies.

If a manufacturer integrates production by carrying out the various distinct operations into which vehicle making is split, namely, pressing out sheet metal parts, casting, machining, assembly and painting activities, its overall optimum size will be dictated both by the maximum optimum of the various processes and by the need to correctly balance these processes. If it is impossible to achieve the output required to balance perfectly various processes with different minimum efficient scales, the car maker will attempt to minimize unit costs at its planned level of operations by using some plant at either above or below its optimum capacity. As far as can be determined from data supplied by manufacturers the minimum efficient scale (that is, the scale at which unit costs are minimized) in the various operations involved in car making is as follows:

Casting of engine blocks	1 million
Casting of other parts	100,000–750,000
Power-train machining and assembly	600,000
Axle machining and assembly	500,000
Pressing of various panels	1–2 million
Painting (undercoats and so on)	250,000
Final assembly	250,000

It can be seen that to reach *maximum* efficiency in production a car firm would need to produce 2 million cars using at least some common body parts. For instance if two models are made at an annual rate of 1 million each the use of, say a common floor pressing could optimize production. In addition the large volumes involved means that various forms of co-operation between firms, such as joint ventures, can help them reach optimum volumes. New technology such as robots and computer-controlled machining centres can reduce the optimum scale of some activities, or at least the cost penalty of sub-optimum scale. However, in many activities, such as engine machining and stamping, large volume is still needed for cost minimization. Furthermore, large volume is still an advantage in spreading various fixed costs per unit, such as research and development, as thinly as possible. Pratten (1971) has provided the following unit cost estimates which cover the range of European capacity bounded by Saab at the lower end and Volkswagen at the upper. It can be seen that an annual production of 500,000 cars is likely to have a cost advantage per unit of around 25 per cent over that of 100,000 units. (See also Rhys, 1972.) The estimates also indicate that further doublings of output would produce reductions in unit cost, albeit of only 5–6 per cent each time.

Output per year	*Index of costs*
100,000	100
250,000	83
500,000	74
1,000,000	70
2,000,000	66

In CV production the power-train (engines, transmissions and axles) optimum requires annual volumes of at least 200,000 a year, although new flexible equipment can reduce the cost penalties of sub-optimum production. Hence volumes of 50,000 could be commercially viable with a degree of product differentiation. In the manufacture of cabs the optimum scale is similar to that of car body pressings. However, the cost penalty involved in producing cabs in much lower volumes is reduced by frequently changing dies in the stamping presses in order to increase utilization and thereby engage in a form of batch production. Engine castings for large diesels have an optimum of around 200,000 units a year while the final assembly optimum for medium, and complicated, heavy vehicles has grown to over 100,000 vehicles a year. This growth was made possible by computer control and the application of more automation to the truck assembly lines, but also improvements in product design that reduced the man-hours needed in heavy truck assembly. As optimum volumes are large in relation to annual output, costs are spread over much longer model runs than are usual on the car side. For instance, Bedford's main truck cab which was introduced in 1960 was still the basis of a unit being made in 1987. Small makers of trucks have been able to keep costs near to the levels achieved by bigger firms either by making items in materials, or by techniques, which involved a lower optimum volume or by buying in from specialists who made cabs, engines, transmissions, axles and so on. However, the huge size reached by European firms such as Daimler Benz and Iveco in the 1970s and 1980s has meant that these integrated producers have attained volumes of production that give them very competitive unit costs. Hence, the position of the smaller firm has become increasingly difficult. In addition the medium-size firms such as Leyland had to reduce in-house production, and buy in and co-operate to try to both obtain modern components and to reduce unit costs to competitive levels. In 1987 another medium-size firm, DAF, extended its co-operation with Leyland to an outright merger. Even then such a firm was small compared with Daimler Benz and Iveco, but a combination of product differentiation and new flexible equipment which could reach high volumes of production by making a variety of items, could give the medium firm the opportunity to manufacture profitably major items such as power-train.

8.2.2 Organization of Labour

In the UK industrial relations problems were, for many years, important in preventing continuity of production and the full utilization of resources. Indeed the proportion of production lost in 1972–4 – the years of boom demand – varied between 10 and 26 per cent of capacity. However, in the 1980s a combination of firm management, high unemployment in the economy, and greater realism on the part of the workforce saw industrial disputes fall to barely measurable levels whilst labour productivity, often through new work practices as well as investment, rose to compare favourably with that in the rest of Europe.

Table 8.3 *Import Penetration into the UK Car Market*

	Total (units)	Share of UK market (%)
1961	22,759	3.0
1969	101,914	10.0
1970	157,956	14.0
1972	450,314	26.4
1973	504,619	27.4
1976	533,901	37.9
1977	698,464	45.4
1978	800,772	49.3
1980	863,080	56.7
1985	1,071,892	58.1
1986	1,053,603	56.0

Source: The Motor Industry of Great Britain, SMMT, London, various years.

8.2.3 Imports and Exports

The growth in imports in the UK car market over the last 25 years is shown in Table 8.3. The surge in imports in 1972 was a reflection of the inability of the UK car industry to supply enough vehicles of the right type. The lack of investment in the 1960s had left the industry with uncompetitive facilities and an ageing model range. At the same time the UK consumer was faced with a greater choice of vehicles, especially in the small to medium range in the mass market than he had enjoyed since the early 1930s, when some fifteen firms had offered their wares. In the period 1975–87 some twenty domestic, West and East European, US and Asian firms were competing in the bargain basement of the UK car market. In addition, because of low productivity in their UK plants the multinationals Ford and Vauxhall produced many of the cars they sold in the UK on the Continent (see Table 8.4). A fall in this activity in the first quarter of 1987 saw imports fall below 50 per cent of total registration for almost the first time in the decade.

It can be seen from Table 8.2 that the UK car industry's export performance has deteriorated since the mid-1960s. From a maximum of 772,000 cars exported in 1969 the total fell to 240,000 in 1985. Initially the CV side held its own rather better with 181,000 units exported in 1969, and 177,000 in 1977. However, by 1985 the decline was more severe than that experienced by cars, with exports falling to 51,500 units.

The greater relative strength of the UK CV industry in the 1970s, especially in the medium van, medium-heavy truck and bus markets, meant that keen UK prices, customer goodwill and relatively adequate stocks made the job of importers more difficult in this market.

However, the catastrophic decline in the competitiveness of BL's heavy goods vehicle products and operations in the latter half of the 1970s, the early EFTA competition in the booming heavy truck market of the 1960s, and later entry by EC firms meant that by the end of the 1970s the very heavy truck market leader in the UK was Volvo of Sweden. Moreover, over 50 per cent of this market was by then in the hands of various foreign producers. Indeed the prime concern of small firms like ERF, Foden and Seddon Atkinson became the restriction of imports rather than the increase in exports. In the car-derived van and medium pick-up markets the Japanese became very active. The UK-based firms BL, Chrysler, Ford and Bedford (GM), used to dominate the medium truck and lightweight bus chassis sectors, and Leyland Vehicles dominated the heavy bus sector. However, in the 1980s imports advanced in these sectors as well, partly due to the high value of sterling in the early 1980s, modern high-quality products and the ageing range of Bedford trucks. Leyland's concentration on buses allowed imports to do well in the coach market. Consequently, in the 1980s foreign competition was experienced in all parts of the CV market.

8.2.4 Demand Characteristics

Cars and CVs provide a flow of transport services. In the case of cars the product is also desired because it confers on its owner various attributes, not the least of which are prestige and status. The relevant dependent variable in the demand equation is not so much the demand for new cars as the demand for car ownership. The latter may involve the purchase of cars of vintages ranging from the new to, say, those over ten years old.

The main independent variables are price and per capita disposable income. Estimates of long-run price elasticity of demand for cars as a whole vary from -0.6 to -1.7 while income elasticities range from 1.1 to 4.2. However, price elasticity estimates for the products of individual firms vary between -2.0 and -7.0. Advertising and demographic, locational and credit factors also influence car demand. Severe short-run changes in car demand are generated by changes in credit terms. For instance, it has been suggested that a fall in the minimum hire-purchase deposit from 33 per cent to 20 per cent of the price of a car increases car demand by the same extent as a 2 per cent growth in national income (Silberston, 1963).

8.3 MARKET STRUCTURE

The UK motor industry must now be viewed as a component of a wider European motor industry. Indeed, unlike the French, West German and Italian industries where most output comes from

Table 8.4 *Shares of UK Market, 1977/1985*

	Share of UK output		Total share of UK market		Share of imports from European plants	
	1977	1985	1977	1985	1977	1985
Rover	49.0	45.0	24.3	17.7	0.4	—
Ford	31.0	30.5	25.7	26.5	6.5	11.7
Vauxhall	7.0	14.5	9.1	16.6	3.0	9.2
'Peugeot'ª	12.5	6.0	6.0	4.0	1.1	2.8
Jaguar	—	3.5	—	0.4	—	—
'Tied' imports^b	—	—	(11.0)	(23.7)	—	—
Other imports	—	—	34.6	34.7	—	—
Other British	0.5	0.5	0.3	0.1	—	—

Notes:
ª In 1977 'Peugeot' refers to Chrysler's UK production and sales even though Peugeot did not buy the latter until 1 January 1979. In 1985 'Peugeot' refers to Talbot production in the UK but Peugeot Talbot sales.
^b 'Tied' imports are those emanating from the other European plants of firms producing cars in the UK. For 1985 Peugeot has been included in this category.
Source: Derived from SMMT data.

indigenous firms, four of the six large UK car makers are foreign-owned. These owners have increasingly viewed the European market and the European industry as an integrated whole. For example, Ford UK's main product and investment strategies are decided for them by Ford Europe while GM has integrated most features of its West German-, British- and Spanish-based operations and model lines. Nissan's UK output does, of course, reflect its Japanese model range and at present no British research and design effort is involved. Only Jaguar in the specialist area, and an increasingly vulnerable Austin Rover are British-oriented companies; even the latter is concentrating its design effort on certain areas, buying in the rest from firms such as Honda, Volkswagen and Peugeot.

Thus, although most output in the UK is concentrated in only six firms, the facilities of four of these are merely complementing other European or Japanese plants. However, the market is less concentrated than output data would imply (Table 8.4) because of intra-European free trade and Japanese penetration of about 11 per cent of the market. (This percentage is constrained by the Japanese agreeing voluntarily to restrict exports to the UK.) The integrated Europe-wide market (including the UK) displays an even greater degree of competition and a relatively low degree of concentration. The top three firms have less than 45 per cent of the total sales (Table 8.5).

Table 8.5   *Share of European Market 1977–85*

	1977	1985		1977	1985
Peugeot-Citroen[a]	18.0	11.6	GMC	10.7	11.4
Ford	13.2	11.9	Rover	4.9	3.9
Renault	11.8	10.7	Daimler-Benz	2.5	3.7
Fiat	11.8	12.2	Others including		
Volkswagen	11.5	12.9	'imports'[b]	15.6	21.7

Notes:
[a] Including Chrysler-Talbot in both years.
[b] The increase in Others largely reflects the advance of Japanese imports.
Source: Derived from SMMT data.

8.3.1   Product Differentiation

Although price competition has always been significant in the motor
industry non-price competition concerned with the differentiation of
products by style and model changes, and by technical, quality and
other marketing variations and tactics is also important.

A style change every three years and a model change every six years
can distinguish a firm's products from its own previous production and
the unaltered offerings of its rivals. However, firms wishing to avoid
the £100 million needed for a major facelift, the £200 million for a
body reskinning and the £450 million for a completely new car, aim to
produce cars with advanced specifications (for example, fuel-efficient,
aerodynamic) and with function-based, rather than stylized, body
designs. By these means they can obtain not only large annual output
volumes but also long-lived production runs as well. Firms try to avoid
head-on competition by stressing differences in their product and by
attempting to provide a different set of characteristics. The firms
wedded to short product cycles are linked with huge European or
worldwide organizations which can spread overheads more thinly.
However, life cycles are becoming longer. The huge costs of model
development and model changes have forced this upon the industry.
Hence, the Ford Fiesta of 1976 will have a lifespan of twelve years,
compared with the usual Ford policy of five/six year product cycles.
The advanced-specification mass producers, however, although often
both large and prosperous, would find it difficult to engage in style and
model competition of the US and Japanese kind without experiencing
increased unit costs and lower profits.

The strategy of long production runs, allied to quality, durability or
engineering specifications, has been followed by the 'quality' car
makers and specialist divisions of larger firms. Attempts have been
made to separate this market from the more price-conscious mass
market by stressing a set of characteristics that imply cars are being built

up to a standard rather than down to a price. Nevertheless, even within the quality market the price variable cannot be ignored.

8.3.2 The Degree of Integration

UK car makers tend to have a greater degree of dependence on outside suppliers than is the norm in the European motor industry. Therefore many major component makers have developed in the UK to supply the 65–70 per cent by value of parts 'bought in' by Rover and Ford, the 70 per cent by Peugeot UK and the 85 per cent by Vauxhall. Although 1,000 suppliers supply 8,000 separate parts to a typical UK car firm, some 30 per cent (by value) of the bought-in content is accounted for by 20 major suppliers including firms such as Lucas, GKN, BBA and Turner & Newall. On the CV side some external economies are enjoyed by vehicle makers who buy in as much as 90 per cent of material costs. As a result quite small UK assemblers were able to reach unit cost levels competitive with those reached by much larger integrated producers, although as discussed above the huge size reached by many Continental truck makers is making this more difficult to achieve, especially as the component supply infrastructure now has a smaller customer base in the UK.

8.3.3 Barriers to Entry

A new entrant would require large marketing outlays to challenge existing product differentiation and brand loyalty and to provide an adequate dealer system. However, such barriers have not proved insurmountable to any existing foreign maker wishing to enter the UK car market. Indeed, the various production and marketing weaknesses evident in the UK industry in the 1960s and 1970s actively *reduced* the marketing entry barriers facing well-established foreign firms. An entirely new entrant would, however, face substantial difficulties.

The major barriers to entry are those stemming from economies of scale and from absolute capital needs. As indicated in Section 8.2.1 the minimum efficient scale for car manufacture would appear to be around 2 million units a year although entry might be risked in the mass market at 1 million units and in the quality car sector at 300,000 units. A firm such as Rolls-Royce survives making only 2–3,000 units a year, while by utilizing the supply infrastructure new makers have been able to enter the UK bus industry at under 1,000 units a year. Heavy CV manufacturers could prosper at either 20,000 a year when buying in, or 60,000 a year when integrated. The high car figures are partly due to economies of scale and partly due to the need to recover model-specific fixed costs as quickly as possible to reduce any vulnerability to model-change competition. The minimum efficient size is greater than the current output of the UK car industry. This shows the importance of integrated production. New technology reduces the volumes needed for economies of scale in a few instances, but in most parts of the production process large scale is still required.

The absolute capital costs needed for car making are huge. A modern press-shop for a volume car producer costs about £120 million with each set of dies costing around £30 million. An assembly plant costs in the region of £200 million. A gearbox plant requires £130 million. A complete engine plant would cost some £250 million when all construction costs and working capital needs are added to tooling and development costs. The total of over £700 million involved here is impressive, but a fully integrated and properly balanced optimum size firm would require much greater expenditures.

8.3.4 The European Community and Market Structure

Within a European context the only major UK-owned producer is the Rover Group (formerly BL) which is relatively small scale in both its car and its remaining CV activities. The other producers are linked to US-, Japanese- or French-controlled European-wide operations. The unified home market of the European Community gave the multi-nationals the opportunity to change their scale of operations by rationalizing and integrating their European activities in West Germany, the UK, France, Spain and elsewhere.

The growth of Continental firms, and direct competition from them within the unified market in the 1970s, put the remaining UK-owned car maker in a vulnerable position as regards size and its potential for achieving economies of scale. In a world context its position was even worse: hence the attempts of the Rover Group (then BL) in 1979–80 to project itself as one of the world's largest *specialist* vehicle makers; and its link with Honda. The measure of the firm's failure to achieve a model-led recovery in 1980–6 was shown by its 1987 strategic plan, which was yet again aimed at projecting Austin Rover as some form of specialist, albeit operating in the volume markets, rather than a producer competing directly with larger firms. The Honda link was one way to remain in the volume market without big production, via the cost-sharing route of collaboration and co-operation.

8.4 MARKET BEHAVIOUR

Although the motor industry in the UK consists of only a few large producers and is oligopolistic in structure, there is little evidence of co-ordinated behaviour or collusion designed to earn a monopoly profit (Rhys, 1978). Indeed, from 1952 to 1968 even though the five UK firms dominated the mass market they competed vigorously. Subsequently, the number of significant competitors increased dramatically with the huge influx of imports during the 1970s. However, the reaction to the high price of sterling in 1979–83 was evidence of price-making, if only temporarily.

3.4.1 Prices and Model Changes

Although the 1970s showed indications of price leadership by either Ford or BL, this was not so much evidence of collusive behaviour as of smaller firms following the barometric, rather than the dominant, price leadership of larger firms who were themselves subject to industry-wide inflationary cost pressures. The higher unit cost operation of smaller firms may have made them loath to lead the price round for any fall in market share would have had immediate adverse effects on their unit costs and profits. The competitive nature of the car market ensures that the prices charged by various UK and foreign firms for comparable models are set close to each other with slight variations being possible because of product differentiation.

Despite the competitive nature of the car market all firms engage in the practice of price discrimination between home and foreign markets and, in domestic markets, between private buyers and fleet users. Furthermore, in 1979–83 the UK car makers refused to reflect new currency parities when sterling compounded the UK's relatively high inflation by appreciating against other European currencies. Hence, UK car prices appeared to be out of line. Arbitrage, or 'parallel importing', on the part of individuals threatened to undermine the official dealer network and the price levels in the UK. Within a short time the level of sterling fell, and relative inter-country prices fell to more usual levels. Nevertheless, during the adjustment period UK producers, and importers charged higher ex-works prices in the UK. This was achieved by controlling entry, and supplies, to the retail sector. Because of the controversy this caused, the European Commission has taken powers to try to prevent excessive inter-country price discrimination in the absence of objectively determined reasons, such as price controls or different tax rates.

Firms have also used non-price variables such as technical innovation, style and model changes in their competitive strategies. In the UK, BL followed a policy of long product cycles of around ten years, partly because of the technical nature of the product and partly because of a lack of funds for replacement. Talbot UK was forced to use long product cycles mainly because of the latter factor and was unable to offer advanced technology as an offsetting variable. Vauxhall and Ford had used a five-year product cycle for their European products but the gradual introduction from 1976 of advanced engineering models forced these companies to lengthen their model runs in order to absorb mounting research, development and tooling costs. The specialist makers maintained styles for a decade and more. During such a period they carefully husband resources to finance a model change which has to be correct or the company's survival is in

immediate jeopardy. Between model changes they stress the quality
and exclusiveness of their products. However, by the mid-1980s the
high standard of Japanese cars meant that *all* firms had to improve the
quality of their products if they were to survive in a competitive
market.

On the CV side, light vans, medium trucks and buses retain their
basic designs for between ten and fifteen years. However, in the field
of heavy trucks, rapid technical developments and the requirements of
safety, environmental and other legislation has reduced the product
cycle from twelve to nine or ten years. In the late 1970s this reduction
put medium-sized firms under pressure and was partly a cause of
Leyland's declining market share as its trucks became outdated. The
1980s saw a continuation of this pressure on life cycles as operating
demands and environmental issues became more important.

8.4.2   Research, Innovation and Patenting

The motor industry today may be regarded as a new infant industry as
tremendous changes in both product and process occurred in the
1980s. Add to this European legislation and directives on, say, lead in
petrol, gas emissions from the exhaust, quietness rules, pricing and so
on, and the challenge facing the vehicle makers becomes even clearer.
Behind all this the manufacturers sought to react to the energy-frugal
late twentieth century by reducing fuel consumption by producing
lighter and more aerodynamic vehicles with fuel-efficient, clean
engines. The British motor industry cut the petrol consumption of its
cars by over 20 per cent between 1978 and 1985.

However, although technical developments are continuous, it is
difficult to foresee a short-term revolution in car design, although such
a possibility on the heavy lorry front is more likely. There appears
little prospect of change from the internal combustion engine in the
near future especially as improved petrol engines and driving habits,
and the spread of diesel power to more and more cars could have
considerable fuel-saving effects. The use of battery-electric technology
may be the most viable alternative, but any social wish to see this
replace internal combustion would have to rely on legislative and
taxation measures to reduce the comparative advantage of oil as an
energy source.

8.4.3   Advertising and Marketing

The most immediate way of bringing products to the attention of the
customer is by advertising. Longer-term marketing strategies involve
the nature and quality of the product, the dealer chain, product
specification and prices.

Advertising on CVs only amounts to 5 per cent of that on cars
although CV registrations are 20 per cent of car registrations. This is

mainly because the CV buyer is more interested in ascertaining the basic economics of a particular vehicle and is unimpressed by generalized advertising aimed either at giving superficial information or at crude product differentiation. Only in the van and coach markets is style competition of any real significance.

With a product as expensive to buy and maintain as a car the distribution network's efficiency and accessibility can be a crucial competitive weapon. In order to try to establish dealers of nearer to optimum size, especially in terms of sales per outlet, UK car makers shed 7,000 outlets between 1970 and 1977. Austin Rover (BL) accounted for 4,600 of these. However, grateful importers snapped up 4000 of these outlets and the ease with which they established their networks illustrates how by this action UK car makers removed a barrier to foreign firms entering the UK market. By 1980 almost 50 per cent of sales outlets were in the hands of importers. This was a major factor in explaining why the foreign car is in such an entrenched position in the UK market, especially in the private motorists' sector, where accessibility to a service point is often important. In the mid-1980s this position remained largely the same. This was reflected in a nearly constant import penetration between 1979 and 1986, during which time a further, if limited, erosion of the UK firms' dealer networks occurred: in 1980 the UK makers had 4,680 outlets, but by 1987 this was 4,000, with Austin Rover accounting for the bulk of the reduction yet again.

8.5 PERFORMANCE

Motor industry firms have some idea of their marginal costs, but long-run prices are usually arrived at by adding a mark-up to average total or variable costs. However, these costs may not be the lowest possible, if the firms concerned are X-inefficient (i.e. they suffer from internal inefficiencies such as poor management). Consequently the absence of reported abnormal profits in the motor industry is not necessarily sufficient evidence that monopolistic practices are not employed. However, given the competitive pressures that exist in the industry, it is probably true to say that there is little evidence of serious long-term welfare loss from this source (see Cowling and Mueller, 1978). However, in the period 1979–83 when UK car prices were high compared with those in other EC countries, a figure of £1.0–1.3 billion welfare loss per year was reported. This added 1½ per cent to the retail price index (RPI). By 1984 the loss had fallen to £650 million (½ per cent on the RPI) (House of Lords, 1984, pp. xlviii–xlix) and by 1986 it was £100 million (0.1 per cent on the RPI).

Although welfare losses have been low, this is not to say that some, albeit competitive firms have not suffered from various inefficiencies of their own. Indeed as rates of return have been low in relation to those

Table 8.6 *Rates of Return on Capital Employed (%)*

	1961	1965	1970	1973	1980	1985
Manufacturing industry	10.0	11.8	11.3	14.4	7.6	10.5
Motor industry	6.4	9.6	3.8	11.0	1.9	3.8

Source: 1961–73: based on evidence contained in Fourteenth Report from the Expenditure Committee, Session 1974–5, *The Motor Vehicle Industry*, HC 617–1, London, HMSO, 1975, p. 407. 1980–5: author's estimation.

of manufacturing industry as a whole it may be questioned whether the use of resources *on their existing scale* by the motor industry was justified (see Table 8.6).

In terms of the profitability of individual companies the UK motor industry in the 1970s and 1980s has not presented a successful picture. Vauxhall and Peugeot Talbot (formerly Chrysler UK and before that Rootes) were chronic loss makers and were saved only by their parent companies from extinction. Rover Group (formerly BL) found it impossible to match the real aggregate profits in the 1960s of the pre-merger constituent firms. In the period 1970–87 only Ford, Rolls-Royce and ERF amongst the vehicle makers reported adequate results with any consistency, and even the latter was badly hit by the slump in the European CV industry in 1979–86 which had left the UK CV industry with about 50 per cent excess capacity for trucks and buses.

Following privatization in 1984 Jaguar's greatly improved efficiency and sales increase due to better quality products, generated record profits. The low level of profits and losses in the 1970s was symptomatic of low productivity, with even Ford suffering severely from this problem. In the 1980s poor financial results were due more to overcapacity and severe competition. However, until the 1980s crude output-per-man figures were not favourable to the UK industry. For instance, in 1975 the Japanese made 37 vehicles per man and the European Continentals averaged 12, while in the UK Chrysler made 11, Ford 9, and BL 5.5. Of course differences in product mix and bought-in content reduce the validity of the above comparisons but value-added figures per man generate the same type of result (Table 8.7).

The earlier unfavourable British results were reinforced by *direct* enquiries, such as those by the Central Policy Review Staff (CPRS), which showed productivity in terms of the number of hours needed to assemble given items with nearly identical facilities. The results indicated that in various assembly operations the UK figure was twice the Continental. This was compounded by other problems such as high warranty costs and the poor utilization of fixed capital arising from a fragmented model range and the consequent shorter production runs. All these inefficiencies increased unit car costs by in excess of 10 per

Table 8.7   *Value Added per Man, 1980 (£)*

Manufacturer	Value added per man, 1980 (£)
GM (USA)	15,308
Daimler-Benz	9,643
Ford (West Germany)	9,521
Volkswagen	9,343
Saab	8,578
Ford (UK)	8,400
Opel	8,065
Volvo	7,573
Renault	7,191
Vauxhall	4,761
BL	3,619
Fiat	3,389
Talbot (UK)	3,318
Ford (USA)	3,064

Source: Author's estimate.

cent of the ex-works price (see Central Policy Review Staff, 1975, pp. 77–94). The factors causing poor productivity were due to overmanning, interruptions to the smooth flow of production and underinvestment in plant and capital equipment. It appeared that BL and Chrysler UK were particularly underinvested. Until the 1980s Ford and Vauxhall suffered mostly from the problems of overmanning, slow work pace and work interruption. By 1986 these problems had been eliminated and productivity equalled that on the Continent. Low productivity had been a long-term feature of the UK motor industry and had not just developed in the 1970s (Table 8.8). The smaller size of UK motor plants, relative to those overseas may also be a source of inefficiency (see Jones and Prais, 1978). (Any tendency for industrial relations problems to increase with the size of plant-employment may be overcome by replacing labour by capital in the larger-output plants.) However, the shake-out in the 1980s saw a great improvement. Overmanning disappeared, plants were rationalized and work practices revolutionized. Nissan's single-union agreement which helped industrial relations also acted as a catalyst to the rest of the industry. However, although the vehicle makers became competitive in productivity the component makers still faced problems. The decline of the UK vehicle makers had reduced their customer base and diminished the flow of new products and their economies of scale. Hence, by 1987 many firms had fallen behind the Continental competition, especially where foundries and electronics were concerned. Indeed, only the few component firms with international operations and markets had a customer base large enough to generate

Table 8.8   *Vehicles Produced per Employee*

	1955	1965	1973	1985
UK	4.2	5.8	5.1	8.5
USA	11.1	.13.9	14.9	12.0
West Germany	3.9	7.1	7.3	12.5
France	3.6	6.1	6.8	9.0
Italy	3.0	7.4	6.8	10.4
Japan	1.2	4.4	12.2	23.5

Source: Central Policy Review Staff, 1975; author's estimate for 1985.

the funds needed for viability. The future facing most of the 2,000 UK component suppliers was a difficult one and decline was likely.

In recent years however the UK's relative position on productivity has improved substantially. Between 1979 and 1986 Peugeot Talbot UK increased its car output per man by 110 per cent, Austin Rover by 250 per cent, Jaguar by 310 per cent, Vauxhall by 130 per cent and Ford by 90 per cent. As a result Vauxhall made 17 cars per man compared with Opel's 16, Austin Rover made 15, Ford (UK) 14 cars per man compared with Ford of West Germany's 16 while, on a different basis, Peugeot Talbot UK made 40 cars per man compared with the French equivalent figure of 35 cars per man. All these figures were as far as possible on a 'like-with-like' basis. So whilst in the 1960s and 1970s the UK motor industry's productivity fell far behind the levels achieved elsewhere in Europe the 1980s saw a dramatic recovery. This was reinforced by the productivity levels forecast to be achieved by Nissan of over 30 cars per man in a UK facility assembling vehicles and manufacturing engines.

This productivity improvement was only reflected by profit making at Ford and Jaguar, although Peugeot Talbot was operating at around break-even in the mid-1980s. Rolls-Royce returned to profits in the 1980s as exchange rates moved in their favour and their customers returned with increased prosperity in the business sector. Austin Rover's new model range did not result in a model-led recovery, and market penetration and loss making worsened in 1985–7. Vauxhall's problems partly stemmed from having to import so many cars and components from West Germany to supply its assembly-only operation in the UK at a time when the West German mark continued to appreciate considerably, especially against sterling. In addition, the period was marked by severe short-run price competition and overcapacity in Europe as a whole.

Many explanations can be put forward for the industry's relative and, indeed, absolute decline. The lower per capita income growth in the UK, the highly cyclical and volatile nature of the economy, poor industrial relations, poor managerial and financial control of companies' activities, poor quality products and the problems caused by the

industry's role as an economic regulator, all played a part. Nevertheless, by 1987, improved models, excellent industrial relations, efficient
plant, new net investment, and renewed faith in the UK by the
multinationals, gave grounds to hope for a recovery in the industry's
affairs.

8.6 PUBLIC POLICY

8.6.1 Finance from the State

A significant feature of the post-1964 period was the emergence of the
state as a source of selective financial assistance as distinct from the
usual general assistance provided in the form of capital grants,
allowances, employment premiums and regional help.

The Industrial Reorganisation Corporation (IRC), established in
1966 with a capital of £150 million, was to bring about a reorganization
of parts of UK industry where organizational inadequacies were the
cause of poor performance. It was, in effect, to encourage mergers. On
only seven occasions during its five-year life did the IRC provide
finance for individual companies, and two of these occasions involved
vehicle makers. The IRC contributed £25 million to help fund Rover
Group (then called BLMC) when it was formed in 1968. Later that
year, after Chrysler took control of Rootes, it invested some
£3 million in the company. This sum included the purchase of some
15 per cent of the equity and thereby enabled Britain to retain a stake
in the concern for a little longer. However, it was the rescue of the
now Rover Group that saw significant state involvement. In 1975 the
government agreed to help to the tune of £1,260 million. In 1980 this
was increased by another £990 million, plus funds from privatization.
This included a £50 million guarantee given by the Department of
Industry (DoI) in late 1974 under Section 8 of the 1972 Industry Act.
As the rescue pre-dated the creation of the National Enterprise Board
(NEB), the Rover Group was taken under state control by Act of
Parliament, with control soon being passed to the NEB. (In 1981
control, and equity, was transferred to the Secretary of State for
Industry.) The rescue of the Rover Group was to be in the form of equity
and loans supplied either by the DoI or by the NEB but in the end all
the money was advanced as equity. This was in effect an interest-free
gift. However, such was the drain on the NEB's resources that its
borrowing powers were increased in 1979 from £1 billion to £3 billion,
although a change of government meant that this was not activated.
The funds given to the Rover Group were for working capital, fixed
investment and model development but no operating subsidies were
allowed. (In 1979 the NEB filled a missing link in the Rover Group
rescue by helping to extend aid to the dealer chain.) In addition, by
1987 government assurances, as distinct from formal guarantees,

underwrote another £1.6 billion of Rover Group's borrowings on the open market. Subsequently this was reduced by a further equity injection by the Government of £680 million. However, the rescue in December 1975 of Chrysler UK by the DoI which put a contingent liability on the Exchequer of £162.5 million, included payments of up to £72.5 million to cover losses by direct subsidy. Smaller amounts of public money have been advanced to motor firms by the Scottish, Welsh and Northern Ireland Development Agencies. (The Scottish organization helped the new Stonefield vehicles concern.) The huge £77 million investment package for the De Lorean car company in Northern Ireland which foundered in 1983 after two years of production had strong social overtones. Assistance to various firms associated with the motor industry (such as foundries) has come from the varied provisions of Section 8 of the Industry Act, while Section 7 selective regional assistance added to general regional assistance provided Ford in 1977–8 with £148 million to pay for a Welsh engine plant and related developments. During the 1980s funds were obtained from special schemes such as the Support for Innovation Scheme, the Microelectronics Applications Project and Flexible Manufacturing Systems, all designed to improve the competitiveness of the industry.

The industry was amongst the greatest contributors to the creation of employment in development areas. In most cases the new locations appeared efficient (National Economic Development Office, 1969), although the Rover Group (then BLMC) claimed in the early 1970s that making trucks at Bathgate imposed a penalty of £52 per unit, and at the same time Chrysler experienced operating penalties of £2 million a year at Linwood. However, by the mid and late 1970s both firms were at pains to show that both locations were suitable, especially Chrysler when it justified transferring some production to Scotland under the post-1976 reorganization. Nevertheless as firms rationalized, the far-flung plants were closed. Scotland's vehicle assembly industry disappeared, some plants on Merseyside closed and component production in South Wales was diminished. This was a case of activities being centralized, rather than the regional locations being inefficient, as the present resurgence of Ford and Vauxhall plants on Merseyside shows.

8.6.2 The Effects of Policy on Vehicle Demand

Change in sales taxes and hire-purchase regulations have severely affected the level of activity in the car market. CVs have not been as severely affected as sales taxes for most business users have had zero incidence since 1956.

The motor industry, by making products whose demand is income elastic, has been subject to the inherent fluctuations (and low growth) in the economy. This instability was reinforced by government's use of he industry as an economic regulator through variations in sales taxes and hire-purchase conditions. The effects of fluctuations were to harm capacity utilization and to make unit production costs higher than need be while destroying forward planning. The effects of government activities on the state of the market was a major factor in the harm done to the industry's profitability in the 1950s and 1960s and hampered its ability to invest in new products and facilities, and to meet overseas competition. The harm done to the industry was officially recognized and resulted in sales tax incidence (and hire-purchase regulations after their reintroduction) remaining almost constant from 1973 until the general increase in value-added tax in mid-1979. The fiscal position was not greatly altered in the 1980s. However, no VAT paid on business cars can be reclaimed whilst the special 10 per cent car tax is discriminatory. The combination of VAT and the car tax tends to make cars that much more expensive relative to most other goods on the UK market.

Other taxes and duties, such as those on fuel and vehicle licences, have been set either on the amount of vehicle use or at low levels, so have had a smaller effect on the demand for cars and indeed CVs. However, a significant increase in fuel tax could affect the incidence of car demand, while a greater awareness by society of the net social costs of vehicle use could induce the UK government or the European Commission to formulate a coherent policy in this area. This would include legislation not only on vehicle noise, and noxious gas emissions, but also on vehicle longevity, vehicle design, vehicle use and so on. Obviously, such changes and changes in general transport policy could affect vehicle demand. For instance, a policy to transfer freight to rail could adversely affect truck demand, while subsidized bus travel could increase the demand for buses. In addition the introduction of pricing schemes aimed at covering the marginal social cost generated by road users could curtail the use of and therefore the annual demand for vehicles. On the other hand more stringent roadworthiness tests could increase the scrappage rate and indirectly, via the second-hand market, the demand for new cars.

8.7 CONCLUSION

The structure, performance and behaviour of the UK motor industry cannot now be properly studied outside a European context. The relatively fragmented European industry contrasts sharply, despite new entrants, with three massive producers in the USA and two clear market leaders in Japan. This difference explains the continued mergers in Europe and the attempts to spread costs by co-operation and collaboration. In the UK four of the largest firms, Ford, Vauxhall, Peugeot and Nissan, are integrated with overseas operations, whilst Austin Rover's survival largely depends upon the success of co-

operation and collaboration. The specialist maker Jaguar depend
upon product differentiation in a specialized niche for its continuing
prosperity. All the major truck producers are now foreign-controlled
with major decisions on model development and component sourcing
being steadily transferred abroad.

REFERENCES

Armstrong, A. G. (1967), 'The motor industry and the British economy',
  District Bank Review, 163, 18–40.
Central Policy Review Staff (1975), *The Future of the British Car Industry*
  (London: HMSO).
Cowling, K., and Mueller, D. C. (1978), 'The social cost of monopoly power',
  Economic Journal, 88, 352, 727–48.
House of Lords (1984), Twenty-seventh Report from the House of Lords
  Select Committee on the European Communities, Session 1983–4, *The
  Distribution, Servicing and Pricing of Motor Vehicles* HL 302 (London:
  HMSO).
HMSO (1976), *The British Motor Vehicle Industry*, Cmnd 6377 (London:
  HMSO).
Jones, D. T., and Prais, S. J. (1978), 'Plant-size and productivity in the motor
  industry: some international comparisons', *Oxford Bulletin of Economics
  and Statistics*, 40, 2, 131–151.
National Economic Development Office (1969), *Regional Policy and the
  Motor Industry* (London: HMSO).
PEIDA (1984), *The UK Vehicle Manufacturing Industry, its economic
  significance* (London and Edinburgh).
Pratten, C. (1971), *Economies of Scale in Manufacturing Industry* (London:
  Cambridge University Press).
Rhys, D. G. (1972), 'Economies of scale in the motor industry', *Bulletin of
  Economic Research*, 24, 2, 87–97.
Rhys, D. G. (1977), 'European mass-producing car makers and minimal
  efficient scale: a note', *The Journal of Industrial Economics*, XXV, 4,
  313–20.
Rhys, D. G. (1978), 'Car market price competition in the mid 1970s',
  Management Decision, 16, 4, 217–31.
Silberston, A. (1963), 'Hire purchase controls and the demand for cars',
  Economic Journal, LXXIII, 289 and 291, 32–53 and 556–8.

FURTHER READING

Central Policy Review Staff (1975), *The Future of the British Car Industry*
  (London: HMSO).
Dunnett, P. J. S. (1980), *The Decline of the British Motor Industry* (London:
  Croom Helm).
HMSO (1975), *The Motor Vehicle Industry*, Fourteenth Report from the
  Expenditure Committee (Trade and Industry Sub-Committee), HC 617,

Session 1974–5 plus volumes of evidence (1975), HC 617–I, HC 617–II, HC 617–III (London: HMSO).

Maxcy, G. (1981), *The Multinational Motor Industry* (London: Croom Helm).

Roos, D. *et al.* (1984), *The Future of the Automobile* (New York and London: Allen & Unwin).

Society of Motor Manufacturers and Traders, *The Motor Industry of Great Britain* (an annual publication) (London).

Chapter Nine

Food Processing

PETER MAUNDER

9.1 INTRODUCTION

Compared with many of the other industries examined in this book food processing is a part of the UK economy whose characteristics and problems have received very little academic study until recent years. The dearth of published material on both food processing companies and products is the more surprising given the inevitable political interest in the availability and price of processed foods. However, there are now clear signs of a growing interest by agricultural economists in the UK in the economics of food beyond the farm gate. Furthermore, diet, nutrition and health considerations regarding food are giving the sector increased attention in the media. Indeed the transformation of agricultural raw materials into processed foodstuffs is now an area of considerable concern amongst consumer organizations and pressure groups.

9.1.1 The Scope of the Food Processing Sector

Food processing does not constitute a clearly defined single industry. There are in fact several food industries within the food processing sector of the economy and they differ widely in terms of their capital intensity of production, nature of markets and variety of product. Any definition of the food processing sector is therefore necessarily arbitrary. It is defined here in terms of twelve of the groups contained in Division 4 (Other Manufacturing Industries) of the 1980 Standard Industrial Classification: 411–416, and 419–423 (organic oils and fats; slaughtering and meat production; preparation of milk and milk products; processing of fruit and vegetables; fish processing; grain milling; bread, biscuits and flour confectionery; sugar and sugar by-products; ice-cream, cocoa, chocolate and sugar confectionery; animal feeding stuffs; starch; and miscellaneous foods). These twelve industries account for about one-tenth of the net output and employment of all manufacturing industries.

Table 9.1 gives some indication of the relative importance of the industries that make up the sector. Over 50 per cent of total employment in the sector is in slaughtering and meat production and

Table 9.1 *The Food Processing Industries: Some Indicators of Relative Importance, 1985*

Industry	Employment	% of total Sales	Capital expenditure
Organic oils and fats	1.5	4.9	2.5
Slaughtering and meat production	21.7	21.3	14.9
Preparation of milk and milk products	8.3	14.8	10.3
Processing of fruit and vegetables	3.3	3.2	3.8
Fish processing	5.6	3.3	5.6
Grain milling	1.3	3.8	2.3
Bread, biscuits and flour confectionery	29.1	11.8	14.2
Sugar and sugar by-products	1.6	3.5	3.2
Ice-cream, cocoa, chocolate and sugar confectionery	10.3	8.3	11.1
Animal feeding stuffs	4.1	9.7	7.8
Starch ⎫ Miscellaneous foods ⎭	13.2	15.3	24.3
Total*	100.0	100.0	100.0
Total Thousands/£m	thousands 493.8	£m 30979.5	£m 960.3

Note: *Totals may not sum to 100.0 because of rounding errors.
Source: Census of Production, 1985, PA1002

bread, biscuits and flour confectionery, although these two industries are much less important in terms of both sales and capital expenditure. One of the reasons for this difference is that both industries are relatively labour-intensive. In contrast, preparation of milk and milk products has a share of both sales and capital expenditure that is higher than its share of employment, a reflection of the high degree of automation that is present in this industry. The capital expenditure figures are of course also likely to be affected by growth prospects.

9.1.2 The Sector's Growth

Although household spending on food in the UK at current prices rose from £13,443 million in 1976 to £30,956 million in 1986 – an increase of 130 per cent – the volume of sales rose only marginally. Measured in 1980 prices, the growth in total sales was just over 7 per cent over this same period. (*Total* consumers' expenditure in real terms rose by 28 per cent.) It is important to note, however, that experience between 1976 and 1986 varied across products. For example, expenditure on

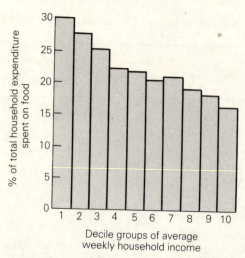

Figure 9.1   *Variation of food expenditure pattern by decile groups of household income*

Source: Family Expenditure Survey 1985, p. 7.

preserves and confectionery grew by 15 per cent in real terms while oils and fats and beverages experienced decline.

The cause of slowly rising food sales is 'the narrow capacity of the human stomach' (Smith, 1776, p. 269). As an individual's income rises, so he or she tends to spend proportionately less on food. This proposition is supported by Figure 9.1 which shows a very clear decline in the proportion of expenditure spent on food as *household* income increases. (Household, rather than individual income is the more appropriate variable here.) An important implication of Figure 9.1 is that the income elasticity of demand for food as a whole is less than unity. (It is clear from data available from the annual reports of the National Food Surveys that income elasticities for many individual food products are *negative*. Indeed, nearly half of all processed foodstuffs come within this category.)

As incomes increase, so the relative importance of different types of food expenditure changes. This is shown in Table 9.2 which takes three household income bands for illustrative purposes. The table also shows the breakdown of food expenditure for 'all income' bands. Not unexpectedly, the basic food products such as bread and flour, butter, margarine, milk, cheese and eggs decline in importance as household income rises, whereas expenditure on 'meals bought away from home' increases dramatically.

It is clear from the above that even with rising real incomes, the food processing sector's scope for expansion is severely limited. The main hope must lie in persuading consumers to replace fresh foods

Table 9.2 *Average Weekly Household Expenditure on Food: by Item and Income, 1985*

	Under £40	Between £175 and £200	£500 or more	All incomes
Bread, flour, biscuits, cakes and cereals	13.6	11.6	8.7	11.3
Meat	22.7	22.0	18.5	21.0
Fish (including fish and chips)	5.1	3.8	3.0	3.8
Butter, margarine, milk, cheese and eggs	17.6	14.7	12.1	14.9
Vegetables and fruit	14.2	13.5	13.1	13.8
Sugar, preserves, sweets and chocolates	4.5	4.4	2.8	4.1
Beverages and soft drinks	6.6	5.4	4.2	5.2
Meals bought away from home, and other foods	15.9	24.5	37.5	25.9
Average expenditure on food (£)	13.55	32.57	59.78	32.70

Note: Columns may not sum to 100.0 because of rounding errors.
Source: Family Expenditure Survey, 1985, p. 14.

with those foodstuffs that have undergone some form of processing, for example, fresh fish with fish fingers or frozen cod steaks. Food processors, therefore, are keen to develop new products which have high added value and in particular are appreciated by women who have jobs and who need to get meals quickly – in other words the so-called convenience foods. However, the demand for fresh foods is currently being encouraged by greater awareness of the problems of obesity and interest by the public in the need for healthy eating. Thus food processors have increasingly had to be aware of the impact of changing consumer tastes influencing the form of food consumed.

9.1.3 Price Elasticities

Price elasticities vary considerably across products, as Table 9.3 illustrates. Of the 103 price elasticities published by the National Food Survey for the period 1979–84 for processed foods (see the source to Table 9.3), over half were lower than −1.0. Other relevant data on price elasticities were given in Section 1.3.

9.1.4 Food Processing and the EC

In recent years, the sector has had to adapt to the higher agricultural raw material costs brought about by the UK's membership of the

Table 9.3   *Price Elasticity of Demand: Some Illustrative Data*

Product group	Product with most elastic demand (elasticity in brackets)	Product with least elastic demand (elasticity in brackets)
Milk	Dried milk (−1.49)	Liquid whole milk (−0.50)
Meat	Pork (−2.15)	Meat products other than uncooked sausages (−0.09)
Fats	All other fats (−1.19)	Vegetable and salad oils (−0.09)
Sugars and preserves	Syrup and treacle (−0.85)	Sugar (−0.50)
Cereals	Wholewheat and wholemeal bread (−2.61)	Breakfast cereals (−0.08)

Source: Household Food Consumption and Expenditure 1984, Table 3.

European Community in 1973. The heavily protected structure of the Common Agricultural Policy (CAP) has meant that UK firms had to adjust to relying on a source of relatively more expensive inputs which has hampered its competitive position in world markets (Harris, Swinbank and Wilkinson, 1983). It is not surprising, therefore, that the sector has sought relief from the high support prices of European agricultural raw materials and pressed for reform of the CAP. (See also Sections 1.4.1 and 9.5.3.)

9.2   MARKET STRUCTURE

9.2.1   Historical Background

The twentieth century has seen some very substantial structural changes in the food processing sector. A brief survey of the sector's development is therefore appropriate. Such a survey also provides a useful historical perspective on the industry's current structure.

The interwar period
Firms engaged in food processing at the start of the present century were, relative to those in other manufacturing industries, typically very small concerns. For example, in 1905 there were only two food firms – Bovril and Huntley & Palmers – among the UK's 50 largest industrial concerns (size is measured here by capital invested)

(Lawrence, 1976, p. 200). The food processor at this time generally supplied a product to the specification of a wholesaler who held the balance of power over both this supplier and his own customers who were mainly one-shop independent grocers. The balance of power, however, began to swing towards the food processors in the interwar period following the development of pre-packaged branded products supported by national advertising. The concentration of production was, however, still generally low in the interwar years. The 1935 Census of Production indicated few instances in the food trades where the three largest firms accounted for 70 per cent or more of employment (Leak and Maizels, 1945).

1950–80

The 1951 Census of Production showed that there had been few marked changes in the concentration of production between 1935 and 1951. Indeed there was only one food industry – ice-cream – which had become more concentrated. Nor was there much change in the market structure of the industries in the early 1950s while trading in food products remained subject to wartime-imposed government controls. It was not until 1953 that government purchasing of cereals and animal feedstuffs ended. In the following year private trading in oils and meat products was resumed. Consumer rationing and price controls on both chocolate and sweet confectionery and sugar ended in 1953. A year later rationing of butter, margarine, cheese and cooking fats ceased although in the case of meat and bacon, a free market did not emerge until mid-1955.

The lifting of wartime controls intensified further the competitive pressures in the food industry which had already been generated by the growth in supermarkets, the development of private brands and the demise of resale price maintenance. The 1956 Restrictive Trade Practices Act also stimulated competition, particularly in grain milling, baking, sugar, butter and cheese. The growing bargaining power of the multiple food retailers from the mid-1950s onwards further increased the pressures on food processors. Whereas in 1960, 500 multiple buying points (head offices) accounted for 27.9 per cent of grocery turnover, ten years later just 202 buying points accounted for 42 per cent of turnover.[1] Smaller food processors lacking a strong brand name were taken over by others or ceased to trade.

In view of the increase in competition, it is hardly surprising to find that in the 1960s there was a notably large fall in the number of food processing firms. Census of Production data show that between 1958 and 1972 the number of food enterprises fell by 40 per cent. Simultaneously, a number of leading food processors tried to extend their product range. This aim of diversification was mainly achieved by take-overs. For example, Cerebos diversified by acquiring A. & R. Scott (porridge oats), pet foods (Stamina Foods), meat pastes (Brand

& Co. and J. & A. Sharwood) and suet (Hugon & Co.) as well as by moving into the animal feeds industry. The Bibby Group which had large interests in this last named industry diversified into foods for human consumption – for example, canned fish and fruit – by acquiring Princes Foods in 1968. In the same year Liebig's Extract of Meat merged with Brooke Bond. Spillers extended their product range into meat processing with the takeovers of Tyne Brand Products in 1967 and of Meade Lonsdale two years later. Schweppes acquired Moorhouses, Hartleys and Chivers – all of which produced jams, jellies and preserves – and also Typhoo Tea. In 1969 it merged with Cadbury. HP Sauce, National Canning (better known for their brand name of Smedleys) and the Ross Group were all acquired between 1967 and 1969 by Imperial Tobacco which already had a stake in the food industry through Golden Wonder potato crisps. All the firms just cited that were taken over had leading brands in their particular sections of the food industry. The value placed by the bidders on these brands was capitalized in the prices paid for them – for example, Schweppes's purchase of Typhoo Tea in 1968 cost £45 million, of which £31 million represented the 'goodwill' the name bore.

The rapid pace of take-over activity led one investment analyst to suggest that food processors bought whichever firms were available for sale, irrespective of the products they manufactured, rather than only those that really fitted in with their true company interests (Capel, 1970). This does not in retrospect seem too extreme a judgement. Indeed, it is supported by the evidence of companies disposing of recently acquired firms. In 1969, for example, British-American Tobacco sold Tonibell Manufacturing, an ice-cream supplier, to J. Lyons, having owned the company for just five years. Then, in early 1970 Associated British Foods (ABF) sold Allied Farm Foods (Buxted chicken) to Imperial Tobacco; they had purchased this company only fifteen months previously.

The proposition that previous acquisitions and attempts at diversification now required a 'sorting-out' strategy by the major food firms also draws support from the consolidations among the leading firms themselves. Cadbury-Schweppes and United Biscuits merged their packaged cake interests to form McVitie & Cadbury Cakes in 1971. Neither firm had found their recent investment in cakes very profitable because of slower growth of this market than had seemed likely in the mid-1960s. In the same year the flour milling and baking interests of Spillers, J. Lyons and the Co-operative Wholesale Society were amalgamated to give the new group, Spillers-French, one-fifth of the bread market. A year later Spillers acquired the pet food interests of Ranks Hovis McDougall (RHM) and in the biscuit industry United Biscuits consolidated its position as market leader by purchasing the biscuit interests of Cavenham Foods.

These mergers contributed to an increase in the concentration of production in many individual food product markets, in many of which the level of concentration was already high. In 1970 a government list of markets in which an individual firm accounted for more than half of output involved seven food markets.[2] In 1973 a further list of products in which a single firm was thought to account for between a quarter and a third of production was prepared. This included no less than 15 food items.[3]

The 1980s

Recent years have seen continued structural change. The reasons behind this change have been varied. First, some firms have sought to diversify their food processing interests by acquisition. For example, Northern Foods has expanded from milk distribution into meat processing through its purchase of Bowyers in 1985. (It had earlier bought Pork Farms in 1978.) In the latter year it also bought the biscuit and cake interests of Adams Foods. In 1984 Tate & Lyle attempted to add tea to its sugar refining interests by acquiring Brooke Bond but was outbid by Unilever. Another company which has rapidly built up a diverse group of food processing interests in the 1980s is Hillsdown Holdings. Hillsdown have since 1981 acquired firms with established brand names but which were not trading successfully. Its expansion programme began with the acquisition of the fruit and vegetable canning firm of Lockwoods Foods in 1981 and this was followed a year later by the purchase of the Daylay eggs, Buxted poultry, Nitrovit animal feed and Ross meat trading interests of Imperial Tobacco. A year later it purchased another Imperial subsidiary TKM Foods (later renamed Smedleys), a producer of canned and frozen fruit and vegetables. Its meat interests were extended with its acquisition of FMC, the largest meat company and leading bacon curer in the UK, in 1983 and of Telfers a year later.

Secondly, some leading firms have sought consolidation in their industries by disposing of certain of their interests which were not perceived as capable by existing management of further market expansion: their sale permitting a realization of cash for use in other parts of the group. An example is the sale by RHM in 1983 of its animal feedstuffs interests to Dalgety. Another example is the disposal by Express Dairies (part of the Grand Metropolitan brewing and food group) of its northern milk division in 1985 to Northern Foods.

Disposals have also resulted where firms with interests in several food markets have resolved to concentrate on their mainstream business as exemplified by the Cadbury Schweppes sale of its food and beverage interests in the management buy-out in 1986. Several companies have disposed of subsidiaries engaged in food *retailing* in order to specialize in processing. Examples here include Fitch Lovell, which in 1982 sold its Key Markets to Linfood (now called Dee Corporation) and the sale by Unilever of Baxters, the second largest chain of butchers shops in the UK, to Union International, soon after it had acquired Brooke Bond in 1984. In 1986 Associated British Foods sold its Fine Fare retail chain to Dee which, together with earlier acquisitions, then became the third largest multiple in the UK. Such disposals reflect the judgement that where a food processor also has retailing interests there are conflicts of interest between the processing and distributive subsidiaries.

9.2.2 Market Concentration

In 1983 the latest year for which Census of Production data were available at the time of writing, the average unweighted 5 firm sales concentration ratio for the 11 industries included in Table 9.1 was 56 per cent. (The sales-weighted ratio was 49 per cent.) Seven of the industries (organic oils and fats; preparation of milk and milk products; fish processing; grain milling; bread, biscuits and flour confectionery; sugar; and ice-cream, cocoa and chocolate and sugar confectionery) had ratios of over 60 per cent. Despite the structural changes that have taken place, the pattern of concentration remained largely unchanged during the early 1980s.

The data in the previous paragraph may disguise the level of concentration in individual food markets. In certain of these markets there is a clear brand leader accounting for one-third or more of total sales. Examples include United Biscuits (biscuits), Kellogg (breakfast cereals), Brooke Bond (tea), Nestlé (condensed milk) and Heinz (baked beans). However, such figures tend to understate the significance of competition provided by small manufacturers who specialize in producing for the major retail chains such as Sainsbury. In the frozen food market, whose value of retail sales in 1986 was £1.5 billion, the market share of the leading firm Birds Eye was less than one-fifth; the share of own labels amounted to 31 per cent. A similar own-label share exists in the market for biscuits and baked beans.

High levels of concentration do not necessarily indicate the presence of market power. It must be remembered that food processors face substantial competition from imports – about one-half of all food imports now enters the UK to some extent processed rather than in fresh form – and that they also face very strong *buyers*. In 1984 the largest ten grocery chains accounted for 78 per cent of grocery turnover[4] (see also section 13.2). Despite the creation of large, diversified multinational companies the balance of market power has shifted from food processors towards their customers and become one of the main issues of current policy, as indicated in section 9.5.2.

9.2.3 Food Processing and the Largest Firms

At the aggregate level, food processing firms are strongly represented in the list of Britain's biggest firms. There are 8 companies with substantial food processing interests among the 50 largest firms as measured by sales. One-fifth of the largest 100 are firms with important food processing interests.[5] Compared with other European countries the UK has more large-sized food companies if 'large' is defined as having more than 500 employees. One study has estimated that the 10 largest firms account for one-third of all food sales (Advisory Council for Applied Research and Development, 1982). It is apparent that the food processing sector is more concentrated than in UK manufacturing as a whole.

9.2.4 Multinational Companies

Foreign-owned firms, especially American ones, are strongly represented amongst Britain's leading food processors. Some have been long established in certain markets. For example, Heinz quickly became the market leader in soups after introducing its first range in 1930 (Walshe, 1974, p. 45). Quaker Oats began production in the UK in 1920, Shredded Wheat (now Nabisco) in 1925 and Kellogg in 1938. General Foods Corporation first produced Maxwell House coffee in the UK in 1956, but the company had owned a British subsidiary, Alfred Bird & Sons, to market imported foods since 1947. But UK firms have also extended their interests in food processing in the USA. Firms such as United Biscuits have become highly diversified conglomerate companies such that food processing activity in the UK is no longer the dominant part of their global sales of food, drink, catering and other products. Firms like Rowntree Macintosh, Dalgety, Tate & Lyle, Unigate and United Biscuits all earn between a fifth and a half of their profit overseas.[6]

9.2.5 Economies of Scale and Barriers to Entry

Data on the nature of scale economies in food production are very sparse. What are available suggest that in a number of product markets the minimum efficient plant size usually accounts for a low proportion of industry sales. In the case of plant bread the proportion was estimated by the Monopolies and Mergers Commission (MMC) at 0.5 per cent of the market; the same source suggested a rather higher figure – 2 per cent – in the case of flour (MMC, 1977a). Scale economies seem to be somewhat more important in potato crisp manufacture where a minimum efficient sized plant accounts for about 10 per cent of industry sales (Bevan, 1974). But even if this latter figure is indicative of the extent of scale economies in other food processing industries it does seem doubtful whether high concentration of food processing is really required in order to realize scale economies, at least in respect of production.

Scale economies in production are therefore unlikely to represent a significant barrier to entry. Problems in winning shelf space in supermarkets and the level of marketing expenses incurred in support of new brands, however, present more formidable problems for entrants to many food markets. There is, moreover, the need for a new entrant to find a novel product so as to challenge existing brands. The high failure of new product development (see Section 9.3.3) makes this issue itself a strong deterrent for potential competitors. Thus the Monopolies Commission (MC) regarded the cost of marketing new brands and risks of product development to be 'substantial' barriers to entry into breakfast cereals (MC, 1973, p. 26).

Where entry involving nationally branded goods does occur it is, as the earlier discussion has indicated, usually by established rather than new firms. (Indeed it is difficult to name even one entirely new food processing firm that has emerged in the past decade in any of the major food markets.) Only established firms are able to finance the often high costs of new plant and of the promotion and marketing of a new brand. For example, the expansion of Golden Wonder crisps from being a small Scottish-based firm to the second largest national concern has been estimated to have cost Imperial Tobacco £10 million between 1961 and 1965 (Bevan, 1974, p. 292): over £70 million in 1986 prices. Bovril reportedly spent £3 million in marketing expenses in addition to some £2.5 million in plant and machinery, a total of about £12 million in 1986 prices, in developing a granulated meat cube to challenge Oxo's domination of the meat and vegetable extract market in 1977.[7]

Entry into the bread and flour confectionery industry is relatively easier than in most other food markets because the perishable nature of the industry's output limits the size of available markets. In-store baking has provided the means by which entry into this industry has been made easier in terms of capital requirements.[8] Furthermore the sale of bread and flour confectionery from the same premises where it is baked involves an entrant in minimal costs of marketing.

The marketing difficulties of entry are much eased when firms supply products for sale by a retail chain under the latter's own name or for the institutional (catering) market. In either case, they can avoid the extensive advertising and marketing costs associated with brand names. Thus Northray Farm Products Ltd was formed in the 1950s by two Lincolnshire farmers to freeze their own products, and it quickly developed a significant market share in own-label frozen peas. Romix Foods began supplying a retail chain with own-label pastry mixes using two machines together costing less than £20 in 1969.[9] The frozen food industry is an example of how entry is not difficult for firms keen to supply the catering and own-label market. Many small specialist ompanies have entered this market and have successfully exploited he potential in serving the rapidly growing number of freezer centres.

Exit may also occur. Even large food firms may find that despite teavy promotional expenditure they have developed an inadequate orand image and have only a low market share. For example, Walls oulled out of the yoghurt market in 1970 and Unigate from canned ouddings in 1978. Both did so having incurred heavy losses in insuccessful attempts to compete with market leaders in these oroducts.

9.3 MARKET BEHAVIOUR

9.3.1 Pricing

Reference has already been made to the changing balance of power between food processors and food retailers in the postwar period. It has been shown that both these stages in the food marketing chains have become more concentrated in character so that situations of bilateral oligopoly have developed in most individual food markets. The expansion of the multiple food retailers at the expense of independent and co-operative food stores – an expansion which was based on the self-service and supermarket style of selling – provided the basis for these food chains to negotiate and secure more advantageous terms from food processors. These terms include not only higher trade discounts off published prices but also cash payments in support of in-store promotional activity. This bargaining between food processors and retailers or 'vertical conflict' provides the essence of competitive pressures facing food processors (Palamountain, 1955). The magnitude of the trading deals secured by the multiple retail chains is rarely made known but in recent times it has caused small independent retailers to call for trading terms offered by food processors to be strictly based on size of orders and not on the bargaining power of buyers. But, as noted in the final section of this chapter, despite an inquiry both by the Monopolies and Mergers Commission and the Office of Fair Trading there has not been any government intervention on this matter.

The oligopolistic character of most food markets has led to some firms becoming price leaders. Associated British Foods (ABF) in bread, Kellogg in breakfast cereals, Brooke Bond in tea and Van den Berghs & Jurgens (a subsidiary of Unilever) in margarine have over the years exerted a significant influence on pricing policy in their respective markets (Mitchell, 1972). In the first of these markets ABF's position as price leader has been based on a lower-cost bakery chain than its main rival, Ranks Hovis McDougall. In the other food markets just cited an important influence on the market leader's pricing policy is the prices charged by the leading multiple chains for their own brands.

9.3.2 The Production of Own-Label Brands

Food processors have had to face another consequence of the movement of power in favour of large food distributors: the development of own-label brands of the multiple food retailers. The enthusiasm for private brands shown, in particular, by the fast expanding Sainsbury and Tesco chains, is readily understandable because overall, private brands have a price differential of 10 per cent or more over the leading national brands. This price advantage reflects the economies obtained by the retailers in marketing and distribution costs in respect of private brands.

The attitude of food processors towards own-label products during the past two decades has in general been unenthusiastic. It is true that the supply of own-label foodstuffs offers the opportunity to use spare capacity and to obtain the benefit of longer production runs. However, food processors have also felt own-label production discourages new product development. They have claimed that low profit margins necessarily limit research effort and that even in cases where manufacturers introduce a superior branded product, they are unable to recoup heavy development costs and to enjoy ultimately an acceptable return on investment incurred.

This argument against own-labels is in fact rarely substantiated by food processors and the alleged highly superior quality of their national brands is debatable. The so-called 'parasitic' effect of own brands on innovation is indeed suspect. For one thing, some of the take-overs in the late 1960s were clearly made to give the large acquiring firms a stake in own-label production, for example, United Biscuits' purchase of Meredith & Drew which specialized in own-label potato crisps and biscuits. The same motive explained Schweppes's acquisition of Moorhouse who produced own-label jam. Indeed some processors have subsidiaries specializing in this trade. These latter include Sol Cafe and SFK (owned by J. Lyons) and Goldhanger (owned by Express Dairy).

Many food processors, however, seem reluctant to devote more than about one-fifth of capacity to own-label products. Some firms, such as Cadbury and Birds Eye (Unilever), resisted the trend towards own-label production for many years, but gradually the number of leading firms opposed to it has dwindled. Own-label products now have a significant share (about one-third) of some food markets such as butter, fruit squashes, instant coffee, tea bags, jam and evaporated milk. Overall, own-label products have not risen much above one-quarter of total grocery sales, which is a share similar to that in the United States market. Nevertheless, own-label products clearly represent an important aspect of the competitive pressures in this sector of the economy.

9.3.3 Innovation

Competition among food processors, and the limited possibilities for expanding the market overall, emphasize the crucial role of new product development. Coffee creamers, soya meals, snack soups, cheesecake, muesli and frozen bakery goods are but a small selection of recent new food products. However, the returns to such development are very uncertain because new products have a high failure rate: up to 60 per cent of new products are withdrawn from sales within five years. One-third of new brands have a life of less than two years (Kraushar, Andrews & Eassie, 1976). Innovation is further examined in Section 9.5.3.

9.3.4 Advertising

In 1982 media expenditure on all foods (fresh and processed) was £277 million (Advertising Association, 1983). This sum accounted for just under 9 per cent of media expenditure when classified by product group. There was little change in this proportion during the previous decade. The ratio of advertising expenditure to total food market sales has for most recent years been just below 1 per cent. Given that this has been below the average for the eight product groups for which Advertising Association data are provided, this figure might suggest that advertising is not a significant aspect of competitive conduct in food markets. However, there are very considerable differences across individual product markets in advertising intensities, as measured by the ratio of advertising to sales revenue. For example in 1980 the ratio was 15 per cent in the case of meat and vegetable extracts and 9 per cent in the cake and pastry mix market. On the other hand advertising expenditure on sugar and canned fruit was just one-fifth of 1 per cent of sales revenue.

Food processors such as chocolate and sugar confectionery firms resort to advertising both to promote their new products and also to maintain sales volume in a market not only static but also dependent on impulse purchasing.

But, this said, the oligopolistic character of the confectionery (and other food industries) itself favours non-price competition. As the Monopolies Commission declared in its report on breakfast cereals, 'the reluctance to compete in price . . . is largely attributed to the structure of the industry' (MC, 1973, p. 25).

9.4   MARKET PERFORMANCE

The source material available for appraising the market performance of the food processing sector of the UK economy is extremely limited, especially if the assessments by the Monopolies and Mergers Commission are ignored. Section 9.5 on public policy reviews the conclusions reached by this body from its study of particular food industries. The focus of attention here, however, is on the sector's profitability, productivity in factor use and technical progress.

9.4.1   Profitability

The rate of return on capital measured at replacement cost, in food processing was for many years after 1960 consistently above the average for all manufacturing industry. But since 1980 food processors have not shared in the recovery in profitability experienced by manufacturing industry as a whole. Despite the steady decline in food prices in real terms, which has helped encourage a small rise in the volume of sales through food retailers (see Section 9.2.2) it is apparent that the greatest share of any resulting benefit has been enjoyed by the major food retailing chains. Their rate of return on capital employed when measured in current-cost terms rose by 6 percentage points between 1980 and 1984 to 16 per cent compared with a static figure of 9 per cent for food processors over this same period.[10]

9.4.2   Productivity

In the light of its profitability record it is appropriate to consider the evidence concerning the sector's efficiency in the use of labour and capital. The Food and Drink Manufacturing Economic Development Committee (EDC), one of the few remaining study groups under the aegis of the National Economic Development Office, reported in 1978 and again in 1982 that the UK food sector compared unfavourably with those of most other developed nations in its record of labour and capital productivity. Its studies suggested that in 1979 value added per worker in the UK food sector was two-thirds that of West Germany and below one-half that in France (Food and Drink Manufacturing EDC, 1978, 1982). Given that in both these two countries the average-sized production unit was, and still is, smaller than in the UK these findings have thrown serious doubt on the sector's long-held belief that its more concentrated market structure placed it at an advantage in terms of its productivity compared with its European competitors.

9.4.3 Technical Progress

While the food processing sector may not be as science-based as the electronics or chemical industries, new product development increasingly involves the application of advances in food chemistry and microbiology. Two examples are the development of textured vegetable proteins based on soya beans and the use of enzymes to produce high-fructose corn syrup. Processed foods contain additives which control the texture, colour and flavour of products and extend their shelf-life. The increasing use of artificial sweeteners, antioxidants, emulsifiers and stabilizers is reinforcing the importance of technical issues.

The innovative character of this sector has been previously indicated. Mergers among leading food firms in the late 1960s were frequently justified on the grounds that only big firms could survive in increasingly competitive world markets. As the size of Britain's leading food firms appears easily large enough to exhaust the benefits of plant economies of scale, it is apposite to consider whether large firms have a higher rate of innovation than small firms.

It is clear that most of the innovations have come from large firms. The research by Townsend *et al.* (1981, p. 46) on this sector indicates that firms with more than 1,000 employees accounted for 83 per cent of the 65 important innovations introduced in the sector in the period 1945–80. The share of innovations accounted for by firms employing fewer than 200 employees was much less than their share of net output. For example, over the period 1945–70 their three innovations, which included the important advance of frozen broilers, represented just 8 per cent of the total number of significant innovations in the industry, compared with their 16 per cent share of the industry's net output (Freeman, 1971, p. 12).

Food research is carried out not only by individual companies but in co-operative industrial research associations, government research institutes, and universities. In 1978 the industry's Economic Development Committee (EDC) considered the level of spending to be low relative to other UK industries and also to food industries in other countries.[11] There is no reason to believe that the picture has changed significantly since then. This concern was later reinforced by a call from the Cabinet Office Advisory Council for Applied Research and Development for a more active funding of basic scientific research (ACARD, 1982).

On the positive side, it is perhaps worth noting that the British Baking Industries Research Association – the baking industry's co-operative research body – has developed one of the industry's more significant technical advances: the Chorleywood bread process. This process which is now used worldwide was quickly adopted in the bread industry: within six years of its launch, it was used to produce three-quarters of the bread made in UK plant bakeries. As shown earlier, innovative activity is inevitably risky. Consequently, some new processing techniques have so far failed to realize expectations. For example, accelerated freeze-drying has not had the general applicability that at first seemed likely, and has only been extensively used for coffee.

9.5 PUBLIC POLICY

9.5.1 The Maintenance of Standards

Producing goods essential to life has ensured that the food processing industries have always been subject to close scrutiny in political quarters. Thus legislation to protect the interests of consumers when buying food has a long history: the first Weights and Measures Act was passed in 1878. The 1955 Food and Drugs Act still provides the basis for government regulations concerning the composition and nutritional quality of food as well as its description. While the aims sought by such Acts do not involve political controversy it is important that such regulations should not be so detailed and slow to adapt that they preclude advantageous substitution of ingredients by food manufacturers. During the 1970s the growing demand for consumer legislation and British entry into the European Community emphasized the importance of these technical matters. This can be briefly indicated by reference to the Food Standards Committee.

Established in 1947 to advise the government in drawing up regulations on the composition of food, this body was probably not well known until the publication of its reports on date marking in 1971 and 1972 and on novel proteins in 1975. The FSC recommended that manufacturers of 'short-life' foods should show a 'sell-by' date on their products and that long-life foods should exhibit a date of manufacture. The merits of open dating had of course been much discussed throughout the food industry and the practice was the subject of favourable prompting by the press.

The attention in the media to the broader question of what people should eat has been a recent phenomenon. There is currently much controversy about the stance of government policy towards what constitutes a healthy diet. Public consciousness about the incidence of coronary heart disease and obesity have clearly affected the pattern of demand for the food industry's products. Thus the demand for high-fibre carbohydrates such as wholemeal bread has risen while consumption of items with a high content of animal fat have declined. These changes in the diet have received the approval of several government bodies, most notably the National Advisory Committee on Nutrition Education (NACNE, 1983) and the Committee on Medical Aspects of Food Policy (COMA, 1984). Whilst the government has accepted the case for foods to be labelled for their fat content critics feel that government policy on nutrition education has been too cautious in the face of vested interests within the food industry (Walker and Cannon, 1984). Whatever the truth of the matter it is clear that a 'healthy diet' has become a subject whereby the government is being pressed to develop a clear and coherent policy on nutritional matters.

The impact of government policies on the behaviour of food processing firms is now considered.

9.5.2 Competition Policies

Restrictive practices

In many of the food processing industries firms agreed after 1945 to strong restraints on competitive behaviour. Analysis of the registered agreements following the passing of the 1956 Restrictive Trade Practices Act shows that in the grain milling, baking and flour confectionery, biscuits, sugar, butter and cheese sections of the industry price competition was effectively minimal (Cuthbert and Black, 1959).

Those firms which were parties to price agreements and which have tried to justify them have not found support in the Restrictive Practices Court. For example, plant bakers in both England and Wales and Scotland – whose agreements were among the first heard in the Restrictive Practices Court – were unsuccessful in defending their agreements.

The Restrictive Practices Court has also had responsibility for hearing applications for exemption from the ban on resale price maintenance under the 1964 Resale Prices Act. For many food grocery products resale price maintenance had in fact largely collapsed by 1960, partly as a result of the ending of the collective enforcement of the practice under Section 24 of the 1956 Restrictive Trade Practices Act. A further important factor in its demise was the growth in competitive pressures both among food processing firms themselves and between the latter as a group and the rapidly growing food retailing chains as discussed previously. Even so, at the time of the passing of the Act profit margins for retailers continued to be fixed by manufacturers of bread, breakfast cereals, confectionery and certain preserves. The first case heard in the court related to chocolate and sugar confectionery. After a lengthy hearing the court ruled in 1967 that the manufacturers had failed to prove their case for exemption from the Act. This decision undoubtedly led many other industries to abandon their plans for justifying resale price maintenance in the court.

References to the Monopolies Commission

The concentration of production in certain individual food markets has been sufficiently high to make several food processing firms potential references to the Monopolies Commission (MC) under the terms of the 1948 Monopolies and Restrictive Practices Act. The fact that hardly any firms were referred for study until 1970 lends support to the view that successive governments believed that competitive conditions were reasonably adequate to maintain acceptable levels of market performance by the constituent units of those industries (Maunder, 1970, p. 458). Since 1970 the MC has reported on the supply of starch (1971), breakfast cereals (1973), frozen foods (1976), bread and flour (1977a), pet foods (1977b), and ice-cream (1979). These references suggest that after 1970 both Labour and Conservative governments had doubts about the strength of competitive pressures in some food markets.

In the case of starch and glucoses the reference to the MC excluded these goods when made up for retail sale. The MC made few criticisms of Brown & Polson which was the leading supplier. The reference of ready-to-eat breakfast cereals in 1971 confined the MC to the issue of prices, and the timing of this reference also suggested the relevance of political pressures. It is surely significant that Kellogg had twice raised its prices within the space of nine months prior to the announcement of the reference! The MC reported that Kellogg's profits had been excessive until 1970 and although they were no longer unreasonable, it recommended that the company's prices be kept under scrutiny. The government accepted the report and thus required Kellogg to seek its approval before making any future price increases. The basis of the MC's view was that competitive forces in the industry were not themselves sufficient to restrain prices. Both the concentration of production and the emphasis on advertising expenditures in support of branded goods by all five major competitors meant that price competition was limited. The MC was convinced that product differentiation had rendered the market insensitive to price competition: it accepted the view that Viota's sale of own-label cornflakes was not restraining Kellogg's pricing policy.

The Heath government's concern with rising food prices provided the setting for its references in 1973 to the now renamed Monopolies and Mergers Commission (MMC) of flour and bread and frozen foods (other than whole frozen poultry). Neither industry was subject to keen criticism from the MMC and this fact was taken by leading firms in both industries as confirmation of the political nature of their original reference.

During the study of the bread industry it was revealed that 77 unregistered price agreements, mainly in respect of discounts offered to retailers, had been in operation between 1968 and 1974. These were later formally registered with the Office of Fair Trading (OFT) and in May 1977 the parties gave undertakings to the Restrictive Practices Court as to their compliance with the requests of the 1956 Restrictive Trade Practices Act. But notwithstanding these agreements, the MMC considered that keen competition existed in the industry at the retail level, and that the identical prices of the three national companies was not evidence of restricted competition. It recognized that statutory controls had exaggerated the relative returns from flour milling as against bread making.

The supply of pet foods was one of the first references (July 1975) to the MMC by the newly created Office of Fair Trading (OFT). The MMC concluded that the monopoly positions of both Pedigree Petfoods and Spillers were not against the public interest. It is particularly worth noting that the MMC offered no substantive criticism of the industry's advertising expenditures as a barrier to entry that had apparently prompted the reference. Moreover, the only recommendation made by the MMC in its 1976 report on the supply of frozen foods concerned the practice of Birds Eye Foods whereby those retailers willing to reserve space in their freezer cabinets were given discounts. After nearly a year's discussion with the OFT the company undertook to drop this restriction of competition, an offer not matched by the other two major suppliers.

In October 1976 the supply of ice-cream was referred to the MMC by the OFT. The MMC in its report published in August 1979 viewed certain trading practices as restricting competition and contrary to the public interest. These practices related to exclusive ties between ice-cream suppliers and retailers both in respect of refrigerated cabinets and in the supply of ice-cream products. After lengthy discussions extending over three years the government announced that forty suppliers had terminated these exclusive ties. The two biggest suppliers – Wall's and Lyons – also relaxed trading terms relating to retrospective bonuses such that retailers had greater freedom of choice in their source of supplier.

Turning now to mergers there have been only three reports by the MMC of take-over bids relating to food processing firms. However, the role of the MMC in government policy towards mergers has none the less been controversial. The decision not to refer to the MMC either the Tate & Lyle bid for Manbré & Garton in 1976 or Imperial Tobacco's proposed acquisition of J. B. Eastwood in 1978 was clearly contrary to the views of both the OFT and the Secretary of State for Prices and Consumer Protection. Sugar-using food processors, such as confectionery firms, and multiple retail chains were critical of the government's decision not to subject the Tate & Lyle bid to scrutiny by the MMC. In both cases fears concerning employment were uppermost in the mind of the government and the Minister of Agriculture in favouring the mergers. In due course, the sugar industry did become the subject of study by the MMC – in 1981 and again in 1987 (MMC, 1981b, 1987).

In the former report the MMC was not enthusiastic about the monopoly supplier of sugar refined from beet sugar, the British Sugar Corporation (BSC), being acquired by the sugar trading firm of S. & W. Berisford and stipulated two conditions to ensure the public interest was not adversely affected. Lord Cockfield, the then Secretary of State for Trade, required Berisford to cease trading in cane sugar refined by BSC's main competitor, Tate & Lyle. Berisford was also required to maintain BSC as a separately accountable subsidiary. In 1986 a take-over bid for Berisford from Hillsdown Holdings prompted a rival bid from Tate & Lyle. The latter's interest in Berisford lay in its keenness to enter the UK beet sugar industry and avoid its dependence on that part of the market reliant on imported cane sugar and subject to regulation by the European Community. Both bids for Berisford were referred to the MMC in May 1986 as was a third bid from Ferruzzi, a sugar firm based in Italy. This decision prompted Hillsdown to withdraw its offer. In its report published in February 1987 the MMC opposed the take-over of BSC by either of the remaining bidders. It pointed out the need for the European Community to reappraise its policy on the refining of beet sugar and imported cane sugar.

The third MMC report of a merger between food processing firms arose from the competing bids of Rowntree Macintosh and Nabisco for Huntley & Palmer in 1982. Nabisco outbid its rival but did not persuade all members of the MMC of the desirability of its proposed course of action. The merger was not opposed by a majority of the MMC but in a note of dissent two members argued that the merger would result in Nabisco and United Biscuits having a combined share of over 70 per cent of the market in snack foods. In their view this would give power to these firms to raise prices and by high levels of advertising, make entry more difficult. A notable aspect of the MMC's inquiry was its suggestion to Nabisco that Huntley & Palmer's snack food business be excluded from the merger proposal. Nabisco declined this proposal – a decision which clearly risked an unfavourable verdict from the MMC. But in the event with a majority verdict from the MMC it gained market share in both the biscuit and potato crisp markets from acquiring Huntley & Palmer.

It was these two food markets which provided another controversial take-over situation four years later. In 1985 United Biscuits and Imperial Tobacco announced that they planned to merge. This merger was widely regarded as a defensive move for both companies since both had been the subject of take-over speculation. The two parties to the proposed merger made determined efforts to avoid referral to the MMC by discussing with the OFT possible disposals of some of their food interests. In the event Imperial was acquired by Hanson Trust which subsequently sold off Imperial's crisp and snack food Golden Wonder subsidiary to Dalgety. But the negotiations by Imperial and United Biscuits with the OFT raised questions for the first time about the detached role of the OFT in advising the government on mergers policy.

The major area of public debate in the food sector has been the 'vertical conflict' between food processors and retailers. The use by the major retailers of their buying power to secure favourable trading rms from food processors has been a controversial issue. The MMC was asked to investigate the matter in July 1977 and published its report four years later. It established that food processors frequently conceded discounts that were not closely related to cost economies of bulk orders.

As the MMC put it in its report on discounts to retailers,

> For the manufacturer who has committed large capital resources to production and who needs a high level of throughput to minimise his unit costs, sales to his largest retail customers are crucial . . . Few food manufacturers are able to resist [retailer] pressures altogether, particularly in respect of products for which there is surplus production capacity.
>
> (MMC, 1981a, p. 31).

The report provided evidence that large retailers have negotiated very favourable trading terms with food processors that exceeded the economies resulting from large orders. But the MMC concluded that

> As competition between retailers has been keen and vigorous, the benefits of these lower buying prices have been substantially passed on to customers in the form of prices which are lower than they would otherwise have been and possibly through improved service. Although the practice may in certain circumstances result in manufacturers' prices to some retailer buyers being higher than they would otherwise have been, competition among retailers reduces the extent to which this results in consumers paying higher prices. It is our view that, in general, retail prices are lower than they would have been in the absence of the practice.
>
> (MMC, 1981a, p. 68)

The MMC's report dismayed organizations representing independent retailers who argued that their members were adversely affected by discrimination and put at an unfair disadvantage in competition with multiple retailers. The OFT was under sustained pressure to reopen inquiry into the matter – which it did in 1984. However, in its update on the MMC report the OFT concluded that its fact-finding exercise did not lead it to differ from the MMC's judgement of the matter (OFT, 1985). None the less the trading relationships between processors and retailers continues to be a contentious issue.

In its 1981 report the MMC recognized that in the longer term the expected continued fall in the number of independent retail shops might eventually result in some lessening in the degree of price competition between the retail chains. Hence it urged that the OFT should keep merger activity by the leading distributors under close scrutiny. The OFT soon found it appropriate to recommend to the Secretary of State for Trade that the MMC examine the proposed merger of Linfood Holdings and Fitch Lovell in 1983. The concern with the continuance of effective competition amongst retailers was uppermost in its report but the MMC declared that even if there was an undesirable imbalance of bargaining power to the disadvantage of food processors it did not think that prevention of the merger would do anything to redress the matter. In the event, as noted earlier, Fitch Lovell retained its independence but sold Key Markets, its retail interests, to Linfood.

CONCLUSION

The above review of public policies has shown how much the food industry has been the subject of government attention during the past decade. Take-over bids, the relationships with food retailers and the concern of consumers about the foods they eat are three issues which have ensured that this sector of the UK economy is subject to much political pressure and media attention. One can be quite confident in forecasting that there will be little change in this situation in the foreseeable future as food processors continue to seek ways of achieving growth in static markets.

NOTES TO CHAPTER 9

1 These figures are derived from 'The Annual Review of Grocery Trading' in the *Nielsen Researcher*, 1961 and 1971 (Oxford: Nielsen).
2 *Hansard*, 799, 6 April 1970, cols 25–6.
3 *Hansard*, 852, 5 March 1973, cols 13–14.
4 Data taken from *The Grocery Marketing Scene* (Oxford: Nielsen).
5 *The Times 1000*, 1986–7 (London: Times Books).
6 'British food companies', *The Economist*, 14 December 1985, p. 65.
7 G. Nuttall, 'All beefed up for battle of the cubes', *Sunday Times*, 26 February 1978. The estimates mentioned in this paragraph relate to the size of the market at the time of the relevant investigation. However the percentages are also likely to be more or less valid for the present, since sales in real terms have been static.
8 One supplier of bakery equipment estimated a capital requirement of £39,000 in 1985. *The Grocer*, 13 July 1985, p. 70.
9 '£250,000 factory expansion by Romix', *The Grocer*, 20 April 1974, p. 85.
10 'Performance of large companies', *Bank of England Quarterly Bulletin*, 25, 3 (September 1985), p. 437.
11 Food and Drink Manufacturing EDC, *Progress Report 1978*, NEDO, p. 10.

REFERENCES

Advertising Association (1983), *Statistical Yearbook 1* (London).
Advisory Council for Applied Research and Development (Cabinet Office) (1982), *Report on the Food Industry and Technology* (London: HMSO).
Bevan, A. (1974), 'The UK potato crisp industry, 1960–72: a study of new entry competition', *Journal of Industrial Economics*, XXII, 4, 281–97.
Capel, James, & Co. (1970), *Food Majors in the Seventies* (London: Capel).
Committee on Medical Aspects of Food Policy (1984), *Diet and Cardiovascular Disease* (London: HMSO).
Cuthbert, N., and Black, W. (1959), 'Restrictive practices in the food trades', *Journal of Industrial Economics*, VIII, 1, 33–57.
Food and Drink Manufacturing EDC (1978), *Productivity Growth in the UK Food and Drink Manufacturing Industry* (London: NEDO).
Food and Drink Manufacturing EDC (1982), *Improving Productivity in the Food and Drink Manufacturing Industry: the Case for a Joint Approach* (London: HMSO).
Freeman, C. (1971), *The Role of Small Firms in Innovation in the UK since 1945*, Research Report no. 6 for Committee of Inquiry on Small Firms (London: HMSO).
Harris, S. A., Swinbank, A., and Wilkinson, G. (1983), *The Food and Farm Policies of the European Community* (Chichester, Sussex: Wiley).
Kraushar, Andrews & Eassie Ltd (1976), *New Products in the Grocery Trades: a UK Study* (London: Kraushar, Andrews & Eassie).
Lawrence, G. K. (1976), '100 years of progress in the food processing industry', Ministry of Agriculture, Fisheries and Food, in *Food Quality and Safety: a Century of Progress* (London: HMSO).
Leak, H., and Maizels, A. (1945), 'The structure of British industry', *Journal of Royal Statistical Society*, 108, parts 1–2, 142–207.
Maunder, W. P. J. (1970), 'The UK food processing and distributive trades: an appraisal of public policies', *Journal of Agricultural Economics*, XXI, 3, 455–64.
Mitchell, Joan (1972), *The National Board for Prices and Incomes* (London: Secker & Warburg).
Monopolies Commission (1971), *Starch, Glucoses and Modified Starch*, HC 615 (London: HMSO).
Monopolies Commission (1973), *Supply of Breakfast Cereals*, HC 2 (London: HMSO).
Monopolies and Mergers Commission (1976), *Frozen Foods*, HC 674 (London: HMSO).
Monopolies and Mergers Commission (1977a), *Flour and Bread*, HC 412 (London: HMSO).
Monopolies and Mergers Commission (1977b), *Cat and Dog Foods*, HC 447 (London: HMSO).
Monopolies and Mergers Commission (1979), *Ice Cream and Water Ices*, Cmnd 7632 (London: HMSO).
Monopolies and Mergers Commission (1981a), *Discounts to Retailers*, HC 311 (London: HMSO).
Monopolies and Mergers Commission (1981b), *S & W Berisford Ltd and the British Sugar Corporation Ltd*, HC 241 (London: HMSO).

Monopolies and Mergers Commission (1987), *Tate & Lyle plc and Ferruzz. Finanziaria Spa and S & W Berisford plc*, Cm 89 (London: HMSO).

National Advisory Committee on Nutrition Education (1983), *Proposals for Nutritional Guidelines for Health Education in Britain* (London: Health Education Council).

Office of Fair Trading (1985), *Competition and Retailing: a Study to Update Information*, in the *1981 Report of the MMC Discounts to Retailers* (London).

Palamountain, J. C. (1955), *The Politics of Distribution* (Cambridge, Mass.: Harvard University Press).

Smith, A. (1776), *The Wealth of Nations*, Book 1, reprinted in A. Skinner (ed.) (Harmondsworth, Middx: Pelican), 1970.

Townsend, J., Henwood, F., Thomas, G., Pavitt, K., and Wyatt, S. (1981), *Science and Technology Indicators for the UK: Innovations in Britain Since 1945* (Brighton, Sussex: Science Policy Research Unit, Sussex University).

Walker, C., and Cannon, G.(1984), *The Food Scandal* (London: Century Publishing).

Walshe, G. (1974), *Recent Trends in Monopoly in Great Britain* (Cambridge: Cambridge University Press).

FURTHER READING

Burns, J. (1983), 'The UK food chain with particular reference to the inter-relations between manufacturers and distributors', *Journal of Agricultural Economics*, XXXIV, 4, 361–78.

Burns, J., McInerney, J., and Swinbank, A. (eds) (1983), *The Food Industry: Economics and Policies* (London: Heinemann).

Guy, K. (ed.) (1984), *Technological Trends and Employment, Vol. 1, Basic Consumer Goods* (Aldershot, Hants: Gower).

Jordan Information Services Ltd (1985), *The British Food Processing Industry* (London).

The Technical Change Centre (1985), *The United Kingdom Food Processing Industry: Opportunities for Change* (London: The Technical Change Centre).

Chapter Ten

Construction

MICHAEL FLEMING

10.1 INTRODUCTION

The construction industry is responsible for the provision, repair, maintenance and demolition of buildings of all kinds, including their internal finishes and services, and also the wide variety of other types of structure – such as roads, bridges and dams – embraced by the term 'civil engineering works'. Over the last decade or so it has suffered a severe contraction in both absolute and relative size: while gross domestic product (GDP) rose by 16 per cent over the period 1973–85, construction output *fell* by 15 per cent. None the less it remains one of the nation's largest industries, currently contributing around 6 per cent of GDP, as against 7.6 per cent in 1973 (a peak year). It is three times as large as agriculture and nearly twice as large as the largest manufacturing industry; it is rivalled in size only by broad service sectors such as distribution. These figures, however, probably understate the relative position of construction because of the importance nowadays of unrecorded work carried out in the 'hidden' or 'black' economy.

The industry is even more important as an employer, particularly of males, a growing proportion of whom are self-employed. It is estimated that about 9 per cent of the total male labour force worked in construction in 1985.[1] The economic significance of the industry, however, is even greater than these figures would suggest, for it is pre-eminent in providing the major part of national capital investment: buildings and works regularly represent around 45–55 per cent of gross domestic fixed capital formation each year (45 per cent in 1985) and constitute over two-thirds of the nation's accumulated stock of fixed capital. A substantial part of the activity of the industry is devoted to the repair and maintenance of the existing stock rather than the construction of additions to it. For these reasons the industry occupies a position of central economic importance.

The demand facing the industry possesses two distinctive characteristics. First, the demand for the product is geographically dispersed but the product itself is not generally transportable. While some work may be prefabricated in factory conditions, the structure must ultimately be provided at a particular location, fixed as it were, to the site and, in the

Table 10.1 *Legal Units by Turnover Size, UK, 1985 (percentages)*

Turnover size (£ thousand in 1983)	Sole proprietors	Partnerships	Companies and public corporations	General govt. and non-profit-making bodies	Total
19–50	72.0	53.8	23.9	40.4	51.3
51–250	26.1	40.5	43.7	26.2	35.1
251–500	1.4	4.0	14.9	14.3	6.7
501–1,000	0.4	1.2	8.8	19.0	3.6
1001–5,000 ⎤			7.0	–	2.6
5001–10,000 ⎬	0.1	0.4	0.8	–	0.3
Over 10,000 ⎦			0.7	–	0.3
Total	100.0	100.0	100.0	100.0	100.0
Base number	82,517	34,205	65,151	42	181,915
Row%	45.4%	18.8%	35.8%	–	100.0%

Notes: Columns may not sum to 100 due to rounding.
  – = nil or less than 0.05%.

Source: Business Monitor PA 1003, London, HMSO, 1986.

case of buildings, connected to mains services (electricity, water, sewers and so on). Thus the advantages which firms in other industries may gain from centralized production in factory conditions do not apply in the construction industry. Secondly, productive activity cannot in general precede the receipt of orders: work has to be carried out under contract, to meet the individual requirements of a large number of separate clients. The only exceptions are in those sectors where builders are able to undertake speculative development in advance of demand – in the main, private housebuilding. Consequently, contractors are faced with a high degree of uncertainty: their work-load is dependent upon their success in winning some of an essentially unpredictable number of highly varied contracts coming forward, the number and value of which can fluctuate very considerably. Differences between one site and another and the exposed conditions of the work itself also add to the uncertainties of contracting.

Together these factors help to explain the organization and structure of the industry and also exercise an important influence on the market behaviour of firms and their economic performance in terms of productive efficiency and technical progress.

10.2 MARKET STRUCTURE

10.2.1 Organization and Structure

Unlike much of manufacturing industry in Britain, which has been subject to a pronounced trend towards higher and higher levels of industrial concentration, the construction industry remains, as it has

Table 10.2   *Number of Firms, Employment and Output by Size of Firm in Great Britain, 1985 (percentages)*

Size of firm (number employed)	Main trades	Number of firms Specialist trades	All trades	Employment	Value of work done (third quarter)
1	38.2	47.6	43.4	7.2	6.4
2–7	51.2	43.4	46.8	24.3	19.2
8–24	7.3	6.8	7.0	16.4	15.5
25–79	2.3	1.8	2.0	14.8	15.6
80–299	0.8	0.4	0.5	13.6	15.5
300–1199	} 0.2	0.1	0.1	12.2	14.7
1200 and over			–	11.5	13.0
All firms	100	100	100	100	100
Total number/value	(73,760)	(94,065)	(167,825)	(941,100)	(£5,974.3m)

Notes: Main trades include general builders, building and civil engineering contractors and civil engineering firms.
   — = nil or less than 0.05%.
Source: Housing and Construction Statistics 1974–85, London, HMSO, 1986.

long been, an industry comprised of a large number of predominantly small firms. The same is true in other countries (Fleming, 1977). In Britain it also consists of a not insignificant public sector: construction labour is employed in direct works departments ('direct labour') by most local authorities and by many other public bodies. Currently only part of this labour is officially classified to the industry but this part constitutes about one-sixth of the total labour force and provides about one-tenth of total output. Their work, however, is predominantly (all but a tenth) repairs and maintenance. Therefore, this chapter will concentrate mainly on the private sector of the industry which is responsible for the greater part of output, particularly of new work.

Tables 10.1 and 10.2 illustrate the structure of the industry. Almost two-thirds of the firms operate as sole proprietors or partnerships, rather than companies, and over half of all firms ('legal units') have turnovers of less than £50,000 (1983 prices). Little more than 3 per cent have turnovers greater than the relatively modest level of £1 million – that is, equivalent to around 30 new houses (Table 10.1). The size structure of the industry is further illustrated in Table 10.2 which gives details of employment and output by size of firm in 1985. It will be seen that out of nearly 168,000 registered firms,[2] about 90 per cent employ fewer than 8 persons. The importance of small firms, however, should not be overemphasized: at the other end of the scale less than 1 per cent of firms (1,167 firms altogether) employed 80 persons or more, but these were responsible for over a third of output and employment.

The structure of the industry appears to have changed markedly over the last few years. Whereas in the first edition of this work it appeared that the mean size of firm had remained much the same over the postwar period, it now appears that the mean size has fallen very considerably from 9.4 to 3.3 *operatives* (that is, employees who do manual work) per firm between 1977 and 1985 (or from 13 to 5 *persons*). To some extent this is a statistical artefact due to the underrecording of small firms on the Department of the Environment (DOE) statistical register in 1977.[3] On the other hand, it does also reflect the underlying economic reality inasmuch as a large number of new small firms have entered the industry (*British Business*, 19 September 1986, pp. 6–7) and it is notable that even the large firms in the industry (the number of which is less likely to be underrecorded) have also declined in size. Further, it is also a reflection of the tendency for an increasing proportion of the labour force to work as self-employed, most of whom (all except working proprietors) are not recorded in the employment data used in the size analyses above.

The multitude of small firms that persists in construction and the apparently unchanging methods of work are sometimes viewed as the cause of – what is held to be – inferior economic performance and are especially contrasted with the trends in manufacturing industry which has been subject to such pronounced changes in structure and production methods. The economic rationale for the structure of the construction industry, however, is not far to seek. It is to be found in factors associated with the nature of demand and the nature of the product itself to which reference has been made.

The geographically dispersed pattern of demand and the non-transportability of the product naturally tend to produce a similarly dispersed organization of construction enterprises and there is in fact a close correspondence between the regional distribution of firms and the regional distribution of work. The work itself is highly diversified by type, size, function, form and method of construction, and in the materials used, and its execution requires the services of many different trades. These services are generally provided by specialist firms operating under subcontract – few contractors carry out the full range of operations required. As Table 10.2 indicates, less than half of the firms are general builders and contractors; the rest specialize in the work of particular crafts or service installations or in the provision of services to main contractors, such as plant hire or scaffolding erection, and most of these firms remain smaller than the general contractors.

Some firms, of course, are prepared to undertake large contracts (many of which would be beyond the capacity of localized builders) anywhere in the country – and indeed anywhere in the world – and these firms have grown to a substantial size (though nowhere near as large as the giants of manufacturing industry). But the number of large contracts available is small and most of the work may be handled by the small and medium-sized local contractors. The actual number of contracts available each year is very large (currently over 100,000 for new work – many of which are subdivided into smaller subcontracts –

Table 10.3   *Size Distribution of Orders for New Work in Great Britain, 1985*

Size of order (value range) (£'000)	Number (%)	Value (%)
25 and under 50	36.1	6.6
50 and under 100	28.8	10.3
100 and under 200	16.8	12.1
200 and under 500	11.5	17.9
500 and under 1,000	3.9	13.7
1,000 and under 2,000	1.8	12.5
2,000 and over	1.1	26.9
	100.0	100.0

| | Total number and values | |
	('000)	(£m)
£25,000 and over	68.8	14,437
Under £25,000	n/a	906
All	n/a	15,343

Source: Department of the Environment unpublished data.

and possibly as many for repair and maintenance work) but only a minority of these exceed £100,000 in value – itself a very low figure, equivalent to a mere three houses or so (Table 10.3).

Indicators of the size of leading companies in the industry are shown in Table 10.4. However, it should be appreciated that the market shares of individual companies are difficult to assess because they are engaged in both construction and non-construction activities at home and overseas and these are not always separately distinguished in company accounts. The table is therefore indicative only. But, it is notable that the relative size of the market leaders is very small: the domestic turnover of construction work of the largest firm in 1985 (£663 million) represented a mere 2–3 per cent of total construction work done in Great Britain in 1985 (£27,850 million). In some sectors of work, however, the degree of concentration may be more marked. In the private housebuilding sector, for example, it appears that the largest firm in 1985 (Barratt Developments) had about 7 per cent of the market (*Financial Times*, 4 February 1986, p. 18).

10.2.2   Conditions of Entry and the Growth of Firms

The relative and absolute cost advantages which often favour large-scale operations and large established firms in manufacturing are of little importance as barriers to entry or as factors encouraging the growth of greater industrial concentration in construction. This is not

Table 10.4 *Leading Firms in the UK Construction Industry, 1985*

Firm[a]	Turnover (£m)				*Average weekly workforce UK All activities*
	United Kingdom		*UK and overseas*		
	Construction[b]	*All activities*	*Construction[b]*	*All activities*	
John Laing	663	n/a	n/a	817	10,200
George Wimpey	(528)	945	1,164	1,581	16,000
Taylor Woodrow	(400)	532	641	812	7,810

Notes:

[a] The firms listed here are the market leaders in the UK. Other firms are larger in terms of total turnover for all activities at home and overseas. Those firms would include Trafalgar House (a large conglomerate: £1,912m), Tarmac (£1,571m) and Costain (£940m).

[b] Covers building, engineering and housebuilding but may include some activities not formally classified as part of the construction industry in official statistics. Figures in parentheses are estimates.

Source: The author is grateful to Savory Milln Ltd for their help in compiling this table.

to deny that some large contracts demand the technical expertise and resources possessed by large contractors but these are the exceptions rather than the rule and in practice their importance is further reduced by the technical conditions of production.

The site-based nature of construction, where each site is necessarily a temporary place of work, and the individuality of most projects ensure that the conditions necessary for the existence of many technical scale economies, namely the centralization of production of standard products using specialized production techniques, do not apply. It is true that some types of scale economy exist but these are related to the size of individual contracts and the degree of repetitive work involved rather than the size of firm undertaking them. As already indicated, however, the majority of contracts are small, few provide any scope for large-scale repetitive work – housing would be the main exception – and, apart from speculative housing, neither the size of contract nor the nature of the work is within the control of the builder. The influence of these factors as entry barriers or in favouring the growth of established firms is therefore limited.

It is also true that specialization of function – an important source of scale economies – does occur in building as elsewhere. But, as indicated above, in building it has been specialization by trade – representing parts of construction work such as roofing, plumbing, and so on – and not by type of building. This fact reinforces still further the tendency towards small scale, because such firms undertake only part of the work on the contract, and facilitates the establishment of new firms by craftsmen in the relevant trades. It is the case that some firms do tend to specialize on particular types of work – for instance, civil engineering and housebuilding represent two sectors in which some firms specialize – but rarely do firms confine their activities solely to one type. There is no technical reason, generally speaking, for narrowing activities to one sector, for many of the basic processes involved in most types of construction work are similar, and the nature of demand itself provides good reason for not doing so. Specialization would make firms more vulnerable to fluctuations in demand because the demand for particular types of work is generally less stable than the demand for construction work generally. There are sound commercial reasons, therefore, for a contractor to broaden his market by tendering for a variety of jobs within his technical and financial capacity. Moreover, it has been shown (DSIR, 1953) that specialist subcontractors are generally more efficient than main contractors doing comparable items of work.

Thus, specialization by trade represents a rational response to the fragmented, heterogeneous and uncertain nature of demand and the technical nature of the construction process itself. It provides great flexibility in coping with the highly varied demands placed upon the industry, for the ability to subcontract parts of a contract as necessary enables contractors to take on jobs over the wide range of sizes that exist in practice with gains, rather than losses, in efficiency.

Ease of entry and the existing structure are further sustained by low capital requirements both in terms of fixed and current assets. The buildings required for most manufacturing processes are not needed by contractors and plant requirements are also limited, because many building processes – especially the craft-based processes – are not amenable to mechanization. The total stock of fixed capital in the industry is equivalent to little more than one year's wage and salary bill, but even this exaggerates the importance of fixed capital requirements for many firms. Much of the capital represents heavy equipment for which the needs of many firms are met by a highly developed plant-hire sector and for which many of the specialist firms have no need at all. Working capital is also limited, for although construction projects may be large (relative to the size of a firm) and have to be financed over lengthy construction periods, the financial requirements are met by regular progress payments from clients and trade credit from materials suppliers. Many contractors increase the self-financing of jobs further by pricing early parts of the work at a high level in order to raise their net receipts in the early stages of the work.

The scope for gaining competitive advantages by other means such as control over raw material supplies or by patent protection is also severely constricted or non-existent. Materials account for a major part of total costs, but they are drawn from a wide range of extractive and manufacturing industries: no one material predominates. It is generally impracticable, therefore, for a contractor to meet his own general materials requirements and there is little advantage in providing for his own needs of a single material (indeed small-scale production could well be disadvantageous). For the materials producer, forward integration into construction provides little advantage because no one contractor is able to provide an adequate outlet, especially as many building materials industries are highly concentrated. The result is that vertical integration is of little importance in construction. Patent protection in such a long-established assembly industry as construction in which traditional craft processes have proved difficult to replace is also of no significance as a barrier to competition. Similarly the nature of demand is such that firms in construction are not able to raise barriers to entry artificially by marketing strategies such as product differentiation and advertising which are so important for branded manufactured products.

In summary then, no natural barriers to entry exist and the scope for artificial barriers is also virtually non-existent. This is not to say, of course, that a new entrant is able to enter and compete in any field of construction, tackling jobs of any size, type, or complexity. But the availability of small-scale work (which trade specialization and a large volume of small repair and maintenance jobs provide) coupled with the limited financial and capital requirements of firms ensure that construction is an industry of easy entry and, given free competition, it is possible for new entrants to extend the range and scale of their activities over time and thus to challenge the larger existing firms. In addition domestic contractors are also open to foreign competition, although in practice it appears to be limited. On the other hand, the large British contractors compete successfully for contracts abroad over a wide front: in recent years the annual value of such contracts has ranged from almost a quarter of domestic orders (1982/3) to one-tenth (1985/6).

10.3 MARKET BEHAVIOUR

10.3.1 Competition and the Market Environment

The large number of firms and the absence of barriers to entry (or exit) provide essential competitive conditions. These are strengthened by the fact that few of the marketing strategies which many manufacturing firms are able to employ to influence their level of sales are open to firms in construction. As indicated earlier, advertising and product differentiation activities are largely ruled out because, apart from design-and-construct companies (discussed later) and speculative builders, contractors have no product as such to sell. Moreover, research and development activity, which is often important as the foundation for product and process innovation in manufacturing industry, also finds little counterpart as a competitive weapon in construction because the design and content of each job are normally outside the control of the builder. Similarly, market conditions are such that there is little or no opportunity or incentive for firms in construction to pursue market power through market dominance attained either by merger or by internal expansion. There has been no growth in the average size of firms in the industry (indeed the reverse is true) and while construction has not been untouched by the intense merger activity of the last 20 years it has not increased concentration.

Naturally, the large number of firms in the industry are not all in competition for the same contracts because of the localized nature of the work and the specialized nature of some contracts. Further, some firms operate under common ownership and control and, therefore, are not truly independent. But in general no contractor is able to exert any control over the market environment in which he operates. Apart from speculative work and contracts obtained by negotiation, firms are dependent for their survival upon their success in competitive tendering. In principle, competitive tendering is a device which enables a client to select the most efficient contractor from among those willing to undertake his particular project. Disallowing the possibility of non-competitive behaviour by contractors in tendering (further considered below), it is the mechanism through which the resource allocation function of the market is performed in construction. The operation of this mechanism, therefore, deserves close attention.

In letting a contract, some clients may prefer to pre-select a contractor (on the basis of their own experience of working with him in the past or on the recommendation of others) and to negotiate the terms of the contract with him. The normal method, however, is to award the job to the contractor submitting the lowest price in competition. Competition may be 'open' in which case any firm may submit a tender, or may be limited to a select list of contractors who are invited to tender. It may be argued that open competition promotes efficiency because it allows each firm willing to undertake the work an equal opportunity of winning the contract. Many associated with the industry argue, however, that the expense involved in the preparation of tenders by an unlimited number of firms is unnecessary and raises the general level of costs – costs which have to be recouped in successful tenders. Further, it is argued that very low prices resulting from indiscriminate tendering lead to bad building, for any builder who has quoted too low a price and is faced with a loss if he does a good job is tempted to cut the quality of his work. Open competition, therefore, is said to be a system which encourages firms that work to the lowest standards and does not ensure value for money. This was the view of official committees in 1944 (Ministry of Works, 1944) and 1964 (Ministry of Public Building and Works, 1964). These committees recommended, therefore, that competition should be limited to a number of firms carefully selected as being capable of, and likely to do, work of the standard required.

Recent surveys have shown that selective tendering is now in widespread use: in the public sector about two-thirds of building contracts and almost four-fifths of civil engineering contracts were let in this way; open competition was used for less than one-fifth of contracts (National Economic Development Office, 1975). Open competition is also apparently little used in important parts of the private sector (Hillebrandt, 1974). The support for selective competition as a means of selecting a contractor, however, must be tempered by other considerations. First, a traditional argument in favour of open competition is that it satisfies, at least overtly, the requirements of public accountability for the expenditure of public money and is a safeguard against corruption through favouritism in the award of contracts. Selective tendering does not necessarily fail to satisfy these requirements but it needs explicit precautions to be taken. Secondly, such tendering may stultify the selective mechanism of the market by sustaining some firms with an established reputation but obstructing the development of others. Up-and-coming firms may be caught in the vicious circle of being unable to gain a place on a select list because they are unable to demonstrate their financial and technical capacity to handle certain types of project and this in turn may be due to their inability to gain contracts of the appropriate type because they are precluded from tendering in the first place. Much, therefore, depends on the way in which select lists of contractors are compiled and maintained. The list may be a standing list or an *ad hoc* list that is compiled specifically for a particular job. In either case it is essential that new firms should be regularly considered for admission to the list, and listed firms regularly considered for promotion or relegation to higher or lower categories on it or removal altogether. Unfortunately, it appears that current practices leave something to be desired in this respect (NEDO, 1975, para. 5.14). Thirdly, because selective tendering may restrict competition to a limited number of firms of a certain type, the possibility of collusion amongst them is facilitated. This is especially true where standing lists are maintained.

The resource savings that the greater use of selective tendering have produced are, of course, impossible to judge. But they should not be overrated. No information is available about how far the number of tenders submitted for each job has been reduced, although Newcombe (1978) has suggested that many local authorities, at any rate, still use fairly large select lists. Against any savings obtained (including those arising from the more timely completion of jobs and perhaps the readier achievement of satisfactory standards) must be put the costs incurred by the client in operating a selective tendering system and also the economic costs involved when the system is not operated with sufficient flexibility to ensure that competition for a particular job takes place among the firms best fitted to carry it out and takes place without collusion. The danger is, therefore, that short-term gains here, as elsewhere, may be bought at the expense of greater long-term losses.

10.3.2 Non-Competitive Behaviour

Given the large number of firms in construction and the large number of contracts let each year, it is impossible for effective collusion to occur on a national scale. It may be easier to organize, however, where the number of potential competitors is limited either by the client – as in selective tendering – or where a natural limitation arises on account of the size, character, or location of the work itself. Contractors may then learn the identity of their competitors and come to some arrangement among themselves about the prices each should submit, coupled perhaps, with some scheme of compensation to be paid to the unsuccessful tenderers by the successful one.

The best-documented example of a more generalized scheme of collusive tendering is one which was operated by the London Builders' Conference (LBC) and investigated by the Monopolies Commission in the early 1950s (HMSO, 1954). In the present context, however, it is notable that the effectiveness of this scheme was limited: out of 6,903 competitions, LBC members won only 1,687 and of these there were only 95 for which the pricing was organized through the conference.

Since 1956 restrictive arrangements of this kind have become subject to registration and investigation under the restrictive trade practices legislation including, since 1968, agreements simply to exchange information about prices. Not all registrable restrictions are in fact registered and in construction a number of unregistered arrangements among contractors tendering for electrical and mechanical engineering services contracts were detected in the 1960s, as a result of which injunctions were obtained against 99 firms (HMSO, 1973). The usual arrangement in these cases was for the exchange of information about prices and the joint determination of the bid to be submitted as the lowest, coupled with a scheme of compensation. Some of the arrangements also involved the giving and taking of 'cover prices', that is prices high enough to ensure that the firm quoting them will *not* win the contract but low enough to appear realistic. A firm may submit a cover price not only when it is a party to a restrictive arrangement but also when it does not wish to increase its work-load but fears a loss of goodwill and possible removal from a select list by refusing to tender or by putting in a clearly unrealistic price.

Just how much collusive tendering still occurs and how much of it is encouraged by the greater use of selective competition is impossible to say. It is perhaps notable that in all the cases of collusion referred to above a limited number of contractors had been invited to tender. Certainly the increased danger of collusion is one to which too little attention is now given by the proponents of selective competition. However, it remains true that selective competition does possess advantages in principle, and it would also seem impossible to sustain a general argument that the construction industry is conspicuously non-competitive. There would seem to be no reason to believe that generalized schemes of the type operated by the London Builders' Conference, if they now exist at all, are any more effective now than they were in the early postwar years. Moreover, while it is undesirable to underrate the importance of the collusive schemes revealed recently, it is notable that they all related to a specialized sector of the industry.

10.4 PERFORMANCE

The economic performance of the construction industry is often compared unfavourably with that of many other industries. It is clear, for instance, that much construction is still carried out in traditional ways and this is contrasted with the increasingly mechanized and automated processes that have transformed production in many other sectors. It is also clear that construction prices tend to rise faster than the prices of other goods: over the period since 1948 the prices of capital goods in general and also of goods and services in general have increased by around 11–12 times compared with 14 times for construction. This difference is mainly explained by the fact that productivity in construction has not increased at the same rate as elsewhere. It is not possible to measure changes in the productivity of the construction industry as a whole over time satisfactorily but it is clear that the disproportionate rise in prices cannot be accounted for by disproportionate increases in the unit cost of factor inputs.

It is a mistake, however, to equate the scope for productivity improvement in such a long-established industry as construction with that available in industries at earlier stages of development and where technological conditions are more favourable. It is also a mistake to regard the failure to increase productivity at a rate commensurate with that attained elsewhere as being a result either of the structure of the industry as such or of the behaviour of contractors themselves. While the price of a particular job and the level of efficiency with which it is carried out are determined by the contractor on that job, many factors which affect his performance – in particular design and technical constraints – are not within his control. The performance of the industry and the scope for improvement can only be considered, therefore, in the context of these factors, and it is these to which most attention is devoted here.

As indicated earlier, most construction projects have to be carried out in accordance with the individual requirements of particular clients. These requirements are normally translated into a particular design and specification by independent architects and/or civil and structural engineers and other consultants who are commissioned by the client. The contractor who is going to be responsible for the physical realization of the project normally plays no part in this process, only appearing on the scene when the process is complete, or virtually complete, and the contract is ready to be let. This division between the design and production stages is a factor of great potential importance, for it precludes any interaction between design and production considerations except in so far as production aspects may be taken into account by the designer. Designers, however, can only do this in fairly general terms, for traditionally they have received little training in such matters and their practical experience is limited to that obtained indirectly in contract supervision – experience that involves transient relationships with different contractors on *ad hoc* jobs. Thus the separation of the design and production functions in construction precludes the close co-operation between designers and producers, which is important from a productivity point of view, and also limits the possibility of the feedback of production experience into subsequent design. This contrasts sharply with the close integration between design and production achieved in much of manufacturing industry where, typically, the main decisions – those concerning product range and quality, volume of output, and techniques and location of production – are all decided within the firm by its own managerial and technical (design and production) staff.

The organizational pattern in construction is one which has evolved over a considerable period of time in response to changes in demand and technical developments. Demands for larger and more complex structures, the introduction of more mechanical and electrical engineering services in them, the use of new materials, and new uses for old materials (for example, pre-stressed concrete) have been met by the employment of specialist design consultants and specialist subcontractors (often nominated by the architect in order to safeguard the standards and performance of this part of the work). Thus considerable fragmention of function and responsibility has developed on each side of the design–production divide. From the point of view of efficiency it gives rise to a fundamental problem to which there is no easy solution. Various responses to it are considered below.

Various ways of integrating design and production may be tried. First, the client and his designer may select a contractor at an early stage of the design process so that he may work in close association with the design team. Since no finished design exists upon which contractors may be invited to tender in competition, the contract has to be negotiated with a selected contractor. The main disadvantage of this approach is, of course, the lack of competition and the difficulty facing the client in ensuring the negotiation of a 'fair' price. In the early 1970s about 14 per cent of building (as opposed to civil engineering) contracts in the public sector were negotiated (NEDO, 1975). Secondly, the builder himself may offer an all-in service – a so-called 'package deal' or 'turnkey' project – in which he takes over responsibility for the whole process from design to erection. An objection which is sometimes made against this solution is that the quality of design suffers because the builder may be more concerned with commercial considerations – subordinating design to production – and that the client forgoes the protection afforded by the architect representing his interests in dealings with the contractor. It also has the disadvantage again that the client forgoes the benefits of competition unless package dealers are prepared to compete on individual projects. Package deals are most used in the private sector for those types of work where requirements are fairly standardized. A recent survey showed that design-and-construct companies handled the design of about one-quarter of factory buildings and one-tenth of office buildings (NEDO, 1974). A third possibility in which designers offer an all-in service of design and construction has been limited by the fact that, until recently, architects were prevented by the rules of their professional institution from also acting as principals of building firms.

Problems arising from the division of functions on the design side itself among independent professionals has found a response in the development of multi-disciplinary practices. A difficulty here, however, is that such practices may not necessarily be able to provide the necessary expertise on all projects and may find it difficult to maintain a balanced work-load for the practice as a whole. A further solution to the design–production dichotomy is the supply of prefabricated 'systems' of construction by firms in manufacturing industry. Developments in this area, however, are best examined under the heading of 'Innovation' which is considered in Section 10.4.2.

In the present context we may note one further disadvantage that has followed from the separation of design from production in the method developed to determine contract prices. In arriving at his tender price, each contractor prices the items in a 'bill of quantities' which is drawn up by a quantity surveyor on behalf of the client for this purpose. The format of the bill is such, however, that while it describes all the work that the construction of a particular building will demand, it does not directly provide information that enables the builder to assess the organizational implications of the job, for it does not indicate the sequencing of operations necessary to complete different stages of the work. It does not reveal, therefore, the extent to which different parts of the work will require contributions from many or few different men or gangs with, as a consequence, many or few potential disruptions to the flow of work. Thus the ease or difficulty of construction implicit in the design may not be recognized by the estimator, with the consequence that the design of buildings which are easy (difficult) to build may not be rewarded with a correspondingly low (high) price. In so far as this is the case, it is clearly an important obstacle to innovation and rationality in design. A solution to this problem is the development of a new form of bill of quantities – an 'operational bill' (Forbes and Skoyles, 1963) – in which the requirements of the design are specified in terms of the sequence of operations required. Its adoption, however, would represent a substantial change in well-established procedures and it has not found ready acceptance.

10.4.1 Site Efficiency

A penetrating analysis of the multifarious factors that affect the efficiency of site work has been made by Bishop (1972). Each contract involves the establishment and control of an *ad hoc* organization of many different gangs and subcontractors who are required to carry out a large number of separate but interrelated operations. Within the constraints imposed by design, therefore, the efficiency of the process depends not only on the rates of output which can be attained in the execution of each of the operations but also on their smooth coordination so as to minimize non-productive time. Much therefore depends on the planning and programming of the work in the first place and, more important, on the effectiveness with which subsequent control is exercised on site for, as Bishop points out, 'on site one *force majeure* follows another' and the best plans and programmes have continually to be changed and updated. It is perhaps not surprising to find, therefore, that site studies reveal variations in the man-hours required on comparable work in the ratio of 3:1 or more (DSIR, 1953; Ministry of Education, 1955; Forbes, 1969).

Considerable attention has been devoted to planning, programming and control problems, especially by the Building Research Station, and although the early promise held out by the application to construction of techniques such as critical path analysis has apparently not been realized (Bishop, 1972), there is little doubt that the greater attention that has been devoted to these problems has been an important source of improvement. Mechanization too has improved productivity either by replacing labour in direct substitution or because the introduction of a particular item of plant has involved the reconsideration of the programming and phasing of work with consequential improvements for that reason. However, it has proved difficult to mechanize many of the craft processes. Mechanization is further considered below. Other sources of variation, and hence scope for improvement, reside not in the overall tempo of the work as a whole, but in the rate of output of individual men or gangs. Improvements here may be obtained by systematic on-the-job training in production methods and by the use of effective incentive schemes (Bishop, 1972). More dramatic sources of productivity improvement have been sought in innovation and it is this aspect of performance that is now considered.

10.4.2 Innovation

As indicated earlier, product and process innovation in construction is largely outside the industry's own control as a result of its service character and the division in the production process between design, manufacture and construction. Innovation in the forms and methods of construction is largely in the hands of designers. Innovations in building materials are in the hands of the building materials industries and their introduction into building is again the responsibility of designers rather than builders. Generally speaking, the builders' responsibility only extends to the execution of work on site where the scope for innovation is limited to organizational matters and the introduction and use of mechanical plant. Innovation in contractors' plant as such, however, is again largely in the hands of manufacturing industry. The diffusion of plant innovations is, of course, more directly attributable to contractors, though yet again within constraints imposed by design.

The scope for the mechanization of site work has proved very limited. Building remains a labour-intensive activity requiring the mixing, placing and fixing of a wide variety of materials and components on-site and involving contributions from many different crafts. The major effect of mechanization in the industry has been the replacement of much manual labour in the activities of excavation, materials handling and concrete mixing. As a consequence, civil engineering is more highly mechanized than building since it involves more of such activities. In building, apart from the development of powered hand-tools, the mechanization of craft processes has made only limited progress and perhaps the main effect of innovations on their work has been through the introduction of new materials such as plastics, new methods of fixing, and a greater degree of prefabrication. With regard to plant diffusion, lack of information makes it difficult to make a proper assessment. One major development in the postwar period has been the introduction of tower cranes, but the criticism is sometimes made that British contractors were tardy in utilizing them given the fact that they had been used on the Continent for twenty years or so before their introduction here in 1951. On the other hand, it must be remembered that the large programme of high-rise building, to which they are particularly suited, had scarcely begun at that time and that, once their safety and suitability in British conditions had been demonstrated, diffusion seems to have been quite rapid (Building Research Station, 1971).

More ambitious attempts to 'industrialize' the construction industry have required technological innovation in building design. They have generally involved the prefabrication off the site of as much of the work as possible, so that the work on-site becomes much more the work of assembly and erection rather than fabrication. There has, of course, been a long-standing trend for many components – such as joinery, pre-cast concrete goods and plasterboard – to be prefabricated, and these have all gradually been incorporated into traditional forms of construction. Similarly new materials have found their place in traditional forms. From time to time, however, special efforts have been made to bring about more comprehensive industrialization, particularly for housebuilding. These occurred after both world wars and again in the 1960s and took the form of attempts to produce sets of parts or 'construction systems', which can be fitted together easily on site, and the development of larger individual components. These attempts have had mixed success. Few of the housebuilding systems developed proved to be successful economically and some of the systems used for housing, education and other buildings have left behind many building failures with heavy maintenance costs; failures of some new systems of road construction and bridge design are also reported. A discussion of the economics of the housebuilding systems will be found in Fleming (1965). Briefly, studies showed that although many systems were successful in saving on-site labour, these savings tended to be confined to the superstructure, leaving a considerable part of the labour-intensive internal finishing work to be performed in largely traditional ways – with increased potential for disruption in the progress of work – and such savings in labour costs as were obtained were outweighed by the higher costs of prefabricated components. Few 'industrialized' housing methods now remain in use for new building.

It is fairly generally accepted that the way forward as far as the 'industrialization' of building is concerned is more likely to be found down evolutionary rather than revolutionary paths. A key aspect of many potential sources of improvement is simplification and standardization of design and production. As far as prefabrication as such is concerned, greater potential appears to be offered through the development of 'component building' – that is, standardization of a range of components which are sufficiently interchangeable in use as to meet general building needs – rather than unique proprietary 'systems' with a limited range of uses. This requires as a prerequisite an underlying system of 'dimensional co-ordination' – that is, a generally agreed set of dimensional constraints within which all designers work. Much has been done to lay the foundations for this approach (DOE, 1978), but it yet remains to be seen how successful it will prove to be in practice.

10.5 PUBLIC POLICY

The government influences the performance of the industry both directly and indirectly in important ways. Particularly important is the government's control and influence over the level of demand on the industry. Direct control is extensive because a large part of demand (well over half in some recent years) comes from public sector clients. Changes can be sudden and large because new construction represents capital investment and governments find it easier to change capital, rather than current, expenditure. In the private sector, the pre-eminence of construction as an investment goods industry, and the fact that the level of investment is more volatile than demand in general, means that construction is again particularly vulnerable to changes in the general economic climate. A persistent criticism through much of the postwar period has been the extent to which a succession of 'stop-go' demand management policies operated by successive governments has had a particularly marked impact on the industry. No more revealing indication of its vulnerability can be given than its experience during the recession from 1973 when the decline in economic activity, coupled with cuts in public expenditure, led to a fall of one-half in the flow of new contracts between 1972 and 1980. Actual output fell less because of compensatory expenditure on repairs and maintenance, as opposed to new work, and because fluctuations in the flow of orders may be absorbed to some extent by variations in construction periods rather than output in any period of time.

The severity of booms and slumps in construction activity are likely to have a particularly adverse effect on the industry in view of its labour-intensive, craft-based nature and the value to a firm of retaining men who are used to working as a team; moreover experience seems to show that recessions often lead to trained men being lost from the industry altogether. The particularly high degree of uncertainty which faces construction firms must preclude forward planning of any worthwhile kind and thus retard investment in plant and labour training. Labour may also be dissuaded from entering the industry in the first place – a factor which may be especially important with regard to the quality of managerial staff attracted to it.

The influence of the government on the level of demand on the industry has, to date, been far more concerned with macro-economic objectives than with the effects on the industry itself. At the industry level, as such, public policy operates in a number of ways. For example, the government has taken a direct interest in labour supply and training matters, by the establishment in 1964 of the Construction Industry Training Board which finances and encourages training. Direct steps have also been taken by the government to foster innovation. Buildings are required to have a long life and have to satisfy stringent performance requirements – many of which are laid down in official regulations concerning public health and safety – but it is not easy to show that new materials and components possess all the performance characteristics required, with the result that designers, the drafters of national standards and the institutions responsible for the provision of finance or insurance cover, all tend to adopt a conservative attitude. This in turn retards innovation and, especially, the diffusion of innovations. With the aim of helping to overcome these obstacles the government established the Agrément Board in 1965 to test new building products and to issue certificate of approval. However, fundamental difficulties remain in the way of demonstrating the likely performance of products in use and perhaps inevitably, cautious attitudes are still prevalent. Government influence is also felt in a more diffuse way through research carried out by the Building Research Establishment which covers a wide field of relevant technical and operational matters. As indicated earlier, the government has also sought to achieve efficiency and economy in building through its encouragement of selective tendering, rather than open competition, as a means of selecting contractors, through the stimulation of 'industrialized' building, and also by support for the formation of public sector purchasing consortia which achieve economies through the bulk ordering of standardized components.

Direct government intervention by means of price controls, financial support or 'restructuring' has been notable for its absence. It is, of course, difficult to exercise control over contractors' tender prices as each price is a unique price for work yet to be done.[4] In contrast with manufacturing industry government assistance to firms in financial difficulties in construction seems to have been restricted to companies which were engaged on public sector work at the time of their difficulties.

The industry has also been little affected directly by the intervention of government anti-trust agencies. The control of restrictive trade practices, particularly collusive tendering, is of most relevance, but the only known instances are the cases referred to earlier and a registered price-fixing agreement between members of the British Constructional Steelwork Association which was abandoned in 1958. Such practices, however, are difficult to detect and it is impossible to judge how widespread they are in the construction industry or what effect the legislation may have had.

In conclusion, it is appropriate to look ahead. It is always hazardous to predict the future but in this industry it is difficult to reject the view that the future path of development will be very similar to the old. In principle, public policy towards an industry, if a 'policy' is thought to be necessary, can focus its attention on structural matters or on matters more directly relating to its behaviour and performance. In the construction industry, public policy to date has been largely concerned with matters relating to behaviour and, especially, performance. The actions with regard to restrictive practices, the placing of contracts, the finance of research (and the dissemination of results), the encouragement of innovation, labour training, and attention to the organization of demand (as opposed to its level) may all be interpreted in this light. No revolutionary improvements have been brought about and, given the nature of the technical processes that have to be performed to satisfy these demands, it would be unrealistic to expect any in the near future. Obviously attention must continue to be devoted to these areas.

Given the nature of demand, the product and the process, the scope for structural change as a means of improving performance must remain limited. Proposals for the extension of public ownership and control, either by the nationalization of construction companies or by the expansion of public direct works departments, are not clear about how the industry's economic performance would be improved given that the techniques of production and the problems of managing and controlling work on unique projects on numerous dispersed sites would remain the same. The organization of the industry has adapted to cope flexibly with the demands placed upon it, and it is questionable how far greater administrative control over productive enterprises in this industry can be expected to provide economic benefits.

Far more important is the need to reduce the severity of the fluctuations in demand from which the industry suffers, thereby removing some of the worst excesses of uncertainty and creating a more favourable economic environment in which it may operate.

NOTES TO CHAPTER 10

1 Based on Department of Employment estimates of employees in employment and self-employed workers in the civilian labour force in June 1985 (*Employment Gazette*, December 1985, p. S12; May 1986, pp. 161–5 and August 1986, p. S9).
2 The discrepancy between the number of firms recorded in Tables 10.1 and

10.2 is due to differences in geographical coverage (UK and Great Britain) and because some firms in Table 10.2 may count as more than one unit in Table 10.1 which relates to the units registered for VAT purposes (some firms may have more than one VAT registration number).
3 The number of firms was more than doubled from 77,000 in 1977 to 168,000 in 1985. For further discussion of statistical problems see Fleming, 1986.
4 However, the industry has not escaped the incidence of price controls altogether: if a tender price is not quoted as a 'firm price' contractors may recoup increases in costs that occur during the construction period, but for a time during the 1970s only part of the labour cost increases could be recouped in this way.

REFERENCES

Bishop, D. (1972), 'Productivity in the building industry', *The Philosophical Transactions of the Royal Society, London*, A272, 1229, 533–63.
Building Research Station (1971), *BRS News*, 18, (Garston, Herts).
Department of the Environment (1978), *An Introduction to Dimensional Co-ordination* (London: HMSO).
Department of Scientific and Industrial Research (1953), *Productivity in House-Building, Second Report*, National Building Studies, Special Report no. 21 (London: HMSO).
Fleming, M. C. (1965), 'Economic aspects of new methods of building', *Journal of the Statistical and Social Inquiry Society of Ireland*, XXI, III, 120–42.
Fleming, M. C. (1977), 'The bogey of fragmentation in the construction industry', *National Builder*, 58, 134–7 and 284–6.
Fleming, M. C. (1986) *Spon's Guide to Housing, Construction and Property Market Statistics* (London: Spon).
Forbes, W. S. (1969), 'A survey of progress in housebuilding', *Building Technology and Management*, 7, 4, 88–91. Building Research Station Current Paper 25/69.
Forbes, W. S., and Skoyles, E. R. (1963), 'The operational bill', *Chartered Surveyor*, 95, 8, 429–34. Building Research Station Current Paper Design Series 1.
Hillebrandt, Patricia M. (1974), *Economic Theory and the Construction Industry* (London: Macmillan)
HMSO (1954), *Report on the Supply of Buildings in the Greater London Area*, House of Commons Paper 264, Session 1953–4 (London).
HMSO (1973), *Restrictive Trading Agreements, Report of the Registrar 1 July 1969 to 30 June 1972*, Cmnd 5195 (London).
Ministry of Education (1955), *Site Labour Studies in School Building*, Building Bulletin 12 (London: HMSO).
Ministry of Public Building and Works (1964), *The Placing and Management of Contracts for Building and Civil Engineering Work. Report of the (Banwell) Committee* (London: HMSO).
Ministry of Works (1944), *The Placing and Management of Building Contracts* (London: HMSO).
National Economic Development Office (1974), *Before You Build* (London: HMSO).

National Economic Development Office (1975), *The Public Client and th*
    Construction Industries (London: HMSO).
Newcombe, Robert (1978), 'Cost of Competition', *Building*, 234, 7041, pp. 95
    97.

FURTHER READING

The primary source of statistical data is *Housing and Construction Statistics*
(London: HMSO, quarterly and annual). For guides to the data available see
the author's works cited below. Useful additional references are:
Bowley, Marian (1966), *The British Building Industry* (Cambridge: Cambridge
    University Press).
Fleming, M. C. (1980), *Reviews of UK Statistical Sources, Vol. 12, Construc-*
    tion and the Related Professions (Oxford: Pergamon on behalf of the Royal
    Statistical Society and the Social Science Research Council).
Fleming, M. C. (1986), *Spon's Guide to Housing, Construction and Property*
    Market Statistics (London: Spon).
Hillebrandt, Patricia M. (1984), *Analysis of the British Construction Industry*
    (London: Macmillan).
Stone, P. A. (1983), *Building Economy*, 3rd edn (Oxford: Pergamon).

Chapter Eleven

Retailing

STUART ELIOT

11.1 INTRODUCTION

The distributive sector is very large in the UK. It was the third largest sector of the economy in 1985, and was second only to finance in the service sector, being larger than government, education and health. Of course the term 'distribution' encompasses more than just retailing – in the UK official statistics it also includes wholesaling, hotels and catering – but retailing is by far the more important of these groups, accounting for about 8 per cent of GNP[1] and 10 per cent of total employment in the UK.

In December 1986 retailing employed some 2,146,000 people. Most of the jobs they occupied required little training or experience, and consequently large numbers of unskilled and young people were employed, together with many married women seeking part-time employment. Moreover, less than 15 per cent of employees were members of a trade union. As a result, pay levels for both men and women were substantially below the average for all industries and services, and in many cases were based on awards made by Wages Councils. However, despite their low average level, wages and salaries still constitute retailers' most important item of expense apart from the cost of goods purchased. In fact, most retail trades have personnel costs which account for between 30 and 40 per cent of gross profit (turnover minus the cost of goods purchased). This means that retailers have a strong incentive to reduce labour inputs, and helps to explain the long-term trend towards self-service and the introduction of labour-saving technology such as electronic point-of-sale equipment.

Other determinants of retail change include the search for economies of scale, changes in real disposable incomes and associated changes in consumer spending, and changes in government policies, demographic and social factors and firms' competitive strategies. Some of these factors will be examined later, but for the moment attention is concentrated on changes in consumer spending.

Table 11.1 draws a distinction between retail spending and non-retail spending (the latter including expenditure on items like travel, housing and fuel) and shows that, although retail sales have risen with the overall level of economic activity, they have accounted for a

235

Table 11.1   *Consumers' Expenditure at Current Prices*

	1975 £ million	% of total	1980 £ million	% of total	1985 £ million	% of total
Food	11,961	18.3	22,876	16.7	29,950	14.0
Alcoholic drink	4,848	7.4	9,955	7.3	15,783	7.4
Tobacco	2,735	4.2	4,821	3.5	7,006	3.3
Clothing and footwear	5,206	8.0	9,873	7.2	14,894	7.0
Durable goods	5,872	9.0	13,437	9.8	21,016	9.9
Other household goods	2,241	3.4	4,723	3.4	7,113	3.3
Books, magazines	943	1.4	1,877	1.4	2,964	1.4
Miscellaneous recreational goods	1,626	2.5	3,542	2.6	5,217	2.4
Chemists' goods	988	1.5	1,917	1.4	3,691	1.7
Other goods	971	1.5	2,355	1.7	3,522	1.7
Total retail spending	37,391	57.2	75,376	54.9	111,156	52.1
Total non-retail spending	27,107	41.5	59,960	43.7	98,748	46.3
Adjustments (e.g., tourism)	840	1.3	1,898	1.4	3,304	1.5
Total consumer spending	65,338	100	137,234	100	213,208	100
Gross National Product	107,043		230,107		354,967	
Total retail spending as % of GNP	34.9		32.8		31.3	

Source: Derived from Central Statistical Office *UK National Accounts*, 1986 edn, London, HMSO.

diminishing share of both total consumer spending and GNP. The table also shows a sizeable decline in the share of consumers' expenditure allocated to food, reflecting a relatively low income elasticity of demand. Declines have also occurred in the shares of tobacco and clothing, the decline in clothing being largely due to the fact that the prices of clothing and footwear have risen by far less than the retail price index as a whole.[2] Most other categories of expenditure have had fairly stable shares of total spending, the main exception being durable goods which have a high income elasticity of demand and hence have achieved a rising share.

One would expect changes in the pattern of spending to be reflected in the turnover of different kinds of retail business, and it can be seen in Table 11.2 that turnover shares of drink, confectionery and tobacco retailers fell slightly between 1978 and 1984, as did the shares of clothing and footwear retailers. Meanwhile, household goods retailers achieved a higher share of retail turnover in line with trends in consumers' expenditure on durable goods. But not all of the changes in Table 11.2 can be predicted from an examination of Table 11.1. Food

Table 11.2   *Market Shares for UK Retailing by Kind of Business (%)*

Kind of business	1978 Turnover	1978 Outlets	1978 Employees	1984 Turnover	1984 Outlets	1984 Employees
Food retailers	37.6	34.2	34.7	38.1	31.1	36.5
Drink, confectionery and tobacco	10.8	16.8	11.6	10.5	16.7	11.2
Clothing and footwear	9.4	16.2	12.4	9.1	16.3	12.3
Household goods shops	13.4	16.5	11.8	14.6	16.7	12.1
Other non-food shops	7.5	11.8	8.5	8.3	14.0	9.2
Mixed retail businesses	19.5	2.6	18.8	18.0	3.2	16.8
Hire and repair businesses	1.8	1.8	2.1	1.4	2.0	1.8
Total retail trade	100	100	100	100	100	100

Source: *Retailing 1980*, Business Monitor SDA 25, 1982 (London: HMSO).
Retailing 1984, Business Monitor SDO 25, 1986 (London: HMSO).

retailers, for example, have managed to increase their share of retail turnover despite the fact that food's share of consumer spending fell by 4 percentage points between 1975 and 1985. The explanation is that many so-called 'food retailers' have widened their product ranges and now sell large quantities of non-foods.

Table 11.2 also shows changes in the shares of retail outlets in different kinds of business. These are often similar to changes in shares of turnover, but the relationship is by no means exact. For instance, even though food retailers have increased their share of turnover, their share of outlets fell quite sharply between 1978 and 1984. This reflects a trend towards fewer, larger shops which has been apparent in many kinds of business, but which has been more pronounced in food.

Between 1961 and 1978, all the main kinds of business saw a decrease in the number of shops, and the total number of shops in Great Britain fell from 577,000 to 350,000 – a decline of 39 per cent or roughly 2 per cent per annum. More recently the decline has slowed down considerably, and Table 11.3 shows an overall reduction of just 2 per cent between 1978 and 1984 (a fall of around 0.3 per cent per annum). However, it should be noted that this small overall change masks wide variations across different types of retailing: from an increase of 20 per cent in mixed retail businesses to a fall of 11 per cent in the number of shops operated by food retailers.

Table 11.3 *Changes in Retail Outlets 1978–84, and Analysis of the Retail Trades in 1984 by Kind of Business*

Kind of business	Changes in outlets 1978–84 (no.)	Changes in outlets 1978–84 (%)	Outlets (no.)	Businesses (no.)	Employees ('000)	1984 Turnover (£m)	Gross margins (% turnover)	Stocks (% turnover)
Food retailers	−12,760	−11	106,843	77,486	850	31,360	21.3	5.3
Drink, confectionery, tobacco	−1,541	−3	57,344	41,992	260	8,686	15.2	8.1
Clothing, footwear, leather goods	−818	−1	56,020	28,684	285	7,476	40.8	18.4
Household goods retailers	−638	−1	57,144	39,379	282	12,000	33.0	17.1
Other non-food retailers	+6,610	+16	47,998	35,350	214	6,869	30.3	19.7
Mixed retail businesses	+1,788	+20	10,900	5,301	391	14,787	32.7	10.8
Hire and repair businesses	+474	+7	6,904	2,597	42	1,163	87.3	3.9
Total retail trade	−6,885	−2	343,153	230,789	2,326	82,342	27.6	10.7

Source: Retailing 1980, Business Monitor SDA 25, 1982 (London: HMSO)
       Retailing 1984, Business Monitor SDO 25, 1986 (London: HMSO).

Table 11.4   *Percentages of Total Retail Trade Controlled by the Top 'x' Organizations*

	'x'	% retail trade
1961	100	21
1971	25	22
1980	12	21
1982	10	22
1984	10	24

Source: Calculated from *Report on the Census of Distribution and Other Services 1961*, 1963 (London: HMSO); *Report on the Census of Distribution and Other Services 1971*, 1975 (London: HMSO); *Retailing 1982*, Business Monitor SDO 25, 1984 (London: HMSO); and the sources quoted in Table 11.2.

1.2 MARKET STRUCTURE

There has been considerable debate as to how retailing might be most appropriately classified in terms of the traditional market forms (Tucker and Yamey, 1973, part 2). It is agreed that neither perfect competition nor monopoly would be an appropriate classification (although local monopolies may be found) and therefore the debate has centred on the choice between oligopoly and monopolistic competition.

One method of classification would be to look at the alleged consequences of different market forms. For example, George and Joll (1981, p. 287) have pointed to the existence of excess capacity in retailing, which is a characteristic of monopolistic competition. However, there is nothing in economic theory to suggest that excess capacity cannot exist in oligopolistic (or, of course, monopolistic) markets. Moreover, much of the excess capacity that exists at certain times may be due to the substantial fluctuations in demand that occur in retailing. If peak demands are to be met, it is inevitable that excess capacity will exist at other times.

An alternative starting point would be to determine whether a market is supplied by a few or many retailers. At first sight this seems relatively straightforward, but the problem with such an approach is that it is not easy to define the relevant market, either in terms of its geographical area or the kind of business. A good illustration of this is that the Monopolies and Mergers Commission (1983) recommended that a proposed merger between Great Universal Stores (GUS) and Empire Stores should be prohibited on the grounds that it would have raised GUS's share of the mail order market from 40 per cent to 47 per cent, and would have increased GUS's power to influence prices and weaken competitors. GUS's objection to this finding was that it

Table 11.5   *Concentration Ratios, 1984*

	% sales accounted for by largest	
	five firms	ten firms
Food	28.2	41.1
Alcoholic drinks	26.3	40.9
Footwear	44.2	53.3
Men's and boys' wear	35.7	45.7
Furniture etc	32.2	41.4
Electrical, gas appliances etc	42.4	55.7
Total retail trade	15.6	23.8

Source: Retailing 1984, Business Monitor SDO 25, 1986 (London: HMSO).

was not only competing with other mail order retailers, but in a much wider market where its share and influence was considerably reduced.

Although it is not easy to fix the boundaries of retail markets and hence to determine precisely the number of suppliers, one firm conclusion that can be reached is that the retail trades are increasingly becoming the province of large businesses. Table 11.4 shows that the last 25 years have seen a marked increase in aggregate or overall concentration in the retail trades: in 1961 the top 100 retailers had 21 per cent of total sales, by 1980 the same percentage was in the hands of 12 retailers and by 1984 the top 10 had 24 per cent. The need to preserve confidentiality does not allow the government to identify individual retailers, but an examination of companies' accounts revealed that the top 5 retailers in 1984 were Marks & Spencer, Tesco, J. Sainsbury, Boots and Asda.

Furthermore, Table 11.5 shows that while concentration may still appear to be quite low in the retail trades as a whole, it is much higher in many individual product markets. In fact, concentration was higher than in retailing as a whole in 33 out of 38 commodity groups identified in official statistics. Moreover, there is evidence that concentration is higher still in regional and local markets (Office of Fair Trading, 1985, p. 26). In many cases the increase in concentration has resulted from the expansion of large multiples (retailers with 10 or more shops) at the expense of small multiples (2–9 shops), single-outlet retailers and co-operative societies (Table 11.6).

The poor performance of the co-operative movement is, perhaps, surprising given that the movement encompasses retailing, wholesaling and manufacturing, and that the movement had a combined retail turnover of some £5 million in 1986 – larger than any other single retailer in the United Kingdom. But whereas the multiples have centralized control systems which facilitate the speedy adoption of best management techniques, the co-operative movement is a very fragmented creature made up of a large number of individual societies, each owned by its own shareholders, and each completely autonomous. The consequences of this include the fact that the movement

Table 11.6   *Percentage Shares of Retail Sales by Form of Organization*

	1971	1976	1980	1984
Single-outlet retailers	41.7	34.1	31.6	29.5
Small multiple retailers	12.6	14.6	14.6	12.9
Large multiple retailers	45.7	51.2	53.8	57.6
Total	100	100	100	100
(of which co-operatives)	(7.2)	(7.1)	(6.5)	(5.3)

Source: *Retailing 1976*, Business Monitor SDA 25, 1978 (London: HMSO); *Retailing 1978*, Business Monitor SDA 25, 1980 (London: HMSO). *Retailing 1982* Business Monitor SDO 25, 1984 (London: HMSO); *Retailing 1984* Business monitor SDO 25, 1986 (London: HMSO).

cannot take full advantage of economies of scale in warehousing, transportation, buying and administration. Also, there are marked differences in managerial ability between one society and another, and there is insufficient cooperation in marketing activities: pricing policies and stock ranges often differ from one society to another, and a wide variety of trading names is used (for example, Leo's, Domus, Shopping Giant). The result is that the movement lacks a coherent trading range (Eliot, 1983). However, in recent times the movement has made strenuous efforts to rationalize its activities and by the beginning of 1987 the number of separate societies had fallen to less than 100 (compared to approximately 1,000 in 1950). Even so, the movement still has a long way to go before it creates the sort of integrated structure which will enable it to compete on equal terms with the multiples.

Table 11.7 shows that (excluding hire and repair businesses) the dominance of large multiples is particularly great in mixed retail businesses. This category includes department store groups like House of Fraser, variety chains such as Marks & Spencer and mail order companies such as Great Universal Stores. Of these, mail order is perhaps worthy of separate mention at this point because it is the main form of non-store retailing.

Government figures show that the mail order companies steadily increased their market share from around 2 per cent of total retail sales in 1961 to 4 per cent in 1980. Much of their early growth was based on their ability to offer extended credit at a time when most consumers found it difficult to obtain substantial credit facilities from conventional retail outlets. Another of their advantages was that customers were able to try out merchandise within the privacy of their own homes and outside conventional shopping hours – an advantage which has assumed greater significance lately with the increase in the number of working wives and increasing traffic congestion in city centres. Nevertheless, since 1980 the growth of mail order has ceased. Indeed, its market share has fallen somewhat. One reason is that credit

Table 11.7   *Percentage Shares of Retail Sales by Kind of Business and Form of Organization, 1984.*

	Single-outlet retailers	Small multiple retailers	Large multiple retailers
Food retailers	21.4	8.2	70.4
Drink, confectionery and tobacco retailers	52.8	10.9	36.3
Clothing, footwear and leather goods retailers	24.0	21.2	54.9
Household goods retailers	35.1	19.9	45.0
Other non-food retailers	52.7	30.0	17.2
Mixed retail businesses	21.4	6.5	72.1
Hire and repair businesses	14.7	8.2	77.1
Total retail trade	29.5	12.9	57.6

Source: as for Table 11.5.

is now more widely available. Another is that mail order's traditional Northern-based, working-class customers have been badly hit by the high unemployment of the 1980s.

One consequence of the increased size of major multiples is that barriers to entry have been rising in many of the retail trades. For example, until recently it was still relatively easy for newcomers to enter the grocery market and obtain a sizeable market share – for example, Asda only entered the market around 1970 and is now ranked among the largest grocery retailers. But the economies of scale available to large retailers – and especially the quantity discounts they obtain from manufacturers – are such that entry on a small scale is becoming much less attractive (see Section 11.4 below).

Furthermore, the quantity discounts are such that many existing single-outlet retailers are facing a very difficult time, although in some trades (and especially grocery) they have been helped by the formation of voluntary groups. Groups such as Spar and VG are sponsored by wholesalers. They provide a wide range of assistance to their members including advice regarding advertising and promotions, site location and stock control; and most important, they centralize buying activities and thus obtain better terms from suppliers. However, it seems unlikely that small retailers will survive if they compete on price alone, and increasingly they will have to rely on other factors such as convenience and opening hours, both of which help to explain the relatively high proportion of the confectionery, tobacco and news-agents trade which is handled by small firms (Table 11.7).

Another survival route taken by many small retailers has been specialization (hence their high share of 'other non-food' trades like booksellers and jewellery), although it must be emphasized that specialization is not confined to independents. Successful multiple specialists include B & Q in the DIY sector, Mothercare which opened its first shop in 1961 and now trades in ten different countries, and the fashion retailer Next which aims to attract the 25–45-year-old working woman with high disposable income.

However, some of the most spectacular multiple growth has resulted from diversification. For example, much of Marks & Spencer's expansion during the last ten years has come from its move into food retailing, with food sales currently accounting for about 40 per cent of its total sales. Meanwhile, food retailers themselves now stock an increasing proportion of non-food products. The result is that while food accounts for just 14 per cent of consumers' expenditure (Table 11.1), the companies classified as 'food retailers' in official statistics account for some 38 per cent of total retail turnover (Table 11.2), and (according to the 1984 Retail Inquiry) they supply 29 per cent of all vehicle accessories sold in Great Britain, 19 per cent of all lawn-mowers and 12 per cent of all flowers, plants and seeds. One factor encouraging this diversification has been the relatively low income elasticity of demand for foodstuffs. Another has been the low gross margins achievable on food compared with non-food products (Table 11.3). Finally, as real incomes and car ownership have increased over time, more consumers prefer to make a large number of purchases on one shopping trip, and stocking a wide range of products helps to attract these customers.

11.3 MARKET BEHAVIOUR

In this section price and non-price competition and retailers' merger activity are discussed.

11.3.1 Price Competition

Retailers' pricing decisions are usually made on the assumption that some (and often most) consumers who enter a shop purchase more than one item. One consequence of this is that the concept of the retailer's demand curve is by no means straightforward because if multiple purchases form any part of a retailer's trade, then it is not possible in principle to analyse that retailer's operations in terms of a series of demand curves for individual products. The reason is that if a retailer stocks a range of products $A_1, A_2, \ldots, A_n$, the demand for A_1 will be influenced by the number of products which comprise the set $A_2, \ldots, A_n$, and by the characteristics, including the price, of each of these products. It is, in fact, more helpful to an understanding of competition in retailing to think of the demand for the overall output of the retailer, for the totality of his products, although even here there are very strict limits to the usefulness of the concept of the demand curve.

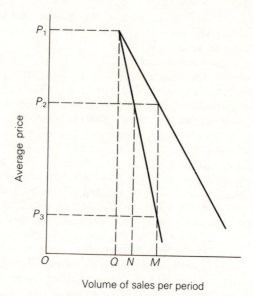

Figure 11.1 *Demand with alternative pricing strategies*

If the demand curve relates to all the retailer's products, price must be interpreted as an average for all the products. It would be easiest to calculate an average price where all the products were measured in the same units, for example, kilos. This would also permit the calculation of a total volume of sales (per period) at that price, and thus the identification of a point on the demand curve.

However, even in this situation a unique demand curve for that retailer cannot be derived. There would be various combinations of price changes that would enable the retailer to change his average price level by, say, 2 per cent, but the change in the volume of sales would probably differ from one combination to another. This is illustrated in Figure 11.1 where the initial price and quantity are P_1 and Q, and a reduction in the average price to P_2 would result in an increase in the volume of sales to N in one instance and to M in another.

Although the inability to derive a unique demand curve means that the usual line of analysis cannot be followed, it does help to explain the nature of price competition in retailing. The pricing policies of retailers can be explained in terms of a search for the most efficient form of price competition. If the firm has decided to reduce its prices and if, for the moment, it is assumed that marginal cost is identical for all products, then the firm will be concerned to obtain the greatest increase in sales volume for a given price reduction. In terms of Figure 11.1, when it reduces price from P_1 to P_2 it will hope to expand sales to M rather than N. Putting the matter the other way round, if the firm wishes to increase sales volume by a given amount, say from Q to M, the more efficient policy is that which requires the smaller reduction in average price – to P_2 rather than P_3.

A broad distinction may be made between two basic alternative strategies that have been adopted by retailers in the search for the most efficient policy: selective and across-the-board price reductions.

A policy of selective price reductions involves large reductions – usually with respect to both the retailer's own normal price and the price currently being charged by competitors – on a small number of products. The basic justification for this policy is that the consumer is able to remember the prices of only a limited number of products, so that there is no point in reducing the prices of a large number. By making a (limited) number of large reductions the retailer seeks to create a low-price image and thus attract more shoppers (Nystrom, 1970). He will reduce the price of those items which he believes to have a high 'transfer effect', to use the term adopted by Holdren (1960). (The transfer effect refers to the change in the *value* of sales of other products following a reduction in the price of one product.)

Items are most likely to have a high transfer effect if their price is high enough to permit a reduction that is easily perceptible, if they account for an appreciable proportion of consumers' expenditure, and if they have been so heavily advertised as to make consumers highly price-conscious. A much lower transfer effect is likely to be attached to products whose price is subject to frequent fluctuations so that there is no well-established market price. Another important factor influencing the selection of products for price reductions is the offer of special terms by the manufacturer, including an allowance towards the cost of advertising the price reduction. (When selective reductions are advertised, the policy is known as 'promotional pricing'.)

The alternative policy which might be adopted by the retailer who wishes to make pricing an important part of his competitive strategy is to reduce the margins on all his products in an attempt to price below his competitors 'across the board'. The prices that are set will not, of course, be lower on those items selected for large reductions by competitors following the other strategy. But it is hoped that an across-the-board policy will also create a favourable price image and so attract consumers.

The operation of these two alternative strategies has been witnessed most clearly in grocery retailing. In the 1950s and 1960s the major gains in market share were made by retailers like Tesco who adopted a policy of selective price reductions. Then in the 1970s the climate changed somewhat. First of all more information was being provided to consumers about the average price levels of different retailers. This information consisted partly of advertising by retailers, and partly of reports issued by bodies such as the Consumers' Association. Second, the 1970s were characterized by high rates of inflation which might have reduced consumers' awareness of normal prices and hence

dampened the impact of selective price reductions. As a result, th
pendulum began to swing and firms such as Asda and Kwik Sav
achieved fairly large market shares on the basis of modest pric
reductions across the board.

However, in more recent years the pendulum seems to have swun
back in favour of those retailers offering selective price reduction
(possibly because of the much lower rates of inflation which are nov
commonplace), and Tesco and Sainsbury in particular have made
impressive gains and now command a combined market share o
almost 30 per cent. Asda, meanwhile, has been faced with a relativel
static market share and has responded by modifying its policies – so
while it still lays the emphasis on across-the-board price reductions, i
has been forced to introduce deeper discounts on a range o
approximately 150 products.

As well as competing on the prices of well-known national brands
some retailers sell a substantial proportion of products under their own
labels. These own-label products are frequently cheaper in the shops
than the corresponding manufacturer brands, this being possible
because retailers themselves buy the products at lower prices from the
manufacturers. Sometimes these lower buying prices may reflect the
fact that manufacturers are willing to accept smaller profit margins in
order to obtain a guaranteed (or at least more secure) outlet for their
products. Also they may reflect the fact that manufacturers' costs of
producing own-labels are usually lower than the costs associated with
well-known national brands: savings may be made on raw material
costs, packaging and selling costs (including advertising). Moreover, it
appears that the cost savings passed on to retailers are such that
retailers often earn higher profit margins on own-labels than on
comparable manufacturer brands even though they sell own-labels at
lower prices.

11.3.2 Non-Price Competition

This can take many forms, but a common characteristic is that they all
tend to increase a firm's average cost at any given level of output.
Another characteristic is that, by comparison with price competition,
non-price competition is often more difficult for competitors to match,
either exactly or quickly. It is therefore analogous to the activities
adopted by manufacturers in an attempt to differentiate their products
from those of their rivals. Research has shown that the determinants of
store patronage vary considerably from one type of shop to another
(Walters, 1985a). However, among the most regularly listed factors are
location, service and stock assortment. The last two of these factors
are dealt with in more detail below.

As shown below, *service* has numerous aspects ranging from the
delivery of goods to the provision of credit and help with after-sales
problems, but perhaps of prime significance are those aspects of

Table 11.8   *Rank Order of Top Five Determinants of Patronage for Retail Outlets*

	Supermarkets	Fast-food outlets	Fashion stores	Department stores	DIY outlets
1	location/ convenience	taste/flavour	value for money	location	location
2	low prices	location	assortment	assortment	low prices
3	assortment	fast service	contemporary	fashion	assortment
4	friendly service	price	quality	quality	quality
5	cleanliness	quality	location	service	knowledgeable service

Source: Walters, 1985a, p. 41.

service which relate to the retailer's staffing policy. Assuming a given size of shop and range of goods stocked, the more staff are employed the less time each customer has to spend on searching for goods, waiting to be served, or waiting to pay. Also, it is not just the number of staff which is important because, as Table 11.8 indicates, technical expertise, knowledgeable service and friendly service may all be major influences on consumers.

Delivery services can also have a crucial influence on patronage, but they are not singled out in Table 11.8, which may be an indication of the fact that they have declined in importance in recent years. This is especially the case where low-price items such as groceries are concerned, partly because of the increasing tendency of many shoppers to buy in bulk using their own vehicles. However, it also applies to more bulky items like furniture since some consumers prefer to save money by purchasing and collecting self-assembly 'flat-packs' from retailers like MFI.

In contrast to delivery, credit is an aspect of service that has received increasing attention. At one time credit was offered to all customers only by mail order houses, but now (as was mentioned earlier) credit is available from a wide variety of sources, and credit cards in particular have boomed. For example, between 1979 and 1986 the number of Barclaycard holders increased from 5 million to nearly 9 million (*Financial Times*, 16 October 1986); and in addition to the major banks, many individual retailers have issued their own cards. The outcome is that credit-financed sales have accounted for an increasing share of total retail sales.

After-sales service has different facets whose relative importance depends on the type of business and product. For instance, purchasers of such products as television sets and washing machines are interested in the speed and reliability of the retailer's maintenance and repair service. As a result, multiples like Comet which made early gains in these markets on the basis of very low prices subsequently added maintenance facilities as part of the 'package' offered to consumers.

For other products like clothing, a more important aspect of after-sales service may be the opportunity for the consumer to have money refunded should the product prove unsuitable.

A second major form of non-price competition is *stock assortment*. By increasing the number and type of commodities stocked, retailers clearly hope to gain revenue from the sale of additional commodity groups. In addition, the sales of existing products are likely to increase as additional customers are attracted by the prospect of being able to find an increasing proportion of their requirements under one roof. Obviously, carrying extra stocks can be very costly, and in reaching decisions about assortment the retailer will have to weigh these extra costs against the loss of potential revenue and goodwill that he may suffer if he reduces his range and cannot meet his customers' requirements.

Table 11.8 shows that *assortment* is ranked in second place as a determinant of patronage for department stores (after location, the importance of which has been demonstrated by numerous studies of pedestrian flows within shopping centres). For many years retail analysts have been predicting the decline of these department stores, largely because they are vulnerable to competition from several sources: the specialist multiple chains selling, for example, clothing and furniture; the large variety chains; and the superstores and hypermarkets which come increasingly close to the department store in the range of goods offered (and often at lower prices and at locations more convenient to the car-borne shopper). Yet despite these developments, the department stores have confounded predictions and clung on to a fairly stable market share. One reason is that they have endeavoured to counter their relatively high prices by attractive combinations of non-price factors including service, assortment and expenditure on furniture and fittings to create a pleasant atmosphere which appeals to customers in higher income groups. Furthermore, all this has frequently been backed by advertising campaigns aimed at creating a favourable overall image.

Of course, department stores are not alone in their use of advertising. For many years retailers spent less money on advertising than manufacturers, being content in the main to use low-cost media such as window-stickers, hoardings and local newspapers. But more recently the advertising expenditure of retailers has risen dramatically. According to the Economist Intelligence Unit (*Retail Business*, April 1986, p. 11) expenditure by retailers on press and TV advertising rose from £44 million in 1974 to £285 million in 1985, the largest advertiser in 1985 being MFI (£19m) followed by Dixons (£11m), the Co-op (£10m) and Tesco (£10m).

Sometimes advertising is used to draw attention to a particular aspect of a retailer's policy (such as a January sale), but increasingly it is seen as a way of developing a distinct image. According to Walters (1985b, p. 42) in the early 1980s 'advertising became vital in distinctive positioning statements which in turn were based upon substantial marketing research and evaluation. In short, the retailer became a brand.'

11.3.3 Merger Activity

Like many other sectors, retailing has seen a spate of mergers and acquisitions in the 1980s. Although the motives varied from one merger to another, in many cases the prime objective was to achieve faster growth. It has already been shown that, in the 1960s and 1970s, much of the multiples' growth was at the expense of small, single-outlet retailers, but, inevitably, the potential gains from this direction are reduced through time. In addition, some of the more successful retailers of the 1980s found themselves constrained by the limited availability of prime retail sites. Consequently much more attention was focused on retail mergers: for example, Burtons took over Debenhams, Dixons bought Currys, Habitat-Mothercare merged with British Home Stores; and in the space of just five years from 1981 to 1986, the Dee Corporation purchased a string of companies including Carrefour, International Stores and Fine Fare, and is now the third largest grocery multiple in the UK.

But not all retailers have followed the merger path, and it is noteworthy that two of the more profitable retailers of recent times – J. Sainsbury and Marks & Spencer – have both achieved their present position through internal growth.

Whether all the recent mergers will prove successful remains to be seen, but an analysis of past mergers by Kerin and Varaiya (1985) gives cause for some doubts. They looked at retail acquisitions in the USA between January 1976 and December 1983 and concluded that 'at a minimum, the results suggest that retailing acquisitions . . . may not benefit shareholders of the acquiring firm'. However, some would argue that changes in technology have improved the chances of success. In particular, the sophisticated computerization of retail operations has made it much easier for companies to run scattered businesses comprised of hundreds of stores.

11.4 MARKET PERFORMANCE

In this section attention is focused on two main indicators of market performance: productivity and profitability. In both cases the evidence requires careful interpretation because of measurement problems, but the difficulties are especially severe with regard to productivity.

In order to establish levels and changes in *productivity*, measures of both inputs and outputs are required. As far as inputs are concerned, most studies have tried to avoid the difficulties involved in constructing an index of total input and instead have used just the number of persons employed as the input index (for example, Ward, 1973; Smith and Hitchens, 1983). With regard to outputs, the main problem is that retailers provide not just a bundle of goods, but also a wide variety of services to which many consumers attach positive values.

Bearing those problems in mind, Smith and Hitchens (1983) carried out a detailed comparison of productivity levels in Britain and the USA and found that American retail productivity (sales per person) was about twice the British level. They concluded that 'while such a comparative performance is nothing to be complacent about . . . when set alongside our record in other sectors this is a relatively good performance . . . distinctly superior to that in manufacturing, public utilities and the extractive industries'.

Smith and Hitchens then went on to investigate in some detail the possible causes of the differences in retail productivity. For example, it is a well-established fact that productivity varies markedly from one retail trade to another,[3] and it was possible that US retailing was biased towards those trades with higher productivity. However, what Smith and Hitchens found was that productivity levels in the USA were higher trade by trade, and differences in the structure of trade were not important. Similarly, variations in the degree of specialization were not of much significance.

In contrast, differences in the size of shop were found to be important:

> on average, US shops are not only physically larger than their British counterparts, but are characterised by a sales area per worker which is about 2.5 times the British figure. No doubt this reflects a more extensive use of self service techniques in US retailing. Certainly it seems to imply that the superior American labour productivity performance is in part due to higher capital intensity – more bricks, mortar and fittings per shop assistant – than in Britain.

Since Smith and Hitchens published their findings, the average size of shop has increased in many UK trades and productivity has almost certainly risen. Nevertheless, UK retailing remains less capital intensive than in the USA, one example of which is that UK retailers have been slow to capitalize on the benefits that technology such as laser scanning electronic checkouts can bring to their operations (*Financial Times*, 30 July 1986 p. 55).

Turning now to *profitability*, data have been published by the Office of Fair Trading (OFT, 1985) on the relative performance of food manufacturers, food retailers and all sectors excluding oil.[4] What the results show is that the historic cost return on capital employed in food manufacturing fell from 19.5 per cent in 1975 to 15.9 per cent in 1983. By comparison, food retailing achieved a small trend increase over the same period (from 20.4 per cent in 1975 to 23.5 per cent in 1983). At current costs the return on capital employed in 1983 was similar in both food manufacturing and 'all sectors excluding oil' (7.9 per cent and 8.9 per cent respectively), but for food retailing the corresponding figure was several percentage points higher at 14.0 per cent in 1983.

During the last ten years or so, manufacturers have often referred to such figures and complained to the government that the larger multiple retailers were abusing their dominant positions and buying power in order to extract large discounts from manufacturers and hence to swell their own profits at the expense of the manufacturers. As a result of such complaints there have been two official investigations of the discounts retailers receive from manufacturers. The first was carried out by the Monopolies and Mergers Commission (MMC, 1981) and the second by the Office of Fair Trading (1985).

Some idea of the magnitude of discounts can be gained from Table 11.9 which estimates the value of certain special terms negotiated by manufacturers with their retail customers. These so-called 'special terms' are typically more favourable than those published in manufacturers' price lists, and include things such as retrospective rebates, contributions to retailers' advertising expenditure and the provision of sales staff at the manufacturer's expense. As can be seen from Table 11.9, the average value of such discounts is substantially greater for manufacturers' top four and top ten customers than it is for others.

To some extent the larger retailers are benefiting from economies that manufacturers achieve in such activities as order processing, order assembly and delivery, although there is some suggestion in the MMC and OFT reports that not all discounts can be fully justified by reference to cost savings. Even so, both the MMC and OFT concluded that the granting of discriminatory discounts was not against the public interest because the benefits of lower buying prices had been passed on to consumers (usually through price cuts but also via improved service).[5]

Furthermore, the OFT stated in its report that it had not been able 'to identify any particular case which amounted to an abuse of buying power or other anti-competitive practice which warranted investigation under the competition legislation'. So perhaps the higher rates of

Table 11.9 *Value of Special Terms Negotiated by Manufacturers with Retail Customers*

Size ranking of customer	MMC report % of gross sales	OFT report % of gross sales
1–4	9.2	10.5
5–10	7.7	9.2
1–10	8.7	10.0
Others	5.6	7.3

Source: Office of Fair Trading, 1985, p. 48.

return earned by larger retailers should be seen as an indication that they have succeeded in meeting consumers' needs. This conclusion would, of course, be consistent with their increase in market share discussed earlier.

11.5   PUBLIC POLICY

Public policy has had a profound influence on retail structure and performance during the last few decades. A major watershed was legislation[6] which led to the progressive abolition of resale price maintenance during the 1950s and 1960s. The effect of abolition was that manufacturers could no longer take steps to ensure that all retailers charged the same price for some given product. Thus the legislation opened the way for retail price competition and was one of the key factors behind the rapid expansion of the multiples and increased efficiency and productivity in the distributive trades (George and Joll, 1981, pp. 286–91).

Since then the retail trades have been affected by numerous measures including Town and Country Planning Acts, price controls, Consumer Credit and Fair Trading Acts, and modifications to the Wages Council system. However, limited space precludes a detailed examination of all these measures; instead the pervasive influence of public policy is illustrated by looking at just two areas: planning controls and consumer protection.

If retailers want to obtain *planning permission* to construct new shops, then in the first instance they must apply to the district councils; but if permission is refused or if conditions are attached to the granting of permission, then retailers have the right to appeal to the Secretary of State for the Environment. Most appeals are conducted via written evidence, but where major developments are concerned a public inquiry may be held, after which the inspector conducting the inquiry must submit a report to the secretary of state who makes the final decision. The secretary of state also has the power to call in for scrutiny any application which in his opinion warrants special investigation, and in practice many of the applications subject to such scrutiny have been for large stores like hypermarkets.

In the 1970s it often proved difficult to obtain planning permission for such stores. The Department of the Environment turned down a high proportion of the applications it 'called in', and many local authorities were equally as restrictive with the result that the pace of change in retailing was slowed down. However, towards the end of the 1970s the attitude of central government changed somewhat and in 1977 it issued new guidance for local authorities in the form of a development control policy note (Department of the Environment, 1977). The note reviewed research findings relating to large new stores and concluded that 'retailing developments which extend choice in shopping, allow more efficient retailing, enable a better service to be given to the public as a whole and make shopping more convenient and pleasant are, in general, to be welcomed'.

Planning permission thus became easier to obtain – but not in all areas because many local authorities were still concerned that the opening of large new stores would lead to the closure of many shops. The result is that superstore and hypermarket penetration varies markedly from one region to another: in the North-West planning permission has been relatively easy to obtain and, in 1985, the region had 15.4 per cent of total superstore sales area in the UK, but only 11.7 per cent of the UK's population. In contrast the South-East had 31 per cent of the UK's population but only 22 per cent of superstore floorspace (Mintel, 1986, p. 11).

In an attempt to bring about more consistency, the secretary of state made the following parliamentary statement in 1985:

> it is not necessary to add more detailed advice to that given in Development Control Policy Note 13 [Department of Environment, 1977] . . . It is important, however, to stress . . . that it is not the function of the planning system to inhibit competition among retailers or among methods of retailing . . . the possible effects of proposed major retail developments on existing retailers is not in this sense a relevant factor in deciding planning applications.

This statement represents a significant shift of policy and is likely to make it much easier to obtain planning permission in the future.

In the *consumer protection* field, there now exists a substantial body of legislation aimed at safeguarding shoppers' rights and, inevitably, this has increased the obligations laid on retailers. One example is the Sale of Goods Act 1979 (which brought together the provisions of earlier legislation, including the Sale of Goods Act 1893). Under the Act consumers are entitled to buy goods which correspond to their description, are of merchantable quality and are fit for the purpose for which they are bought. These rights apply regardless of whether the goods are bought for cash, by hire-purchase or conditional sales agreements, and in all cases the obligations are imposed on the person transferring the goods, and not on the manufacturers. Moreover, consumers cannot lose their rights by signing them away or as a consequence of notices exhibited in a shop or on the back of a receipt.

Another example of the legislation is the Fair Trading Act of 1973 which provided for the establishment of the Office of Fair Trading. The Office is under the guidance of the Director General of Fair Trading, and he is charged with safeguarding consumers' interests and can investigate both general consumer trade practices and the activities of individual traders. In addition, the Director General is responsible for screening all proposed mergers and if he thinks that a merger will operate against the public interest, then he can recommend a detailed investigation by the Monopolies and Mergers Commission, provided that the value of assets acquired exceeds £30 million or that the merger would produce a situation where one firm controlled at least 25 per cent of the market. In practice few retail mergers have been referred to the Commission, but the situation may change because the Monopolies and Mergers Commission report on discounts (1981) expressed concern that 'retailing might come to be dominated by a very few retailers to such an extent that competition would suffer and the consumer would be worse served than at present'. It was therefore considered 'important to keep a particularly close watch on future mergers in the distributive trades'.

Finally, a new Consumer Protection Act was introduced in May 1987. The Act had two main aims. One was to introduce strict product liability so that consumers would no longer have to prove negligence when claiming compensation for damage or injury caused by unsafe or defective products. The other was to strengthen the provisions of the 1968 Trade Descriptions Act. That Act made it an offence to give false descriptions of goods orally, in writing, or in advertisements; and it also required that, where a retailer claimed a price reduction (for example, in a 'sale'), then he must have charged the old price for at least 28 days in the previous 6 months. However, the 1968 Act was weakened in various ways by appeal cases, and therefore the intention of the Consumer Protection Act was to remedy the defects and make it a criminal offence to give consumers misleading indications about the prices of any goods or services.

11.6   CONCLUSION

The last two decades have witnessed major changes in the structure of the retail trades, in the competitive strategies adopted by retailers, and in the legislative framework within which retailers operate.

The immediate future is likely to see a continuation of the trends discussed in this chapter, although one important development could be a greater emphasis on multinational retailing. At this point in time few retailers have extensive operations overseas, but for reasons already mentioned (such as the limited availability of prime retail sites and the possibility of tighter merger controls) the major multiples may find it difficult to achieve their growth targets within the confines of the UK, and may therefore look increasingly to other countries. For instance, both Marks & Spencer and J. Sainsbury 'have carefully built up their knowledge of the US market and may make a substantial acquisition there in the next few years' (*Financial Times*, 30 July 1986).

NOTES TO CHAPTER 11

1 The *National Income Blue Book* (Central Statistical Office, United Kingdom National Accounts, 1986 edition) shows that in 1985 the distributive trades as a whole accounted for 13.2 per cent of GDP.
2 In the ten years from 1975 to 1985, the retail price index rose by 177 per cent but the price of clothing and footwear rose by only 77 per cent. As a result, even though there was an increase in the quantity of clothing bought, there was a fall in the share of consumer spending going on clothing.
3 For example, an analysis of the 1984 Retail Inquiry showed that turnover per person varied from £26,231 per annum, in clothing and footwear retailing to £42,553 per annum in household goods.
4 The data relate to trading profit and are based upon the published accounts of large industrial and commercial companies, adjusted as necessary to achieve consistency in measuring trading profit and capital employed on historic and current cost bases.
5 The OFT carried out a survey of a large number of products and found that the average gross margin of those products was not significantly different as between multiples and independents, which is 'not inconsistent with the proposition that the benefits of lower buying prices are passed on in the form of lower selling prices' (Office of Fair Trading, 1985, p. 12).
6 Collective resale price maintenance (that is, enforcement of retail prices by a group of manufacturers) was prohibited by the Restrictive Trade Practices Act 1956, and enforcement by an individual manufacturer was restricted by the Resale Prices Act 1964.

REFERENCES

Department of the Environment (1977), *Development Control Policy Note 13: Large New Stores* (London: HMSO).
Eliot, S. J. (1983), 'The crisis in the co-operative movement', *Retail and Distribution Management*, 11, 4, 8–14.
George, K. D., and Joll, C. (1981), *Industrial Organisation*, 3rd edn (London: Allen & Unwin).
Holdren, B. (1960), *The Structure of a Retail Market and the Market Behaviour of Retail Units* (Ames, Iowa: Iowa University Press).
Kerin, R. A., and Varaiya, N. (1985), 'Mergers and acquisitions in retailing: a review and critical analysis', *Journal of Retailing*, 61, 1.
Mintel (1986), 'Grocery superstores', *Retail Intelligence*, July–September, 7–49.
Monopolies and Mergers Commission (1981), *Discounts to Retailers*, HC311: Session 1980–81 (London: HMSO).
Monopolies and Mergers Commission (1983), *Great Universal Stores and Empire Stores*, Cmnd 8777 (London: HMSO).
Nystrom, H. (1970), *Retail Pricing: An Integrated Economic and Psychological Approach* (Stockholm: Swedish Institute of Economic Research).
Office of Fair Trading (1985), *Competition and Retailing* (London).
Smith, A. D., and Hitchens, D. M. W. N. (1983), 'Comparative British and

American productivity in retailing', *National Institute Economic Review*, 104, 45–57.

Tucker, K. A., and Yamey, B. S., (eds) (1973), *Economics of Retailing* (Harmondsworth, Middx: Penguin).

Walters, D. (1985a), 'Evaluating the role of concessions in assortment planning', *Retail*, 3, 2, 39–42.

Walters, D. (1985b), 'Relative differentiation for competitive advantage', *Retail*, 3, 3, 42–4.

Ward, T. S. (1973), *The Distribution of Consumer Goods: Structure and Performance* (London: Cambridge University Press).

FURTHER READING

Craig, C., and Wilkinson, F. (1985), *Pay and Employment in Four Retail Trades*, Research paper no. 51 (London: Department of Employment).

Department of Trade and Industry (Business Statistics Office), *Retailing 1984*, Business Monitor SDO 25, (London: HMSO).

Journal of Retailing (New York: New York University).

Mintel, *Retail Intelligence* (London: Mintel Publications).

Reports of the Monopolies and Mergers Commission, e.g. (1981) *Discounts to Retailers*, HC 311: Session 1980–81; (1985) *Dee Corporation and Booker McConnell*; Cmnd 9429; (1985) *Lonrho and House of Fraser*, Cmnd 9458.

Retail Business (London: Economist Intelligence Unit).

Chapter Twelve

Rail Transport

KEN GWILLIAM

12.1 INTRODUCTION

12.1.1 Rail Transport as an Integrated National Monopoly

The 1947 Transport Act took into public ownership the whole of the British railway system, together with the bulk of the public road haulage industry. This nationalized public transport system was to be managed by a British Transport Commission (BTC), organized for operational purposes into a number of separate modal executives. Road haulage was largely denationalized after 1953, and the 1962 Transport Act separated the BTC into five autonomous nationalized industries, of which British Rail (BR) was the largest.

Although some of the peripheral activities which originally belonged to BR (for example, British Transport Hotels and the Sealink shipping company) were privatized in the early 1980s, and the National Bus Company has been privatized in 1986/7, the main railway system of the United Kingdom remains as a unitary nationally owned company. The only rail operations outside its control are the publicly owned urban underground systems in London, Glasgow and Newcastle upon Tyne and a number of very small private railways, mostly operated by enthusiasts for tourist purposes, which are not considered in this chapter.

Thus rail transport is seen as a 'natural monopoly', and government policy towards rail transport has been that of trying to find the appropriate institutions, objectives and controls for this statutory monopoly within a transport sector which is competitive and increasingly predominantly privately owned.

12.1.2 The Current Rail Market

At the end of 1986 BR operated a passenger network of over 14,000 kilometres of route, with some 2,400 stations. On this network it operates about 310 loaded train-kilometres a year carrying 30 billion passenger-kilometres. This accounts for 6 per cent of the total passenger-kilometres by mechanized transport in the UK but, because of the relatively long average rail trip length, only 2 per cent of passenger journeys.

The passenger business is divided into three main sectors, with very differing characteristics.

The *Inter City* sector is the main user of 3,400 route-kilometres and about 100 stations, although Inter City trips may originate at any station. The main Inter City network radiates in five main corridors from London, but the sector also includes the cross-country trunk route from the North-East to the South-West. Half of the total business is to and from London, and half of the trips exceed 160 kilometres in length. In this sector rail transport provides for both business and non-business trips in competition mainly with the private car over the shorter ranges, with the deregulated coach industry over distances of up to 400 kilometres (mainly for non-business trips), and with air transport for the very long distance, predominantly business, trips. It operates with an average load factor of about 40 per cent.

The *London and South-East* sector (renamed Network SouthEast in 1986) is the main user of 3,300 route-kilometres and about 900 stations. It accounts for 43 per cent of loaded train mileage and 60 per cent of passenger rail trips. Although it carries only 3 per cent of all mechanized journeys in the London region, it carries about one-third of London commuters and dominates the longer-distance segment of the commuting market, carrying over 80 per cent of those commuting from outside the old GLC boundary. It mainly competes with the private car over the longer distances, though there has been growing competition since 1980 from commuter coaches. In some areas there is also direct competition with London Transport underground railways. This part of the BR network suffers from very heavy peak demands but has much equipment that is underutilized for long periods of the day and, despite its promotional efforts for off-peak traffic, has an average load factor of only 25 per cent.

The *Provincial* services of BR include branch-line services, stopping services on the main lines and some rail services in the metropolitan areas other than London. The sector is the main user of about 7,700 km of route and about 1,400 stations. It accounts for 32 per cent of loaded train-kilometres and only 16 per cent of passenger-kilometres and consequently has an average load factor of only 20 per cent. It competes with car and bus, the latter competition being expected to become more fierce as deregulation of the stage bus industry bites after 1986. Before the abolition of the metropolitan counties in 1985 there was planned integration of rail and other transport services in the major conurbations, with rail services operated to standards and fares set by the political authority, and with compensatory direct grants from the local authority under Section 20 of the 1968 Transport Act. Although the formal provisions still remain it is not at all clear how much of the financial support will in the long run survive.

The *Freight* business is divided into two sectors, freight and parcels. The freight sector has a gross income of about £550 million, which is one-sixth of the total gross income of BR. In 1985/6 it lifted 140 million tonnes, of which 98 million was bulk movement of coal and coke, iron and steel. The average length of haul is only 71 miles, despite the comparative advantage that rail might be expected to have over longer distances. This low figure is largely due to the relatively short hauls of trainload coal and coke. But it is also a' perennial problem for BR that rail technology shows a comparative advantage in longer-haul freight of which there is relatively little in the UK. It is hoped that the building of the Channel Tunnel, due for completion in 1993, will radically alter this situation by opening up new international rail markets.

The *parcels* sector has a gross income of about £100 million, derived in approximately equal proportions from parcels trains and from parcels carried in passenger trains. In recent years it has lost its previous monopoly position in the long-distance carriage of mail and newspapers, but has been successfully expanding its own express 'Red Star' system.

12.2 THE RAIL TRANSPORT MARKET

12.2.1 The Nature of the Product

Rail transport, like all public transport services, cannot be stored; if not used at the moment of its production it is wasted. Whilst in some markets, such as the trainload movements of bulk freight, it is possible to produce only on demand, in most cases the immediately perishable and to some degree indivisible nature of the product makes it inevitable that capacity will be provided which is surplus to demand. In these circumstances the art of management is to plan and market services in the best way to meet the corporate objective, which, as shown later, is not always profit. The complexity of scheduling rail services means that there can be a lead time of over a year on revision of timetables, leaving railways very vulnerable to unforeseen increases or reductions in demand.

12.2.2 Supply Characteristics – the Cost Structure

This inherent inflexibility can be exemplified very clearly by looking at the rail cost structure. If rail costs are grouped into those which are invariant with respect to the size of the business (fixed costs), those which vary with the size of network operated (semi-variables), and those which vary directly with the amount of service provided (variables), (see Table 12.1) it can be seen that a large proportion of the total costs are committed independently of the level of service provided.

Table 12.1   *The Structure of Rail Costs in 1985*

	£ million	%
Variable		
Train services	1,150	39.8
Semi-Variable		
Terminals	321	11.1
Miscellaneous traffic expenses	77	2.7
Track and signalling	688	23.8
Fixed		
Administration and general	653	22.6

Source: Transport Statistics Great Britain.

Further than this, of course, the marginal cost of the extra passenger or rail container on a train which has space for it is very low.

12.2.3   Demand Characteristics – Market Segmentation

It is difficult to make valid generalizations about the characteristics of demand because of its heterogeneity but some introductory observations may help in understanding the market performance of BR.

For passenger transport the factors of paramount importance are income, price and quality of service. The effects of income are complex. Increasing income is associated with increasing car ownership, which would normally be expected to militate against the use of public transport. On the other hand rail transport is a 'superior' good and as incomes rise there is a tendency for the amount of personal transport demanded to increase more than proportionately and certainly for rail transport to be substituted for bus, and for long journeys, for car transport. Thus, as the 1976 Consultative Document on Transport Policy (HMSO, 1976) showed, the higher income groups are responsible for a disproportionately large share of expenditure on rail transport, partly because business travel undertaken by higher income groups is taken largely at full fares.

The evidence on price elasticities fits well within this pattern. For business travel, price elasticity appears to be low, whilst for other purposes higher elasticities prevail (Jones and Nichols, 1983; Glaister, 1983). In particular, recent evidence of competition between rail and express bus services for the custom of students and old age pensioners suggests fairly high elasticities and cross-elasticities in these markets (Douglas, 1987).

Competition between rail and the private car, and to a lesser extent between rail and air seems to depend more on quality of service. The ability of accelerated rail services to compete with air on the routes from London to Leeds, Birmingham and Manchester and with the

private car for transport to the South-West has demonstrated relatively
high service elasticities. Similarly improved speed and reliability
associated with electrification has contributed to the expansion of the
long-distance commuting market in the South-East.

For freight transport service factors also have been shown to be
important in the modal choice studies (Edwards and Bayliss, 1970).
Whilst price is clearly not irrelevant it seems that the ability to provide
a quality service, well integrated with the rest of the production and
distribution system of the sector concerned is paramount. The decline
of the BR general merchandise business has been attributed partly to a
failure to concentrate sufficiently on rail freight service quality
(Gourvish, 1986).

12.2.4 British Rail within the Transport Market

Given that BR has a statutory monopoly in rail transport the
interesting questions of market structure are not internal to railways
but concern its relationship in the transport market with its customers
and competitors.

The rail share of both the freight and passenger markets in the UK
has been falling steadily (see Table 12.1). But in recent years this has
represented increasing specialization of function and a growth of road
transport rather than an overall decline in rail traffic. Between 1972
and 1977, the rail freight business increased in a number of major bulk
categories (coal and coke, earths and stones, chemicals). More
recently it has begun to hold its own in some categories of general
cargo when speed and certainty of delivery could be assured. Similarly
in the passenger market, InterCity has maintained its market by a
combination of steady improvement in quality (associated with the
High Speed Train and more recently electrification) and effective use
of discriminatory pricing. Despite fare increases, BR also maintains its
leading role in providing for commuters into London from the South-
East because of its quality of service advantage.

One of the dominating characteristics of the transport sector is that
the road network is substantially more dense than the rail network
(250,000 route miles compared with 11,000). Thus rail transport is
dependent either on traffics that both originate and terminate very
close to the sparser network or on adequate arrangements for modal
transfer. In the passenger market the history of competition between
bus and rail has often meant that bus stations and railway stations were
far apart and there has been relatively little attempt to co-ordinate
services or time-tables.

The problem has been even more intense for freight where the costs
of terminal handling are a large proportion of total costs, hence
militating against multi-modal transport. The traditional rail response
to this has been to offer its own road collection and delivery services,
hence attempting to offer a door-to-door service at least within the one

organization. But this was always a costly arrangement and after the transfer of the rail delivery fleet to National Carriers Ltd in 1968 traditional transhipment traffic declined.

A technically more attractive alternative means of handling general merchandise is by containerization. Because the transfer of whole containers from road to rail vehicles was much cheaper than the manhandling of goods, and because it gave improvements also in speed and security, this was felt to be the best way of maintaining the railways' general merchandise market. The Freightliners company was set up to develop this potential. More recently the Speedlink concept of guaranteed overnight delivery of general cargo traffic has been addressed to the same characteristic of quality of service.

Even more crucial than the co-ordination among modes of transport may be the co-ordination between the transport function and the rest of the production and distribution system. In this respect the own-account road haulage fleet has an obvious initial advantage in terms of total control over distribution management. The corollary of this is that BR has also had to seek means of providing services equally closely linked to the rest of the production and distribution process. In some markets it has been very successful. The 'merry-go-round' trains carting coal between mines and power stations are physically well integrated with both the mining and power supply industries. More generally, government support for investment in private sidings under Section 8 of the 1974 Railways Act is selectively redressing a trend that has seen the number of private sidings reduced from 6,000 to 2,000 over the last 15 years. Increasingly the evidence on freight transport suggests that the crucial decisions are those concerning investment in facilities, terminals and fleet, particularly those by customers which will effectively tie consignors to rail transport for the bulk of their traffic.

12.2.5 Labour

About two-thirds of the operating expenses of BR are accounted for by staff costs, a proportion not dissimilar to that of the bus and road haulage industries. Efficient use of labour is hence of great significance. Not surprisingly, in a traditional labour-intensive industry facing increasing competition and the need for technical change, the management of change has been a source of substantial conflict between the BR board and its unions.

There are three major rail unions. The National Union of Railwaymen (NUR), with a total membership of 126,000 and 83,000 employed by BR, is a general union with members in most grades and functions. The Amalgamated Society of Locomotive Engineers and Firemen (ASLEF) and the Transport and Salaried Staffs Association (TSSA) are smaller unions with more specialized memberships of footplate staff and non-manual staff respectively. Inter-union rivalries

Table 12.2 Rail Transport, 1948–85

	Train-km (million)	Pass-km ('000 m)	% of all pass-km	Tonne-km ('000 m)	% of all tonne-km	Network ('000 km)	Staff ('000)
1948	588.3	34.2	n/a	35.4	n/a	31.5	649
1955	584.6	32.7	18.6	36.2	37.3	30.7	565
1960	604.2	34.7	15.6	30.5	30.6	29.6	515
1965	518.8	30.1	10.5	25.2	20.9	24.0	365
1970	469.9	30.4	8.8	26.8	19.4	19.0	274
1975	404.8	30.3	9.0	20.9	15.0	18.1	230
1980	396.6	30.3	7.0	17.6	10.9	17.6	205
1985	341.6	29.7	7.0	15.3	9.0	16.7	168

Source: Transport Statistics Great Britain.

have been a notable feature of the industry for many years.

As Table 12.2 shows, the labour force employed by BR has been reduced dramatically even over the last decade when the output has remained fairly stable. This has resulted from a combination of revised operating practices (for example, single-driver operation, elimination of guards on fully fitted freight trains); the introduction of new technology (new rolling stock needs less maintenance with the result that the workshop staff employed by British Rail Engineering Ltd (BREL) has fallen from 88,000 to 17,000 over the last decade); and revised management structures (a whole tier of line management has been taken out and headquarters staff reduced).

The impact of these policies has varied greatly. In some areas there remain staff vacancies (for example, there were said to be 10,000 unfilled vacancies in London and the South-East at the end of 1986) whilst in others there is little hope of alternative employment either within the function or the locality affected. Relatively attractive redundancy and early retirement provisions, and some attempts to provide assistance for small business developments in released properties (for example, Shildon and Swindon engineering works) may sweeten the pill, but still leave it basically unpalatable. The resistance of the unions to the introduction of labour-saving devices (such as one-man operation of trains) in these circumstances is understandable.

It is also worth noting that rail employment is still relatively low wage employment in the UK (Gwilliam et al., 1979) although both BR and the Department of Transport have insisted that labour shortages in the South-East are not the consequence of the tightness of the subsidy arrangements but are a reflection of the unattractiveness of the unsocial hours of work.

12.3   THE DEVELOPMENT OF RAIL POLICY

12.3.1   The Decline of Rail Transport

Over the period of public ownership of the railways there has been a substantial decline in both the level of demand for rail transport, and in the resources used in the industry, as Table 12.2 shows. The rail transport share of both freight and passenger markets has fallen to less than one-third of the levels prevailing in 1955.

Three features of Table 12.2 are particularly notable. First, the absolute decline in rail transport is much less startling than its relative decline. Secondly, the reduction in labour force and network size greatly exceeds that in output of train-miles or traffic carried, thus showing dramatic improvement in the productivity of the assets employed. Thirdly, since 1975 network size, output of train-kilometres and patronage have been broadly maintained, with only employment continuing to decline.

As shown later, in Section 12.4.1, the performance of the rail system has improved substantially over the period, both in terms of the physical productivity of the assets used and in terms of the quality of the product. Despite this, however, the cost of rail transport to the consumer has been increasing relative to that of other modes, as Table 12.3 shows. The consequence of this history of declining traffic and increasing costs has been a significant increase in the financial deficit of the railways. In the years immediately after nationalization the Railway Executive was able to show a surplus on operating account, but was not able to cover its apportioned share of the central charges of the BTC. Over the next four years rail finances improved, and in 1952 the railways produced an overall surplus. But the improvement did not continue. By 1956 there was a surplus on operating account which had reached £104 million by 1962, giving an overall deficit in that year of £156 million. That deficit has increased steadily in money terms since then, as Table 12.4 shows.

It should be noted, however, that the bulk of the increase in real terms had occurred by 1975. Even in money terms the deficit is now

Table 12.3   *Passenger Transport: Consumer Cost Indices (1960 = 100)*

	1960	1965	1970	1975	1980	1985
Rail fares	100	135	175	366	831	1,064
Bus and coach fares	100	132	189	366	871	1,263
Purchase price of cars	100	87	102	172	400	512
Running cost of cars	100	118	147	284	557	813
Total consumer expenditure	100	114	145	261	502	693

Source: Transport Statistics Great Britain.

Table 12.4 Total Financial Support to British Rail (£ million)

	1972	1973	1974	1975	1976	1977	1978	1979	1980	1981	1982	1983	1984	1985	1990 (Target)
Current	141	189	391	514	494	520	571	675	727	875	987	997	1,035	1,001	550
1985 prices	614	753	1,344	1,424	1,195	1,105	1,089	1,126	1,012	1,088	1,144	1,099	1,098	1,001	

Source: Transport Statistics Great Britain.

being reduced following the introduction of new arrangements for the control of the finances of the nationalized industries and new tougher financial policies imposed by the Conservative government in the early 1980s.

12.3.2   Rail Policy before 1974

Several factors contributed to the deteriorating financial situation. Increased competition from the road haulage industry after denationalization in 1953 caused losses in freight traffic and revenue. Changes in industrial structure, particularly the decreasing movement of the staple rail traffics of coal and iron ore, accentuated this loss. The growth of car ownership, and the decreasing competitiveness of rail, led to similar losses in the passenger market.

Initially the problem was seen as that of investing to increase rail productivity and secure the transition of the system to a new stability. In 1955 the government accepted a modernization plan with an estimated cost of £1,240 million. The programme provided for improvements of track and signalling, replacement of steam locomotion by diesel or electric traction, the modernization of passenger rolling stock and stations, and the remodelling of freight services using continuously braked wagons and modernized depots. In the event capital costs were 30 per cent greater than anticipated and benefits much slower to accrue than expected. By 1962 there was a record deficit.

Even before this date rail policy had come under review. In 1960 the Select Committee on Nationalised Industries reported critically on the way railways were being managed (HMSO, 1960) and in 1961 a special committee of investigation under the chairmanship of Sir Ivone Stedeford advised a thorough reorganization of nationalized transport.

The 1962 Transport Act implemented this reorganization. The BTC was split into five separate industry boards and the newly created British Railways Board (BRB) given the remit to break even as soon as possible. To this end nearly £500 million of capital debt was written off, a further £700 million suspended, and support grants for up to £450 million provided for a period of five years at the end of which financial viability was expected. The 1962 Act also removed the obligation to act as a common carrier, and, with the exception of passenger fares in London and freight rates for services competing with coastal shipping BRB was given commercial freedom. Dr Richard Beeching was appointed as chairman in June 1961 with the remit to reshape BR policy within this new remit. To this end he undertook a thorough review of the rail business, published in March 1963. (HMSO, 1963)

The main thrust of the Beeching Report was that the railway system was overextended and underutilized. One-third of the route mileage carried only 1 per cent of the train mileage, whilst one-third of the tations produced only 1 per cent of the traffic. Almost half of the passenger rolling stock was used for high-peak requirements only. Local passenger services and wagon load general merchandise freight were seen to be particularly unremunerative. It was therefore proposed to close over 2,000 stations and 5,000 miles of route to passenger traffic, to substantially reduce the carriage and wagon fleet and to rationalize the rail workshops accordingly. This was the 'Beeching axe'.

The programme was not totally negative. The review showed coal and mineral traffic to be still profitable despite its recent decline and identified express passenger traffic and a revamped general freight service operating full trainloads of demountable containers (the 'liner train' concept) as potentially so. Thus the programme of conversion from steam to diesel traction was to be continued and a major investment to be made in the new freight system.

The forecast financial improvements were not achieved for a number of reasons. Liner trains did not make the expected impact and wagon load traffics were not cut as rapidly as proposed. The sundries traffic thus became more rather than less unprofitable whilst continued stagnation of the basic industries prevented the expected growth in profit from the coal and mineral traffic. Many of the proposals implied increases in labour productivity without providing for a share of the gain to be taken in wage increases. The depreciation costs of the new equipment were probably underestimated. And, above all, the government did not, in the event, allow the rate of service withdrawal proposed by Beeching. Thus, despite the Beeching revolution, the financial position continued to deteriorate. By 1968 the deficit was back to £150 million and another comprehensive review of transport policy was undertaken. The 1967 review, implemented in the 1968 Transport Act, was the product of a Labour administration with Barbara Castle as Minister of Transport. It might therefore have been expected to involve a much more planning-oriented, pro public transport stance than that undertaken in 1962 by a Conservative government.

That was not, in effect, the case. The 1968 Transport Act implemented the proposals of the Geddes Committee report (HMSO, 1965) to deregulate the road haulage industry and the transport sector moved a step further in the direction of reliance upon competition between modes in a managed market. Although there was provision in the 1968 Act for a new type of restriction on the road haulage industry in the form of special authorizations being required to be able to carry bulk traffics, long-distance traffics and large vehicle loads, implementation of that provision was made conditional on BR being able to offer an equivalent service in terms of price, speed and quality. In the event that part of the proposals was never implemented and the freight market became freely competitive.

The basic philosophy of the regime was that railways were to compete in the market and were to be commercially viable. The main thrust of the 1968 Act therefore was to reconstruct the basis on which rail transport was to compete in the market, to relieve them of the burden of historic debt and to compensate them directly for any remaining non-commercial obligations. A further £1,262 million of capital debt was therefore written off leaving the board with a book value of only £365 million, reducing debt servicing charges by £54 million in 1969. In addition the transfer to the newly formed National Freight Corporation of the loss-making sundries services and half of the Freightliner company improved the accounts by a further £18 million per annum. A grant of £15 million per annum was also to be paid for up to five years to finance the elimination of surplus track capacity. As far as continuing obligations were concerned the Act provided that specific subsidies should be paid for any unremunerative service which the government required BR to continue to provide.

The achievement of a small surplus after grant in 1969 and 1970 seemed to suggest that balance of compensation payments had been set about right. But once again the deficits escalated in the following two years and a further review of rail policy was instituted.

12.3.3 Rail Policy since 1974

In 1973 the government and BR undertook a joint policy review. The outcome was that both parties accepted that the commercial remit of 1968 could not be achieved, even with the subsidy provisions, unless there was a substantially smaller rail network. Moreover, it appears to have been accepted that no politically accepted pruning could be achieved within the existing framework. So it was the framework, rather than the rail network, which would have to change.

The 1974 Railways Act used the powers and terminology suggested by EC regulations on railways to specify a 'public service obligation' (PSO) to maintain the network and level of service broadly at the level then obtaining. The system of specific subsidies was replaced by a blanket compensation for the achievement of this objective. This was set at £300 million per annum for the next five years, inclusive of operating deficits and new capital requirements. The existing capital debt was again written down from £439 million to £250 million.

Even this regime proved difficult to live with. Faced with the great inflationary pressure arising from the 1973 oil crisis the government imposed restraints on the pricing freedom of the nationalized industries which prevented BR from using the main instrument at their disposal to reconcile a fixed service obligation and financial target with escalating costs. By 1976 the cash requirement had risen to £450 million and BR management felt it necessary to argue that if government wished to maintain the 1974 Act network it would have to provide increased resources for the task.

In 1976 and 1977 the problem was confronted in the context of another transport sector policy review. The 1977 Transport Policy White Paper (HMSO, 1977) maintained the concept of the public service obligation and its compensatory grant, but recognized that this would have to be determined annually in the light of current circumstances. Moreover, rail objectives, and the consequential obligation, were to be specified separately for the distinctly separate markets in which BR operated. Everything henceforth would turn on the annual negotiation of the PSO grant and the sector objectives. The rationality of the subsidy structure and procedures have been widely criticized (Gwilliam, Nash and Palmer, 1982).

12.4 MANAGEMENT OF THE RAILWAY BUSINESS

12.4.1 Sector Management

In the early 1980s railway management structure was subject to its most radical reorganization since nationalization. The main responsibility for the commercial performance of the railway system has traditionally been vested in regional general managers, who controlled both supply and marketing of services within their region. Operational standards were set by the four major functional directorates (Operations, Civil Engineering, Mechanical and Electrical Engineering, and Signals and Telecommunications). Under these arrangements it was possible to integrate the provision of the various types of rail service (freight, InterCity passenger, local passenger) and to maintain high levels of technical competence in the supply functions. However, as government became increasingly interested after 1974 in the way in which revenue support was being used, and increasingly keen to set stiff targets for those services which they considered to be best provided on a purely commercial basis in competitive markets, the limitations of the structure began to become more apparent. The separate-market-based way in which the railway was being viewed from outside did not have a counterpart at the highest level of management structure. Decisions on the level of technical service to be provided did not have a clear commercial basis. No one appeared to have the responsibility or the grasp to ensure that there was not significant overprovision of jointly used facilities.

Sector management is the response to these perceived problems. The railway is divided into five main businesses (freight, parcels, InterCity passenger, provincial passenger, and London and South-East). All operational assets, and their associated costs, are assigned to one of these sectors; where more than one sector uses an asset there is a procedure for charging out costs to the secondary user. The sector directors have their separate financial targets and are expected to manage the assets allocated to them to achieve those targets. Separate sector results have appeared in the Annual Accounts since 1982. The

Regional General Managers become production managers providing services within their region for all of the sector directors. The traditional functions become part of the supply organization, with line staff reporting to the regional general manager and the functional directors taking an essentially advisory technical role on standards. The management thus becomes 'business-led' rather than technically led.

The structure is not without its potential anomalies. Because running a single train over a section of track may lead to a passenger sector having to accept primary responsibility for the infrastructure there may be an institutional bias against the provision of some services which might be justifiable on the margin. At the local level it is the responsibility of regional general management to look out for and circumvent such anomalies, whilst at the national level it is the responsibility of the Managing Director (Railways) to prevent their occurrence.

12.4.2 Corporate Planning

The focal document for rail strategy is the corporate plan which sets out, sector by sector, the financial and operational goals on a five-year rolling basis. It is made consistent with resource requirements and availability and is the basis of the discussion between the board and the Secretary of State for Transport of the PSO grant requirements and the investment requirements. When approved it forms the framework for action planning by regional general management which has the responsibility to provide services according to plan and budget. The ability to monitor performance effectively against plan has been greatly improved in recent years by the introduction of computerized management information systems.

12.4.3 Cost Allocation

The setting of sector objectives in financial terms requires costs to be allocated between the sectors. Where an asset is used exclusively by one sector (for example, a freight wagon) no problem occurs. Some assets, however, are used by several sectors in circumstances where a reduction of use by any one might reduce the total amount of the asset required (for example, some classes of locomotive). BR calls these common costs and they are usually allocated in proportion to use. In other cases the asset is indivisible and, though shared between sectors in use, would not be reduced if any particular user ceased to need the asset (for example, a single-track rail route). These are referred to as joint costs.

In cases of pure jointness of cost any allocation between joint users is essentially arbitrary. It was for this reason that for many years BR preferred to look at activities in terms of the contribution which they made to the joint costs of the system rather than attempt to produce separate sector accounts.

Since the adoption of sector management such an approach is unacceptable and hence an exhaustive allocation is necessary. All assets, including infrastructure, are allocated to a 'prime user'. For infrastructure the procedure for charging costs to secondary users is called 'sole user with surplus add-back'. On this convention the prime user takes such costs as it would incur if it were the only user, and had adjusted capacity to the optimal level for its own purposes. Other sectors are then charged the increments which result from adjusting to take their needs also into account. When this has been done the total may still not add up to the actual costs either because there is presently capacity which is surplus to the total need or because the facility is outdated and therefore of a higher cost than would be necessary with perfect adjustment. This is the 'surplus add-back' which is allocated to the prime user, and which acts as the stimulus to the prime user to optimally adapt the assets under its control to current needs. The most recent improvement is the adoption of 'location costing' whereby individual elements of infrastructure cost are identified, rather than the whole of a cost component being allocated on a historically based averaging procedure.

For costs other than infrastructure the use of assets, and thereby the allocation of costs, is undertaken through a computing system called SPAMS (Sector Performance Accounting and Monitoring System). Within this system the sectors determine and underwrite the requirement for resources in advance of the annual budget, and retain sponsorship of assets and their associated costs until they are either taken over by another sector or are taken out of the system.

In allocating cost responsibilities between sectors the principle is that only avoidable costs are charged to the freight and parcels sectors, so that they would only be responsible for infrastructure of which they were the sole user. As between passenger sectors the arrangement is more complex, with InterCity at the other end of the spectrum in terms of accepting cost responsibility.

Similar problems arise in revenue allocation when a trip begins in one sector and terminates in another. Again a convention is necessary, which in this case reflects the proportion of the trip mileage on the two sectors and the proportion of the trains available for serving the trip in the two or more sectors. BR readily concedes that these procedures do not unambiguously and precisely give a commercial basis for deciding whether a particular activity is covering its 'full costs' or not. But it considers that the benefit obtained from making every asset and cost the particular responsibility of some business manager outweighs that defect.

12.4.4 Marketing and Pricing Policies

Sector management has also given a new focus for product development, marketing and pricing initiatives. For each of the sector managers attention to the specific market potential, and the extraction of revenue from that potential, is just as important as control of costs.

In the freight business, the trainload movement of bulks remains the major revenue earner, with the 'merry-go-round' movement of coal between mines and power stations the most prolific service. But it is no longer a growth sector and there has been a renewed interest in recent years in containerized traffic and in wagon load traffic operated to give higher speed and certainty of delivery. Both the Freightliner and Speedlink concepts were concerned centrally with reconciling quality of service with the unfavourable condition of less than trainload consignment size. In the passenger business tighter financial constraints and fiercer competition, both from airlines and from the coach industry after its deregulation in 1980, have led to the need to devise more efficient pricing strategies and devices. The answer has been sought in market segmentation and price discrimination. The theory is simple enough. If the total market can be separated into segments exhibiting differing price elasticities then gross revenue can be increased by charging different prices to the two segments.

The practice is very difficult. First it is necessary to identify segments with significantly different elasticities. Then a device must be found for implementing fare differences which does not permit those willing to pay a higher fare to take advantage of a lower one – the problem of countering revenue dilution. Finally the effects of the price structure must be monitored to ensure that the elasticities have not been so altered by the policies pursued as to render them inefficient. For example, increasing price usually puts BR on to a section of the demand curve with higher elasticity so that a policy of charging up in the markets showing inelastic demands may eventually exhaust its potential for increasing gross revenue. There is some concern that that is what is happening now in the business market.

Some discriminatory devices such as student and senior citizen railcards entitling the bearer to travel at reduced rates, may be easy to implement and to monitor. But these devices leave a large segment of the population unaffected and are not capable of discriminating between business trips, for which the demand elasticity is typically believed to be low, and personal trips which may be more price-elastic. Over the years BR has endeavoured to develop a strategy for exploiting this difference. The present structure distinguishes between the standard fare and saver, or reduced fares, on the basis of time of travel. This has the advantage of charging higher fares for those trains which it is believed that the timing of business activities will ensure that business travellers will be forced to use (and hence have a low fare elasticity) and which also exhibit high marginal costs of

provision because they are undertaken at the periods of peak vehicle
requirement.

12.4.5 Quality of Service

Quality of service is important to BR for two rather different reasons.
In the commercial sectors, particularly in respect of business travel,
demand may be rather more responsive to changes in quality than to
changes in price. Hence there is a commercial inducement to identify
the qualitative aspects which are most highly valued and to supply
them. The 1985/6 'Customer Care' campaign bore that emphasis. BR
clearly believes that, despite evidence that increased standard fares
have taken BR on to a section of the demand curve with a price
elasticity close to unity, it is still possible to recoup, through increased
fares, the costs of further improvements in quality in this market. In
the supported sectors, the quality of service is an essential part of what
the government is buying, so that there is an interest, both from BR
and from the Department of Transport in identifying measures of
quality which can be set as objectives, and against which performance
can be measured. BR has for many years collected and published
statistics on punctuality for trains of various categories. This is now
being supplemented by information on such factors as train failures
and cleanliness. The secretary of state has welcomed the developments
in this direction, though so far there has been no attempt either to
cost the effects of setting different standards, or to relate the level of
support to the achievement of standards. Both would appear to be
necessary if this form of control of the supported sector is to be really
effective.

12.4.6 Investment

BR presently invests about £400 million per annum, most of which
takes the form of replacement of track, rolling stock, terminals and
other facilities. In recent years the investment programme has been
seen as the key both to improving the quality of service offered to
customers and to reducing the requirements for revenue subsidy
through reducing operating costs.

The criteria and techniques used in appraising projects stem from
the way in which the objectives of the board are defined. Financial
appraisal is normally used (rather than cost–benefit analysis) as a
corollary of the commercial remit of the undertaking as a whole. But
the existence of the 1974 Act obligation to maintain the network of
services broadly as existing at the beginning of 1975 implies that where
replacement investment is necessary to secure the continued achievement of that objective it shall be undertaken irrespective of its
profitability. In those circumstances, the criterion used is to invest in
the least-cost method of replacement. For anything over and above the

minimum necessary to maintain the objective, and for all investments in assets not directly necessary to the objective, a discounted cash flow analysis is undertaken using a discount rate (7 per cent real in 1986) approved by the government.

The railway investment programme, although initiated and planned by the board, is subject to government review and control in a number of ways. First, the total size of the annual programme is limited by the external financing limit and the fiscal controls which are decided in the annual public expenditure review. Secondly, the Department of Transport maintains a running review of the business plans of the board and agrees with the board the five-year investment programme which is intended to reflect agreed strategies and plans. Thirdly, the Secretary of State calls in for detailed scrutiny each year a number of specific projects (normally projects exceeding £5 million in value).

Some chairmen of BR have found it necessary to complain bitterly of these constraints. During the chairmanship of Sir Robert Reid since 1982, however, there has been a much closer relationship between BR and the Department of Transport with greater security of investment funding appearing as the quid pro quo for the acceptance of much tighter limits on the PSO settlement.

There remains a fundamental incomparability between the financial appraisal applied to rail projects and the cost–benefit appraisal of road schemes, which has been recently reviewed. In their report (Buchanan and Partners, 1984) the consultants showed that it would be possible to apply similar techniques to rail investment. The government have stated that cost–benefit analysis may be applied to rail schemes where there is clear evidence of unusually large external effects (such as the North London Line electrification scheme) but have reiterated that they do not consider there to be any systematic bias against rail investment and that no general change of technique is to be introduced.

12.5 PERFORMANCE

12.5.1 Assessing Performance

Assessing the performance of a nationalized undertaking is very difficult in the absence of a competitive benchmark. *Ad hoc* reviews of performance have been undertaken by statutory bodies (HMSO, 1980) and parliamentary committees (HMSO, 1960). The 1980 Competition Act extended the powers of the Monopolies and Mergers Commission to efficiency audits of the nationalized industries and an inquiry into rail services in the South-East commenced in late 1986. The Audit Commission now also reviews the financial controls and performance of the nationalized firms (National Audit Office, 1986). In all of these studies the issue of the appropriate indicators of performance arises.

In the 1978 White Paper on the nationalized industries (HMSO, 1978) the government required each industry to construct indicators of performance, in addition to the financial measures, that could be reported and monitored. In so doing it recognized that the objectives of the nationalized industries are diverse, and that where profit maximization is not the objective the bottom-line result may not be an adequate criterion of performance. Hence BR constructs indicators of financial performance on a sector-by-sector basis, of physical productivity of specific assets used, and has recently been required by the Secretary of State for Transport to publish measures of quality of service. The 1985/6 Annual Report and Accounts contained a list of 39 performance indicators for the rail business. The difficulty of finding a benchmark is addressed by publication of comparisons within the organization over time, and, where possible, with similar organizations in other countries. Too much attention must not be focused, therefore, on any one simple indicator, but the whole set looked at in the round to obtain an impression of how effectively the system is performing. Bearing that caveat in mind, however, some indicators of recent performance may be stated. The base for the time series comparisons is taken in 1972, which was the last 'normal' year before the oil crisis.

12.5.2 Financial Performance

The net financial performance of the rail system deteriorated very rapidly and substantially in real terms in the three years after 1972 but then fluctuated about the plateau level until 1980 when there was a jump to a new plateau that was maintained for three years. Since then it has improved steadily (that is, the deficit has declined in real terms – see Table 12.4) and as shown later the plan is for this improvement to continue so that by the end of the decade the support level will be less than 60 per cent of its plateau level.

To understand this performance it is possible to look separately at revenues (which are themselves the product of outputs and prices) and costs (the product of inputs and prices). The outcome can also be disaggregated by sector.

For passenger traffic the trends differ substantially between sectors. InterCity traffic declined substantially between 1974 and 1976, and again from 1979 to 1982, but this has been against an overall upward trend so that patronage in 1985 is some 15 per cent above the level of 1972. That has been achieved with a less than proportionate increase in train-kilometrage. Patronage in London and the South-East rose slowly until 1978 but has declined since then to a level very similar to that in 1972, with similar amount of train service offered. The provincial sector has declined slowly over the period to a level about 10 per cent below that in 1972, despite the maintenance of an approximately constant level of performance.

Prices, in real terms, have increased steadily to a level 35 per cent

above those in 1972. But during that period price discrimination has
increased substantially with the result that a larger proportion of
passengers are now using fares below the standard, so that real receipts
per passenger-kilometre actually fell below the 1972 level in 1982, and
by 1985 were still only 5 per cent above those of 1972.

On the cost side, the passenger service requirement of the 1974 Act
objective has meant that the train-kilometres have been maintained.
This has been achieved with a total staff level reduced from 234,000 in
1972 to 173,000 in 1985. With freight train-kilometrage having been
reduced only slightly this shows an increase of train-kilometres per
employee over the period of about 23 per cent. During that time real
weekly earnings have increased by about 13 per cent, which is slightly
greater than the average for all industries. Rail employment in the UK
remains, however, a relatively low paid sector, certainly in comparison
with the position of rail employment in some other European countries
(Gwilliam *et al.*, 1979). The sector contributions to this financial
outcome vary enormously. Freight and parcels sectors are expected to
be commercial and, with the exception of the period of the miners'
strike in 1984, have broadly covered the costs allocated to them. The
operating ratios (costs as a proportion of revenues) of the passenger
sectors are shown in Table 12.5. Whilst InterCity and London and the
South-East (LSE) have regularly shown a surplus over direct operating
expenses they have failed by a considerable margin to meet total costs.
Provincial has failed to cover even its direct operating expenses and
covers only about one-quarter of its total allocated costs.

12.5.3 Physical Productivity

Some indicators of the physical productivity record of the rail system
are set out in Table 12.6. This shows that the number of train-miles per
member of staff employed has been increasing steadily. The intensity
with which rolling stock is being used is increasing at a similar pace.
The density with which the infrastructure is being used has increased
much less quickly, and the average load factors of the trains actually
run has remained fairly constant.

Table 12.5 *Operating Ratios of the Passenger Sectors, 1980–6*

	Direct cost						Full costs		
	1980	1981	1982	1983	1984/5	1985/6	1983	1984/5	1985/6
InterCity	63	73	80	68	70	65	139	145	131
LSE	72	72	86	77	74	73	147	146	140
Provincial	147	162	200	179	177	167	403	404	372
Total passenger	n/a	n/a	101	88	86	82	181	181	169

Source: British Rail Annual Report and Accounts.

Table 12.6 *Physical Productivity in BR, 1972–85*

	1972	1977	1981	1985
Train-km per member of staff	1.99	2.15	2.21	2.39
Loaded train-km per route-km	21.7	22.0	22.1	29.4
Passenger-km per loaded train-km	99	94	95	98
Net tonne-km per loaded train-km	275	349	357	312

Source: British Rail Annual Report and Accounts.

In international terms BR productivity per man appears to be about average, though if the BREL staff employed on traction and rolling stock maintenance (which is contracted out in many railways) is excluded the performance appears to be above average. But the hours worked per man in BR appear to be substantially longer than those in other countries, and in the specific area of train crew productivity BR performance has been substantially worse than in other countries largely due to different manning arrangements. Recent action by BR management, including one-man operation of trains, has been directed to reducing these disparities.

12.6 PUBLIC POLICY AND THE FUTURE

12.6.1 Privatization

The main BR system has not been considered one of the prime candidates for privatization in the programme of the Conservative governments since 1979, despite the privatization of its ancillary businesses (shipping and hotels), the introduction of franchising in some of its support services (catering), and increasing commercialization of its property assets. The most extensive proposition has concerned the organization of its engineering subsidiary BREL. This has been divided into two divisions concerned with maintenance and new-build respectively, with BREL being required to compete with the private sector for new-build business. Late in 1987, proposals for the privatization of BREL were announced. Whilst it is unlikely that a Labour government would renationalize any of the subsidiary activities that have already been privatized it might well reverse a privatization of BREL.

Other schemes of privatization have been more speculatively discussed. Where individual lines are largely separate from the rest of the network (for example, London Fenchurch Street to Southend) it has been suggested that they might be sold in their entirety. Or, more radically, it has been suggested that by dividing responsibility for infrastructure from that of operations it would be possible to allow private train operators to compete for paths in the network (Starkie, 1984). Such proposals have been dismissed by rail management as unworkable given the complexity of handling traffic on a rail network and likely to be inefficient in the separation which is implied between the planning and provision of infrastructure and operations.

12.6.2 Finance

As part of the process of control of rail finances the government now sets financial targets for the rail system as a whole and for some of its sectors. In the 1986 statement the Secretary of State indicated that he wished the PSO grant requirement to be reduced from the level of £992 million that had existed in 1983 to £555 million in 1989/90 (all in 1986/7 prices). He also indicated that the InterCity sector would cease to be eligible for any PSO support by that date. Whilst he indicated that it was the responsibility of the board to determine fares he specifically referred to the need for 'a significant reduction' in the grant requirement for Network SouthEast, and to the expectation that rail fares in the provincial sector would not undercut those of deregulated bus services.

12.6.3 Transport Policy Framework

There has been a considerable measure of agreement over the years on the general framework of rail transport policy. Both Labour and Conservative governments have attempted to secure efficient allocation of resources through competition between the modes in the freight and InterCity passenger markets. Whilst the Labour Party in opposition has indicated that it would not pursue the same restrictive financial policies to the public sector as the Conservative government, and has argued that there should be more consultation with local authorities and consumer interests in setting the rail targets, the difference appears to be one of detail rather than of principle. Hence we may expect a continuation of the arrangements whereby rail transport is viewed as a commercial activity in the freight and long-distance passenger markets but as a social service within the provincial and London commuting markets.

There appear to be two fundamental weaknesses in this structure. First, there is the association of the 'social' role with the railway sectoral division. Many rich people use the subsidized rail services for leisure purposes and poor people make essential trips on the commercial InterCity network. To subsidize trips of the former and not the latter is anomalous. Secondly, the 1974 Act objective of maintaining services broadly as they then existed has the apparent effect of increasing the support for those services which are least popular, and ossifying the provision of public transport service in a mode which is, because of its high proportion of fixed costs, particularly unsuited to the economic provision of service where demand is sparse. The replacement of rail by bus services in these situations appears to be eminently sensible. Though the 1985 Transport Act gave BR powers to take such action subject to the protection of some kinds of service by statutory closure procedures, there remains the anomaly that rail replacement bus services have a greater degree of protection and a more secure source of finance than other bus services. Such a structure owes more to political than to economic reasoning.

REFERENCES

Buchanan, Sir Colin, and Partners (1984), *Economic Evaluation Comparability Study; Application of the SACTRA Framework and COBA Principles to Rail Investment*, Department of Transport (London: HMSO).

Douglas, N. (1987), *A Welfare Assessment of Transport Deregulation* (Farnborough, Hants: Gower).

Edwards, S. M., and Bayliss, B. T. (1970), *The Industrial Demand for Transport* (London: HMSO).

Glaister, S. (1983), 'Some characteristics of rail commuter demand', *Journal of Transport Economics and Policy*, 17, 2, 115–32.

Gourvish, T. R. (1986), *British Railways 1948–73: A Business History* (Cambridge: Cambridge University Press).

Gwilliam, K. M., Nash, C. A., Mason, K. R., Prideaux, J. D. C. A., Wicks, P., Gunton, F. R. and Jacques, P. (1979), *A Comparative Study of European Rail Performance* (London: British Railways Board).

Gwilliam, K. M., Nash, C. A., and Palmer, J. (1982), 'Rail transport subsidy policy in Great Britain', *Rail International*, 15, 2, 23–32.

HMSO (1960), *British Railways*, Report of the Select Committee on Nationalised Industries, HC (session 1960/61) (London).

HMSO (1963), *The Reshaping of British Railways*, British Railways Board (London).

HMSO (1965), *Road Carriers Licensing*, Ministry of Transport (London).

HMSO (1976), *Transport Policy: A Consultative Document*, Department of Transport (London).

HMSO (1977), *Transport Policy*, Cmnd 6836 (London).

HMSO (1978), *The Nationalised Industries*, Cmnd 7131 (London).

HMSO (1980), *British Railways Board: London and South East Commuter Services*, Report of Monopolies and Mergers Commission, Cmnd 8046 (London).

HMSO (1983), *Railway Finances*, Report of a Committee chaired by Sir David Serpell (London).

HMSO (1986), *Departments of Energy, Trade and Industry and Transport; Effectiveness of Government Financial Controls over the Nationalised Industries* (London).

Jones, I. S., and Nichols, A. J. (1983), 'The demand for intercity rail travel in the United Kingdom', *Journal of Transport Economics and Policy*, 17, 2, 133–54.

National Audit Office (1986) *Departments of Energy, Transport and Trade and Industry: Effectiveness of Government Financial Controls over the*

Nationalised Industries, Report by the Comptroller and Auditor Genera (London: HMSO).
Starkie, D. (1984), 'BR: privatisation without tears', *Economic Affairs*, 15–19.

FURTHER READING

Bagwell, P. S. (1982), *The Railwaymen; Vol. II: The Beeching Era and After* (London: Allen & Unwin).
Bonavia, M. R. (1981), *British Rail: The First 25 Years* (Newton Abbot, Devon: David & Charles).
Dodgson, J. S. (1983), 'British Rail after Serpell', *Three Banks Review*, CX1, 22–37.
Harris, J., and Williams, G. (1980), *Corporate Management and Financial Planning. The British Rail Experience* (St Albans, Herts: Elek).
Nash, C. A. (1985), 'Paying subsidy to British Rail – how to get value for money', *Public Money*, 5, 1, 35–40.
Pryke, R. W. S., and Dodgson, J. S. (1975), *The Rail Problem* (London: Martin Robertson).

Chapter Thirteen

Domestic Air Transport

PETER JOHNSON

13.1 INTRODUCTION

For the purposes of this chapter, domestic air transport covers all scheduled passenger air services between points in the UK. The growth of such services between 1975 and 1986 has been relatively rapid. Table 13.1 shows that between these years, the growth of air travel in the UK (measured in terms of passenger-kilometres) was 67 per cent, twice that of road, and over 12 times that of rail. Air travel also grew over three times faster than real GDP. Despite this rapid growth, however, domestic scheduled air services still only account for a tiny proportion of the total passenger-kilometres travelled in Great Britain – less than 1 per cent in 1986. Growth has been erratic. Indeed between 1976 and 1977 and between 1980 and 1981, output, in terms of passenger seat-kilometres used, fell.[1] On both occasions airlines cut back the seat *capacity* flown by more than the fall in output.

Table 13.1 *Passenger Transport in Great Britain, 1975–86: Estimated Passenger-Kilometres*

Mode	(Billion) 1975	(Billion) 1986	% Increase 1975–86
Road			
Buses and coaches	55.0	41.0	−25.5
Cars and taxis	294.4	424.3	44.1
Motor and pedal cycles	7.92	10.11	27.7
All road	357.32	475.41	33.0
Rail	35.1	36.98	5.4
Air	2.22	3.70	66.7
All modes	394.64	516.09	30.8

Note: The table gives, for each mode, the degree of detail available from official sources. The extent to which the figures are rounded varies between modes.
Source: Transport Statistics, Great Britain, 1975–1985, HMSO, London, 1986, Table 1.1; and Department of Transport.

Total employment in air transport and supporting services in Great Britain has remained fairly static at around 46,000. This figure covers employment based in Great Britain and associated with any kind of air transport operation including international flights (by both British and foreign airlines). Non-scheduled domestic and cargo operations are also included. If the share of air transport movements is used as a basis for allocating employment to different types of operation (see Section 13.5.2) domestic scheduled services account for about 17,500 employees in Great Britain.

Only UK airlines are permitted to operate domestic services in this country. Table 13.2 provides various measures of the importance of these services in the total operations of UK airlines. Clearly, the choice of measure is critical in assessing the relative importance of domestic services. The higher frequency of these services, their shorter-haul nature and their use of smaller aircraft mean that they are more important in terms of the first three measures given in the table. The insignificance of domestic services when judged on the last three measures reflects the absence of wide-bodied aircraft and long hauls on these routes.

The ratio of seat-kilometres used to seat-kilometres available is one variant of the *load factor*, a measure of capacity utilization. The overall load factor in domestic scheduled services has remained fairly constant: only once in the last ten years has it fallen outside the range 60.8 to 63.3. It should be noted that this load factor cannot be inferred from the data given in Table 13.2 on the *proportion* of the total seat-kilometres (used and available), accounted for by domestic services.[2]

Table 13.2 does not of course provide data on the importance of domestic scheduled flights in *all* air transport using UK airspace, because the activities of foreign airlines are excluded.

Nearly 55 per cent of all passengers uplifted[3] on domestic routes in 1986 were accounted for by the eight trunk routes out of London. A

Table 13.2   *The Importance of Domestic Scheduled Services, UK Airlines, 1986*

Measure	Domestic scheduled services as a percentage of all scheduled and non-scheduled passenger services[a]
Aircraft flights	29.2
Passengers uplifted	20.1
Aircraft-kilometres flown	10.9
Seat-kilometres available	5.0
Seat-kilometres used	4.1
Tonne-kilometres used	3.8

Note: [a] Sub-charter operations performed on behalf of UK airlines are excluded.
Source: Calculated from data in Table 1.5 in *UK Airlines Annual Operating, Traffic and Financial Statistics 1986* CAA, London, 1987.

runk route is defined here, somewhat arbitrarily, as one which carries
more than 100,000 passengers per year and which is not characterized
by substantial seasonal fluctuations. The London–Channel Islands
routes, which carry well over 0.5 million passengers a year, but which
are highly seasonal – in 1985, for example, January traffic was only
36 per cent of August levels – are referred to separately below. On
each trunk route, both Heathrow and Gatwick are served by
competing carriers. Up to 1979, British Airways (BA) served *both*
airports on the Aberdeen route but in that year it was replaced by
Dan-Air at Gatwick. Two of the trunk routes are now also served
(directly or indirectly) by Air UK out of Stansted. Jet aircraft carry the
majority of the traffic on the trunk routes.

Four of the trunk routes – Belfast, Edinburgh, Glasgow and
Manchester – may be regarded as *primary*. In 1986, Edinburgh and
Glasgow each carried well over, and Belfast just under, a million
passengers. Manchester carried 876,000. A characteristic exclusive to
the primary trunk routes is the operation by British Airways of a
'shuttle' service. This service guarantees a seat to any passenger who
arrives at the departure gate up to ten minutes before departure. If the
scheduled aircraft is full, the airline provides a 'back-up' aircraft to
carry the excess traffic. The supply of seats for any scheduled service is
therefore completely elastic. By treating the shuttle service to all four
destinations as a single system, BA is able to obtain economies of
massed reserves in the provision of back-ups. High volume, high
scheduled frequency and non-seasonal business demand are seen as
essential ingredients for such a service (Watts, 1983).

In addition to the trunk routes, there are a further three, largely
non-seasonal, routes out of London (Birmingham, East Midlands and
Inverness) each of which accounted in 1986 for well over 60,000
passengers a year. These three routes, served mostly by jet aircraft,
accounted for another 3 per cent of total domestic passenger carryings.
The remaining domestic scheduled services may be grouped as follows.

(1) *Provincial routes.* These routes operate between the main
provincial centres of population. Some are relatively substantial:
Manchester to Belfast, for example, carried over 140,000 passengers in 1986. Those provincial services carrying over 30,000
passengers in 1986 – roughly enough to support a Monday to
Friday return jet service given an appropriate pattern of demand –
accounted for nearly 9 per cent of all domestic passengers.
Provincial services use a wider variety of aircraft types than the
trunk routes.

(2) *Channel Islands and Isle of Man Services.* About 23 per cent of
domestic passengers were carried on these routes in 1986. Most
airports in the UK have a summer service to the Channel Islands,
although over a quarter of all passengers fly from London. In 1980,
British Airways gave up many of these routes as they were unable

to make them pay. Smaller, independent airlines have been more successful.

(3) *Scottish internal services.* These mostly thin services – carrying about 5 per cent of the total – include both mainland and island services. Many of the latter perform a 'lifeline' function. Over the years, their positive externalities have been regarded as large enough to justify public subsidies. Loganair, for example, an independent airline which, along with British Airways, provides most of the island services is currently subsidized by the Scottish Office on two routes: Glasgow to Skye and Glasgow to Tiree and Barra and by the Western Isles Islands Council on the Stornaway–Benbecula–Barra route. Virtually all the Scottish routes use propeller aircraft.

(4) *Other routes.* This 'miscellaneous' group, which covers the remainder of UK domestic passengers, is largely accounted for by 'third-level' services which are operated by small aircraft with a capacity of less than 25 seats (Civil Aviation Authority, 1979 para. 5). Some of the services that have already been referred to are of this type. An important function of third-level services is to feed major airports, notably Heathrow and Gatwick with interline traffic. For example, over half of the passengers travelling between London and Norwich transferred airlines at the former (CAA, 1985a, p. 21).

About 60 per cent of domestic scheduled passengers are travelling for business purposes (CAA, 1980, Appendix A). Many passengers flying internationally use domestic flights to get to or from the airport served by the international flight. The proportion of such interlining passengers tends to be inversely related to the length of the domestic journey (CAA, 1985a, para 2.11). For example in 1984, 90 per cent of passengers travelling· on the Birmingham–Heathrow route were interlining on to international services, whereas only 22 per cent of Glasgow–Heathrow and 28 per cent of Edinburgh–Heathrow passengers did so. A higher proportion of Gatwick domestic passengers interline than is the case at Heathrow[4] (CAA, 1985a, para. 2.7). The 'add-on' price for the domestic leg is usually (but not invariably) less than the normal fare which is charged when the passenger is only travelling domestically.

An airline may be prepared to sustain losses on its domestic services because of their role as feeder routes for its international operations, which may be highly profitable as a result of the market protection afforded by bilateral agreements. If an airline has no domestic services, it may attract fewer international passengers since it is known that, *ceteris paribus*, a traveller prefers to stay with the same airline on both the domestic and international legs, rather than to change carriers. British Caledonian, for example, has been prepared to lose money on its domestic routes into Gatwick because its international operations are based there.

The product sold on domestic schedules is highly perishable. Once an airline has decided to fly on a particular route, an unfilled seat on that aircraft 'perishes' once the aircraft door is shut. Unused seat capacity cannot be stored. This characteristic of air travel – which of course is shared by many other goods and services – has important implications for pricing policy. These are considered in Section 13.4.1.

13.2 DEMAND AND COSTS

13.2.1 Demand

The travel decision

For most purposes, domestic air services, like competing forms of public transport, may be considered an intermediate product. Most individuals travel from A to B for some purpose other than the 'consumption' of the travel itself. Where there are consumption benefits – more likely for leisure than for business travellers – these are usually small.

A passenger who has already made the decision to travel, will choose air where the total costs of so doing are less than those incurred by using alternative methods. The relevant cost comparison is the door-to-door one. 'Cost' here includes not only monetary expenditure – on, for example, fares and meals – but also an assessment of the value of travel time involved. Such an assessment would have to take into account that not all travel time may be wasted.

The true cost of flying will also be affected by what Douglas and Miller (1974, p. 28) call 'schedule convenience'. An intending passenger may have a desired departure time of (say) 10.00 a.m. Such a time is optimal from that passenger's viewpoint. Now the *actual* departure time may differ from this desired departure time for the following reasons. First, there may be no scheduled departure at 10.00 a.m. Thus the passenger may experience 'frequency' delay measured by the difference between the two times. Secondly, the passenger may be unable to obtain a seat on the next best departure time, because the aircraft is full. The resultant delay has been labelled as 'stochastic delay' by Douglas and Miller. It is 'the expected length of delay a potential passenger faces because of the chance that his most preferred scheduled departure will be booked up and he will have to select another and possibly even a third or fourth, and so on' (Douglas and Miller, 1974, p. 82). Where a shuttle service is in operation, stochastic delay is effectively eliminated. The sum of frequency and stochastic delay is the expected schedule delay. It should be noted that schedule delay may not all be wasted time, although the time may be used less efficiently. Schedule delay can be avoided by the use of private transport. It may sometimes lead to a switch of transport mode or even to the abandonment of a journey. In addition to schedule delay, there may also be delays caused by such factors as congestion and mechanical breakdown.

Differences in the level of comfort and safety will affect the cost comparison. Relevant comfort considerations as far as air travel is concerned include the amount of leg-room, type of aircraft, pleasantness of the aircrew and the load factor: most passengers prefer to have an empty seat beside them. (It is important to remember the effect of the load factor on service quality whenever changes in the former occur. For example, to see an increase in the load factor as simply an increase in productivity – raising the number of passenger seat-kilometres travelled with virtually no increase in inputs – is to take too narrow a view of 'output', since the nature of that output has changed.[5]

Typically, air transport is more expensive (in terms of monetary expenditure) but quicker than surface modes. The longer the trip, the more likely it is that the value of time saved through air travel will outweigh the differential in monetary expenditures, particularly where the journey length is above that at which it is necessary for surface but not air travellers to have an overnight stay.

As indicated earlier, the majority of domestic passengers are business travellers, whose expenses are paid for them. For such travellers, it will be the costs to the employer, rather than to the individual, of the different transport modes, that will be most relevant in the transport decision.

Elasticities
One of the few studies to consider demand elasticities in UK domestic air transport (Transport and Road Research Laboratory, 1981) examined the London–Glasgow/Edinburgh trunk routes. This study found that (real) price elasticities were low on both routes: for London–Glasgow, the best estimate was −0.07 and for London–Edinburgh −0.26. Business travellers dominate both routes, although rather more leisure traffic travels between London and Edinburgh, a factor which may explain the greater fare-sensitivity on this route. The findings of the TRRL study relate only to the price ranges actually experienced over the period studied; at much lower prices, traffic is almost certainly more price-sensitive.

Demand was found to be much more responsive to price with elasticity estimates of around −1.0 – in a recent cross-section study of 135 US low-density commuter routes where again business travel predominates (Meyer and Oster, 1984, p. 31f). However, these routes mostly involved much shorter distances than the Scottish routes. As indicated earlier, the shorter the route, the more competitive, *ceteris paribus*, other modes are likely to be with air. The same US study also provides estimates of frequency and journey time elasticities. Frequency elasticities of around 0.5/0.6 were found, but this result must be seen in the context of the *level* of frequencies operated on these routes: on average, fewer than four flights a day. It would be expected that as the frequency level rises, so the frequency elasticity would fall (for supporting evidence, see Meyer and Oster, 1984, p. 40). Demand was found to be highly sensitive to journey time: the relevant elasticity was around -1.5. Again, however, it would be expected that these elasticities would decline with increases in sector length (and hence journey time).

Meyer and Oster also reviewed studies of air travel in high-density corridors in the USA (1984, p. 37f). Most of these studies showed demand to be much more price-responsive than that in the commuter studies, reflecting the relatively better availability of alternative modes of transport in these corridors. The studies also report lower frequency elasticities. Such findings are expected given the higher level of frequencies.

No direct estimates of income elasticities are available, although the TRRL study did show that air traffic on the Scottish routes was much more responsive to the level of economic activity (variously measured) than to the price, a finding supported by other work on the London–Glasgow route (Johnson, 1987).

13.2.2 Costs

The costs of operating domestic air services may be divided into three main categories. First there are those costs which arise primarily as the result of owning (or renting), flying, and maintaining aircraft. These may be referred to as *capacity costs* (Douglas and Miller, 1974, p. 8). Major items under this heading include flight and cabin crew training, salaries and expenses, fuel and oil, maintenance, depreciation and fees paid to the aviation authorities. An airline can alter its capacity costs by changing the size and composition of its fleet and/or its schedules. But once these are decided, it has little room for manoeuvre and the number of passengers will not substantially affect this category of costs.

Capacity costs do not increase proportionately with the size of aircraft. There are three main reasons for this non-proportionality. First, crew costs do not tend to increase in direct proportion to the size of aircraft. Secondly, many items of electronic and other equipment – radar, for example – do not have to increase proportionately with the size of the aircraft. Some may not increase at all. Finally, there are economies of increased dimensions in the construction of the aircraft itself.

The second category of costs, *traffic costs*, covers expenditure which is largely determined by the amount of traffic carried. Passenger meals, embarkation fees and agents' commissions are the most important items. Some of these costs are invariant with respect to sector length. There may also be an element of indivisibility in their provision: a reservations desk requires a minimum number of staff to service it in any given time period, irrespective of the number of passengers that use it. Airlines may however seek to avoid the problem of indivisibilities by contracting out some of these services.

The final cost category – *overheads* – covers general management and certain central functions such as personnel.

Capacity costs account for the bulk of operating costs. For example, in the case of British Midland Airways (BMA) the second largest domestic airline in the UK, operating costs amounted in 1984 to 76 per cent of the total. (*All* BMAs operations are included in the calculation.) (Traffic costs accounted for nearly 20 per cent, and overheads 4 per cent.) It should be noted too that a substantial proportion of costs – particularly those relating to fuel, oil and fees, together mounting to over 50 per cent of the total – lie outside the direct control of the airline.

Two further features of costs in air transport should be noted. First, costs per seat-mile of any aircraft decline with sector length (at least up to the aircraft's design range). This decline arises because many capacity costs do not vary with sector length. For example, most of the costs associated with take-off and landing remain the same whatever

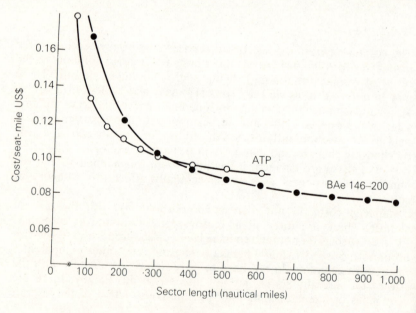

Figure 13.1   *BAe 146–200: ATP Cost comparison*

Source: British Aerospace.

the sector length. The fall in seat costs as sector length increases is illustrated in Figure 13.1 which is based on British Aerospace's data for two of its aircraft, its new 64-seater (turbo-prop) ATP which made its first flight in 1986, and the 100-seat version of its BAe 146-200 jet. Both aircraft are suited to domestic operations. The graph is intended for illustrative purposes only and is not based on the costs of any particular actual or potential operator. For sector lengths below 330 miles, the ATP is cheaper per seat-mile than the BAe 146 but is more expensive over longer distances. The graph is drawn with respect to a given load factor (60 per cent).

Secondly, the marginal costs of carrying an additional passenger on a flight up to the capacity of the aircraft are small.

Unit cost comparisons between *airlines* of different sizes are made hazardous by wide variations in output mix. This mix relates to the breakdown between short- and long-haul routes, and between the types of aircraft used and passengers carried. The choice of airports used by airlines may also affect costs since airport charges differ. Differences in congestion at airports and weather conditions will all be reflected in cost data.

However, if a passenger trip on a given sector is taken as the basic unit of output and if consideration is limited to a hypothetical airline serving only that sector, then the long-run average costs of passenger trips of that airline are likely to decline at least initially, as capacity costs are spread over more passengers. The airline will be able to utilize more cost-efficient aircraft and to achieve a higher throughput of 'indivisible' terminal and other facilities as the scale of output increases. Economies of massed reserves, particularly in the provision of spares and maintenance, may be generated. Certain indivisible centralized resources and functions such as computerized reservation systems may be more fully used. Pecuniary economies in the purchase of inputs may be achieved.

On the other hand, the larger airline may suffer from greater inflexibility and higher administrative costs. The smaller airline may be able to contract out certain activities in such a way that it effectively secures the benefits of economies of scale across the market place. BA, for example, provides airport services for Brymon Airways at Heathrow and Gatwick. Some companies, such as Servisair, specialize in providing such services for airlines.

Once the simplified picture of a single-route airline is abandoned the relationship between size and unit costs (both measured with respect to some generalized measure, such as available seat-kilometres) becomes more complex. It is true that some of the economies mentioned above may be achieved irrespective of route structure. However, others may be directly dependent on it. An airline may, for example, obtain network benefits through economies of scope (Morrison and Winston, 1986b, p. 6). Such economies arise whenever it is cheaper to provide two services together rather than separately. Some cost advantages may depend on how far an airline's fleet is standardized (HMSO, 1969, p. 67f).

A number of cost comparisons of airlines of different sizes have been undertaken in the United States, and the conclusions are similar: costs tend to be approximately constant over the ranges studied (see, for example, Douglas and Miller, 1974, pp. 13–17, and the survey in Winston, 1985). The problem of cost comparisons referred to earlier should, however, be borne in mind when considering these results. Furthermore the studies do not cover the whole size spectrum. Nevertheless the results do suggest that merger proposals of larger airlines that are based on an economies of scale justification should be treated with some caution.

Many small airlines are able to operate in markets which the larger airline would find it uneconomic to serve. In 1980 BA relinquished its rights to 26 domestic routes in a cost-cutting exercise. These routes were subsequently awarded to, and operated by, a number of smaller independent operators. Where a small airline is likely to face difficulty is in markets where it is competing directly with a large airline. The latter may have a number of marketing advantages, most obviously in the number of connections it may be able to offer, although even here the small airline may be able to enter a contractual arrangement with another large airline to reduce this competitive disparity. Many small airlines in the USA, for example, have 'code-sharing' arrangements with a large airline which provide access to the latter's network. Such an arrangement may not be without its problems. The difficulties that may arise from a link-up between small airlines and a large one is illustrated in British Caledonian's experience with its commuter network experiment. This network was set up in 1983–4. The arrangement involved a number of third-level carriers adopting a distinctive logo and an aircraft livery aligned to British Caledonian's colour scheme. It was hoped that the single, recognizable British Caledonian banner would generate increased feeder traffic and thereby benefit all the airlines involved. However, in 1984 Genair, a key airline in the arrangement, collapsed. This failure inevitably had some adverse impact on British Caledonian's own image as an airline. The link-up also raised difficulties over the maintenance of consistent quality standards across a number of independent airlines.

13.3 THE STRUCTURE OF THE INDUSTRY

13.3.1 The National Picture

Table 13.3 provides an indication of the overall structure of the industry. The measure of size used – available seat-kilometres – provides a measure of capacity. Airlines that do not operate a domestic scheduled service are excluded from the table. Some of these omitted airlines belong to the same group as those listed in the table – for example, British Airtours is part of BA – and they may therefore have some indirect impact on domestic operations. Not all the airlines listed in Table 13.3 are independent of each other. BMA acquired 75 per cent of Loganair's shares from the Royal Bank of Scotland in 1983. (The other 25 per cent are held by Loganair's Managing Director.) Manx Airlines was formed in 1982 by BMA in conjunction with the British and Commonwealth Shipping Company, through its subsidiary Air UK, to run services to the Isle of Man. BA has a 14 per cent stake in the voting shares of the Plymouth-based Brymon Airways.

Some of the smaller airlines have been or are part of larger groupings which have interests in other industries. The Royal Bank of Scotland's ownership of Loganair and British and Commonwealth's Shipping Company's ownership of Air UK are two examples that have already been noted. Such an arrangement may enable a small airline to survive financial difficulties in a way that might not be possible if it were independent. For example, it is very unlikely that Loganair would have survived the first oil shock in 1973–4 if it had not had the backing of a large parent company. The existence of such a company may also strengthen the hand of a small airline when it competes with a large airline, especially if the latter is not part of an even bigger organization.

BA clearly dominates the domestic scene although its share of capacity has been falling. (Its share was 61 per cent in 1980.) The current dominance of BA is largely the result of political rather than

Table 13.3 *Domestic Scheduled Services: Market Structure, 1986*

Airline	Available seat-kilometres, domestic scheduled services	% of total domestic scheduled services	Domestic scheduled services as % of airline's available seat-kilometres, on all scheduled and non-scheduled services
British Airways	3,185,663	54.1	4.4
British Midland Airways	1,068,598	18.1	84.0
Dan Air Services	446,492	7.6	4.9
British Caledonian	411,018	7.0	3.4
Air UK	237,273	4.0	40.5
Manx Airlines	121,882	2.1	97.0
Loganair[a]	96,588	1.6	97.7
Guernsey Airlines	92,949	1.6	94.0
Brymon Airways	65,258	1.1	65.4
Others (10 airlines)	165,025	2.8	27.2
Total	5,890,746	100.0	5.0

Notes: [a] Loganair is owned by British Midland Airways. See text.
Source: Derived from *UK Airlines Annual Operating, Traffic and Financial Statistics 1986* Table 1.5, CAA, London, 1987.

market forces. British European Airways (BEA), the predecessor of BA's domestic operations was formed as a nationalized corporation in 1946, and was given a monopoly of domestic routes. This privileged position of BEA was eroded in the early 1950s (Baldwin, 1985, p. 23) although it was only in 1960 that BEA's monopoly was formally removed from the statute book. However, even when licences were granted to competitors in the 1960s on key domestic routes, frequency limitations were imposed on the new entrants, though not on BEA (HMSO, 1969, p. 82). Given the presumption in favour of incumbent firms that has underlain much of domestic air regulation in the 1970s, it is hardly surprising to find BA in its current position.

The table also shows that for three of the four largest airlines, domestic scheduled services constituted only a small proportion of total operations, whereas for the smaller airlines the proportion is very much larger.

There has been a good deal of structural change among the smaller airlines. An illustration of such change is provided by the history of Air UK.[6] This airline was formed in 1980 as a result of a merger between British Islands Airways/Air West, Air Anglia and Air Wales. All these companies were already members of the British and Commonwealth Shipping Group. British Island Airways can itself be traced back through its various antecedents – Jersey Airlines, Manx Airlines and Silver City Airways – to the early postwar period. British Islands Airways/Air West was established in 1979 following British and Commonwealth's acquisition of Air Westward. Air Anglia, which itself was formed from a merger of Norfolk Airways, Anglia Charter and Rig Air, became part of British and Commonwealth in 1979. Air Wales was absorbed into Air Anglia in 1979. Much of this consolidation activity reflects the financial vulnerability of small airlines who often operate seasonal or low-density routes and who frequently seek to expand too rapidly. Some commuter airline operations have been short-lived: for example, Metropolitan Airways, which was set up in 1982 and ran third-level services linking a number of provincial cities failed in 1985. Genair, another small third-level company lasted for a similar period. The airlines in the 'Other' category are very small, often operating only a few small aircraft.

13.3.2 Competition on Individual Routes

The data in Table 13.3 give no indication of market structure on individual routes. As indicated in Section 13.1, all the London trunk routes have separate airlines operating out of both Heathrow and Glasgow. Heathrow and Gatwick services do provide some competition for each other, although Heathrow is far superior to Gatwick in terms of frequencies and interlining opportunities. (Heathrow serves well over 100 destinations not served by Gatwick, whereas there are under 40 destinations served only by the latter. Where a destination is served by both airports, frequencies from Heathrow are usually much higher.)

On three of the four primary trunk routes (Belfast, Edinburgh and Glasgow), BA's shuttle also competes 'head to head' with a conventional service by BMA out of Heathrow, although the latter has less than a third of the traffic on all three services. On the Manchester service, Dan Air provided a competing conventional service for a short period in 1985–6. When it originally came on to the route in April 1985 it offered three daily services. BA however increased its frequency in response to Dan Air's entry and the latter airline was unable to sustain its operations at their original level. It withdrew completely at the end of 1986 (*Air Travel*, 25 November 1986). On the four non-primary trunk routes there is only one Heathrow operator (BA on one route, BMA on three).

Surface modes provide some competitive challenge to the trunk routes, although for reasons given in Section 13.1 this challenge is less important the longer the route.

On the other domestic routes, head-to-head competition normally only arises where a particular sector forms part of different multi-sector routes operated by more than one airline. For example, Edinburgh–Aberdeen is served by BA and Air UK, but only as one part of longer routes. (Air Ecosse also operated on this sector until it was forced to stop trading early in 1987.) Indirect competition between airlines arises from a number of sources. A few routes have competing services out of Heathrow and Gatwick. On the Belfast–Manchester and Belfast–Glasgow route services into Aldergrove compete with those into Harbour. Furthermore some provincial airports such as Newcastle and Teesside and Manchester and Liverpool have catchment areas that overlap. Many cross-country routes face very little effective competition from surface modes, but the traffic is often so thin that the viability of an air service is marginal anyway.

Even though direct competition may be limited, an airline still faces the possibility that its licence may be revoked and given to a new entrant. Where such a threat is effective, it may have the same effect as the presence of actual competition.

13.3.3 Barriers to Entry

As Section 13.1 indicates, an airline wanting to enter a particular route has to obtain a licence from the Civil Aviation Authority (CAA). The CAA's licensing policies, and the statutory framework within which it is required to operate, have varied over the years. Licensing has become more liberal in the 1980s, but the CAA has also refused some important applications.

The ease with which an airline may enter a route, once it has received a licence, depends on numerous factors. If the route does not already have an airline operating on it, the entrant may have to incur costs to make the new air service known. If a competing airline is already established on the route, there will already be some public awareness of the existence of a service. However, the new entrant may then face the costs of attracting passengers away from the incumbent in order to ensure the viability of its service. It may face at least two difficulties here. The first concerns the relationship between market share and frequency. If, as some analysts believe (Meyer *et al.*, 1981, p. 216), there is an S-shape relationship between frequency and market shares, the entrant, if it is intending to operate at relatively low frequency, may be placed at some market-share disadvantage. Its cost per passenger may therefore be higher. The second problem arises when the incumbent operator has a more extensive route network. Such a network may facilitate more convenient interlining than that available to the potential entrant's passengers. The network may also mean that the incumbent is able to offer a more attractive 'frequent-flier' discount. Such discounts are related to the *overall* use of an airline's services.

An entrant has a number of options open to it when challenging an incumbent. Price discounts, improvements in the quality of service (through, for example, raising the level of in-flight catering, introducing more convenient timings or better aircraft), and promotional activities, are all possibilities. An important consideration in the entrant's choice of strategy will usually be the likely response of the incumbent.

Much debate has been generated on the extent to which airline markets in the absence of regulated entry are contestable (see, for example, Baumol, Panzar and Willig, 1982, p. 7, and Shepherd, 1984). A market is said to be perfectly contestable when entry is absolutely free (the entrant is at no disadvantage relative to the incumbent firm(s)), and exit is absolutely costless (any firm can leave the market without impediment and can recoup all losses incurred in the entry process, that is, there are no sunk costs). A perfectly contestable market will ensure maximum economic welfare in a market, even if there are only a few operators. From the discussion in the previous paragraphs, it seems clear that the sunk costs of entering a market are unlikely to be zero, a condition for perfect contestability, because of the initial costs of establishing loyalty, especially if an incumbent airline has a 'national carrier' status. (There may also be some sunk costs incurred in securing and setting up airport facilities.) Nevertheless, Morrison and Winston (1986) have shown that at least in the USA, potential competition, defined for any sector as the number of airlines that serve at least one of the airports involved but not the sector, does have a disciplining effect on the market. Such a finding suggests that it may be important to foster potential competition. Interestingly the CAA has recently placed some emphasis on encouraging the development of at least one potential competitor for each market (CAA, 1985b, para. 3).

3.4 MARKET BEHAVIOUR

3.4.1 Pricing

A profit maximizing airline, with a given schedule and fleet, will wish to maximize its revenue from its route network. This may sometimes mean carrying passengers whose fares cover only (the very low) marginal network traffic costs.

Price discrimination between groups of passengers with different price elasticities plays an important part in the maximization of revenue. Typically, discrimination is achieved by attaching different restrictions to tickets. For example, BMA offers Key and Standby Fares, apart from the normal economy fare on its domestic services. The Key Fare is only available on certain services and full payment must be made at the time of booking. There are substantial cancellation charges (100 per cent on London routes). The Standby Fare can only be used if there is spare capacity on a flight; seats cannot be booked in advance. The more severe the restrictions an airline places on a fare, the cheaper it is. And the more restrictions a passenger is able to accept, the higher that passenger's price elasticity is likely to be.

There are at least two constraints on price discrimination. First, if the airline makes the fare structure too involved, it may find its potential customers become disaffected. Secondly, and more importantly, it may not always be possible to discriminate between passengers without incurring some revenue dilution, caused by passengers switching from the higher fare, which they would have paid in the absence of discrimination, to the lower fare. The possibility of revenue dilution in respect of Standby Fares tends to be higher where the intending passenger knows that the load factor is typically low. Thus a Standby Fare may only tend to raise total revenue where the likelihood of obtaining such a fare is not high. Sometimes an airline will impose a seat limit on different fare types to restrict the amount of transferring that may be done. Indeed an airline may decide to keep some seats empty, in order to preserve its higher-revenue tickets. *Some* dilution of revenue may be acceptable, provided the loss of revenue from existing passengers is exceeded by the gain in revenue derived from price discrimination.

An airline's freedom of manoeuvre may be constrained by the existence of a competing operator. In the UK 'head-to-head' competition has tended (not surprisingly) to generate a similar range of fares. Airlines have sought to avoid price wars not only because of the possibility that such wars might attract regulatory intervention or prohibition but also because, in markets where price elasticity is low, a price war would be self-defeating. For example, when BMA came on to the Heathrow–Glasgow route in 1982, BA was explicit about its intention of avoiding a price war (*The Times*, 28 July 1982).

An airline may be able to utilize its aircraft for other purposes when they are not being used on scheduled passenger services. For example Loganair is contracted to provide night mail services in Scotland. Any price above marginal cost for such operations will be worthwhile from the airline's viewpoint.

13.4.2 Non-Price Behaviour

In its economic control of the industry the CAA has traditionally focused on prices. Airlines have been largely free from regulation in the non-price dimensions of business behaviour, although on occasions the CAA has imposed a frequency limitation. Even in the present more relaxed regulatory regime, where all price changes are automatically approved unless objected to, price is still subject to more regulatory attention (all proposed price changes have to be filed with the CAA) than non-price behaviour. Douglas and Miller (1974) have shown that in pre-deregulation days in the US airline industry, controls on pricing forced airlines into non-price competition, most obviously on frequencies, and thereby generated a sub-optimal outcome in terms of economic welfare. Deregulation in the United States has since led to a wide variety of price/quality combinations being offered (Bailey and Williams, 1986).

13.4.3 Behaviour of Smaller Airlines

The smaller UK airlines have played an important role in developing new domestic networks partly as a result of their inability to gain access to established routes. For example, Air UK and its predecessors have provided services from Norwich. Air UK has also started to operate services from Stansted. BMA has developed services from the East Midlands and Brymon from Plymouth. The smaller airlines have, as noted earlier, also been able to operate successfully on routes abandoned by BA. Occasionally they have obtained a licence to *replace* BA.

Their history is not one of clear financial success. Margins have often been very tight. In the 1980s, operating profits have averaged 4 per cent of operating revenues for major UK airlines[7] in the private sector (*UK Airlines*. CAP 521, CAA: London, Table 2.2), and it is likely that for many smaller airlines operating domestic scheduled services this percentage is even lower. Small adverse changes in business conditions can generate substantial losses and it is hardly surprising to find that airline failure has been a common event. The airlines that have managed to survive have been those which have developed clear strategic objectives and which have sought expansion at a modest pace. Despite the mixed fortunes of the small airlines, they have nevertheless played a key role in testing out new markets and in providing services that the national carrier has been unable or unwilling to offer.

13.5 PERFORMANCE

It has already been shown that domestic scheduled air transport in the UK has grown rapidly in recent years. However, experience has varied considerably across routes, as may be seen from the growth records of the Heathrow routes: while the primary trunks experienced an increase in passenger carryings of 50 per cent over the period 1980–6, two routes – Liverpool and Birmingham – experienced substantial decreases (54 and 20 per cent respectively).

In the first column of Table 13.4, the growth (in terms of used seat-kilometres) of the main airlines offering domestic scheduled services over the period 1980–5 is shown. British Airways has shown relatively little growth. What growth there has been has come from the expansion of passenger numbers on existing routes, rather than from the opening up of new routes. British Caledonian has experienced a slight decline. Most of the other airlines in the table, apart from Air UK – which engaged in substantial rationalization of the routes it inherited when it was formed – have shown considerable growth, much of it coming from the development of new routes. Some of these airlines were very small and young in 1980, hence rapid growth could

Table 13.4   *Growth and Load Factors on Domestic Scheduled Services, 1980–6*

	% increase 1980–6 in seat-kilometres used	Load factor: unweighted average 1980–6
Air UK	−10.8	60.4
British Airways	10.4	64.2
British Caledonian	−2.4	57.4
British Midland Airways	65.3	59.2
Brymon Airways	75.8	54.2
Dan Air Services	99.1	61.3
Guernsey Airlines	1057.9	75.2
Loganair	167.7	59.7
Manx Airlines	_a	63.0[b]
Others	194.1	48.6[c]
Total	28.8	62.0

Notes: [a] Manx Airlines did not exist in 1980. However, if Air UK, British Midland Airways and Manx Airlines are grouped together (the first two airlines own the third), the percentage increase between 1980 and 1986 is 56.9 per cent.
[b] 1982–6.
[c] Not all the other airlines existed in each year 1980–6. The load factor given is the unweighted average for all the 'airline years' available.

Source: As for Table 13.3.

be expected. Growth may not of course imply long-term viability. Air Ecosse, included in 'Others' in the table, grew by nearly 400 per cent over the period 1980–5, yet went into liquidation in 1987. Indeed it might be argued that *too* rapid growth contributed to its demise.

Table 13.4 also provides data on load factors. Of the major domestic operators, British Airways has the highest load factor, reflecting the relatively dense nature of the routes it serves. Load factor data must be interpreted carefully. As indicated in Section 13.2.1, the load factor is one determinant of the quality of output. It is also affected by numerous factors such as the nature of demand, and the available aircraft designs. It may sometimes be appropriate for a profit maximising airline to operate on low load factors. At the same time, however, it is evident that airlines that have developed financial difficulties have often shown low levels of capacity utilization. (For example, Genair had an average load factor between 1981 and 1984 of 40.2 and Metropolitan averaged 39.5 between 1982 and 1985.) The table shows that, overall, over a third of seat capacity is unused. This spare capacity could of course be utilized at very low marginal cost. Its presence therefore raises the question of the extent to which appropriate pricing policies could lead to its utilization while increasing revenues for the airlines.

A number of studies of airline efficiency have been undertaken in recent years. These have, however, been subject to criticism on several grounds (see the review in CAA, 1977). In any case they do not single out UK domestic operations for separate study. The problem of separating out domestic operations from other services is also present in the analysis of profitability. Neither the CAA nor the airlines publish financial data on domestic operations alone. (As Table 13.3 shows some airlines are almost exclusively concerned with such operations but they are mostly the smaller airlines.) However, what evidence there is suggests that although domestic operations can sometimes be highly profitable – the recent experience of Manx Airlines is an instance of this – margins are often tight and volatile.

13.6   PUBLIC POLICY

13.6.1   Regulation

Types of regulation

All countries regulate (to varying degrees) their domestic air transport industries. The maintenance of safety standards is one key objective of such regulation. Even in the USA, where deregulation has proceeded further than anywhere else, the Federal Aviation Administration continues to regulate and monitor a wide range of technical aspects of airline service. It might of course be argued that even the safety dimension of airline operations should be left to the 'free market' thereby allowing customers to make up their own minds about which price/safety combination they wish to purchase, but so far no government has been prepared to tolerate the accident rate that might result from such a policy.

Regulation has, however, usually extended well beyond technical considerations to economic matters and it is on such regulation that attention is focused here. In the UK, economic controls have been concerned with two key areas: entry and pricing. Control of entry has in turn revolved round two issues. The first is the financial fitness of the potential entrant. This test – which is also still applied in the USA – reflects the view that customers should be protected from financially precarious or crooked operators. It is puzzling, however, why air transport operators – as opposed to, say, the manufacturers of machine tools – should be subject to a vetting procedure beyond that laid down in the Companies Acts, especially as the financial fitness test is not usually seen as being crucial to the maintenance of safety. The second is the appropriateness of allowing a newcomer on to a particular route. It is this second issue concerning entry that is discussed below.

Controls on entry and pricing

The traditional argument for the control of entry on to a particular route has been that many routes and networks are characterized by natural monopoly and that to allow more than one competitor into the market would raise unit costs and may even mean that *no* airline could be profitable. The empirical evidence on airline costs however raises doubts about how valid the natural monopoly argument is. Another argument for controlling entry has been that by such means, incumbent firms may then be willing to fulfil the 'common carrier' obligations of providing a regular and full scheduled service even though some of the services, taken by themselves, may be loss making. An airline protected from entry may also be willing to offer unprofitable low-density services in order to provide a comprehensive network. There are, however, likely to be other ways – for example, direct subsidization – to ensure the provision of such services.

There is another argument for entry controls that is particularly relevant for the UK. Airport capacity at two key airports – Heathrow and Gatwick – is currently fully utilized at certain times of the day.[8] With such a situation some controls are necessary. However, a pricing system for runway 'slots' which equated demand with supply would represent an alternative approach to these problems (see below).

A key argument for the control of air fares is that where entry is constrained – artificially by regulation and/or by other barriers to entry – incumbent firms may be able to exploit their protected positions by raising prices. (Monopoly power may be particularly enhanced where surface modes do not offer strong competition.) Thus the need to control prices arises in part at least from controls on entry.

The regulatory system in the UK

Regulation of air transport goes back to before the Second World War (Baldwin, 1985, p. 17). Since the formation of the (short-lived) Air Transport Licensing Authority – the first licensing body – in 1938, the regulatory machinery has gone through a number of changes. The present system revolves round the activities of the CAA, a body formed in 1971 following the report of the Edwards Committee on the air transport industry (HMSO, 1969).

Under the Civil Aviation Act 1982, the CAA's primary responsibilities are

> to secure that British airlines provide air transport services which satisfy all substantial categories of public demand . . . at the lowest charges consistent with a high standard of safety in operating the services and an economic return to efficient operators . . . and with securing the sound development of the civil air transport industry of the United Kingdom.

It is also required 'to further the reasonable interests of users of air transport services'. In exercising its licensing functions the CAA has to have regard to the most effective use of UK airports; it is required to look at the effect the granting of a licence would have on an existing service; and it must undertake its activities in such a way that it imposes on the industry and the services the industry provides the minimum restrictions consistent with its duties. The CAA's statutory objectives are clearly open to a wide variety of interpretations. In its *Statement of Policies on Air Transport Licensing*, the CAA (1985b) declared itself in favour of competition as a means of achieving the objectives of the 1982 Act. However, this declaration was heavily qualified and left a continuing role for the CAA as assessor of the costs and benefits of competition in particular situations. For example, it saw itself as always carefully weighing 'short term gains in user satisfaction . . . against the longer term need for the sound development of an efficient and competitive industry' (para. 3). Clearly, in the view of politicians and administrators the 'free market' could not be relied upon to provide optimal outcomes. This view was expressed (for example) in the CAA's refusal to allow either Air Ecosse or Air UK to compete with BA on the Heathrow–Aberdeen route in 1984 (see *Decision on Air Transport Licence Application: 11/84*, CAA: London). The CAA accepted that some passengers would transfer to the new carrier (presumably they would only do this if there were gains to be obtained). It also accepted that BA could remain profitable following entry and that the new carrier would provide greater choice to consumers. Nevertheless it did not think that these benefits would outweigh the losses experienced by users of other services which might be displaced at Heathrow as a result of entry. It did not however explore the question of how far such displacement might be desirable, given the competing claims on limited resources, and the current system of non-price allocation of runway capacity.

The US experience of domestic deregulation – a model for the UK?

In the United States economic regulation of domestic air transport has almost entirely disappeared following the 1978 Airline Deregulation Act. In 1985 the Civil Aeronautics Board – the US equivalent of the CAA – was wound up. Numerous studies have pointed to the welfare gains – notably from lower prices and greater frequencies – that have resulted (see, for example, Bailey *et al.*, 1985, and Morrison and Winston, 1986b). For several reasons, however, caution must be exercised in the interpretation of these results particularly in a UK context. First, these studies are not without their problems. For example, they do not typically take into account the decline in quality that has resulted from higher load factors that deregulation has generated. Secondly, it is not at all clear that the US industry has reached any equilibrium. Considerable structural changes are still going on; at the time of writing, the industry has become more concentrated (in terms of the concentration ratio) at national level than it was prior to deregulation. While the level of concentration in individual markets may be the most relevant structural consideration for welfare purposes, nevertheless the strength of individual airlines at a national level may have an important influence on their behaviour in these markets. If a tight oligopolistic structure emerges this may eventually lead to a reduction in any welfare gains that deregulation has generated to date. Thirdly, the US industry, though oligopolistic, does not have a dominant airline in the kind of position which for political and historical reasons, BA holds in the UK. BA's position, with its grandfather rights to Heathrow was a key reason why the CAA abandoned its proposal – which was strongly endorsed by the government (HMSO, 1984) – to liberate entry on certain key domestic routes in the UK (CAA *Official Record Series 2*, No 652 January 1985). The CAA had proposed to exclude services using Heathrow and Gatwick because of capacity constraints there. The opposition to the proposal centred on the argument that with these two key airports excluded the extent to which airlines would be exposed to free competition under the proposal would vary considerably. For example, some small airlines had all their business in the areas where entry controls would have been relaxed, whereas BA had about 3 per cent of its traffic there. It was argued that BA's dominant position protected by its access to Heathrow and Gatwick would have given it an unfair competitive advantage.

The key to the regulation versus deregulation debate for UK domestic air transport is the continued existence of a dominant supplier which has favoured access to limited runway resources. The enforced separation of BA's domestic operations from its international activities, and the introduction of appropriate pricing policies at airports might reduce the need for any intervention. Neither is likely to happen in the near future at least. BA's successful opposition to the CAA's proposals (CAA, 1984) that it should lose some international routes to British Caledonian indicates its high level of lobbying skills. Thus some form of regulatory intervention may be desirable. It must be remembered, however, that such intervention has its own costs; these costs may be greater than the benefits obtained. Even if this is not the case, it is an open question how far the airline industry needs its *own* agency to do this (as opposed to the more general anti-trust framework that applies to the rest of UK industry).

13.6.2 Airports

Domestic scheduled services account for just under 38 per cent of all air transport movements (ATMs) at UK airports. At some airports such services account for the majority of ATMs. At Heathrow and Gatwick, however, domestic scheduled services account for only 28 and 19 per cent respectively. In 1984 the number of passengers per domestic scheduled ATM was 69.3 at Heathrow and 47.4 at Gatwick (CAA, 1985a, p. 15). All other scheduled services had 128.3 passengers per ATM at Heathrow and 99.7 at Gatwick. Since 1974, the number of passengers per ATM on domestic scheduled flights has grown only very slowly – hardly at all at Heathrow – whereas on other scheduled flights it has risen substantially. This difference in growth is due to the increasing importance of larger aircraft in international flights and the greater number of third-level domestic services now being allowed to use Heathrow.

These 'per ATM' passenger numbers are of particular significance given the current excess demand for runway slots at Heathrow and Gatwick. The scheduling committees (made up of the airlines) at each airport seek to resolve this problem by pushing the excess demand to other times. A guiding principle in the allocation procedure is that those airlines which already have a slot have a prior claim to it, a 'grandfather right'. Substitution of such an administrative mechanism by a pricing or auctioning system would have a number of advantages. It would no longer bestow, as a result of historical factors – a key right and windfall gain on an airline.[10] Those airlines that valued a particular slot the most would be able to obtain it. *Any* airline would thus be free to use Heathrow or Gatwick. Prices would reflect the superior network advantages at Heathrow. (If the government wished for various reasons to encourage the development of Gatwick, it could pay a direct subsidy.) It is likely that the ATMs with lower numbers of passengers would become less important under such an arrangement although the type of passenger carried on these operations – frequently business travellers – might be willing to pay a higher price for the convenience of landing at Heathrow than many leisure passengers on international flights.

Equating supply and demand through price is not of course without its problems. International flights and the associated bilateral agreement present particular difficulties. Again, many international airlines are state owned or favoured. Continued access to Heathrow may be important to their status and they may therefore be paid subsidies in order to achieve it. BA by virtue of its size may be better placed, simply by virtue of its size and greater ability to cross-subsidize, to bid for slots than a small independent UK airline seeking to build up its network. Some of these arguments have been rehearsed in CAA (1986).

There may be ways in which these problems could be overcome and in this context it will be interesting to see the effect of the introduction of a 'buy/sell' procedure for slots at the four US airports where prior to the innovation, the demand for slots exceeded their supply. Under the new procedure, an airline may, within certain restrictions, sell its grandfather right to a slot to another airline, and retain the proceeds. No system is ever likely to be perfect – the US innovation has been criticized on the grounds that it generates windfall gains for the airlines from publicly provided resources – but it would certainly be worth exploring the issue of whether a pricing mechanism would generate more satisfactory signals than the present arrangement. Such a mechanism could be implemented through an appropriate airport pricing strategy, rather than through the grant of buy/sell rights to airlines. A market pricing approach to runway slots would be reinforced by an organizational structure for airports that consisted of three *competing* London airports, each run by a separate company. The privatization of the British Airports Authority (BAA), which operated all three airports provided an opportunity for introducing such a structure. The BAA management, however, successfully opposed this strategy. One interpretation of this opposition to a more competitive environment – a factor highlighted by Kay and Thompson (1986) – is that it stemmed from management's desire to maintain its own security through the retention of a strong market position.

13.6.3 Privatization of BA

In 1987, BA was privatized. Prior to its sale, BA experienced an improvement in both labour and total factor productivity (Ashworth and Forsyth, 1984, p. 56). These authors argue, however, that much of the (quite substantial) improvement in labour productivity may be explained by greater expenditure on other inputs and that even after the recent increases in total factor productivity, BA was still relatively inefficient by comparison with international airlines and British independents. Such findings must however be treated with care because of the problems associated with comparisons of this kind. BA's profitability showed a dramatic turn-round in the early 1980s, although possibly over half of this was attributable to favourable movements in the exchange rate (Ashworth and Forsyth, 1984 p. 125). Although BA's domestic services constitute only a small proportion of its total activities, it is likely that much of what is true for BA as a whole, is likely to be true for its domestic operations. (The latter is however subject to rather more competitive pressure.)

It is too early to say how far BA's productivity will continue to increase now that it is in the private sector. Changes of ownership may do little to improve BA's efficiency if its market position is maintained by regulation. As Kay and Thompson (1986) point out it is not ownership as such but the interaction of ownership and competition that promotes efficiency.

13.7 CONCLUSION

The domestic air transport industry has experienced very rapid, if erratic growth in the last ten years, and looks set to continue to grow more rapidly than GDP. The industry's development has been heavily influenced by public controls, most notably through the CAA, the British Airports Authority, and the political influence exercised over BA's operations during its nationalized phase. The CAA has now adopted a more relaxed regulatory stance; and the BAA and BA have been privatized. It remains to be seen how far these changes will affect the industry. These are grounds for arguing that they will make little difference.

POSTSCRIPT

On 21 December, 1987, BA acquired BCal for £250m, after a fierce protracted battle which included a rival bid from the Scandinavian airline, SAS. BA's bid for BCal was reported on by the Monopolies and Mergers Commission (*British Airways plc and British Caledonian Group plc. A Report on the Proposed Merger*. 1987. Cm 247. HMSO: London). The MMC approved the bid, following undertakings by BA, one of which was that within a month of take-over, BA would return to the CAA all BCal's domestic route licences. BA would also not oppose any application by a competitor for these routes, although it retained the right to reapply for the licences. It remains to be seen whether any smaller UK airlines could compete head to head with BA/BCal on the relevant domestic routes, or could make a sufficiently strong case to the CAA for sole rights, thereby displacing the new merged airline. (Although BA undertook not to rely on its rights as an incumbent in any reapplication it is difficult to see how the CAA could avoid taking the merged airline's incumbency into account in its decisions.)

NOTES TO CHAPTER 13

1 Passengers carried also fell between 1979 and 1980. Clearly this fall was concentrated in the shorter distances.
2 The reason for this is that the figures are heavily affected by the very high load factors achieved on charter flights – exceeding 80 per cent – over typically much longer distances than domestic flights.
3 Numbers of passengers uplifted is the traffic measure used in CAA statistics and it is therefore utilized here. Since the trunk routes are also among the longer-distance services, a passenger seat-kilometre (used or available) measure would almost certainly give a bigger share to the trunks than that quoted in the text. 'Passengers uplifted' relates to all (not only scheduled) domestic operations.
4 See CAA, 1985a, para. 2.10.
5 For a given number of passengers and a given aircraft, the load factor may of course be changed by altering the number of seats in the aircraft. However the change in load factor occurs, the effect on product quality must be considered.
6 The following draws heavily on the information contained in the 'World Airline Directory', *Flight International*, 29 March 1986.
7 A major airline is one whose fleet has an aggregated maximum take-off weight exceeding 200 tonnes. Charter airlines are included.
8 For a decision where airport capacity constraints played an important part in the licensing decision, see *Decisions on Air Transport Licence Applications, 11/84*, CAA, London.
9 *True* excess demand at Heathrow and Gatwick may be higher since a number of airlines may not bid for slots because they know they will not get them. It is also likely that Heathrow would generate greater excess demand than Gatwick if every airline put in a bid for their most preferred option. Many airlines are at Gatwick because they cannot get into Heathrow.
10 Asworth and Forsyth, 1984, p. 13, estimate that BA's privileged access to Heathrow may confer on it an implicit subsidy in the order of £50 million. This figure relates to all BA's activities, not only its domestic service.

REFERENCES

Ashworth, M., and Forsyth, P. (1984), *British Airways*, IFS Report Series no. 12 (London: Institute for Fiscal Studies).

Bailey, E. E., Graham, D. R., and Kaplan, D. P. (1985), *Deregulating the Airlines* (Washington, DC: Brookings Institution).

Bailey, E. E., and Williams, J. R. (1986), 'Sources of economic rent in the deregulated airline industry', Mimeo (Pittsburgh: Carnegie Mellon University Graduate School of Industrial Administration).

Baldwin, R. (1985), *Regulating the Airlines* (Oxford: Clarendon Press).

Baumol, W. J., Panzar, J. C., and Willig, R. D. (1982), *Contestable Markets and the Theory of Industrial Structure* (New York: Harcourt, Brace Jovanovich).

Civil Aviation Authority (1977), *European Air Fares*, CAP 409 (London).

Civil Aviation Authority (1979), *Domestic Air Services*, CAP 420 (London).

Civil Aviation Authority (1980), *Passengers at the London Area Airports* 1978, CAP 420 (London).

Civil Aviation Authority (1984), *Deregulation of Air Transport. A Perspectiv* on the Experience in the United States, CAA Paper 84009 (London).

Civil Aviation Authority (1985a), *Air Traffic Distribution in the London Are* CAP 510 (London).

Civil Aviation Authority (1985b), *Statement of Policies on Air Transpo* Licensing, CAP 501 (London).

Civil Aviation Authority (1986), *Air Traffic Distribution in the Londo* Area – Draft Advice to the Secretary of State, CAP 517 (London).

Douglas, G. W., and Miller, J. C. (1974), *Economic Regulation of Domesti* Air Transport: Theory and Policy (Washington, DC: Brookings Institution)

HMSO (1969), *British Air Transport in the Seventies. Report of the Committe* of Inquiry into Civil Air Transport (The Edwards Committee), Cmnd 401 (London).

HMSO (1984), *Airline Competition Policy*, Cmnd 9366 (London).

Johnson, P. S. (1987), *Airline Deregulation and New Entry: A Case Study o* the London–Glasgow Route, Durham University Economics Departmen Working Paper no. 82.

Kay, J. A., and Thompson, D. J. (1986), 'Privatisation: a policy in search of a rationale', *Economic Journal*, 96, 18–32.

Meyer, J. R., and Oster, C. V. (1984), *Deregulation and the New Airline* Entrepreneurs (Cambridge, Mass.: MIT Press).

Meyer, J. R., Oster, C. V., Morgan, I. P., Berman, B. A., and Strassman D. L. (1981), *Airline Deregulation. The Early Experiences* (Boston, Mass. Auburn Publishing Co.).

Morrison, S. A., and Winston, C. (1986a), 'Empirical implications and tests of the contestability hypothesis', Mimeo (Washington, DC: Brookings Institution).

Morrison, S. A. and Winston, C. (1986b), *The Economic Effects of Airline* Deregulation (Washington, DC: Brookings Institution).

Shepherd, W. G. (1984), '"Contestability" vs. Competition', *American* Economic Review, 74, 572–87.

Transport and Road Research Laboratory (1981), *Rail and Air Travel between* London and Scotland: Analysis of Competition using Box–Jenkins Methods (by Jenkins, G. M., Abbie, E., Everest, J. T. and Paulley, N. J.) Transport and Road Research Laboratory, Laboratory Report 978 (Crowthorne, Berks).

Watts, R. (1983), 'Simplifying flying: development of shuttle operations', in *Economics of Air Transportation*, Proceedings of the Seventh World Airports Conference organised by the Institution of Civil Engineers, 24–26 May (London: Thomas Telford).

Winston, C. (1985), 'Conceptual developments in the economics of transportation: an interpretative survey', *Journal of Economic Literature*, XXIII, 57–94.

FURTHER READING

The best statistical source on the industry is the CAA's publications on operating traffic and financial statistics. The monthly publication is *UK*

Airlines – Monthly Operating and Traffic Statistics; the annual publication is *UK Airlines: Annual Operating, Traffic and Financial Statistics*. Most of the financial statistics in the latter relate to the total operations, domestic and non-domestic, of airlines, but some traffic and operating data for domestic activities only are available.

The CAA has published a number of useful reviews on issues relating to the industry including

Domestic Air Services, 1979 (CAP 420).
Deregulation of Air Transport: A Perspective on the Experience of the US, 1984 (CAA Paper 84009).
Airline Competition Policy, 1979 (CAP 500).
Competition on the Main Domestic Trunk Routes (CAA Paper 87005)

The CAA's current policies are given in its *Statement of Policies on Air Transport Licensing – January 1985*.

Remarkably little has been published on the economics of the UK industry. The Edwards Committee Report – *British Air Transport in the Seventies*, Cmnd 4018 (HMSO: London, 1969) – though dated, still provides a good discussion of the underlying economic issues. Two recent Institute of Fiscal Studies reports, *British Airways* (1984) and *Privatising London's Airports* (1985), also provide an economic analysis of some important topics.

Administrative and political aspects of regulation by the CAA are considered in Baldwin, R. (1985), *Regulating the Airlines* (Oxford: Clarendon Press).

Chapter Fourteen

Insurance

BOB CARTER

14.1 INTRODUCTION

The insurance industry has for five hundred years been making an increasingly important contribution to Britain's social welfare and economic development by providing for the sharing (or spreading) of risks and for the investment of personal savings.

Firms are exposed to unexpected changes in the supply of resources and in the demand for their products which may result in windfall profits or losses. Other uncertain events, such as accidents, fires, floods and disease, result only in loss for the individuals or organizations concerned. Insurance is designed to deal with this latter class of so-called 'pure risks'. Each policyholder pays a premium related to the expected value of the losses he/she may suffer if an insured loss-producing event occurs during the period of insurance, and the insurer undertakes to compensate any policyholder who does so suffer a loss. Thus the financial losses of the unfortunate few are spread amongst many.

A broad distinction can be drawn between long-term and general (non-life) insurance business. The former consists mainly of life insurance and pensions where the insurer spreads the risk over time, undertaking to pay the policyholder either: (1) a certain sum upon his/her death (or under endowment policies, his/her survival to a specified date); or (2) with pension contracts, an annuity during his/her lifetime after retirement. Most life policies remain in force for ten or more years during which time the insurer accumulates a fund to meet the eventual claims, and the large savings element of the majority of the contracts substantially adds to those funds, making life offices major institutional investors.

General insurances are typically for periods of only one year, but the funds held by insurers to meet their liabilities to policyholders may still exceed the total premiums for the year.

Theoretically, only risks that: can be measured objectively, are independently exposed to loss, give rise to losses capable of monetary valuation, and are fortuitous so far as the policyholder is concerned, are suitable for insurance (Berliner, 1982). Few risks fully measure up to such conditions, but that does not deter insurers from devising new types of insurance.

308

The performance of insurance contracts depends on chance in that the insurer only promises to pay if some uncertain event occurs. Insurance, however, differs from gambling in that a policyholder: (1) must have an insurable interest in the subject-matter of the contract (that is, he/she must stand to suffer financial loss if the insured event does occur); and (2) other than for insurances on human life, he/she is only entitled to be indemnified to the extent of any loss incurred. Nevertheless there is a problem of moral hazard: although few individuals try to profit by deliberately bringing about an insured loss, carelessness and the inflating of claims are common events which insurers try to control by surveys, policy conditions and the investigation of claims.

14.1.1 The British Insurance Industry

The industry's operations extend worldwide. UK and foreign insurance companies and Lloyd's of London syndicates underwrite in Britain both UK and overseas risks, though much of the latter business consists of reinsurances.[1] Many British insurance companies also have overseas branch offices and subsidiary or associated companies. Tables 14.1 and 14.2 show the development of the domestic and worldwide premium incomes of UK-incorporated insurance companies and Lloyd's. A significant part of the premium income growth, particularly since the early 1970s, is due to inflation and, in the case of overseas premiums, the fall in the external value of sterling. Table 14.3 provides a better indicator of the development of the industry compared with the UK economy as a whole.

Throughout the 1950s and 1960s, life premiums increased faster than national income. After the 1973 oil crisis, real growth of life insurance was adversely affected by inflation and the economic recession so that for a time premium income fell as a percentage of national income. Likewise the demand for all classes of non-life insurance grew rapidly in the 1960s in response to the rise in real incomes and the developments in technology, the law and social behaviour, such as the changing attitudes towards liability for personal injury. The post-1973 stagflation interrupted the real growth of premium expenditures, and in many countries intensified competition between insurers for non-life insurance business.

As noted earlier, premium income generates funds for investment so that the postwar period has also witnessed a substantial increase in the invested funds of insurance companies (see Table 14.4).

The freedom UK insurance companies enjoy in the investment of their funds enables them to hold diversified portfolios of assets (see Table 14.5) (Clayton and Osborn, 1965; Dickinson, 1971; Wilson Committee, 1978; Dodds, 1979). Although the net acquisitions of fixed and variable interest securities vary significantly from year to year, over the long term they tend to maintain a ratio of around 3:2. The

Table 14.1   *Net Written Premiums in the UK*

	1977 £m	% of total	1980 £m	% of total	1985 £m	% of total
Long-term business						
Ordinary long-term	3,555	41.9	6,008	43.0	13,885	48.2
Industrial branch	514	6.0	886	6.3	1,201	4.2
Total, long term	4,069	47.9	6,894	49.3	15,086	42.4
General business						
UK risks Motor	1,033	12.2	1,827	13.1	2,617	9.1
Fire & accident	1,685	19.8	2,785	19.9	4,920	17.1
Other motor, fire & accident business written in UK	772	9.1	1,317	9.4	1,207	4.2
Reinsurance	n/a		n/a		2,194	7.6
Marine, aviation transport	931	11.0	1,166	8.3	2,782	9.7
Total general business	4,421	52.1	7,095	50.7	13,720	47.6
Total all business	8,490		13,989		28,806	

Notes:
1 The figures represent the premiums for insurances and reinsurances, written in the UK by British and foreign companies established in Britain, Lloyd's and friendly societies, less premiums for reinsurances ceded abroad.
2 The figure for 'Other motor, fire & accident' relates to insurances and reinsurances of overseas risks written in the UK.
Source: Association of British Insurers, *UK Market Statistics, 1984.*

extent to which the companies match the maturity dates of their assets to their liabilities is shown by the higher proportion of the general insurance funds held in cash and other short-term assets (8.8 per cent) compared with the long-term (life) funds (2.7 per cent).

Finally, the contribution that insurers and brokers make to the balance of payments is shown in Table 14.6. So far the foreign companies operating in Britain have done relatively little to reduce Britain's favourable balance of trade in insurance services.

14.1.2   The Supply of Insurance

The following five characteristics of insurance business significantly affect its supply.

1) *Variable costs* comprise the largest proportion of total costs (Carter, 1979), with commissions paid to intermediaries plus claims payments accounting for around three-quarters of the premiums for most classes of non-life insurance. This gives an insurer considerable flexibility in the volume of business he can profitably write.

2) *Uncertainty*: at the time of sale an insurer cannot know whether a particular insurance will result in a claim, so that the final cost of writing one more contract is always uncertain. However, insurance

Table 14.2 *Worldwide Net Written Premiums of British Insurers Including Lloyd's*

	1958 £m	% of total	1968 £m	% of total	1978 £m	% of total	1985 £m	% of total
Ordinary life & annuities	438	25.4	1,225	30.9	4,793	34.7	16,226	42.8
Industrial life	178	10.3	277	7.0	573	4.2	1,201	3.2
Total life	616	35.7	1,502	37.9	5,366	38.9	17,427	46.0
Marine & aviation	203	11.8	499	12.6	1,193	8.6	2,782	7.3
Other non-life	907	52.5	1,959	49.5	7,238	52.5	15,487	40.9
Reinsurance	n/a		n/a		n/a		2,194	5.8
Total non-life	1,110	64.3	2,458	62.1	8,431	61.1	20,463	54.0
Total	1,726	—	3,960	—	13,797	—	37,890	—

Source: 1958–68: derived from the *Annual Abstract of Statistics*; 1978: *Policy Holder Insurance Journal* 97, 33, 1979 and Lloyd's; 1984: Association of British Insurers, *Insurance Statistics 1981–85*, and Lloyd's.

Table 14.3 *Net Written Premiums as Percentage of Gross National Product (at Factor Cost)*

	1958	1968	1978	1985
Net premiums for UK domestic risks				
Long-term (life)	na	na	3.3	4.4
General (excluding marine & aviation)	na	na	2.2	2.2
Worldwide business of UK insurers				
Long-term	3.0	3.9	3.6	5.7
General (including marine & aviation)	5.4	6.4	5.6	6.7

Source: As for Tables 14.1 and 14.2, *National Income & Expenditure*.

Table 14.4   *Total Investments of Financial Institutions at End of Year Market Values*

	1967	1977	1985	% of total	Annual growth rates 1967–77	1977–85
	£m	£m	£m		%	%
Insurance companies						
Long term funds	10,086	33,088	128,820	37.7	10.7	18.5
General funds	1,872	6,723	18,759	5.5	11.9	13.7
	11,958	39,811	147,579	43.2		
Superannuation funds	6,246	24,100	157,376	46.1	14.5	26.4
Investment trusts	4,022	6,563	18,085	5.3	5.0	13.5
Unit trusts	788	3,432	18,633	5.4	15.9	23.5
Total	23,014	73,906	341,673	100.0		

Notes:

1 Insurance companies' figures exclude balances held by agents; the 1967 figures relate to British Insurance Association members only and are at book values. Also the growth rates for 1967–77 are based on book values.

2 Superannuation funds: holdings of local authority funds are as at 31 March of the following year.

Source: Financial Statistics, HMSO.

Table 14.5   *Distribution of Insurance Companies' UK Funds by Class of Asset at 31 December 1985*

Class of asset	Long-term funds (£m)	(%)	General funds (£m)	(%)
Cash and other short-term assets	3,200	2.48	2,070	11.03
British government securities	30,456	23.64	4,778	25.47
Local authority securities	656	0.51	54	0.29
Overseas government securities	1,803	1.40	1,549	8.26
Loans and mortgages	4,268	3.31	381	2.03
Company securities:				
Ordinary shares UK	43,123	33.48	4,870	25.96
Overseas	11,550	8.97	1,394	7.43
Other securities UK	4,232	3.29	975	5.20
Overseas	728	0.57	788	4.20
Unit trusts	7,960	6.18	—	—
Property and land	20,162	15.65	1,595	8.50
Other	682	0.53	305	1.63
	128,820	100.00	18,759	100.00

Notes:

1 All holdings are at market values except mortgages and loans and part of 'Other' which are at book value.

2 Agents' balances have been excluded.

Source: Financial Statistics, May 1987.

operations are based on the principle of risk combination: the larger the number of independent exposure units that a company insures, the smaller will tend to be the relative variation in its actual from its expected aggregate claims costs. It can further reduce the risk of insolvency due to fluctuations in claims costs by reinsuring and maintaining free reserves. An increase in the volume of business written will enable an insurer to retain larger risks and/or operate with relatively smaller free reserves.

3) *Investment earnings*. Normally premiums are paid at the inception of an insurance contract so providing an insurer with the funds to meet prospective claims' liabilities. The investment of those funds provides an additional source of earnings, including capital gains, which can be taken into account in the fixing of premiums.

4) *Regulation*. Governments regulate both the entry of new insurers to their markets and the operations of established insurers. Amongst the constraints imposed on insurers, the solvency regulations limit the amount of business an insurance company can transact relative to its capital and free reserves.

5) *Ancillary services*. Insurers provide various pre- and post-sales services, including advising on loss prevention, and assisting in reducing losses. The costs of such services are built into premium loadings, though for large commercial insurances they are sometimes charged for separately.

14.1.3 The Demand for Insurance

The demand for insurance arises from a desire for economic security. Whether individuals will consider buying insurance and if so, the prices they will be prepared to pay, is determined by such factors as their perception of the risk, and how risk-averse they happen to be (Friedman and Savage, 1948). Similarly firms make their insurance purchasing decisions in the light of their corporate objectives and attitudes to risk (Carter and Crockford, 1974; Carter, 1978). Demand is also related to the size of possible loss. To insure against very small losses is neither necessary nor economic because of the relatively high premium loading required to cover the costs of handling small claims.

Since the Monopolies Commission decided in 1972 that the total market demand for fire insurance was relatively price-inelastic, buyers of insurance have become far more responsive to premium rate fluctuations for all classes of insurance. Firms respond to increases in premium rates by devoting more resources to loss prevention (Doherty, 1976), and by retaining more of their own risks instead of fully insuring (Carter and Crockford, 1974).

The demand for an individual insurer's products tends to be highly responsive to both the price level and, in relation to the renewal of existing policies, to price changes (Reynolds, 1970). A 1977 survey of British motorists revealed that, *ceteris paribus*, the average motorist

Table 14.6 *The Contribution of Insurance and Other Services to the UK Balance of Payments (£ million)*

	1978	1981	1984	1985
Insurance companies: Underwriting overseas business and profits from overseas branches and affiliates	313	260	361	436
Portfolio investment	81	226	702	976
Total	394	486	1,063	1,412
Lloyd's: Underwriting overseas business	354	254	220	729
Portfolio investment	70	128	344	479
Total	424	382	564	1,208
Insurance brokers:	237	314	535	664
Total insurance (gross)	1,055	1,182	2,162	3,284
Less profits of UK branches, subsidiaries etc. due to overseas parents	13	29	−34	−34
Net earnings of the insurance industry	1,042	1,153	2,196	3,318

Source: UK Balance of Payments, 1985, HMSO.

would have been tempted to change insurers if offered a 13 per cent premium reduction, and 27 per cent of the respondents would have switched for only a 5 per cent price cut (Louis Harris International, 1977).

The demand for life insurance is complicated by most life and pensions contracts combining both protection and savings elements. Not only is it difficult to define and measure the prices of such contracts, but they are also in competition with savings products available from other financial institutions (Finsinger, Hammond and Tapp, 1985; Carter, Chiplin and Lewis, 1986). Also the determinants of demand differ between the various types of contract that have been designed to cater for individual's differing needs. For example, although the demand for all types of personal life insurance is directly, and generally more than proportionately, related to changes in personal disposable income, the demand for certain types of contract is particularly affected by the demand for new mortgages.

4.2 THE STRUCTURE OF THE BRITISH INSURANCE MARKET

At the end of 1985 there were 841 insurance companies authorized to write insurance business in the UK. However, after excluding the companies writing no new business, the specialist companies providing insurance only to a limited class of persons, and over 150 subsidiaries of other authorized insurers, the 'commercial' insurance market can be taken as consisting of around 450 companies and groups, of which some 40 per cent are British-controlled. In addition there are some 370 Lloyd's syndicates, backed (in January 1986) by 28,597 underwriting members (including 4,911 overseas members), and a few friendly societies that write life insurance.

Companies are authorized by the Department of Trade and Industry to transact specific statutorily defined classes of insurance (including reinsurance) business. Most of the major British companies operate as 'composites' transacting both long-term (life) and general (non-life) insurance business. Other companies specialize, mainly in the writing of life or marine and aviation insurances; in the life market the specialists account for over 40 per cent of total premiums. The insurance market is less concentrated than many other industries, but as shown in Table 14.7 a few companies still write substantial shares of the total business. The relative ease of new entry to the market tends to counteract the periodic increases in market concentration resulting from mergers between the major companies (Richards and Colenutt, 1975).

Many foreign insurers have established or acquired UK-incorporated subsidiaries, but only a few write substantial UK domestic insurance accounts, the majority being interested mainly in the overseas business placed on the London market. The share of the total premiums written in the UK by foreign-controlled companies rose from 14.0 per cent in 1970 to 17.1 per cent in 1980 for general insurance, and from 11.8 per cent to 13.1 per cent over the same period for long-term insurance.

Lloyd's of London grew out of Edward Lloyd's coffee house where in the seventeenth century merchants gathered to transact marine insurance (Gibb, 1957). Today, Lloyd's provides a major international market for the insurance and reinsurance of large and unusual risks. The Corporation of Lloyd's itself writes no insurances but provides the facilities for the individual underwriting and broking members to carry on their business. Today the underwriting members remain individually liable without limit for their underwriting debts, but belong to syndicates managed by professional underwriters.

Generally the British insurance market is highly competitive. The cost advantages of the large companies are insufficient to shield them from competition from either the smaller companies, or from new entrants which nowadays often are members of large foreign insurance

Table 14.7 *Concentration Ratios in British Insurance Based on Net Premium Incomes, 1984*

		General insurance %	Ordinary insurance %
(a)	Worldwide business of British insurers (including Lloyd's)		
	3 largest companies	33.6	21.5
	6 largest companies	53.6	33.3
	Lloyd's	21.3	—
(b)	Insurances & reinsurance written in the UK (including Lloyd's)		
	3 largest companies	22.0[a]	19.0
	6 largest companies	37.2[a]	31.7

Note: [a]estimated from 1983 figures.

Sources: Tables 13.1 and 13.2; company accounts; Carter, R. L., and Godden, A. H. (1984), *The British Insurance Industry* (Brentford, Middx.: Kluwer).

groups. Also Lloyd's is a major competitive force in the market and a source of many product innovations.

14.2.1 Insurance Intermediaries

Although in recent years some insurance companies, particularly amongst the life offices, have been increasing their direct marketing efforts by employing full-time salesmen, newspaper advertising and direct mail, most insurances are handled by intermediaries. Some companies deal only with full-time registered insurance brokers, and Lloyd's syndicates accept business only from the 260 registered Lloyd's brokers (though special arrangements have been made for other brokers to deal directly with the motor syndicates under schemes arranged by Lloyd's brokers). However, many other individuals and firms, such as accountants, solicitors, and garage proprietors, act as part-time insurance agents, and there are several thousand other full-time intermediaries trading under various titles. In the mid-1960s the big four clearing banks, the Trustee Savings Bank (TSB) and the Scottish banks extended their activities into insurance and are now estimated to control about 30 per cent of UK life and pensions brokerage (Diacon, 1985). The banks' lead has been followed by the motoring organizations, and following the enactment of the Building Societies Act 1986, the major societies are planning to extend their insurance activities.

The Insurance Brokers (Registration) Act 1977 restricted the use of the title 'insurance broker' to suitably qualified and experienced persons who possess adequate financial resources and conduct their *business* in an ethical manner; unfortunately it did not prevent people *from* trading as full-time insurance intermediaries under other titles. *The* Financial Services Act 1986 requires all independent intermediar-*ies* engaged in 'investment business', including life insurance, to be *authorized* by the Securities and Investments Board or a recognized *self*-regulatory organization. The Association of British Insurers has *issued* codes of practice governing the selling of general and long-term *insurances* issued by non-broker intermediaries.

Fewer than a dozen major broking firms control well over half of the *total* business handled by brokers (Kitcat & Aitken, 1982). All of the *major* firms are active in overseas markets and most have branches, *subsidiaries* or affiliates in many parts of the world. In the 1970s several *large* British and American broking firms merged or entered into working *relationships* which gave the Americans easier access to Lloyd's.

14.2.2   The London Insurance Market

London is the world's leading international insurance market. Lloyd's obtains three-quarters of its premium income from abroad, and brokers bring in large amounts of direct and reinsurance business which is placed with both British and foreign-controlled companies (Economists Advisory Group, 1984).

The formation in Britain of specialist reinsurance companies lagged behind their development in Europe. Even today only one British reinsurance company, the Mercantile and General Reinsurance Company (a part of the Prudential group), figures amongst the world's ten largest reinsurers, which are mainly German, Swiss or American (Carter, 1983). Since the 1970s the large British direct insurance companies have strengthened their reinsurance interests by forming specialist reinsurance subsidiaries, and by participating in the for-mation of international joint-venture reinsurance companies.

14.3   MARKET BEHAVIOUR

14.3.1   Pricing

Although at the time of sale the eventual cost of an individual insurance contract is uncertain, the premium is usually agreed and paid by the policyholder at that time. Therefore, an insurer must base his price on an estimate of the expected administration and claims costs. Given the delay between the receipt of premiums and the payment of claims, the insurer can allow for the potential investment income that he can expect to earn. Thus the basic premium formula for a non-life insurance is as follows:

$$P = (p \times \bar{c}) (1+r)^{-t} + L$$

where

P = the premium;

$(p \times \bar{c})$ = the estimated loss expectancy given by the probability of a loss occurring (p) multiplied by the average size of claim ($\bar{c}$);

r = the rate of interest that can be earned on invested funds;

t = the average delay between the receipt of premiums and the payment of claims;

L = the loading of the premium to cover marketing and administration costs, to provide a profit and to contribute to contingency reserves.

The loss expectancy gives the risk premium which the insurer must charge to cover the expected claims cost of the contract; the discount factor allows for the estimated investment earnings on the funds held to provide for the potential claims. The contingency element of the premium loading is to provide some protection against the risks that actual claims may exceed the expected claims or that investment earnings may prove to be less than estimated. The premium rating process is thus a form of cost-plus pricing incorporating a profit margin. However, if an insurer wishes to acquire new business or retain existing insurances he cannot ignore the premiums offered by competitors (Benjamin, 1977; Carter, 1979). Also there is evidence that increasingly insurers are prepared to use marginal cost pricing to enter markets or adjust their market shares.

The pricing of some long-term life insurances takes the form of a single premium payable at commencement, but mainly policyholders are charged level annual premiums which must allow for mortality rates rising with age, so that as time passes the numbers of insured lives still living and paying premiums will be falling while the number of claims will be rising. Therefore premiums must be fixed at a level in excess of that required to cover the claims expected in the early years to provide a fund to cover the shortfall in the premiums receivable over the claims payable in the later years (Franklin and Woodhead, 1980).

The ease and accuracy with which loss expectancies may be estimated, and so premiums calculated, varies according to the class of insurance, and between the mass risks (that is, personal and small business insurances), and large industrial and commercial insurances (West, Bishop and Bellinger, 1986). An insurer can use past loss experience to classify the mass risks into reasonably homogeneous groups according to observable risk factors; for example, lives insured are classified by age and sex, and shop premises are classified for fire insurance according to the type of trade, building construction and similar factors. If an underwriter fails to recognize important differences between groups he runs the risk of losing to more observant, discriminating competitors those policyholders with lower-than-average loss expectancies (Scurfield, 1968). The underwriter of large industrial and other risks is faced with the dual problems of relatively small numbers of exposure units, often subject to varying risk factors, and of policyholders who demand that their premiums reflect their own rather than an industry's loss experience, so that premium rating becomes individual case- rather than group-related.

Life insurance companies use mortality rates derived from observations of large numbers of lives, which normally change significantly only over many years. Moreover, claims are always for the full sum insured. Therefore, loss expectancies can be estimated with a high degree of accuracy, and large companies can expect to experience relatively small random variations in mortality experience. The main element of uncertainty lies in the rate of interest used in the calculation of premiums for the discounting of future premiums and claims. Nowadays premium rating for life insurance is a relatively precise process using, subject to the pressures of competition from other insurers (and from other savings institutions too), conservatively low discount rates. Competition is, however, beginning to undermine the traditional classification of life risks solely according to age and sex: an increasing number of insurers now also distinguish between smokers and non-smokers.

Matters are more complicated for non-life insurers. First, they have to consider both the probability of one or more losses occurring during the period of insurance, and the variations in the size of losses. Secondly, non-life risks are more heterogeneous. For the mass risks a well-established insurer can draw upon a large volume of past loss statistics, and in the case of motor insurance most companies pool their experience to enable the Motor Risks Statistics Bureau to produce market data. Despite improvements in statistical analysis and in the application of actuarial techniques, subjective judgement still remains important in estimating the influence on future loss experience of changing economic, social, legal, technological and other factors which over relatively short periods can significantly affect the probability and/or severity of loss. Inflation, for example, may substantially increase average claims costs, so that in fixing premiums the insurer must allow for future inflation to the date when the last claim can be expected to be settled (Carter, 1979). In the case of liability insurances claims brought by injured third parties may remain outstanding, increasing in cost, for years.

The pricing of the insurances of large risks presents the underwriter with his greatest challenge, and although the analysis of past experience may provide some bench marks for particular groups of risks, the adjustments for individual experience cannot be based solely on objective factors.

Pricing behaviour in relation to non-life insurance has undergone several major changes over the last twenty years. Before 1968 the premiums for many classes of UK non-life insurance were subject to minimum price agreements, known as tariffs, to which most of the large insurance companies subscribed. Under the pressure of intense competition from new companies in the 1960s, the motor insurance tariff was abandoned in 1968, shortly followed by most other tariffs, but it was not until 1986 that the fire insurers finally accepted the 1972 recommendation of the Monopolies Commission that the commercial fire tariff should be terminated. Although there is a good case for banning price fixing agreements, there is merit in the collective pooling of loss statistics to provide a sounder statistical base for rate making than would be available to any individual insurer (Carter and Doherty, 1974).

The second major change has been in the bringing of investment income into the calculation of premium rates. The escalation of interest rates in the 1970s led to so-called cash flow underwriting with companies competing for liability and other classes of insurance that generate large funds to obtain the investment income.

Finally, changing public attitudes has led to pressures from official and other bodies for the banning of premium discrimination on grounds of sex, race or other uncontrollable conditions (Carter, 1986).

14.3.2 Marketing

Although the situation is changing, most insurances are still marketed through independent intermediaries who are remunerated by the insurers through the payment of commissions on premiums. In particular, brokers handle the majority of large industrial and commercial insurances and insured pension schemes (Kitcat & Aitken, 1982).

During the 1980s most insurance companies have been reassessing their approaches to marketing, particularly of personal insurances. Greater emphasis is being placed on discovering consumers' needs, redesigning existing products and introducing new products. Also companies are adjusting to the developments in information technology. For example, computer programs have been designed for the underwriting of the simpler personal insurances; networks are being developed linking brokers to participating insurers' computers to enable them to obtain competing quotations; and the computerizing of policy records is enabling companies to make better use of client information for direct-mail marketing campaigns. Companies are also increasingly using press and television advertising and sponsorship to increase consumer awareness; however, although insurers' sales promotion expenditure has been rising rapidly in the 1980s it is still low relative to many other industries (Carter, Chiplin and Lewis, 1986; Dyer and Anderson, 1986).

The life offices in particular are caught up in the so-called financial services revolution, and are being forced to reconsider their future roles. Over forty life offices now manage unit trusts, and the trend is for them to market units directly as well as indirectly through their linked life insurance policies. A few of the major companies have decided to become integrated financial institutions capable of offering clients a wide range of financial services; for example, several have acquired chains of estate agents, and one company offers a cash management account through its banking subsidiary.

A major development in the marketing of personal insurances has been the rapid growth of the insurance business of the banks. Besides their insurance broking interests, Barclays, Lloyds and the TSB banks own three of the most successful life offices selling mainly linked life insurances. It is likely that in the next decade the leading building societies will make a similar impact on the insurance market.

Finally, most large industrial, commercial and local authority buyers of insurance have formed their own insurance departments to handle the purchase of insurance. Some deal direct with their insurers, though many still employ the services of brokers (Association of Insurance and Risk Managers in Industry and Commerce, 1983). Some companies have formed their own broking subsidiaries and some have set up, mainly in overseas tax havens, their own insurance companies, known as captive insurers, to insure some of their risks.

14.4 PERFORMANCE OF INSURERS

The characteristics of an insurance company are similar in many ways to those of the producers of goods so that essentially the same measures of performance may be employed, such as the growth of output/turnover, profits and net worth; efficiency; and innovative record. Some of the conventional measures do, however, pose conceptual problems for all financial institutions; for example, what are the appropriate measures of their output and profitability? (National Association of Insurance Commissioners, 1970; Benjamin, 1976; Abbott, Clarke and Treen, 1981).

Business growth is normally measured in terms of premium income, but to measure the real growth of business adjustments may be needed for inflation and changes in foreign exchange rates. Also there may be substantial differences between the growth of gross premiums and premiums retained net of reinsurance. As life business comprises mainly long-term contracts, a large part of a company's premium income will be attributable to policies effected in earlier years. Therefore, a better measure of its progress may be new business premiums, though these may fluctuate due to the incidence of single-premium business (Richards and Colenutt, 1975; Diacon, 1985).

Premium income is a poor measure of the physical output of an insurance company because a rise in premium income may be attributable to an increase in premium rates or in the size of insured risks, rather than in the number of policies handled.

Efficiency: there are both conceptual and data availability problems in attempting to measure an insurer's efficiency (Monopolies Commission, 1972). The most widely employed partial measure is the ratio of management expenses plus commissions to written premiums. However, the relative costs of handling different classes of insurance vary considerably, and differences between two insurers' ratios may be attributable to the quality of the policy, claims handling, and ancillary services provided. Nevertheless time-series data do indicate whether insurers are becoming more or less efficient. For example, between 1968 and 1977 the nine largest British insurance companies cut their general insurance expense and commission ratios by one-tenth on average, an improvement that has been maintained.

Claims payments: the amount of the claims paid in a year is an inadequate indicator of the proportion of the premiums which an insurer is returning to its policyholders. The overwhelming majority of the claims paid by a life insurer in any year will relate to policies that were issued in earlier years, and the difference between the eventual aggregate earnings from, and the cost of the claims of, the new policies issued in the current year will not be apparent for many years.

Even with general insurance many of the claims paid during a company's financial year will relate to insurances in force in previous years, while many of the claims reported on current insurances may still be outstanding at the year-end. Therefore, it is necessary to measure both paid and outstanding claims (Benjamin, 1976; Abbott, Clarke and Treen, 1981). The main measure of claims performance is the ratio of claims incurred to premiums earned. This ratio is not, however, an entirely unambiguous measure of performance. A low ratio indicates that the insurer is returning to policyholders little of the premiums they have paid by way of claims payments – though a new life office would not expect many claims in its early years. A very high claims ratio on the other hand may indicate that unless remedial measures are taken the company will become insolvent, or if the high claims ratio only applies to one class of insurance, that some policyholders are being subsidized by others.

Profitability. The problems of measuring the profitability of insurance business differ somewhat between long-term and general insurance. The profitability of a life office can only be judged on the basis of periodic actuarial valuations of its assets and liabilities (Franklin and Woodhead, 1980).

The calculation of the profit earned in any financial year on general insurance depends to a large extent upon the valuation of unearned premiums and outstanding claims, in that the emergence of profits (or losses) is affected by under- or over-reserving in earlier years. A distinction is usually drawn between so-called underwriting profit and total profit. Essentially the underwriting result consists of premiums – (claims + expenses)

Investment income earned on the funds is added to obtain the total profit, though whether realized and unrealized capital gains should be counted too is a matter for argument (National Association of Insurance Commissioners, 1970; Carter, 1979). Between 1981 and 1985 UK insurance companies incurred on average an annual aggregate underwriting loss on their worldwide general insurance business of 11.67 per cent of their net written premiums: investment income converted those losses into a profit of 3.38 per cent. The profitability of the insurance industry, expressed as a return on capital employed, has been low over the last decade. In the 1970s there were grave doubts regarding the ability of the industry to raise the capital required to finance the inflation-induced growth of premium income (Plymen, 1977; Kelly, 1978). In the event, from 1974 to 1981 inclusive the nine largest composite companies raised £622 million in rights issues.

Innovation. The industry has a good record of innovation. Computers have changed organization and working systems, have enabled companies to handle more business with smaller staffs, and are changing the marketing of insurances. New types of insurance have been designed to meet new risks ranging from hang-gliders to satellites, and new forms of contract have been devised to allow larger buyers of insurance to retain part of their own risks. Brokers have played an important role in such developments.

Solvency. The function of an insurance company is to provide security for its policyholders so that its solvency measured by its ratio of free reserves to premium income is of primary importance.

During the 1970s and early 1980s general insurance claims have increased faster than premiums, and even after allowing for higher investment earnings due to high interest rates some companies have experienced overall losses. Paradoxically, however, solvency margins have also risen to record levels due to rights issues and, more important, the rise in the market prices of assets.

14.5 PUBLIC POLICY AND INSURANCE

14.5.1 Supervision

The public interest in the insurance industry differs from the protection of the purchasers of goods. Insurance consumers initially receive in return for the premium paid only a promise of financial security, which may prove to be worthless if the insurer becomes insolvent. Not only may some policyholders then suffer possibly crippling financial losses, but third parties, such as accident victims who are unable to obtain compensation, may be affected adversely too. Other aspects of consumer protection relate to the pricing of insurance contracts; the information made available to consumers at the point of sale; an insurer's relationship with, and the rewards offered to, intermediaries; the manner in which claims are handled; and possible conflicts of interest between a life office and its policyholders in the investment of their funds.

The size of the investment funds controlled by insurers, and the impact of insurance/reinsurance imports on the balance of payments, have led many governments, particularly in the Third World, to intervene in regards to such matters too.

The present UK insurance regulatory system has evolved for over a century, but major changes have been made since the mid-1960s due to company failures leading to pressure from the consumer lobby, and the government's obligation to comply with European Commission directives. Whereas the British government has concentrated on trying to ensure that insurance companies are financially secure and well managed, most EC governments also control such matters as premium rating and investment policy.

The current position regarding insurance supervision in the UK is as follows:

Insurance companies are supervised by the Department of Trade and Industry (DTI) under the provisions of the Insurance Companies Act 1982 and the Industrial Assurance Acts 1923 to 1958. The DTI controls entry to the market by granting authorization only to companies that meet minimum capital requirements, are owned and managed by 'fit and proper' persons, produce an acceptable business plan and make adequate reinsurance arrangements. Authorized companies must meet minimum solvency standards, annually submit detailed returns, conduct an annual actuarial valuation of their long-term business, and comply with marketing and other regulations. If a company fails to comply with any of the regulations the DTI has powers to intervene and, if insolvent, to petition for its winding up.

If an authorized insurance company should run into financial difficulties, other companies carrying on the same class of business can be called upon by the Policyholders Protection Board to contribute to a levy to safeguard the financial interests of the company's UK private policyholders or, in connection with liability insurance, third parties who would be prejudiced by its failure. The problem with such guarantee funds is that they may distort competition by reducing the potential penalty for policyholders of insuring with less reputable companies.

Regulation of the marketing of, and admissible assets for, investment-type life insurances falls within the Financial Services Act 1986. When the Act becomes fully operative insurance intermediaries engaging in investment business will be required to operate either as company representatives or as authorized independent intermediaries, and both company representatives and independent intermediaries will have to comply with conduct-of-business rules covering the giving of advice, advertising and the remuneration of salesmen.

Lloyd's: the supervision of the Lloyd's market still largely operates through self-regulation by the Council of Lloyd's under the Lloyd's Acts 1871 to 1982. Following a series of market scandals in the 1970s, the 1982 Act made fundamental changes to the constitution of Lloyd's giving the council and the new chief executive more powers to regulate the activities of the underwriting syndicates. The Act also required Lloyd's brokers by 1987 to dispose of their interests in the underwriting agencies that manage the syndicates.

Intermediaries: the requirements regarding the registration of insurance brokers and the authorization of all independent intermediaries conducting 'investment business' have already been noted above. A major new feature of the Financial Services Act 1986 was the obligation placed on independent intermediaries to disclose to clients the commission receivable on the sale of any life policy or unit trust.

14.5.2 Control of investments

Insurance companies are largely free to invest their funds as they please, and periodically their decisions are criticized as being contrary to the public interest, not least in relation to their investments in land and property, and since 1979 in overseas securities.

Another concern has been the increasing concentration of financial power in the hands of insurance companies and pension funds; for over twenty years personal holdings of ordinary shares have been falling, though the privatization programme has lately helped to reverse that trend, as individuals have channelled an increasing proportion of their savings through institutions, which consequently have increased substantially their share of the total market value of quoted shares (Erritt and Alexander, 1977; Wilson Committee, 1980). However, the institutions' holdings are spread over many hundreds of independent, often competing, institutions so that there is little fear of collusive action to control industry.

The Committee of Inquiry on Small Firms reported in 1971 that as a general rule the size of individual investments preferred by life offices precluded the provision of finance except to the largest of 'small' firms. Since then not only have life offices continued to provide funds for the Industrial and Commercial Finance Corporation and its successor, Investors in Industry, which have been a major source of finance for small firms, but many have formed or helped to finance venture-capital institutions and other institutions providing loans and leasing facilities for small firms (Carter, Chiplin and Lewis, 1986). The difficulties involved in lending to small firms may deter some investment managers, but if there is a large unsatisfied demand for finance at terms reflecting the higher transactions costs and risk involved, then life offices, which largely compete on their investment performance, have every incentive to meet it.

The counterpart to the criticisms relating to small firms is that by favouring larger firms life offices have contributed to the increase in industrial concentration in Britain. In particular Prais (1976) claims that the supply of relatively cheap debenture funds to large firms during the 1950s and 1960s helped to finance the merger boom. That may be so, though it certainly was not the intention of the life offices when they set out to increase the proportion of corporate securities in their investment portfolios. Likewise it may be argued that by supporting rights issues institutions have helped to finance the present merger boom, but equally they have been active in providing finance for management buy-outs as conglomerates have divested themselves of some of their subsidiaries.

In the 1970s life offices were criticized for investing too little in British industry. After the decline in the proportion of new acquisitions allocated to corporate securities in the mid-1970s, the latest available figures show that in 1983/5 UK corporate securities accounted for 23.7 per cent of total net acquisitions: neither the distribution of UK securities between industrial and other companies, nor the proportion of the funds invested in unit trusts allocated to UK corporate securities, is known.

As far as the criticism that UK financial institutions have been channelling funds abroad at the expense of investment in Britain is concerned, it is worth noting that at the end of 1985 almost 11 per cent of the long-term business and 20 per cent of the general business assets were invested abroad compared with 3 per cent and 11 per cent respectively at the end of 1979. The higher proportion of general funds invested abroad can be attributed at least in part to the more international composition of the non-life companies insurance portfolios and the obligations they have to hold assets in the country of risk.

Periodically it is urged that there should be some official direction of the investment of institutional funds. In 1986 the Labour Party both resurrected an earlier TUC idea of a national investment bank in which the insurance companies and pension funds would have to invest 10 per cent of their funds, and proposed the imposition of tax penalties on companies that do not repatriate excess funds back to the UK.

Finally, life offices frequently have been criticized for allegedly not becoming involved in the companies in which they invest but selling their shares when things go wrong. In practice often the size of their investments is such that they cannot readily dispose of their shares. Moreover evidence presented to the Wilson Committee and the findings of other researchers (Midgley, 1975) show that the life offices are more active than it would appear. Further involvement would necessitate access to information not available to shareholders, so raising considerable problems in relation to insider dealing and market competition.

14.5.3 International Trade

Although much of the international trade in insurance, and more particularly reinsurance, services is conducted on a cross-frontiers basis, a direct insurer that wishes to write a large volume of insurance business in any country needs a local presence in order to provide the pre- and post-sales service which policyholders require.

Whereas over the last thirty years there has been considerable progress in reducing the obstacles to international trade in goods, the trend has been in the opposite direction for services (Griffiths, 1975; Carter and Dickinson, 1979; Bickelhaupt and Bar-Niv, 1983). Many governments, particularly amongst the developing nations, have either totally excluded foreign insurers from their domestic markets or have made it very difficult and/or costly for them to remain, and local residents have been prohibited from placing their insurances abroad.

Apart from over forty countries that have nationalized their insurance industries, other countries have restricted foreign insurers from supplying their services in order to develop their own domestic insurance industries, to retain insurance funds for internal investment and to reduce the balance of payments costs of insurance/reinsurance imports. Developing countries have been encouraged, arguably misguidedly, to pursue such policies by the United Nations Conference on Trade and Development (Hindley, 1982). It must be emphasized, however, that the problem is not simply a North v. South issue; few if any countries impose no restrictions on foreign insurers, and many developed as well as developing countries pursue highly protective policies.

The effect on the British insurance industry has been twofold. Insurance companies have been forced to close down their offices in many countries and in others to transfer to local nationals a majority interest in their former wholly owned subsidiaries. At the same time cross-frontiers insurance trade has become concentrated mainly on reinsurance.

Although the desire of governments for self-sufficiency in insurance is understandable, like other protective policies, the costs may far exceed the benefits. Until the late 1970s there had been little research into international insurance transactions so that policies had been formulated with little theoretical understanding or empirical evidence of the consequences. For example, some governments have sought to retain locally a high proportion of the insurances of very large industrial complexes, giant tankers and jumbo jets, or insurance against natural (for example, earthquakes, hurricanes) or man-made (for example, Bhopal) catastrophes, where one loss might substantially exceed the country's total annual premium income. United Nations Conference on Trade and Development (UNCTAD) now acknowledges that there are advantages in spreading the risk of such losses, and the funds to meet them, internationally (UNCTAD, 1977; Carter and Dickinson, 1979).

The effects on the balance of payments of international insurance transactions are even less well understood: even when attempts are made to quantify the various elements, the results are often confused and incomplete (Dickinson, 1977). The fact that over the long term insurance imports may result in a net foreign exchange cost is not alone a sufficient reason for restricting trade. In many cases it may be a reasonable price to pay given that otherwise the occurrence of very large losses could badly undermine the solvency of local insurers and adversely affect the balance of payments and the economy generally. Access to the types of insurance and the ancillary services which major international insurers and reinsurers can provide is important to many industries, and if local firms are denied access to such facilities it may place them at a competitive disadvantage internationally. Also resources that would be employed in producing insurance services locally may be better employed producing import substitutes or commodities for export. There is no reason why some countries should not possess a comparative advantage in the production of insurance services.

The steps that have been taken by the EC to create a common market in insurance are the most significant reversal of the protectionist trend. However, after a quarter of a century of negotiations only the first stage of 'freedom of establishment' (that is, the right of an insurance company with a head office in one member state to establish branch offices in other member states) has been achieved. 'Freedom of services' (that is, the right of an insurer established in one member state to sell its services across national frontiers) is still under negotiation.

On a wider scale, the industrialized countries that are members of the Organization of Economic Co-operation and Development (OECD) are currently examining the existing barriers to insurance trade preparatory to negotiations on measures to achieve some liberalization. Since the late 1970s the American government has been pressing for services, including insurance, to be brought within the GATT multilateral trade negotiations, and despite strong opposition from some of the developing countries it was agreed in 1982 that GATT should look into the possibility of incorporating services in future negotiations. However, it is unlikely that there will be any widescale moves towards a more liberal trading environment within the foreseeable future.

NOTE TO CHAPTER 14

1 Reinsurance is a system whereby one insurer can transfer to another insurer, known as a reinsurer, part of the liabilities he has accepted under contracts of insurance he has written. Thus insurers can further spread large risks which exceed their own underwriting capacities.

REFERENCES

Abbott, W. M., Clarke, T. G., and Treen, R. (1981), 'Some financial aspects of a general insurance company', *Journal of the Institute of Actuaries*, 108, 119–88.

Association of Insurance and Risk Managers in Industry and Commerce (1983), *Report on the Status, Salary and Conditions of Service of Full Members* (London).

Benjamin, B. (1977), *General Insurance* (London: Heinemann).

Benjamin, S. (1976), 'Profit and other financial concepts in insurance', *Journal of the Institute of Actuaries*, 103, 233–81.

Berliner, B. (1982), *Limits of Insurability of Risks* (Englewood Cliffs, NJ: Prentice-Hall).

Bickelhaupt, D. L., and Bar-Niv, R. (1983), *International Insurance* (New York: Insurance Information Institute).

Carter, R.L. (1978), 'Risk management: a British point of view', *Zeitschrift für die Gesamte Versicherungswissenschaft*, 1/2, 135–56.

Carter, R. L. (1979), *Economics and Insurance*, 2nd edn. (Stockport: P. H. Press).

Carter, R. L. (1983), *Reinsurance*, 2nd edn (Brentford: Kluwer).

Carter, R. L. (1986), 'Public policy and insurability', *The Geneva Papers on Risk and Insurance*, 11, 39, 145–56.

Carter, R. L., Chiplin, B., and Lewis, M. K. (1986), *Personal Financial Markets* (London: Murray).

Carter, R. L., and Crockford, G. N. (1974), *Handbook of Risk Management*, updated (London: Kluwer).

Carter, R. L., and Dickinson, G. M. (1979), *Barriers to Trade in Insurance* (London: Trade Policy Research Centre).

Carter, R. L., and Doherty, N. A. (1974), 'Tariff control and the public interest', *Journal of Risk and Insurance*, XLI, 3, 483–95.

Clayton, G., and Osborn, W. T. (1965), *Insurance Company Investment* (London: Allen & Unwin).

Committee of Inquiry on Small Firms (1971), *Financial Facilities for Small Firms*, Research Report no. 4 (London: HMSO).

Diacon, S. R. (1985), *The UK Insurance Industry: Structure, Development and Market Prospects to 1990* (London: Staniland Hall).

Dickinson, G. M. (1971), *Determinants of Insurance Company Asset Choice* (Hove, Sussex: Withdean).

Dickinson, G. M. (1977), 'International insurance transactions and the balance of payments', *Geneva Papers on Risk and Insurance*, 6, 17–35.

Dodds, J. C. (1979), *The Investment Behaviour of British Life Insurance Companies* (London: Croom Helm).

Doherty, N. A. (1976), *Insurance Pricing and Loss Prevention* (Farnborough, Hants: Saxon House, D. C. Heath).

Dyer, N. and Anderson, R. (1986), *Marketing Insurance: a Practical Guide* (London: Kluwer).

Economists Advisory Group (1984), *The Future of London as an International Financial Centre* (London: Lafferty).

Erritt, M. J., and Alexander, J. C. (1977), 'Ownership of company shares', *Economic Trends*, 287, 96–107.

Finsinger, J., Hammond, E., and Tapp, J. (1985), *Insurance Competition or Regulation*? (London: Institute of Fiscal Studies).

Franklin, P. J., and Woodhead, C. (1980), *The UK Life Assurance Industry* (London: Croom Helm).

Friedman, M., and Savage, L. J. (1948), 'The utility analysis of choices involving risk', *Journal of Political Economy*, LVI, 279–304.

Gibb, D. E. W. (1957), *Lloyd's of London* (London: Macmillan).

Griffiths, B. (1975), *Invisible Barriers to Invisible Trade* (London: Macmillan, for Trade Policy Research Centre).

Hindley, B. (1982), *Economic Analysis and Insurance Policy in the Third World* (London: Trade Policy Research Centre).

Kelly, R. (1978), 'The profitability of insurance companies', paper presented to the 1978 annual conference of the Chartered Insurance Institute.

Kitcat & Aitken (1982), *British Insurance Broking: A Statistical Report* (London: British Insurance Brokers Association).

Louis Harris International (1977), *A Survey of Motor Insurance* (London: Sentry Insurance Co.).

Midgley, K. (1975), *Companies and their Shareholders – the Uneasy Relationship* (London: Institute of Chartered Secretaries and Administrators).

Monopolies Commission (1972), *Report on the Supply of Fire Insurance*, HC 396 (London: HMSO).

National Association of Insurance Commissioners (1970), *Synopsis of the Report on the Measurement of Profitability and Treatment of Investment Income in Property and Liability Insurance*, NAIC proceedings, Vol. II, New York.

Plymen, J. (1977), 'Profitability and reserve strength of non-life insurers', *Journal of the Chartered Insurance Institute* (new series), 2, part 1, 28–31.

Prais, S. J. (1976), *The Evolution of Giant Firms in Britain* (Cambridge: Cambridge University Press).

Reynolds, D. I. W. (1970), 'Motor insurance rate fixing', paper presented to the Institute of Actuaries Students Society.

Richards, K., and Colenutt, D. (1975), 'Concentration in the UK ordinary life assurance market', *Journal of Industrial Economics*, XXIV, 2, 147–59.

Scurfield, H. M. (1968), 'Motor insurance statistics', *Journal of the Institute of Actuaries Students Society*, 18, 3, 208–20.

United Nations Conference on Trade and Development (1977), *Insurance of Large Risks in Developing Countries*, TD/B/C.3/137 (Geneva: UNCTAD Secretariat).

West, B. R., Bishop, J. H., and Bellinger, R. (1986), 'Underwriting – art or science?', *Annual Conference Papers 1986* (London: Chartered Insurance Institute).

Wilson Committee (1980), Committee to Review the Functioning of the Financial Institutions, Report, Cmnd 7937 (London: HMSO).

FURTHER READING

Carter, R. L. (1979), *Economics and Insurance*, 2nd edn (Stockport: P. H. Press).

Carter, R. L., and Dickinson, G. M. (1979), *Barriers to Trade in Insurance* (London: Trade Policy Research Centre).

Committee to Review the Functioning of Financial Institutions (1980), *Report*, Cmnd 7937 (London: HMSO).

Diacon, S. R. (1985), *The UK Insurance Industry: Structure, Development and Market Prospects to 1990* (London: Staniland Hall).

Diacon, S. R., and Carter, R. L. (1984), *Success in Insurance* (London: Murray).

Dodds, J. C. (1979), *The Investment Behaviour of British Life Insurance Companies* (London: Croom Helm).

Doherty, N. A. (1976), *Insurance Pricing and Loss Prevention* (Farnborough, Hants: Saxon House, D. C. Heath).

Economists Advisory Group (1984), *City 2000: the Future of London as an International Financial Centre* (London: Lafferty).

Finsinger, J., Hammond, E., and Tapp. J. (1985), *Insurance: Competition or Regulation?* (London: Institute of Fiscal Studies).

Franklin, P. J., and Woodhead, C. (1980), *The UK Life Assurance Industry* (London: Croom Helm).

Monopolies Commission (1972), *Report on the Supply of Fire Insurance*, HC 396 (London: HMSO).

The following are useful sources of statistical material:

Annual Abstract of Statistics (London: HMSO).

Business Monitor MA16 (London: HMSO).

Carter, R. L., and Godden, A. H. (1984), *The British Insurance Industry*, 1984/5 edition (Brentford, Middx: Kluwer).

Financial Statistics (London: HMSO).

Insurance Business: Annual Report (London: Department of Trade and Industry, HMSO).

Insurance Statistics (London: Association of British Insurers).

Chapter Fifteen

Medical Care

IVY PAPPS

15.1 INTRODUCTION

15.1.1 Postwar Development of the Industry

The postwar history of medical care in the UK is essentially the story of the National Health Service (NHS).[1] The 1946 National Health Service Act nationalized one thousand voluntary hospitals and two thousand local authority hospitals, made provisions for universal free access to a GP and provided for free dental and ophthalmic services as well as free supplies of dentures, spectacles and medicines. Thus, when the NHS was set up, all services could be obtained free at the point of use. These services were to be paid for by a combination of National Insurance contributions, rates and general taxation.

The system set up in 1948 was administered by the Ministry of Health and, latterly, by the Department of Health and Social Security (DHSS) and contained three administrative entities: (1) the Regional Hospital Boards which allocated funds to hospital management committees and controlled the hospital sector, with the exception of that part of the finance of teaching hospitals which was the responsibility of the University Grants Committee; (2) the Local Executive Councils which were concerned with non-hospital medical services such as those provided by GPs, dentists, pharmacists and ophthalmic practitioners; and (3) the local authorities which had the responsibility of providing support services such as antenatal and postnatal care, midwives and so on. Although this structure survived for 26 years until the reorganization of the NHS in 1974, problems of co-ordination among the three entities were almost inevitable. For example, the decision on whether to discharge a patient from hospital will depend, among other things, on the level of support services which will be available to the patient at home, but because decisions about the amount and type of resources allocated to hospitals and support services were made by different authorities, there was no reason to expect that the mix of hospital and domiciliary services would be efficient. For such reasons, the reorganization of the NHS emphasized centralization by placing all health services in a given area under the

Table 15.1 *NHS Expenditures, Manpower and Hospital Beds, Selected Years, UK, 1949–85*

	1949	1959	1969	1979	1985
Expenditure[a]					
£ million (current prices)	446	735	1,796	9,195	17,352
% of GNP	4.0	3.5	4.6	4.7	5.7
Manpower (number or whole-time equivalents)					
Hospital medical and dental staff	11,941[c]	15,726	26,514	38,312	44,859
Hospital nursing and midwifery staff	146,679[c]	213,133	320,036	433,490	500,165
Other hospital staff	196,169[c]	259,410	354,749	452,610	454,018
GPs	22,091[c]	23,102	24,239	27,696	29,684
Dentists and ophthalmic practitioners	18,697[c]	11,196[b]	19,440	24,550	17,713[b]
Other non-hospital staff	9,529[c]	n/a	8,919	9,561[d]	9,667[d]
Total	405,066[c]	522,567	753,897	986,219	1,056,101
Total as % of total labour force	2.0	2.1	2.9	3.7	3.8
Hospital beds (thousands)	453[c]	563	542	463	421

Notes: [a] Financial years
      [b] Dentists only
      [c] England and Wales
      [d] Great Britain

Source: Central Statistical Office, *Annual Abstract of Statistics* (London: HMSO).

control of the Regional Health Authority (RHA) which was, in turn, made responsible directly to the DHSS.

The history of the NHS has not, on the whole, been one of steady growth. Table 15.1 shows that, although total expenditure at current prices has dramatically increased since 1948, the proportion of GNP devoted to the NHS has only grown from 4.0 per cent in 1949/50 to 5.7 per cent in 1985/6 and, moreover, that this proportion actually fell during the 1950s. On the other hand, manpower in the NHS has been growing rapidly both in absolute terms and as a proportion of the labour force, the most dramatic increases being in the manpower used by hospitals. While manpower used by the NHS as a whole has almost doubled between 1959 and 1985, hospital medical staff have almost trebled, while the number of GPs has increased only by about 28 per cent. The large increase in hospital manpower compared with the 25 per cent *decrease* in hospital beds suggests that there has been considerable substitution between factors of production in the hospital sector. Indeed, it appears that the factor mix (and possibly the output) in the NHS is now very different from that used when the service first started.

It was originally thought that expenditure on the NHS would eventually fall as a healthier population required less medical care. However, initial expenditures were much higher than expected and continued to grow during the earlier years in absolute terms (though not as a proportion of GNP). As a result, there was a demand for the introduction of charges both to inhibit 'frivolous' demands for medical services and to raise some revenue. In spite of protests by some Labour MPs, charges for spectacles and dentures were introduced in 1951 and prescription charges in 1952. With various minor changes, such charges have persisted for most of the subsequent period.

Although the NHS provides almost all medical care in the UK, a private sector has persisted. Largely in order to persuade doctors to support the NHS, private beds were allowed in NHS hospitals after 1948. There has also been a small amount of private non-hospital medical care. This private sector has always been small in the postwar years. In 1983, about 7 per cent of the population were covered by private medical insurance plans and, in 1977, private expenditure on medical care accounted for about 1 per cent of total expenditure (Lee Donaldson Associates, 1978). In spite of its size, the existence of the private sector has generated substantial political heat.

15.1.2 The Nature of the Product

There are several distinctive features of the medical care industry.

(1) The real output of the industry is ultimately an improvement in the health status of the patient, but it is extremely difficult to measure this output directly. The output of an industry producing services

which are marketed – for example, hairdressers – is measured by the value of those services. However, it is still very difficult to define the price per unit of output because the quality of services is certain to vary a great deal. Such problems are multiplied for the output of the NHS because there is no direct information about the value which consumers place on it.

(2) There is a very close connection between supply and demand factors – particularly in the case of hospital treatment. Doctors not only supply medical services but also, to some extent, demand them by acting as the patient's agent because the patient seldom has sufficient technical knowledge to make a decision about the treatment he needs. Typically, he will go to a doctor for advice and this doctor will demand services on the patient's behalf while at the same time supplying some of the services. Such an interaction makes it possible that the usual assumption of the independence of supply and demand curves will not be as useful as it has been in the analysis of other industries.

(3) Because modern hospital care involves large and often unexpected expenditures, most countries have evolved a system of finance which provides medical care free at the point of use. The NHS does so by government finance and provision of medical services; in the United States there is some government finance, but most medical services are provided by the private sector and financed by private insurance; most other countries have schemes which consist of various mixes of these two types. The common feature of all of these schemes is that, for at least some medical services, the price faced by the patient when he is making his decision about the amount and type of care which he will demand is less than the marginal cost of care. This implies that a misallocation of resources in medical care is likely to result unless some additional allocative mechanism is introduced. Moreover, the fact that the service is free at point of use introduces some elements of moral hazard. Because some close substitutes for medical care (such as more sensible life styles and some proprietary medicines) are still priced at marginal cost, the patient has an incentive to substitute medical care for these alternatives, some of which may be more efficient from a social point of view.

(4) Like most other services, nearly all the output of the medical services industries is geographically immobile and must be consumed at the point at which it is produced. This feature of the industry has obvious implications for the regional distribution of the consumption of medical care.

15.1.3 Supply Characteristics

One of the reasons for the unexpected increase in NHS costs is the advances in medical techniques made over the last thirty years that

Table 15.2   *Proportion of Beds Occupied in Each Specialty, 1959 and 1985 (%), England and Wales*

	1959	1985[a]
All specialties	100	100
Medical		
General medicine	6.97	8.83
Paediatrics	1.37	1.36
Infectious diseases	1.64	0.23
Diseases of the chest	4.79	0.68
Neurology	0.21	0.57
Cardiology	0.08	0.42
Sexually transmitted diseases	0.06	n/a
Other	0.71	2.27
Geriatrics and chronic sick	12.04	19.43
Surgical		
General surgery	7.06	7.08
Ear, nose and throat	1.41	0.95
Traumatic and orthopaedic	3.66	5.95
Neurosurgery	0.19	0.42
Gynaecology	1.91	2.42
Other	2.39	3.94
Obstetrics and GP maternity	4.08	4.09
Psychiatric	44.92	38.33
Other	6.51	2.92

Note: [a] England only.

Sources: DHSS, *Health and Personal Social Service Statistics for England, 1986* (London: HMSO); and DHSS, *Digest of Health Statistics for England and Wales*, 1970 (London: HMSO).

were not anticipated by the founders of the NHS. Advances in the treatment of cardiac cases and the development of spare-part surgery, for example, provide effective treatment for patients who would otherwise have died or lived much more restricted lives. Because the techniques involved are very expensive, they have increased the average cost per case. On the other hand, some innovations have decreased the average cost per case. The development of an effective drug treatment for tuberculosis replacing the long and costly treatment of the disease in sanatoria is a case in point (see Section 5.4). However, new medical techniques which have increased costs have almost certainly predominated.

Partly as a result of changes in medical techniques, the mix of cases treated in hospital has changed, as shown in Table 15.2. There has been a dramatic fall in the proportion of beds devoted to diseases of the chest, probably due to the development of antibiotic drugs, while there has been a large proportionate rise in cardiology and neurology, probably as a result of the availability of new techniques.

It is difficult to say much of any interest about the supply of medical services in the UK. As far as the output of medical services as a whole is concerned it is not possible to examine the response of the NHS to changing prices and, thus, identify a supply curve.[2] By its very nature there are no prices for NHS output to which the service could respond, even were that considered desirable. More seriously, the reaction of the NHS to changes in the relative prices of its inputs cannot be examined in order to infer the form of the production function which the service faces. There is nothing in its organizational structure which would ensure that the NHS operates on its production frontier. Friedman (1985) shows that the efficiency with which the NHS and the institutions within it use their inputs depends on the arguments of the objective function of the decision-makers. He discusses the possibility that decision-makers may seek to maximize quantity and quality of medical services, the total budget of the organization, or the incomes of medical practitioners, and shows that not all of these objectives are consistent with an efficient combination of inputs.

It is, of course, possible to discuss the supply of various factors of production to the NHS and this is an interesting and fruitful field for research which has, unfortunately, been poorly worked so far. Obviously, for non-specialized factors of production, such as ancillary workers, the supply could be expected to be perfectly elastic at the going wage, for the NHS, even though a large employer, can scarcely be large enough to affect the wages of unskilled labour. A similar argument may well be relevant for drugs. Because the market for pharmaceuticals is international and the NHS is a small buyer in world terms, it might be expected that supply of pharmaceuticals is perfectly elastic at the world price. However, because of patents, each pharmaceutical company has a monopoly over its own drugs, and if it can combine this with control over resale, then it can engage in discriminatory pricing.[3]

The more interesting questions concern those of the supply side of medical manpower. Very little information exists about the supply curves of doctors and nurses in the UK although some factors which should be considered in any investigation may be suggested. First, and especially in the case of doctors, the manpower tends to be internationally mobile. For example, Lindsay and Seldon in Lindsay (1980) claim that a 1 per cent decrease in the rate of return to medical training results in a 1.7 per cent increase in emigration. However, more information about the determinants of international flows of medical manpower would be helpful.

Second, the NHS has a major role in training doctors as well as using them. As long as there is an excess demand for places in medical schools, the supply of doctors will depend not only on individual decisions but also on decisions taken by NHS administrators about the number of medical school places. Perhaps because of this, most of the work concerning the supply of manpower to the NHS has been concerned with manpower planning.

15.1.4 Demand Characteristics

It is tempting to interpret Table 15.1 corrected for inflation, as providing information about the income elasticity of demand for medical care in the UK. This interpretation would be mistaken for three reasons. First, it is difficult to argue that the government's decision about spending on medical care is the same as that which would result from the sum of individual decisions if the NHS did not exist. Indeed, the rationale for the NHS is that it does provide a pattern of medical services which differs from that resulting from individual choice. Thus, although it may be argued that decisions about NHS expenditure reflect some kind of public income elasticity of demand, it is unlikely to be comparable with the income elasticity of demand that is estimated for marketed goods.

Second, and probably more important, there is some reason to think that the relative price of medical care has changed over the period. Lee Donaldson Associates (1978) show that in 1976 costs per claim for private medical care were three-and-a-half times larger than they were in 1966 while the retail price index was only 2.8 times larger. Although this is by no means conclusive evidence, it does suggest when taken together with the experience of the USA where the index of prices for medical care has been rising faster than the retail price index, as discussed by Feldstein (1981), that Table 15.1 reflects substitution as well as income effects.

Third, the demand curve has probably shifted because of a change in the age structure of the population – in particular, because of the large increase in the number of old people. Maynard and Bosanquet (1986) discuss this and other reasons for an increased social demand for medical care.

More sophisticated techniques are, therefore, needed to estimate price and income elasticities of demand. Newhouse (1981) and Pauly (1986) summarized much of the work that has been done on own-price elasticity of demand for medical services. Although all of this work refers to US data, the results are sufficiently consistent to be interesting. Almost all studies conclude that the own-price elasticity of demand is negative (as expected) though small.[4] Most estimates of price elasticities of demand for various types of services are found to be numerically less than unity and, indeed, are seldom significantly different from zero. Moreover, Newhouse (1981) concludes that 'estimated income elasticities have varied from near zero to approximately 1.0'.

Newhouse and Phelps (1974) provide information about cross-price elasticities of demand between hospital treatment and visits to a doctor's surgery and find that they are small and frequently not significantly different from zero. This suggests, somewhat surprisingly, that patients do not see these services as very close substitutes. On the other hand, because a visit to a GP is often a necessary prerequisite to hospital referral, the services may be complements in a large number of cases. The small and insignificant cross-price elasticities of demand may not, on closer inspection, be so surprising.

Some other interesting work has also been carried out by Kleiman (1974) and Pryor (1968) on the interaction between the public and private provision of medical care. Pryor argues that they are perfect substitutes so that changes in public provision will be exactly offset by changes in private provision. Using cross-section data on 16 countries, Kleiman develops a model which suggests that only 20 per cent of changes in public provision are offset by changes in private provision – but again his results are not statistically significant. Indeed, one of the striking features of the large amount of work on the estimation of price and income elasticities of demand is that, although similar results are obtained by using different data sets, few of these results are statistically significant.

15.2 MARKET STRUCTURE

15.2.1 Concentration

With the NHS supplying 98 per cent of hospital throughput and most GP services, the degree of concentration in the supply of medical services in the UK is clearly very high. Although there has been some attempt to allow choice in general practice by making it legally possible for patients to change their GP without changing their place of residence, it is, in practice, quite difficult to do so. There is also the possibility of competition among different areas of the NHS – for example, the use of a casualty department of the local hospital rather than the patient's own GP – but such possibilities are likely to be few. It is thus difficult to avoid the overwhelming impression of the NHS as the monopoly supplier of medical services, a position which allows very little choice to patients.

The degree of concentration among the suppliers of factors of production is also of interest. The British Medical Association (BMA) represents the majority of doctors in the NHS and not only engages in negotiations about salary and conditions of work but also has considerable influence, as an expert pressure group, over the determination of the number of medical school places. The BMA, therefore, has important monopoly power. Since the NHS is almost the sole employer, the medical labour market provides the interesting spectacle of a bilateral monopoly tempered only by international flows of manpower.

15.2.2 Barriers to Entry

The NHS maintains its monopoly position largely because of the advantage it enjoys as a result of its method of finance. There is no way by which a patient can opt out of the NHS. Thus, a patient pays a price for private medical care *in addition* to the amount he has already paid for the NHS and not *instead of* this amount, as would be the case in most other industries with competing firms. This price advantage enjoyed by the NHS has been reinforced by an increase in the standard of services provided by the NHS – for example, the move toward smaller wards which has increased patients' privacy. In this way, the services provided by the NHS and those of the private sector have become more homogeneous and the incentive to enter the private sector has been reduced. This is not to say that the product of the private sector is not differentiated from that of the NHS. There are virtually no queues in the private sector while it might take up to two years to obtain a minor operation in the NHS. Some people are willing to pay in order to secure treatment at a time convenient to them.

However, such 'queue jumping' by private patients has raised considerable political storms and led to calls for the removal of private beds from NHS hospitals – if not for the total abolition of private practice. Although there has been little evidence that the abolition of private beds would reduce waiting lists significantly, the political arguments have concentrated on this aspect. However, a more cogent argument may be that private patients receive a subsidy from the NHS. Culyer and Cullis (1974) suggest that, on the basis of average cost pricing, private patients do not bear the full capital costs of their beds in NHS hospitals. If this is the case, the abolition of private beds from NHS hospitals would increase the cost for private patients who would then have to be treated in private hospitals. These increased costs would tend to decrease private practice.

15.2.3 Cost Structures

Because it is so difficult to measure the ultimate output of medical services – a change in health status – most of the research on costs has concentrated on measuring the costs of intermediate outputs such as costs per patient-week in hospital, cost per case, and so on.

In one of the few studies using UK data, Beresford (1972) examines the behaviour of costs per patient-week and costs per case as a function of throughput. (Throughput is defined as the number of cases per occupied bed per week. Therefore, multiplying the reciprocal of throughput by seven gives the average length of stay in days.) He finds that costs per patient-week rise with throughput. The early days of any course of treatment are relatively costly and, because increasing throughput raises the number of 'early days', this positive relationship is hardly surprising. On the other hand, he finds that costs per case at

irst fall rapidly with increases in throughput and then tend to level off
at a throughput of about 0.7. This suggests that hospital costs per case
could be minimized by speeding up throughput so that the average
length of stay was fewer than 10 days. However, it should not be
inferred from this evidence that hospitals 'should' speed up their
throughput to this level. Beresford's evidence, while useful, refers only
to *hospital* costs. By reducing length of stay in hospital, some of the
costs of care may be shifted from the hospital to the domiciliary health
services and, perhaps more importantly, to the family. It is not obvious
that social efficiency would be increased by reducing hospital stay. In a
more recent study of maternity units, however, Steele and Gray (1982)
find that marginal costs of specialist maternity hospitals are approximately constant whether output is measured in terms of deliveries or
bed-days, but the evidence for GP units is ambiguous.

Beresford's study refers only to optimal use of existing resources but
it would also be useful to have some information about the optimal
pattern of investment in new hospitals. Unfortunately, the information
about the size of hospital that minimizes average costs is inconclusive.
Feldstein (1967), correcting for the effects of case mix, concludes that
the optimal size of hospital is either 310 or 900 beds (the latter figure is
relevant if the larger hospitals which had a lower throughput could
achieve the throughput of the smaller ones) while Culyer *et al.*[5]
conclude that the optimal size is about 500 beds. Similarly conflicting
results are obtained when data from other countries are used. The
paucity of information about economies of scale has not, of course,
prevented policy recommendations about the optimal size of hospitals.
Gray and Topping (1945) recommended that a district general hospital
should ideally have about 800 beds in order to take advantage of
economies of scale while some time later, the Bonham-Carter Report
(HMSO, 1969b) argued that the optimal size was even larger (about
1000–1750 beds).

The same lack of evidence underlies policy towards health centres
and group practices. The thinking behind these innovations is that they
'must' provide economies of scale and, therefore, be more efficient
than the single-GP practice. As a result, they have received
considerable official encouragement. Bailey (1970), however, casts
some doubt on this faith. Using US data, he finds no evidence of
economies of scale of this type although his methodology is open to
some criticism. Later work by Kimbell and Lorant (1977) suggests that
group practice exhibits first increasing and then decreasing returns to
scale. There is clearly a need for more work in this area. For the NHS
in particular, it is most important that better estimates of the
underlying cost structures in each part of the service are provided so
that planning can be carried out on a firmer basis than has been
possible hitherto.

A parallel line of inquiry has investigated the optimal input mix by
attempting to estimate hospital production functions and, again, the

results are inconclusive. Using NHS data, Feldstein (1967) found, for example, that too little was being spent on doctors and too much on nurses while Lavers and Whynes (1978), also using NHS data, found the opposite.

15.3 MARKET BEHAVIOUR

15.3.1 Non-Price Resource Allocation

Waiting lists for hospital beds have been a problem since the early days of the NHS and, in spite of a doubling of throughput capacity, have remained remarkably constant. The persistence of waiting lists is often viewed in one of two ways. One interpretation is that the NHS is failing to meet medical need and that more hospital beds should be provided. The other interpretation is that waiting lists measure the excess demand generated by the zero price and indicate the existence of resource misallocation; the problem would be solved by the privatization of medical care.

However, both interpretations fail to take account of the special characteristics of medical care and the NHS.

First, medical need is not an unambiguous concept – particularly in the context of hospital treatment. There are often various ways in which a particular condition may be treated and the doctor's choice of treatment will depend in part on non-medical factors. For example, the choice between drug therapy in hospital or the same therapy at home may depend on both the facilities available to the patient at home and the availability of hospital beds. Secondly, even if medical need could be defined unambiguously, Lindsay and Feigenbaum (1984) show that the willingness of patients to join the queue depends on the expected waiting time so that an increase in supply (reduction in expected waiting time) will increase the rate at which patients are willing to join the queue. It may even increase the length of the queue. For both these reasons, the waiting list may not be readily interpreted either as a measure of the failure to meet medical demand or as a measure of excess demand for hospital services.

Thirdly, although privatization would reduce waiting lists to zero, it will not necessarily improve the efficiency with which resources are allocated since it would almost certainly be accompanied by a growth in medical insurance which again would provide medical care free at the point of use. There is some concern in the USA[6] about the problems of controlling the use and the cost of hospital services financed by insurance.

Fourthly, there is no theoretical reason why the NHS could not achieve an efficient allocation of resources if that were its objective. Although the market equilibrium achieves an efficient allocation of resources by the use of prices,[7] the same allocation could be achieved (albeit with some difficulty) by NHS planners. Thus, the existence of waiting lists is neither a necessary nor a sufficient condition for a misallocation of resources. Moreover, if a major objective of the NHS is the replacement of the market allocation by public decisions, then the reintroduction of the price system simply misses the point.

15.3.2   Regional Allocation of Resources

If this last view expressed in the previous section is correct it may be more appropriate to replace the concept of *demand* by a concept of *need* as developed by Culyer (1976), based on the idea that individuals as a group would like to make medical care available to everyone whether or not they would or could have purchased it themselves in a free market. There are some problems with this view, but it does appear to be consistent with some popular opinion. If this is in fact the case, it might be expected that an important aspect of an NHS based on need would be equal access to health producing facilities. It should be noted that this does not necessarily imply equal access to medical care because some environments are more unhealthy than others. Thus, where medical care is not equally accessible, the concept of need would require it to be concentrated in areas of greatest need – that is, in areas of highest incidence of disease and illness. Ideally, this concept would apply to individuals but data on individual access to medical care are very scarce.[8] However, regional statistics on medical care which give a fairly comprehensive view of the regional distribution of resources are available.

Table 15.3 shows that there are very large regional variations in medical care which do not appear to be related in any systematic way to medical 'need'. Indeed, Noyce *et al.* (1974) show that in 1971/2 there was little significant positive correlation between various indicators of medical need and NHS expenditure but that there was some significant negative correlation in the case of the birth rate. Moreover, Culyer claims that the 'general pattern in the early 1960s was, it would appear, in proportionate terms not so very different (as far as the hospital services are concerned) from what it was after the First World War' (1976, p. 115).

It seems, therefore, that the introduction of a NHS based on need did not change the regional distribution of medical resources from that which existed under a system based primarily on demand. It was the recognition of such persistent regional inequalities which led to the setting up of the Resource Allocation Working Party (RAWP) in 1975. Its report (HMSO, 1976) confirmed the existence of these inequalities and proposed a formula to relate future financial allocations to need in such a way as to penalize currently well-endowed areas and favour those whose facilities are poor relative to their needs. In a situation of increasing real resources devoted to the NHS, relatively well-endowed areas would simply not gain resources at the rate they would have

Table 15.3 *Selected Health Authorities Expenditure Per Capita, Financial Years 1974/5 and 1983/4*

	£ per capita		% deviation from UK average	
	1974/5	*1983/4*	*1974/5*	*1983/4*
Trent	61	232	−16.4	−13.1
NW Thames	85	268	+16.4	+0.3
NE Thames	82	299	+12.3	+12.0
SE Thames	79	280	+8.2	+4.9
Oxford	68	216	−6.8	−19.1
W. Midlands	63	237	−13.7	−11.2
England	72	258	−1.4	−3.4
Wales	75	279	+2.7	+4.5
Scotland	84	328	+15.1	+22.8
Northern Ireland	86	331	+17.8	+24.0
United Kingdom	73	267		

Note: The two authorities with the highest per capita expenditure and the two with the lowest were chosen in each year.

Sources: Central Statistical Office, *Regional Trends*, 1986 (London: HMSO); Central Statistical Office, *Regional Statistics*, 1976 (London: HMSO).

expected under the old allocation system. However, with static funding, such areas would be forced to lose resources to others. Thus, an attempt to apply the RAWP formula may be one of the reasons why there is talk of a crisis in the NHS (for example, in the NW Thames RHA). However, Table 15.3 shows little significant change in the regional distribution since 1974/5. Trent and W Midlands had the two lowest per capita expenditures in 1974/5 and had the second and third lowest in 1983/4 while the lowest in 1983/4 was Oxford which was not particularly well favoured in 1974/5. Similarly, the relatively good positions of NE Thames and SE Thames did not change much.

15.3.3 Manpower Planning

Because of the abolition of market signals in medical care in the UK and because the NHS trains a large proportion of the specialized manpower which it uses, the NHS has from the start engaged in various manpower planning exercises.[9] Such exercises have been *ad hoc* rather than part of a continuous planning procedure and have come to very different conclusions. The Goodenough Report (HMSO, 1944) suggested only a cautious increase in the stock of doctors. The government ignored this advice and increased the number of doctors by over 20 per cent. The Willink Report (HMSO, 1969a) came to the conclusion that there was a potential surplus and recommended that medical school admissions should be reduced by 10 per cent. This recommendation was followed but Lafitte and Squire (1960), using somewhat different assumptions, concluded that the Willink requirements had been underestimated by about 17 per cent. Partly because of this criticism of the Willink Report, the government set up yet another working party to review its data and conclusions. The Platt Report (HMSO, 1961) made suggestions about the career structure of doctors and expressed concern about the shortage of British doctors. Paige and Jones (1966) using a somewhat different methodology estimated that 'a shortage of doctors in 1975 is unavoidable'. The next official exercise was contained in the Todd Report (HMSO, 1968) which also estimated a shortage.

In each case the forecast requirements of GPs were greater than the actual amount while for hospital doctors the reverse was the case. It would be difficult to argue that manpower planning in the NHS has been a success. Forecasts have been made on the basis of *ad hoc* assumptions about future trends. Such 'ad hockery' is illustrated by the definition of 'shortage'. The manpower planners' shortage has no close relationship with the economist's concept of excess demand which refers to the differences between quantities demanded and supplied at a particular price. The planners calculate the required number of doctors in some future time period as a function of population and, perhaps, the distribution of population and project the estimated doctors available at that time as a function of net migration rates, output of medical schools, and other factors. The difference between the two is the shortage (or surplus) of doctors. Notice that neither the required number of doctors nor the estimates of those available depends on doctors' salaries. That is, there is no attempt to adjust the projected factor mix used by the NHS in response to changes in the relative price of different factors of production nor to allow for the individual response of doctors to changes in salaries – particularly relative to salaries abroad. For example, planners have seriously under- or overestimated emigration and immigration of doctors and this has led to errors in forecasts. Moreover, the sporadic nature of the exercise has made it impossible to improve the forecasts by making gradual adjustment to the plans.

Maynard and Walker (1978) took a somewhat different approach. They recognized explicitly that each set of manpower requirements has a particular cost and, therefore, prepared different manpower scenarios together with their implied costs based on various assumptions about population, the development of the NHS, doctors' salaries and so on. This seems a much more promising approach to the planning problem.

15.4   PERFORMANCE

There are very great difficulties involved in measuring the performance
of the medical care industry in the UK. Because the output of the NHS
is not marketed, a simple measure of the rate of return on capital, such
as the ratio of profits to net book value, cannot be used. Moreover,
because the true output of the industry is a change in health status, the
output itself is difficult to measure and even more difficult to value. In
addition, part of the activities of the NHS are research into and
development of new medical techniques along with the training of a
new generation of medical personnel. These activities are often
inseparable from the day-to-day work of treating patients. Therefore,
some effects of inputs used at present will not be felt until the future.
As a result, analysts are faced with the familiar problem of allocating
costs incurred in the production of joint products.

Because of such difficulties, it is impossible to produce a single
measure of performance for the NHS and it is necessary to examine
the suitability of various measures which have been used.

15.4.1   Indicators of Health Status

Indicators of the health status[10] of the country as a whole – such as the
infant mortality rate or life expectancy rates – have been used to show
the performance of the country over time or compared with other
countries. For example, although the UK's infant mortality rate has
fallen dramatically from 63.1 deaths per 1,000 live births in 1930 to
10.1 in 1983, the country's performance is poor relative to others such
as Denmark where the rate fell from 79.6 to 7.7 and Japan where the
rate fell from 124.5 to 6.2 over the same period.

However, the relative performance of medical care in the UK
cannot be assessed from such trends because they do not provide any
information about expenditure on medical care. Moreover, it is by no
means certain that all – or even most – of the improvement in these
indicators can be attributed to changes in medical care. Some (for
example, Hartwell, 1974; Perlman, 1974a, Newhouse and Friedlander,
1980; and Hadley, 1982) argue that the changes reflect such factors as
better nutrition and better living conditions rather than improved
medical care.

Even if the effects of medical care could be disentangled from those
of other factors, the health indicators discussed so far are much too
crude. After all, most modern medicine is not about saving or
prolonging life but about making life more comfortable by relieving
pain, increasing mobility and so on. There has been a good deal of
recent work on the production of a more satisfactory index of health
status taking such factors into account but much still remains to be
done.

15.4.2 Measures of Inputs

Comparisons can be made of inputs – such as expenditures on medical care as a proportion of GNP or number of doctors per thousand population – but such figures cannot, of course, tell anything about the effectiveness with which the country is using the inputs to produce changes in health status. Moreover, a low proportion may reflect lower prices as a result of the monopsony power on the part of the NHS rather than a lower quantity of inputs. Therefore measures of inputs can indicate nothing about the relative performance of the medical industry in different countries.

15.4.3 Cost–Benefit Analysis

Instead of attempting to measure the performance of the NHS as a whole, cost–benefit analysis could be used to calculate the rate of return to particular types of treatment. This approach raises difficult problems because it necessitates the placing of values on human life[11] and on the reduction of pain and suffering. It also requires information about the probable effects of the treatment. Eventually, the development of this approach may permit a move towards some kind of evaluation of the NHS as a whole but, even if it does not, it is valuable for planners in the NHS to obtain some idea of the relative rates of return being earned by various treatments.

Because of the difficult problem of the evaluation of benefits and because so little is known by the medical profession about the natural history of or the effects of treatment on many diseases, it is difficult to find satisfactory examples of cost–benefit studies in the NHS.[12] Most so-called cost–benefit analyses are really cost-effectiveness studies; that is, they measure the effectiveness of different ways of achieving the same goal without considering whether the attainment of the goal is worth even the lowest costs. However, a recent development in cost-effectiveness analysis will make it possible to overcome this last problem for resource allocation within the NHS. It has long been recognized that the purpose of the NHS is not only to prolong life but also to improve the quality of life. Ludbrook (1981), for example, argues that to compare the costs of an additional expected year of life occurring as a result of dialysis with that of transplantation to measure the relative cost-effectiveness of these two treatments for renal failure ignores the differences in the quality of life experienced by the patient after these treatments. There have, therefore, been attempts[13] to take into account the differences in the quality of life to produce a quality-adjusted life year (sometimes known as QUALY) which is calculated by weighting a year of life by an index of quality obtained from psychometric evidence. This technique not only allows for a more precise comparison to be made between different treatments of the same clinical condition but also for comparisons of the cost-effectiveness of widely differing activities within the NHS.

15.5   POLICY

Obviously, much of what happens in the industry is a result of government policy. The discussion in this section will, however, concentrate on an examination of the effects of possible changes of policy towards the NHS and the interaction between the NHS and policy in other areas.

15.5.1   Charging for Medical Services

It is unlikely that any government in the near future will change the NHS so radically that health care in the UK would be provided largely by the private sector, but it has often been suggested that a larger proportion of medical services should be financed by user charges. For example, it is suggested by some that charges should be raised to cover more – or perhaps all – of the cost of the prescription. At present, there is a charge of £2.40 per item on prescription while the average cost to the NHS is almost £5. It has also been suggested that a charge should be made to hospital patients to contribute towards the residential costs of hospital care. Such charges to patients are justified on the grounds that although there may be good reason for the social provision of medical care, there is no good reason why those in hospital should receive food, laundry and so on for no charge while those not in hospital (some of whom are also ill) have to finance these items themselves. To give some idea of the amounts involved, if each hospital patient were charged £2 per day, then £250 million per year could be raised (or about 1.5 per cent of the total NHS expenditure).

The arguments for user charges are that they would both raise revenue for the hard-pressed NHS and help to reduce pressure on NHS services by inhibiting demand. A little thought suggests that these two aims are not consistent. If demand is price elastic, then charges will be more effective in limiting demand than in raising revenue while, on the other hand, if demand is price inelastic, charges will be more effective in raising revenue than in inhibiting demand. Because what little evidence is available suggests that the demand for medical services is relatively inelastic,[14] the introduction of charges would be expected to increase revenue to the NHS, without having any substantial effect on the pressure of demand. The Merrison Report (HMSO, 1979) rejected these user charges on the basis of the inequities which might be introduced by them and because of high administrative costs. It seems unlikely, therefore, that such charges will be introduced without more examination.

On the other hand, however, the supply of some hospital services have been privatized. Some RHAs have allowed private companies to tender for contracts to supply hospital services such as laundry, cleaning and catering. Moreover, Wales has two kidney dialysis units run by private firms on behalf of the NHS and 12 English RHAs are reported to be considering such schemes. Supporters of this policy point to cost savings while opponents argue that the savings are achieved only by paying low wages and reducing the quality of service. Systematic studies are required to resolve these arguments.

15.5.2 Substitutes for Medical Care

It was argued earlier that one of the problems encountered in manpower planning is the tendency to assume fixed coefficients of production. A related difficulty may arise when considering the NHS as a whole. When medical need is observed, it is tempting to meet this need by expanding the NHS. However, it may be more efficient to allocate resources so as to avoid the medical need ever arising. For example, it may be more efficient to increase resources for health education and medical research rather than for medical treatments of often dubious efficacy.[15]

Moreover, some activities, which involve care rather than cure, for example, a large amount of geriatric provision, are carried out by the NHS. It is possible that such activities could be carried out more cheaply and perhaps more effectively by some other body. It would probably be widely agreed that society has a responsibility to provide such caring activities, but it is not at all clear that the NHS should be its agent. A searching examination of the role and scope of the NHS could well yield surprising and useful results.

15.5.3 Illness and the UK Economy

In 1984, the UK lost 27.1 million working days because of strikes. In the same year, more than 350 million working days were lost through illness. The effect of illness on the economy is, therefore, very large. Indeed, working days lost through illness have actually risen since 1948 (when they were about 140 million). It cannot however be concluded that the NHS has failed to improve the health of the working population. The increase in working days lost may be due to more generous sick pay arrangements or to an income effect which means that more prosperous workers are prepared to take longer periods of sick leave at lower pay rather than to return to work at full pay before they feel completely well.[16]

This brief discussion illustrates some of the difficulties of measuring the value of the output of the NHS. Not only is it difficult to place a value on health, the concept of health itself is not unambiguous. Whether people feel well enough to go to work depends not only on the medical care they receive from the NHS but also on a range of other factors – some of which may be policy variables such as sickness benefit – that change the relative costs of sickness. Policy towards the

NHS cannot therefore be viewed in isolation from other policies. The development of efficient services to meet the health needs of a modern population with rising incomes requires a hard look at what those needs are, whether they are being met by the NHS or, indeed, whether they can be met by conventional medical care, and to what extent more efficient substitutes are available. The fact that medical care in the UK is almost entirely provided by the public sector makes it all the more necessary that policy-makers know as much as possible about both the interaction between individual behaviour and demands on the health services (for example, smoking and lung cancer) and the interaction between other government policies and use of the NHS (for example, sickness benefits and demand for sickness certificates). Without such awareness, increasing expenditures on the NHS could well be, at best, inefficient or, at worst, useless.

NOTES TO CHAPTER 15

1 For more detailed description of the history of the NHS, see Watkins (1978) and Abel-Smith (1978).
2 The NHS pays GPs' fees for special services such as cervical smears, and it might therefore be possible to estimate supply curves for such services in response to changes in the real value of the fees. However no such estimates are known to the author.
3 See Chapter 5 for a more detailed discussion of the structure of the pharmaceuticals industry.
4 However, Feldstein (1974) argues that price elasticities of demand will be biased downward if a correction is not made for quality differences.
5 Quoted without publication details in Culyer (1976, p. 64).
6 See, for example, Feldstein (1981) and Friedman (1978).
7 See Culyer (1985).
8 Le Grand (1978) provides some information about access to medical care by different social classes.
9 See Maynard and Walker (1978) for a more detailed discussion of manpower planning in the NHS.
10 See Culyer *et al.* (1972) and Culyer (1983) for discussion of the problems of existing indicators and of the way in which more satisfactory indicators may be developed.
11 See Jones-Lee (1976) for a summary of earlier attempts to value human life and for his own estimates.
12 Blades *et al.* (1986) provide references to a number of studies most of which deal with the methodology of applying cost–benefit analyses to health rather than actually analysing quantitatively the rate of return to particular programmes in the health service.
13 See Kind *et al.* (1982) and results summarized in Maynard and Bosanquet (1986).
14 Section 5.3.2 in this book provides a discussion of the price elasticity of demand for drugs and challenges the conventional view that such demand is wholly inelastic.

15 Cochrane (1972) provides an interesting discussion of how little is known about the efficacy of common treatments for common diseases.
16 Doherty (1980) and Fenn (1981).

REFERENCES

Abel-Smith, B. (1978) *National Health Service. The First Thirty Years* (London: HMSO).

Bailey, R. M. (1970), 'Economies of scale in medical practice', in Klarman, op. cit.

Beresford, J. C. (1972), 'Use of hospital costs in planning', in M. M. Hauser (ed.), *The Economics of Medical Care* (London: Allen & Unwin).

Blades, C. A., Culyer, A. J., Wiseman, J., and Walker, A. (1986), *The International Bibliography of Health Economics*, Vols. 1 and 2 (Brighton, Sussex: Wheatsheaf).

Cochrane, A. L. (1972), *Effectiveness and Efficiency: Random Reflections on Health Services* (London: Nuffield Provincial Hospitals Trust).

Culyer, A. J. (1976), *Need and the National Health Service* (London: Martin Robertson).

Culyer, A. J. (1985), *Economics* (Oxford: Blackwell).

Culyer, A. J. (ed.), (1983), *Health Indicators: An International Study for the European Science Foundation* (Oxford: Martin Robertson).

Culyer, A. J., and Cullis, J. G. L. (1974), 'Private patients in NHS hospitals: waiting lists and subsidies', in Perlman, op. cit.

Culyer, A. J., Lavers, R. J., and Williams, A. (1972), 'Health indicators', in A. Shonfield and S. Shaw (eds), *Social Indicators and Social Policy* (London: Heinemann).

Doherty, N. A. (1980), 'Disincentives to work under the UK Industrial Injuries Scheme', *International Journal of Social Economics*, 7, 7, 341–52.

Feldstein, M. S. (1967), *Economic Analysis for Health Service Efficiency* (Amsterdam: North-Holland).

Feldstein, M. S. (1974), 'The quality of hospital services: an analysis of geographic variation and intertemporal change', in Perlman, op. cit.

Feldstein, M. (1981), *Hospital Costs and Health Insurance* (Cambridge, Mass.: Harvard University Press).

Fenn, P. T. (1981), 'Sickness duration, residual disability and income replacement. An empirical analysis', *Economic Journal*, 91, 158–73.

Friedman, B. (1978), 'On the rationing of health services and resource availability', *Journal of Human Resources*, XIII (Supplement), 57–75.

Friedman, L. S. (1985), *Microeconomic Policy Analysis* (New York: McGraw-Hill).

Gray, A. N. H., and Topping, A. (1945), *London Hospital Survey*, Ministry of Health and Nuffield Provincial Hospitals Trust (London: HMSO).

Hadley, J. (1982), *More Medical Care, Better Health? An Economic Analysis of Mortality Rates* (Washington, DC: Urban Institute Press).

Hartwell, R. M. (1974), 'The economic history of medical care', in Perlman, op. cit.

HMSO (1944), *Report of the Inter-Departmental Committee on Medical Schools*, Goodenough Report (London).

HMSO (1961), *Report of the Joint Working Party on the Medical Staffing Structure in the Hospital Service*, Platt Report (London).

HMSO (1968), *Royal Commission on Medical Education*, Todd Report, Cmnd 3569 (London).

HMSO (1969a), *Report of the Committee to Consider the Future Numbers of Medical Practitioners and the Appropriate Intake of Medical Students*, Willink Report (London).

HMSO (1969b), *Report of the Committee on the Functions of the District General Hospital*, Bonham-Carter Report (London).

HMSO (1976), *Report of the Resource Allocation Working Party*, RAWP Report (London).

HMSO (1979), *Royal Commission on the National Health Service*, Merrison Report, Cmnd 7615 (London).

Jones-Lee, M. W. (1976), *The Value of Life: An Economic Analysis* (London: Martin Robertson).

Kimbell, L. J., and Lorant, J. H. (1977), 'Physician productivity and returns to scale', *Health Services Research*, 12, 4, 367–79.

Kind, P., Rosser, R., and Williams, A. (1982), 'Valuation of quality of life: some psychometric evidence', in M. W. Jones-Lee (ed.), *The Value of Life and Safety* (Amsterdam: North-Holland).

Klarman, H. E. (ed.) (1970). *Empirical Studies in Health Economics* (Baltimore: Johns Hopkin University Press).

Kleiman, E. (1974), 'The determinants of national outlay on health', in Perlman, op. cit.

Lafitte, F., and Squire, J. R. (1960), 'Second thoughts on the Willink Report', *The Lancet*, 7150, 538–42.

Lavers, R., and Whynes, D. (1978), 'A production function analysis of English maternity hospitals', *Socio-Economic Planning Sciences*, 12, 2, 85–93.

Lee Donaldson Associates (1978), *UK Private Medical Care. Provident Schemes Statistics, 1977*, Report for the Department of Health and Social Security.

Le Grand, J. (1978), 'The distribution of public expenditure. The case of health care', *Economica*, 45, 178, 125–42.

Lindsay, C. M. (ed.) (1980), *New Directions in Public Health Care: A Prescription for the 1980s*, 3rd edn (San Francisco: Institute for Contemporary Studies).

Lindsay, C. M., and Feigenbaum, B. (1984), 'Rationing by waiting lists', *American Economic Review*, 74, 3, 404–17.

Ludbrook, A. (1981), 'A cost-effective analysis of the treatment of chronic renal failure', *Applied Economics*, 13, 3, 337–50.

Maynard, A., and Bosanquet, N. (1986), *Public Expenditure on the NHS: Recent Trends and Future Problems* (London: Institute of Health Services Management).

Maynard, A., and Walker, A. (1978), *Doctor Manpower 1975–2000: Alternative Forecasts and their Resource Implications*, Royal Commission on the National Health Service, Research Paper no. 4 (London: HMSO).

Newhouse, J. P. (1981), 'The demand for medical care services: a retrospect and prospect', in van der Gaag and Perlman, op. cit. 85–102.

Newhouse, J. P., and Friedlander, L. J. (1980), 'The relationship between medical resources and measures of health', *Journal of Human Resources*, 15, 2, 200–18.

Newhouse, J. P., and Phelps, C. E. (1974), 'Price and income elasticities for medical care services', in Perlman, op.cit.

Noyce, J., Snaith, A. H., and Trickey, A. J. (1974), 'Regional variations in the allocation of financial resources to the community health services', *The Lancet*, 7857, 554–7.

Paige, D. C., and Jones, K. (1966), *Health and Welfare Services in Britain in 1975* (Cambridge: Cambridge University Press).

Pauly, M. V. (1986), 'Taxation, health insurance, and market failure in the medical economy', *Journal of Economic Literature*, XXIV, 2, 629–75.

Perlman, M. (1974a), 'Economic history and health care in industrialized nations', in Perlman, op. cit.

Perlman, M. (1974b), *The Economics of Health and Medical Care* (London: Macmillan).

Pryor, F. L. (1968), *Public Expenditures in Communist and Capitalist Countries* (London: Allen & Unwin).

Russell, L. B. (1979), *Technology in Hospitals: Medical Advances and their Diffusion* (Washington, DC: Brookings Institution).

Steele, R., and Gray, A. M. (1982) 'Statistical cost analysis: the hospital case', *Applied Economics*, 14, 5, 491–502.

van der Gaag, J., and Perlman, M. (eds) (1981), *Health, Economics and Health Economics*, Contributions to Economic Analysis Series no. 137 (Amsterdam: North-Holland).

Watkins, B. (1978), *The National Health Service. The First Phase* (London: Allen & Unwin).

FURTHER READING

Blades, C. A. Culyer, A. J., Wiseman, J., and Walker, A. (1986), *The International Bibliography of Health Economics*, Vols. 1 and 2 (Brighton, Sussex: Wheatsheaf).

Culyer, A. J., and Jonsson, B. (eds) (1986), *Public and Private Health Services* (Oxford: Basil Blackwell).

Culyer, A. J., and Wright, K. G. (eds) (1978), *Economic Aspects of Health Services* (London: Martin Robertson).

HMSO (1979), *Report of the Royal Commission on the National Health Service*, Cmnd 7615 (London).

Mooney, G. H. (1986), *Economics, Medicine and Health Care* (Brighton, Sussex: Wheatsheaf).

van der Gaag, J., and Perlman, M. (eds.) (1981), *Health, Economics, and Health Economics* (Amsterdam: North-Holland).

Some statistical sources:

Alderson, M. (1974), *Central Government Routine Health Statistics*, Reviews of UK Statistical Sources, Vol. III (Oxford: Pergamon Press for The Royal Statistical Society and the Social Science Research Council).

Alderson, M. R., and Dowie, R. (1979), *Health Surveys and Related Studies*, Reviews of UK Statistical Sources, Vol. IX (Oxford: Pergamon Press for The Royal Statistical Society and the Social Science Research Council).

Department of Health and Social Security (annual) *Health and Personal Social Service Statistics for England* (HMSO).

Department of Health and Social Security (annual) *Hospital Costing Return* (HMSO).

Lee Donaldson Associates (1978), *UK Private Medical Care*, Provident Schemes Statistics, 1977, Report for the DHSS.

Chapter Sixteen

Tourism

PETER JOHNSON

16.1 INTRODUCTION

16.1.1 What is Tourism?

Tourism is currently seen as a major growth industry. It is also regarded by government as a significant provider of new jobs, a role which led to the transfer of the responsibility for tourism policy from the Department of Trade and Industry to the Department of Employment at the end of 1985.

Which activities are most appropriately included within the definition of tourism is a matter of some debate, but a useful starting point is the definition given by Burkart and Medlik (1981, p. 319): 'Tourism denotes the temporary, short term movement of people to destinations outside the places where they normally live and work and their activities during their stay at these destinations.' This definition embraces not only the holiday traveller but also the person travelling on business. Tourism then is not synonymous with leisure. The definition also includes, for example, the person travelling to see relatives, to attend a funeral or to make a hospital visit. It is clear therefore that the consumers of tourism are a highly diverse group. However they are all involved in the transfer of spending power from one location to another.

Tourism involves the provision of many different types of output, including transportation (without which tourism cannot occur), accommodation, entertainment, tourist attractions, catering, travel agency and tour operation. These activities in turn require inputs from a wide range of industries. For example hotels are a major market for the food, laundry and construction industries. Again, retailing is a major beneficiary of tourism spending. Given space constraints, this chapter will inevitably have to focus attention on a few key activities in what is, by nature, a very diverse industry.

Tourism is not separately identified in the Standard Industrial Classification. It does however make some economic sense to group together under one heading industries that are producing services that are seen by consumers as complements. And even if the *purpose* of 'temporary, short term movement' varies significantly from one person to another, the bundle of services required is often similar. Also some producers of tourism services are able, after fairly simple adjustments, to adapt their output to meet the demands of different types of tourist. Thus, for example, an airline is able to alter relatively easily the mix of first-class and economy seats in its aircraft as the balance of business and leisure demand changes.

For some statistical and analytical purposes the term 'tourist' is restricted to those people whose visits last at least 24 hours. Thus day trippers are excluded. Such a division is somewhat arbitrary. However, some kind of dividing line is necessary if tourism is not to embrace all kinds of travel away from home, such as shopping at the local retailer, commuting to work, and so on. Unless otherwise stated this convention is adopted throughout this chapter.

16.1.2 Types of Tourist

As far as UK tourism is concerned, consumers may be divided into three main groups. The first two of these involve international movements.[1] The first group consists of those UK residents who travel abroad. As Figure 16.1 shows, there has been a very substantial expansion of such tourists since 1977. Their expenditure has also risen at an impressive rate (Table 16.1, col. 3).

The biggest growth has been in visits to Western Europe which now account for 88 per cent of all visits. (Travel to North America grew in volume up to 1981, but has since declined.) Expenditure by UK residents while abroad does of course represent an outflow on the current account of the balance of payments. It is for this reason that this group is sometimes seen as generating 'import tourism'. Data in Table 16.2 indicate that by far the most rapidly growing component in import tourism in the last ten years has been holiday travel and that an increasing proportion of holiday traffic is using inclusive tour arrangements. The proportion travelling by air has remained fairly constant at just under two thirds.

The second group is made up of those overseas residents who visit the UK. Figure 16.1 indicates that the growth of such visits has been much slower and more erratic than the flow of UK residents abroad, with the numbers declining between 1978 and 1981 and between 1985 and 1986. Trends in the number of visits have been broadly matched by those in real expenditure (Table 16.1, col. 1). Up to 1985, the fastest growing category of visits from overseas was those from North America, which in that year accounted for over a quarter of the total. (However, the United States' bombing of Libya in 1986 led to a substantial fall in these visits.) Such incoming visits do of course provide a source of foreign earnings and are thus often labelled 'export tourism'. In contrast to trends in import tourism, holiday visits to the UK have grown much more slowly than business traffic (Table 16.2). The relatively rapid growth in business traffic is reflected in the much

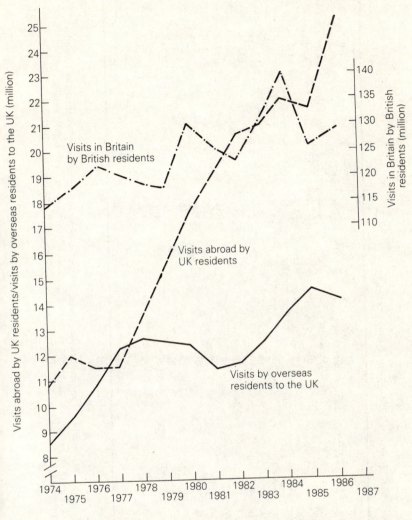

Figure 16.1   *Trends in tourism, 1974–1986*

Note: Data on visits in Britain by British residents for 1984 onwards are not strictly comparable with those for years prior to 1984.
Source: HMSO, 1985b, pp. 8–9; *Overseas Travel and Tourism* (MA6), various years; English Tourist Board, *Annual Report and Accounts, 1985/6*; British Tourist Authority.

Table 16.1 Real Expenditure on UK Tourism, 1974–86 (in 1980 prices)

Year	(1) Expenditure by overseas residents in UK (£m)	(2) Expenditure by British residents in Britain[b] (£m)	(3) Expenditure by UK residents overseas (£m)	(4) Net effect on Balance of Payments (1) minus (4)
1974	2241	4492	1337	+904
1975	2560	4519	1419	+1141
1976	3218	4365	1325	+1893
1977	3681	4108	1329	+2352
1978	3410	4217	1651	+1759
1979	3310	4497	2151	+1159
1980	2961	4550	2739	+222
1981	2628	4070	2931	−303
1982	2582	3645	2901	−319
1983	3051	4078	3014	+37
1984	3296	4268[a]	3095	+201
1985	3629	4210[a]	3176	+453
1986	3361	4384[a]	3534	−173

Notes:
[a] Data calculated on a new basis from 1984.
[b] Expenditure in current prices by British residents in Britain was deflated by the index used in MQ6 (see Sources) to deflate the expenditure by overseas residents visiting the UK. It should be noted that the figures in column (2) include and those in column (1) exclude transport costs.

Sources: Overseas Travel and Tourism (MQ6) 3rd quarter, 1987; HMSO, 1985; English Tourist Board Annual Report and Accounts for 1985/6; British Tourist Authority.

Table 16.2 The Nature of Import and Export Tourism

	Import tourism						Export tourism					
	All visits	Holiday (inclusive tour visits in brackets)	Business	Other	Visits made by sea	Visits made by air	All visits	Holiday (inclusive tour visits in brackets)	Business	Other	Visits made by sea	Visits made by air
1976 (% of total)	100.0	60.8 (33.5)	17.8	21.4	37.4	62.5	100.0	48.6 (13.9)	17.9	33.5	41.1	58.9
1986 (% of total)	100.0	70.8 (41.6)	13.5	15.7	35.4	64.6	100.0	42.6 (11.6)	23.3	34.1	36.7	63.3
Growth 1976–86 (%)	112.2	147.2 (163.5)	61.0	57.3	100.8	119.0	27.4	11.8 (5.8)	66.6	29.2	13.9	36.8

Note: 1986 data are provisional.
Source: Overseas Travel and Tourism, MA6 (various years)

faster expansion of air traffic: the business traveller is more likely to travel by air than the holidaymaker.

The last column of Table 16.1 shows the net effect, excluding transportation, on the balance of payments (in 1980 prices) of the two international visitor flows since 1974. The contribution of tourism to the current balance was much less in the 1980s than in the 1970s. Even the substantial balance in 1985 was considerably lower than any in the period 1974–9.

The final group of tourists are those domestic residents who travel at home. These tourists are consumers of 'domestic tourism'. As Figure 16.1 shows the number of domestic tourism trips – a stay of one night or more – has behaved rather erratically since 1974 although the overall trend is upward. (It should be noted that domestic tourism in Figure 16.1 relates to Britain rather than the UK. Trends for both are however likely to be very similar.) Expenditure (Table 16.1, col. 2) has been similarly erratic. It has still not reached (in real terms) the peak achieved in 1980.

About 60 per cent of domestic tourism is accounted for by holiday travel, and a further 29 per cent by business and conference travel. Over 70 per cent of all domestic trips utilize the car as the main form of transport. The dominance of the car, which is a postwar phenomenon, further emphasizes the indirect importance of a wide range of industries (including petrol refining and motor manufacturing) to tourism.

In 1986, the number of visits taken by UK domestic tourists (estimated by applying the UK : Britain population ratio to the figures for British domestic tourism visits) was nearly nine times that taken by export tourists. However, since the number of nights per visit and expenditure per night both tend to be lower for domestic tourists, the expenditure by such tourists was only about a third higher (Table 16.1). Tourism expenditure, particularly in relation to employment, is further discussed in Sections 16.1.3 and 16.5.

The determinants of tourism flows are complex. Not surprisingly, however, fluctuations in total real expenditure by domestic residents on tourism at home and abroad (very roughly the sum of columns 2 and 3 in Table 16.1) follow fluctuations in real personal disposable incomes. It is likely that such income is also an important influence on the tourism expenditure of overseas residents and hence on their propensity to travel to the UK. The *nature* of tourism demand (in respect, for example, of destination, length of stay and mode of travel) is also likely to vary with the level of income. Another important influence on demand is exchange rates (British Tourist Authority, 1984). These rates are a crucial determinant of the tourism 'terms of trade' and thus, *inter alia*, the distribution of total expenditure between domestic and foreign tourism, which are to some extent substitutes. For example, between 1977 and 1981 the weighted terms of trade deteriorated significantly (Thomas, 1986) and this adverse movement was in part responsible for the growing share of total tourism expenditure by domestic residents spent on import tourism during that period. It also provides at least part of the explanation of why export tourism declined in importance over the same period. Movements in exchange rates are also likely to affect the destinations of those who travel internationally.

Further influences on tourism demand are 'fashions', tastes and a wide range of non-economic influences. (The bombing of Libya by the United States in 1986 referred to earlier, is an example of the importance of such influences.)

The different influences on tourism demand may work in opposite directions. For example, the effects of the gain in UK price competitiveness after 1981 (Thomas, 1986) did not translate into a decline in import tourism because of the positive effects of rising disposable incomes in the UK. (As indicated above however travel to North America *did* decline following the relatively severe drop in the dollar value of sterling.) On the other hand, export tourism rose strongly after 1981 because the gain in UK competitiveness and rising disposable incomes in the main countries from which overseas tourists to the UK came worked in the same direction.

Another complicating factor in the analysis of tourism demand is the many different *types* of tourist demand. The determinants of each are likely to vary: what is important for (say) holiday demand may be less significant for the business traveller. Only a multi-variate model, which acknowledges the existence of these different demands, is likely to explain satisfactorily why total tourism demand varies in the way it does.

16.1.3 Employment

As Section 16.1.1 indicated very many UK industries are involved in providing output which is directly or indirectly relevant to tourism. Since 1986, the Department of Employment has categorized some industries as 'tourism-related'. Table 16.3 provides data on employees in employment in these industries in Great Britain. The industries involved are of course concerned with a much wider clientele than people who are away from home for at least one night. However, a more detailed breakdown is not available.

Between 1982 and 1987 the total number of employees in these industries expanded by over 15 per cent. (The fastest growth occurred in catering.) Much of the overall expansion, however, was in part-time jobs. For example, over the period June 1982 to June 1987, 71 per cent of the total increase in the number of female jobs in the industries represented in the first three rows of Table 16.3 plus the hotels segment of 'Accommodation' was accounted for by an increase in part-time employment (Similar data for all the industries covered in that table are not available.)

Two further characteristics of Table 16.3 are worth noting: first, a substantial majority of the jobs in the industries for which data are available are held by females; and secondly, part-time employment plays a dominant role (except in the accommodation sector).

Table 16.3 does of course omit a number of activities that are directly concerned with tourism. The most obvious of these is transportation. Like many of the industries in Table 16.3, transportation covers a wide range of activities only some of which relate to tourism. Thus although it is known that, *overall*, the transport industries most likely to provide services for tourists[2] have declined over the period 1982–7 (by about 12 per cent), it is not possible to say whether growth in the tourism-specific elements has been positive or negative.

Table 16.3 also excludes a number of other tourist-related activities such as those relating to tour operating and travel agency, concerts, theatres and stately homes.

Data on *self*-employment in tourism-related industries is rather sparse. However, it has been estimated (*Employment Gazette*, November 1987, p. S60) that in 1981, there were 158,000 people in this category, and that between 1981 and 1986 self-employment in 'Hotels and Catering' – a rather wider grouping than that contained in the first four rows of Table 16.4 – rose by 28 per cent (compared with a 24 per cent increase for all industries).

Employment in tourism is further discussed in Section 16.5.2.

16.1.4   The Supply of Tourism

In the UK, the tourist industry is concerned with supplying all three types of tourist identified in Section 16.1.2. Domestic tourists require transport, accommodation, leisure and recreational facilities and tourist 'attractions'. Export tourists also require the same services in the UK although the latter will often use foreign carriers to get to and from the UK. Import tourists typically use UK carriers for their transport. Tour operators provide services to both types of international traveller although UK operators are most heavily involved with import tourism.

The price elasticity of supply depends on how narrowly the particular type of output under consideration is defined, and on the time period that is involved. For example, 'accommodation in central London', and '*four star hotel* accommodation in central London' are unlikely to have the same supply elasticities and both are likely to have higher elasticities in the longer term.

Much existing capacity in the tourism industry cannot easily be altered in the short run. The marginal costs of taking another passenger on an aircraft or ship that is already scheduled or of providing hotel accommodation for another visitor is therefore often very low *up to capacity limits*. This may also apply to a range of tourist attractions

Table 16.3 *Employment in Tourism-Related Industries, Great Britain, 1982–7*

Industry	Number of employees ('000s) June 1982	Number of employees ('000s) June 1987	% growth: June 1982 to June 1987	Female employees: % of total, June 1987	Part-time employees: % of total, June, 1987
Restaurants, cafes, etc.	194.1	238.1	22.7	62.6	55.3
Public houses and bars	236.0	281.2	19.2	72.7	76.1
Night clubs and licensed clubs	138.5	146.6	5.8	60.0	76.5
Accommodation	267.4	293.2	9.6	63.7[a]	40.5[a]
Libraries, museums, art galleries, sport and other recreational services	336.8	396.8	17.8	n/a	n/a
Total	1,172.8	1,355.9	15.6	n/a	n/a

Note: [a] Hotel trade only.
Source: Employment Gazette, November 1987.

such as gardens and stately homes. Of course the supply of some 'natural' tourist attractions such as the Northumberland coast or the South Downs cannot be increased in supply even in the long run. (These attractions may however be *reduced* by such factors as soil erosion.) The fixity of capacity has important implications for pricing as Section 16.3.1 shows.

It should be remembered that typically as output in the tourist industry changes, so the quality of that output also changes. A crowded hotel, beach, boat or aircraft usually represents lower quality than an underutilized counterpart. It may also be the case that the private costs of supplying tourism output do not reflect the social costs. For example, the coach operator may not incur all the additional congestion costs that his activities generate.

These issues were taken up rather graphically more than twenty years ago by Mishan. He argued that travel on the scale then being promoted by the tourism industry

> rapidly and inevitably disrupts the character of the affected regions, their populations and ways of living. As swarms of holiday makers arrive by air, sea and land, by coach, train and private automobile, as concrete is poured over the earth, as hotels, caravans, casinos, night clubs, chalets, blocks of sun flats crowd into the area and retreat into the hinterland, local life and industry shrivel, hospitality vanishes, and indigenous populations drift into a quasi-parasitic way of life catering with contemptuous civility to the unsophisticated multitude . . . what a few may enjoy in freedom the crowd necessarily destroys for itself . . . Unless international agreement can be reached to control further tourist damage our children will inherit a world almost wholly bereft of undisturbed natural beauty (1967, p. 105).

Although Mishan was primarily addressing himself to foreign travel the underlying point he was making has obvious implications for holiday tourism in the UK.

Many firms engaged in selling tourism engage in 'bundling' a number of different services, with the customer paying an inclusive price for travel, accommodation and sometimes recreational services. There may be a number of reasons for such bundling. It may be attractive to the customer who may save on transactions costs, because the search costs involved in finding the integrated package required may be avoided. It may generate savings in production costs by permitting closer co-ordination of complementary outputs. And it may sometimes permit a tour operator if it is in a strong market position to raise its profitability by the extraction of more consumer surplus (Phlips, 1983, p. 176f).

A tour operator (or other intermediary) may also achieve cost savings through bulk purchase. These economies may be real deriving for example, from the reduction in risk and transactions costs for the supplier and/or be the result of market power. Such cost savings may however, be obtained even when bundling is absent. (Some inter- mediaries, for example specialize in the provision of hotel rooms.)

16.1.5 Demand

Some of the evidence on price elasticities for rail and air transport were reviewed in Chapters 12 and 13 respectively. Leisure and holiday traffic tends to be much more responsive to price than business traffic, a difference which has led to price discrimination in favour of the former.

Witt and Martin (1985) also found in their study of overseas holiday visits by UK residents to major destinations that the demand for travel involving surface modes tends to be more elastic (and more likely to be greater than unity) than that for air. The greater price-sensitivity of demand for surface travel probably in part reflects the generally lower per capita incomes of those using that mode.

Accommodation too faces demand categories with very different elasticities. It is hardly surprising therefore to find hotels offering packages – either direct to the public or through travel agents – which provide cheaper tariffs for those customers whose demand is more price-elastic. Such customers are usually able to agree to certain restrictions which their counterparts with less price-elastic demand are unable to accept.

The study by Witt and Martin suggests too that the income elasticity of demand for foreign holidays tends to be greater than unity, Leisure visits *to* the UK by overseas residents are also highly income elastic: a recent study gives an income elasticity of 2.8 (British Tourist Authority, 1984). These findings conform with the results of other studies (see those quoted in Burkart, 1980; see also Edwards, 1976).

There is some seasonality in the demand for tourism: in 1986, 41 per cent of all visits abroad by UK residents, and 37 per cent of overseas residents' visits to the UK were made in the third quarter. (A slightly lower percentage applied to domestic tourism.) Holiday, rather than business visits are the principal source of this seasonality.

16.1.6 Expenditure

One striking characteristic of the real expenditure data in Table 16.1 is its erratic record. For example, between 1980 and 1982, expenditure by British residents in Britain (column 2) fell by nearly 20 per cent while in the following two years it rose by 17 per cent. Expenditure by overseas residents in the UK (column 1) has also shown considerable volatility, a reflection more of trends in the numbers of visits by such residents, than of changes in expenditure per visit. Such variations make planning by companies more difficult and may act as a disequilibrating force on industrial behaviour and performance.

16.2   MARKET STRUCTURE

As the previous section has shown, very many industries, and parts of industries are involved in the production of tourism. It is not therefore meaningful to talk of the structure of the tourism industry as a whole. Nowhere is this more apparent than in the analysis of the many thousands of tourist attractions – such as museums, castles, cathedrals, leisure centres and art galleries that exist. Each is likely to vary in the extent to which it faces local and national competition (from similar or different attractions). It does however make sense to consider the structure of particular sectors of the tourism industry. Some key sectors are considered below.

16.2.1   Tour Operation

The concept of the package holiday in which tour operators specialize can be traced back to Thomas Cook's commercial innovativeness in the mid nineteenth century (Swinglehurst, 1982). The development of mass transportation (and the resultant lowering of unit costs in real terms) and rising real incomes since that time brought steady growth, but it was in the postwar period – particularly in the 1960s – that the most rapid expansion occurred. Commercial and technological developments in air and sea[3] transport have played a key role in this acceleration. While some UK tour operators provide UK holiday packages for both overseas and UK residents, the bulk of the business is concerned with UK residents travelling overseas. It is therefore on this latter activity that this section concentrates.

The structure of the market, as far as airborne foreign packages is concerned may be obtained from data on Air Traffic Operators Licences (ATOLs) issued by the Civil Aviation Authority. Each tour operator requires an ATOL when it buys airline seats that are then resold to passengers either as part of an inclusive tour or in some other form. The scrutiny associated with the issuing of such licences and subsequent monitoring is intended to reduce the likelihood of financial collapse and to ensure that where such collapse does occur, the holidaymaker is protected from financial loss. In September 1986, the total licensed turnover of ATOL holders was £2,911 million and the total number of return seats was nearly 12 million. Using ATOL statistics, Table 16.4 shows the level of concentration in the industry.

In the first half of the 1980s concentration remained fairly static, but it jumped substantially in 1986. According to the Monopolies and Mergers Commission (HMSO, 1986), British Airways, Horizon and

Table 16.4 *Concentration in the Foreign Holiday Package Market*

Year (at 5 April)	% of total market			Total number
	Top 5	Top 10	Top 30	
1981	34	48	72	6,662
1982	38	52	73	7,067
1983	38	52	69	7,938
1984	34	46	68	8,624
1985	37	49	70	8,647
1986	48	60	n/a	9,844

Note: The figures relate to bonded or *authorized* holidays. Such figures do not conform precisely to holidays *taken*, but the correspondence is likely to be very close.
Source: HMSO, 1986, p. 10; and Civil Aviation Authority.

Thomson have remained in the top five since 1976 and of those Thomson (part of a Canadian group) has consistently remained the market leader. Intasun came from the ninth largest in 1976 to the second largest in 1985. Cosmos on the other hand was second in the late 1970s but was seventh in 1985. There is thus clearly some movement in the ranking of the largest firms. These firms are surrounded by a substantial number of smaller operators who inevitably provide some competitive constraint on the leaders.

Tour operators vary considerably in the types of product they offer. The larger companies tend to offer a range of tours from general holidays to those which cater for specialist activities and interests. The latter type of holiday has grown substantially in relative importance in recent years. Such market 'segmentation' has in fact been an important source of growth for the bigger operators. The smaller companies usually specialize in terms of activity and area.

Economies of scale do exist in the buying of transport and accommodation, but these economies can be achieved at sufficiently low levels for the smaller specialists to be competitive. Some tour operators have expanded by vertical integration. For example, both Thomson and Intasun own their own airlines (Britannia and Air Europe respectively). Both also engage in direct selling, thereby performing a travel agency function. Some airlines have integrated forwards to offer their own package tours – such integration enables the airlines better to protect their own passenger demand – while some travel agents have integrated backwards into tour operation.

The main requirement for entry into airborne foreign packages is the financial resources required to obtain an ATOL and to commence operations. Those operators using other forms of transport must, if they are members of the Association of British Travel Agents (ABTA) (see Section 16.2.4) take out a bond to cover their customers in the event of loss. (The British Coach Council, 120 members of which offer package tours, and the Passenger Shipping Association, which has 35 package operators, offer a *voluntary* bonding scheme.) The tour operator does not of course have to undertake the hotel and transport investment its operations require.

Once the tour operator has contracted for accommodation and transport – often up to a year ahead – it cannot escape the payments to which it is committed, no matter what level of utilization it is in fact able to obtain. If it cannot fill the contracted capacity at the prices it has planned, it will have an incentive to start discounting in order to obtain at least some contribution to its contractual commitments, even though it may not cover them. Accommodation and transport charges – which account for 60–70 per cent of total costs (Burkart and Medlik, 1981, p. 73) – therefore represent a fixed capacity cost similar to that faced by transport and hotel operators (see Section 16.2.2 below).

It must be remembered that new operating firms – whether crossing over from another industry or entirely new – are not the only form of entry which may constrain the activities of incumbent firms. Self-supply is always an option. Such supply will occur where the customer perceives that the difference in price that he would have to pay to organize the trip independently is less than the transactions costs involved in such organization.

16.2.2 Hotels

As Table 16.5 shows licensed hotels account for only 14 per cent of the total nights spent by British residents in Britain. (The picture for accommodation for *UK* tourists *in the UK* is likely to be similar to that given in Table 16.5). The proportion of nights and expenditure spent by tourists from overseas in hotels is almost certainly considerably higher, but even when allowance is made for the latter, it is unlikely to alter the overall accommodation picture of the availability of a very considerable range of (generally cheaper) alternatives to hotels, for example, guest houses and self-catering. The availability of these alternatives places some restriction on the pricing freedom of the hotelier, particularly at the cheaper end of the market.

Within the hotel industry itself, the level of concentration is low. Even the largest hotelier, Trusthouse Forte, with 260 hotels (HMSO, 1987, p. 33) has less than 1 per cent of the total number (its share of the number of beds and revenue is probably higher but is still likely to be under 10 per cent). In particular locations however – such as central London and areas of outstanding natural beauty – a hotel may have considerable market power, especially where planning restrictions and other considerations inhibit further development.

The larger hotels are able to achieve some economies in marketing, purchasing and operations, although many of these advantages may be obtained by an independent hotel if it joins a consortium arrangement

Table 16.5 *Accommodation for British Tourists in Britain, 1985*

	% of total number of nights	% of total expenditure
Licensed hotel	14	38
Unlicensed hotel/guest house	5	6
With friend or relative	42	23
Camping/caravanning	19	14
Other	20	19
Total	100	100
Nights (million)	500	
Spending (£ million)		6,325

Source: British Tourism Survey 1985 (British Tourist Authority/English Tourist Board), p. 10.

such as Best Western. Furthermore, as far as the provision of accommodation itself is concerned, the advantages of size are very limited, as evidenced by the co-existence side by side of hotels of very different sizes. Where, however, the larger hotels may obtain an advantage is in respect of the provision of specialist on-site facilities, such as swimming pools. Even here, the smaller hotel may overcome its disadvantage by allowing non-residents – possibly from neighbouring hotels – to use its facilities. According to Burkart and Medlik (1981, p. 149) about 50 per cent of the total costs of normal working and sometimes considerably more are necessary to make the facilities available at all, irrespective of the volume of business. The presence of high fixed costs may sometimes lead the hotelier to offer some of his rooms at prices significantly below their average total costs, but above their average variable costs, if such a strategy would generate a higher contribution to fixed costs than would otherwise be the case.

Entry is relatively easy, although a major hurdle especially in city centres may be the availability of land and planning consent.

16.2.3 Transportation

The two key areas here are air and sea transport.

Air
Domestic scheduled air transport has already been considered in Chapter 13. Many of the economic issues associated with the operation of international scheduled and charter operations are also present with domestic scheduled services and need not be rehearsed again here.

Of the total seat-kilometres available, two airlines on international scheduled routes account for 95 per cent of the total: British Airways

(79 per cent) and British Caledonian (16 per cent). These routes are of course highly regulated; new entry may only occur following bilateral agreement between the governments concerned. While there has been some relaxation of regulation on certain European routes in recent years – most notably to the Netherlands – most are still closed to new entry and even on the routes which have been liberalized, many of the cheaper fares remain subject to considerable restriction. On the North Atlantic, a number of low-cost airlines have entered in recent years but many have had to pull out because of financial problems.

In the non-scheduled inclusive tour market, there is rather less concentration with the six largest accounting for 87 per cent of the total seat-kilometres available. The biggest with 30 per cent of the market is Britannia Airways, a subsidiary of Thomson. (These companies are now becoming increasingly involved in international scheduled operations.) A number of scheduled operators also provide charter services on a small scale and are likely to act as a constraint on the leading airlines. The Civil Aviation Authority has adopted a much more relaxed attitude towards the licensing of charter operations so that provided an airline can meet the financial and technical requirements, it will be licensed. Load factors are nearly 40 per cent higher in inclusive tour operations than in domestic operations, reflecting the lower (negative) elasticity of demand with respect to such factors among holidaymakers than among business travellers.

Sea transport

The short sea crossings to Belgium, the Netherlands and France which take the bulk of Continental traffic[4] are dominated by European Ferries which carries over half of the passengers and cars on these routes (HMSO, 1986, p. 8). During the 1970s there was substantial competition from other services, notably the hovercraft, and a number of operators opened up new routes. (Between 1970 and 1981, for example, 32 new Anglo-Continental routes were opened although P & O was the only operator to commence services on the short sea crossings.) Although competition has increased, geographical accessibility, higher frequency (and hence lower unit costs) and shorter length of time at sea, still give the short sea crossings some market advantages, which is reflected in the often relatively higher profits of the operators involved on these crossings (HMSO, 1981, p. 53), and in the higher exit rate of operators on *other* routes, notably the North Sea.

Ship operating costs represent about 60 per cent of the total cost of running a ferry. The most significant items of ship operating costs are crew, fuel, capital charges, maintenance and insurance. These costs do not vary significantly with the number of passengers on any given ship. Nor do they rise proportionately with the size of ship, reflecting the existence of economies of increased dimensions. Harbour dues, management, marketing and publicity also do not rise proportionately.

It is the existence of these economies that has led to the development of ever larger ferries. A further 5–15 per cent of ferry costs are accounted for by harbour charges.

Entry may be impeded by a number of factors. It may be difficult for a new entrant to secure sailing times at a busy port that do not place it in a commercially disadvantageous position *vis-à-vis* established operators. Suitable times may be particularly difficult to secure where the established operator owns the port in question. The problems may be further compounded where the frequency of service is already high and where, as a result, commercially viable entry requires the newcomer to enter with more than one ship. (When P & O entered the Dover–Boulogne route in 1976 it was initially able to secure a 'slot' for only one ship at Dover even though it required another ship to compete effectively.)

In 1981, the Monopolies and Mergers Commission reported (HMSO, 1981) on a proposed merger between European Ferries and Sealink (British Ferries). Although the previous decade had seen an increase in new routes to the Continent, the commission took the view that the merger would be against the public interest, because it would lead to a major reduction in competition, particularly on the short sea routes whose geographical and commercial advantages give them some protection from rivals. The commission also considered that a merger would increase the companies' influence over the access of potential entrants to the ports.

16.2.4 Travel Agency

The vast majority (over 90 per cent) of travel agents are members of ABTA. At the end of 1986, there were 2,806 such members with 3,657 branch offices. In addition, there were 544 tour operators in membership.[5] In recent years there has been a growth – through openings and acquisitions – in large agency chains: between 1981 and 1986 the number of agencies with over 100 branches grew from two to six (largely at the expense of the medium-size multiples). Thomas Cook, Pickfords and Hogg Robinson, the market leaders, have together over 900 outlets (compared with under 600 in 1984). At the same time the number of agencies has grown rapidly. There are no figures available on market concentration, but the Monopolies and Mergers Commission estimated (HMSO, 1986, p. 11) that the five largest travel agents sold around 25 per cent of foreign package holidays[6] in 1985 and operated around 20 per cent of all ABTA and tour operator outlets.

Whether or not extensive economies of scale exist in travel agency is rather unclear. There is some scope for economies in computerized accountancy, advertising and other centralized services, but the larger operations may suffer a staffing cost disadvantage (HMSO, 1986, p. 12).

The travel agency, like the tour operator, provides an intermediary role. Apart from the costs of setting up in business and becoming known it is an activity that is relatively easy to enter, in that there are few legal or 'artificial' restrictions on entry. Furthermore, incumbent firms always face the possibility that their role may be taken over by the customer and/or the producer of the travel, accommodation or tour. (Over a quarter of all foreign package holidays are sold by tour operators either directly or through agencies they own.)

16.3   ASPECTS OF MARKET BEHAVIOUR

16.3.1   Pricing

Demand in many parts of the tourism industry is characterized by considerable fluctuations over time. Seasonal fluctuations are particularly marked in holiday tourism (Section 16.1.5). Substantial variations also occur on a weekly or even daily basis in some sectors. Business demand for hotel rooms is much higher on weekdays than at weekends. And cross-channel routes experience far greater levels of demand for sailings during the day than at night. Costs may also vary across time periods.

Faced with these variations, it usually pays the profit maximizing firm to charge different prices in each time period to reflect the differences in marginal revenues and costs. Such differential pricing – which is only possible because the output is non-storable – will typically, though not invariably, lead to lower prices in off-peak periods, thereby ensuring fuller utilization of capacity than would otherwise occur. If it diverts traffic away from the peak, then the total capacity employed can also be reduced. However, only if a precise knowledge of cost and demand schedules is available is it possible to say whether the differences in price amount to price discrimination.

A number of tourism sectors have experienced price wars in recent years. During 1980, following the abandonment of revenue pooling arrangements, extensive price cutting occurred on the cross-channel routes. In 1981–2, Laker's activities on the North Atlantic route led to retaliatory action by the major airlines. Then in 1985, following Thomson's initiative, the major tour operators began an intense price war.

The precise circumstances surrounding the price cutting has varied. Potential or actual new entry – for example, Laker on the North Atlantic, new operators, and indeed the possibility of a fixed link, across the English Channel – may play an important part in stimulating price rivalry, as may unexpected changes in demand. Thomson's efforts on the other hand were in part directed against the rapid market growth of a rival (Intasun) which had (and still has) the reputation for selling a low-priced product. Price cutting may seem a particularly attractive option where short-run marginal costs are low and where excess capacity exists. Section 16.2 showed that several parts of the tourism industry have the former characteristic and that they are unable to adjust capacity very easily. However, such a strategy may ultimately be self-defeating and lower profitability if revenue dilution occurs. Even if such dilution does not occur, a price-cutting strategy may be insufficient to stave off a financial crisis if the excess capacity is too great (several tour operators went into liquidation in the summer of 1987 for this reason). Equilibrium may once again be achieved where entry has been thwarted or accom-modated, and capacity adjusted downwards (or demand increased). Firms may attempt to find stability through agreement – for example, in late 1980 a number of ferry operators sought permission from the Office of Fair Trading to engage in discussions to reach an agreement on certain minimum fares – but such an agreement may fall foul of anti-trust legislation. (The ferry operators' request was turned down.)

In travel agency, the scope for direct price competition at least as far as inclusive tours are concerned has been constrained by a number of factors. In recent years, some travel agents – notably the larger ones – have offered inducements such as 'free' insurance, 'free' transport to the airports, and spending vouchers to customers who purchase tours through them. A few agents have offered reduced brochure prices. Most tour operators have opposed the offering of pecuniary and non-pecuniary inducements, and have included a prohibition clause in their contracts with agents.[7] However, the Monopolies and Mergers Commission (HMSO, 1986) found that tour operators' attempts to impose this prohibition restricted competition among agents and was against the public interest. The commission argued that the restriction was constraining the value and incidence of inducements offered by agents. Interestingly, however, the commission took the view that agents should not be permitted to offer a direct *discount* on the brochure price (because of the legal nature of the relationship between the principal, that is, the operator, and his agent) even though they should be allowed to provide cash *inducements*. The Monopolies and Mergers Commission's recommendation was given statutory backing in July 1987 (*Financial Times*, 10 July, 1987). The rationale for such a distinction appears to be legal rather than economic.

It might be argued that a more widespread use of inducements by travel agents would put pressure on tour operators to offer larger commissions (normally around 10 per cent) so that the agents' own margins did not suffer. However, travel agents were already free to compete on the quality of their service (including location); there is no reason to think that one dimension of competition should put any greater pressure on the commission terms than any other. The new freedom of travel agents does however widen the choice of competitive strategies open to them.

16.3.2 Exclusive Dealing: the Case of ABTA

ABTA travel agents may not sell any foreign package holiday not organized by an ABTA member. Furthermore ABTA tour operators may not sell their holidays other than through an ABTA travel agent. The agreement, known curiously as the Stabilizer, was defended in the Restrictive Practices Court in 1982 as being necessary to protect the public financially. The court accepted this defence, arguing that even if the risk of failure amongst ABTA members was no higher than elsewhere, 'the nature of the failure when it occurs and the repercussions that flow from it are unusual and call for an unusual degree of protection for the consumer' (*Industrial Court Reports*, 1985, p. 28). Certainly there was a considerable public outcry following the series of business collapses in 1974. However it is not at all clear why, if financial protection of a given minimum standard for consumers is considered necessary, it should be enforced through an exclusive dealing arrangement of a trade association, rather than through statutory provisions.

16.3.3 Segmentation, Diversification and Innovation

In recent years a number of tour operators, particularly the larger ones, have followed a strategy of market segmentation, producing (for example) separate brochures for particular destinations and/or age groups. Such a strategy in part reflects the saturation of the market for 'general' holidays and the growing sophistication of consumer tastes. In both cases the large company is able to obtain the benefits of a specialist image, while retaining any advantages of scale. Such a combination puts smaller independent specialists under increased market pressure. The trend towards market segmentation is also apparent in the hotel industry.

Alongside such segmentation, and in part a cause of it, has been the development of a number of commercial innovations. Two key innovations in tour operation over the last decade or so have been the development of inclusive camping holidays (in which the tour operator supplies a ready erected tent on a site) and of holidays for the older generations. Independent specialist companies (Eurocamp and Saga respectively) played a major role in both innovations, although a considerable number of larger companies are now offering these types of holidays. Unlike innovations in manufacturing, where patents and industrial secrecy may provide some protection for the innovator's market position, new developments in tourism are not so easily protected in the market place, except through the development and maintenance of a strong brand image and the ability to keep a step ahead of rivals in further development.

The development of new types of tourist attraction – such as theme parks and garden festivals – may generate costs and benefits that do not enter into the accounts of the attraction itself. There may therefore sometimes be a case for public assistance. However if such assistance is provided through (uncoordinated) local channels, it may lead to overprovision. Public assistance in tourism is considered in Section 16.5.

Unfortunately, virtually all the research on innovation in the UK has been undertaken in manufacturing. Key questions on tourism innovation, such as those relating to the optimal conditions for its generation and diffusion, and to the role of public finance and support, thus remain unanswered.

16.4 PERFORMANCE

Relative to GDP and consumer spending, expenditure by domestic and overseas residents on tourism in the UK grew more slowly in real terms between 1974 and 1986: the data in Table 16.2 suggest a growth rate of around 15 per cent – whereas the growth of GDP and consumer spending was 20.2 and 26.5 respectively. The industry did of course go through extensive fluctuations over the period. However employment in tourism-related industries grew relatively fast (see Section 16.1.3; total employment in Britain hardly rose at all between 1982 and 1986, the period covered in Table 16.3). These figures show that care must be taken before granting the tourism industry the accolade of 'the fastest growing industry'.

Some measure of the overall performance of the UK tourist industry in terms of its 'market' share of world tourism may be gauged from Table 16.6. This table must be treated very cautiously: definitions of the relevant tourism flows often differ significantly from country to country, and even where they are consistent, methods of statistical collection may vary. Furthermore domestic tourism is excluded from the calculations. Nevertheless the data do provide some albeit rough guide to the relative position of the UK. In the 1980s, there may have been a slight increase in the UK's share of arrivals, but the 'high' of 1976–78 has not been repeated. The gain in the 1980s reflects the rise in UK price competitiveness (see Section 16.1.2), a rise which resulted from factors largely outside the direct control of the tourist industry itself.

It is difficult to reach any firm conclusions on the profitability of the tourism industry, because comprehensive data are not published. Many of the larger companies have interests outside tourism – for example, P & O, which owns North Sea Ferries and European Ferries, is also engaged in freight shipping and housebuilding – and it is difficult to exclude these non-relevant activities from published accounts. And of course the self-employed do not have to disclose their results. However, it is known that a number of sectors of the UK

Table 16.6   *The UK and World Tourism*

Year	(1) International tourist arrivals: all countries (thousands)	(2) Visits to UK by overseas residents (thousands)	(3) UK share: $\dfrac{(2)}{(1)} \times 100$
1975	214,357	9,490	4.4
1976	220,719	10,808	4.9
1977	239,122	12,281	5.1
1978	257,366	12,646	4.9
1979	273,999	12,486	4.6
1980	284,841	12,421	4.4
1981	288,848	11,452	4.0
1982	286,958	11,636	4.1
1983	293,944	12,464	4.2
1984	315,359	13,644	4.3
1985	332,991[a]		

Note: [a] estimate.

Sources: Compendium of Tourism Statistics, 1986 (World Tourism Organisation: Madrid), p. 154. Business Monitor MQ6 *Overseas Travel and Tourism* Fourth Quarter, 1986 (HMSO: London).

tourism industry show low profitability, in part as a result of intense competition. For example, in the first half of the 1980s, net profits as a percentage of turnover for the biggest 30 ATOL holders averaged only 3.7. A low level of profitability for foreign package holiday operators was also reported in the study by the Monopolies and Mergers Commission (HMSO, 1986, p. 19), which found net margins of less than 1 per cent in the sample of companies they examined. In travel agency the Monopolies and Mergers Commission found that in the early 1980s small travel agents were trading with very low or negative profitability (HMSO, 1986, pp. 21–2). The larger travel agencies were however doing very much better and were experiencing substantial increases in profits. It is also the case that some of the larger hotel groups have very satisfactory levels of profit. For example, Trusthouse Forte, the leading hotel group, has sometimes achieved a rate of return significantly above that for all industries.

Relatively high profits may be a reflection of superior efficiency and/or of market power derived, for example, from substantial entry barriers. Although there may be some sectors of the industry where the latter explanation is more appropriate – for example, a hotel may have a key location which is protected by planning restrictions – it is more likely, given the structure of much of the industry (see Section 16.2), that the former will be valid.

16.5 GOVERNMENT SUPPORT FOR TOURISM

The present pattern of government involvement in tourism may be traced back to the Development of Tourism Act 1969.[8] This Act set up the British Tourist Authority (BTA) with the responsibility to promote tourism to Britain from overseas, to advise the government on tourism matters affecting Britain as a whole and to encourage the provision and improvement of tourist amenities and facilities in Britain. In practice most of the BTA's efforts have gone into overseas promotion of Britain. The 1969 Act also set up three statutory domestic promotion agencies: the English, Scottish and Welsh Tourist Boards (ETB, STD and WTB, respectively). A key function of these boards is to administer the provision of financial assistance for tourism projects under Section 4 of the Act. This section, which is applicable to all types of tourism projects (including, for example, hotels, leisure amenities and information facilities), provides for grants, loans and interest relief grants, although most assistance is in the form of grants. Between 1983 and 1986, total investment in assisted projects under this section was £250 million, of which £34 million was given in assistance.[9]

About 57 per cent of the BTA's income of £30 million in 1985/6 came from government grant-in-aid. The comparable percentage of the ETB's income of 20.3 million was 83 per cent. This latter percentage includes government funds for tourism projects. Tourism promotion is thus substantially publicly financed.

Responsibility for the BTA and the ETB lie with the Secretary of State for Employment, while the STB and the WTB are answerable to the Secretaries of State for Scotland and Wales respectively. This has meant that the funding mechanism for the different tourist boards has varied. The Secretaries of State for Wales and Scotland have very considerable discretion on how much to spend on tourism once their block budget has been allocated whereas the Secretary of State for Employment has to agree his budget with the Treasury on a programme basis. The Trade and Industry Committee of the House of Commons has pointed out (HMSO, 1985a, p. xviii) that these different financial arrangements for allocating funds have led to substantial variations in the amount spent (relative to the size of the industry) in different parts of the UK. For example the committee estimated that in 1984/5, Scotland spent, relative to tourism turnover, over four times the amount spent in England on Section 4 assistance. (For Wales, it was over three times.) There may be an underlying rationale for such differences – for example, both Scotland and Wales may have to counteract a 'distance' disadvantage when promoting tourism outside their boundaries – but, if such a rationale exists, it should at least be explicit and be evaluated in some way.

The ETB has set up 12 non-statutory regional boards which undertake a number of the ETB's functions on its behalf. These regional boards are financed from a variety of sources: about 21 per cent of their income comes from the ETB, the rest coming from local authorities (14 per cent), commercial membership (15 per cent) and other sources (50 per cent). (ETB, *Annual Report and Accounts, 1985–6*.)

The activities of the BTA and the tourist boards raise at least two questions. First, why is government promotion of British tourism overseas necessary? There are almost certainly economies of scale in promotion and a single body might therefore be justified, but this is not necessarily an argument for a *public* body; the existence of economies of scale may not of itself provide any bar to commercial provision. A more attractive justification derives from the argument that potential visitors are likely to base their decisions on whether or not to visit Britain in terms more of the country's overall attactive-ness – including its weather and natural beauty – rather than on the promotion of individual facilities. If this is the case, then there is a strong incentive for individual tourism-providing firms to 'free-ride' and thus to generate a sub-optimal allocation of funds to promotion. Such arguments may however be used to justify virtually any level of public funding. It is therefore important that the expenditure of bodies such as the BTA should be subject to constant rigorous assessment. Publicly financed promotion of tourism through the tourist boards may to some extent be justified on grounds similar to those that might be used in respect of the BTA. However, the activities of these boards raise the question of the extent to which they increase total demand for tourism in the UK (by home and overseas residents), and the extent to which they simply compete against each other for a given level of demand, and thereby engage in promotion which is self-cancelling.

Second, what is the underlying rationale for Section 4 assistance? The tourist boards emphasize the importance of ensuring that Section 4 assistance is not given where funds would otherwise be provided, that is, that the principle of additionality is adhered to. Quite apart from the issue of how assessments of additionality can be made in particular applications – at least one study of grant assistance (Archer and Shea, 1980, p. 95) has raised some doubts about the extent to which tourist board grants are truly additional – this principle raises the fundamental question of why, if a project would not be able to go ahead without public assistance, it should do so *with* it. There may be two main reasons: capital for a commercially viable project may be unobtainable because of imperfections in the capital market; and there may be external benefits which do not appear in the private return, but which if taken into account would make a commercially non-viable project socially worthwhile. The validity of the first of these arguments has not been demonstrated in any rigorous form; the second argument, like that used to support the BTA's activities, is rather open-ended and needs to be applied precisely in each case of Section 4 assistance. It must be said too that such assistance may not necesarily be the most appropriate way of meeting (where it exists) the kind of market failure discussed above.

A more general argument that has sometimes been used to justify public support for tourism is the job generating role of the industry, particularly among the young and in depressed regions (Manpower Services Commission, 1986). Public finance may be used to stimulate employment through demand promotion and/or measures to increase the industry's competitiveness in supply. Promotion of tourism may indeed increase demand, but its effect relative to that of more fundamental factors such as exchange rates and real incomes, not only in the UK but throughout the world, is likely to be marginal. On the supply side, it should be noted that measures may sometimes *reduce* employment, by encouraging labour saving innovation.

Any assessment of the employment effects of policy in this area faces two key problems. The first relates to the estimate of what employment would have been in the absence of policy in the firms that are the *direct* beneficiaries of policy, that is, what employment additionality there is. The second concerns the effects of the policy on employment in firms *other than the beneficiary firms*. These effects may be worked out through the demand for inputs, the employment multiplier[10] and competitive displacement. The ultimate impact may be positive or negative. It is clear therefore that an examination of actual employment in beneficiary firms is very unlikely to provide a guide to net employment generation.

16.6 CONCLUSION

The tourism industry in the UK is likely to continue growing, albeit erratically, in the foreseeable future. (Some idea of the untapped potential demand may be gained from the fact that 40 per cent of British people do not yet take a holiday of four nights or more.) However, this growth is likely to be subject to a wide range of political, social and economic influences, many of which are outside the direct control of the UK. Such influences generate uncertainty and volatility and put many of the firms involved in the industry in a vulnerable position. Any assessment of the industry's record and potential and public policy towards it, should be seen in that context.

NOTES TO CHAPTER 16

1 Day excursionists are included in the figures.
2 The relevant industries have been defined as Transport and Communication (Division 7) *less* Road Haulage, Miscellaneous Transport and Storage, Postal Services and Telecommunications. Even this definition is too wide. For example, much sea transport which is included as a relevant industry is

concerned with freight. Unfortunately there is no way in which appropriate adjustments can be made.

3 It is common to think of air travel as being most affected by innovation. But the pace of development in sea transport has also been dramatic. In 1962, a drive-through ship carrying 850 passengers and 120 cars could be turned round in 1½ hours. The new 26,000 tonne ships brought into service in 1987 can turn round in about the same time while carrying 2,300 passengers and 650 cars. (*The Times*, 3 April 1987, p. 5.)

4 According to the Monopolies and Mergers Commission (HMSO, 1981, p. 27) nearly two-thirds of all tourist vehicle journeys in 1980 between the UK and the near Continent used these routes.

5 Some members of ABTA are both travel agents and tour operators.

6 Such holidays account for about 43 per cent of the total sales of the larger agents and about 55 per cent of the total sales of the smaller agents (HMSO, 1986, p. 11).

7 Up to 1984 such prohibition was included in a standard agency agreement drawn up by ABTA for its members. In that year however it was prohibited by the Restrictive Practices Court in re Association of British Travel Agents Ltd's Agreement: *Industrial Court Reports*, 1984, pp. 12–15.

8 Some form of government support can be traced back to the 1920s. In 1929, the government first provided an annual grant of £5,000 to the Travel Association of Great Britain which for the following 40 years was the government's main vehicle for promoting travel to and within the UK: HMSO, 1985a, p. xvii.

9 Taken from the *Government's Expenditure Plans 1987–8 to 1989–90* HM Treasury, Cm 56-II, January 1987, p. 114.

10 For a discussion of multipliers in tourism, see Archer, 1977.

REFERENCES

Archer, B. H. (1977), '*Tourism Multipliers: the State of the Art*, Bangor Occasional Papers in Economics, no. 11 (Cardiff: University of Wales Press).

Archer, B. H., and Shea, S. (1980), *Grant Assisted Tourism Projects in Wales: an Evaluation* (Cardiff: Wales Tourist Board).

British Tourist Authority (1984) *Econometric Modelling of Tourist Visits to the UK*, Final Report (London: British Tourist Authority).

Burkart, A. J. (1980), 'Tourism' in P. S. Johnson (ed.) *The Structure of British Industry* (St Albans, Herts: Granada), pp. 362–3.

Burkart, A. J., and Medlik, S. (1981), *Tourism: Past, Present and Future*, 2nd edn (London: Heinemann).

Edwards, A. (1976), *International Tourism Development Forecasts to 1985* (London: Economist Intelligence Unit).

HMSO (1981), *European Ferries Ltd. Sealink Ltd*, A Report by the Monopolies and Mergers Commission, HC 68 (session 1981–2), (London).

HMSO (1985a), *Tourism in the UK. Vol. I: Report and Proceedings of the Committee*, Trade and Industry Committee, HC 106–1 (session 1985–6 (London).

HMSO (1985b), *Tourism in the UK. Vol. II: Minutes of Evidence and*

Appendices, Trade and Industry Committee, HC 106-11 (session 1985–6) (London).
HMSO (1986), *Foreign Package Holidays*, A Report by the Monopolies and Mergers Commission, Cmnd 9879 (London).
HMSO (1987), *Trusthouse Forte PLC and Enterprises Belonging to Hanson Trust PLC*, A Report by the Monopolies and Mergers Commission, Cm 96 (London).
Manpower Services Commission (1986), *Tourism in North East England: A Context Statement*, MSC, Northern Regional Office, mimeo.
Mishan, E. J. (1967), *The Costs of Economic Growth* (London: Staples).
Phlips, L. (1983), *The Economics of Price Discrimination* (Cambridge: Cambridge University Press).
Swinglehurst, E. (1982), *Cook's Tours. The Story of Popular Travel* (Poole, Dorset: Blandford).
Thomas, D. E. L. (1986), 'Tourism in the UK: an industry riding on the exchange rate', *Service Industries Journal*, 6, 3, 398–416.
Witt, S. F., and Martin, C. A. (1985), 'Forecasting future trends in European tourist demand', *Tourist Review*, 4, 12–19.

FURTHER READING

The key statistical publications for international flows of tourists is the Business Monitor: *Overseas Travel and Tourism*, which is published both quarterly (MQ6) and annually (MA6). For domestic tourism, an important summary statistical publication is the *British Tourism Market*, produced by the ETB, jointly with the BTA and WTB. The *Digest of Tourism Statistics*, published periodically provides data on a wide range of tourism topics and also contains extracts from BTA surveys. A useful, but now rather dated survey of tourism statistics is Lewes, F. M. M., Parker, S. R., and Lickorish, L. J. (1974), *Leisure and Tourism (Reviews of UK Statistical Sources, IV)* (London: Heinemann).

A good recent review of policy issues associated with tourism may be found in the Trade and Industry Committee's report on *Tourism in the UK*, HC 106, session 1985–6 (London: HMSO).

Surprisingly, relatively little academic work has been undertaken on the tourism industry, but readers might consult the following.

Archer, B. H. (1977), *Demand Forecasting in Tourism*, Bangor Occasional Papers in Economics no. 9 (Cardiff: University of Wales Press).
Archer, B. H. (1977), *Tourism Multipliers: the State of the Art*, Occasional Papers in Economics no. 11 (Cardiff: University of Wales Press).
Burkart, A. J., and Medlik, S. (1981), *Tourism: Past, Present and Future* (London: Heinemann).
Medlik, S. (1978), *Profile of the Hotel and Catering Industry* (London: Heinemann).
Organization for Economic Co-operation and Development (annual), *Tourism Policy and International Tourism in OECD Member Countries* (Paris: OECD).

Notes on the Contributors

Bob Carter is Norwich Union Professor of Insurance Studies in the Department of Industrial Economics, Accountancy and Insurance at the University of Nottingham. His other academic appointments have been at Brighton Polytechnic and the American Graduate School of International Management. His main research interests are in international insurance and reinsurance and risk management. He has acted as a consultant to the European Commission and the Association of British Insurers. He is a Council Member of the Insurance Brokers Registration Council and the Insurance Ombudsman Bureau. Recent publications include *Reinsurance* (2nd edition 1983), *Success in Insurance* (with S. R. Diacon, 1984), *Personal Financial Markets* (with B. Chiplin and M. K. Lewis, 1986).

Anthony Cockerill is Senior Lecturer in Economics at Manchester Business School, University of Manchester. Previously, he has held posts at Cambridge, Leeds, Salford and UMIST. His main research interests are in international differences in industrial structure and performance and he has written widely on the economics of several industries. He has been Economic Adviser to three Parliamentary Select Committees. Recent publications include *Structure and Performance of Industries* (1984), with T. T. Jones, and an edited book (with J. F. Pickering), *The Economic Management of the Firm* (1984).

Stuart Eliot is a Lecturer in Economics in the Department of Management Sciences, University of Manchester Institute of Science and Technology. His current research is concerned with the causes and consequences of retail mergers. He is also economic consultant to the Co-operative Union, the National Federation of the Co-operative Movement in the UK. Research carried out in this capacity includes an evaluation of the factors affecting the viability of small shops, and an analysis of retailing in inner city areas.

Michael Fleming holds a Personal Chair in Economics at Loughborough University. He was educated at Oxford University and has held appointments at the Building Research Establishment and the Queen's University of Belfast. His main research interests are industrial economics and the economics of housing and construction. He is joint editor of the series of monographs sponsored jointly by the Royal Statistical Society and the Economic and Social Research Council entitled *Reviews of United Kingdom Statistical Sources* and is author of two reviews in the series. Recent publications include *Spon's Guide to Housing, Construction and Property Market Statistics* (1986) and *Spon's House Price Data Book* (1987).

Ken Gwilliam is Professor of Transport Economics at the University of Leeds Institute for Transport Studies. His previous appointments were at the University of Nottingham and University of East Anglia. He has acted as Specialist Adviser to the House of Commons Transport Committee on several occasions, most recently in its inquiry into rail finances. He has also been expert adviser to the Director General of Transport for EEC. For 5 years he was a Director of the National Bus Company. He was researched widely in transport economics and his publications include a major study *Comparative Performance of European Rail Systems*.

Peter Johnson is a Senior Lecturer in the Department of Economics, Durham University. His previous appointments were at the University of Nottingham and University College, Cardiff. His research is concerned with the employment implications of tourism and the economic analysis of new and small firms. He has acted as an academic consultant to the Manpower Services Commission and the Economic and Social Research Council in the latter field. He has also served as a council member of the Small Business Research Trust. Recent publications include *British Industry: An Economic Introduction* (1985) and *New Firms: an Economic Perspective* (1986).

Danny Hann is now an economist with the CEGB. Previously he was Shell Research Fellow in the Energy Economics Centre at the University of Surrey where he obtained an MSc in economics and a PhD in energy sea oil, the development of government energy policies and the economics of politics and bureaucracies. Recent publications include *Government and North Sea Oil* (1986) and, with Chris Rowland, *The Economics of North Sea Oil Taxation* (1987).

Brian Hill is a Senior Lecturer in the Department of Economics, Nottingham University. His main teaching and research interests are in agricultural economics. In this field he has acted as consultant to the United Nations Food and Agriculture Organisation, the Agricultural Economic Development Committee of the National Economic Development Office and the Open University. He is author of three books, various journal articles, and has participated in several broadcast discussions of agricultural matters.

Peter Maunder is a Senior Lecturer in the Department of Economics at Loughborough University. As a trained teacher who taught in a school before reading for a higher degree, he is much involved in economics education and examining. He is General Editor of *Economics*, Journal of the Economics Association, and has both written and edited a number of occasional papers for Heinemann, *Government Intervention in the Developed Economy* (1979), *The British Economy in the 1970s* (1980) and is joint author of *Economics Explained* (1987). He is Joint Chief Examiner of Advanced Level Economics for the University of London Schools Examination Board.

Ivy Papps is a Lecturer in the Department of Economics, Durham University. Her previous appointments were at the University of Sussex and Chicago State University. Her main research interests lie in the economics of the public sector and she is currently concerned with the economic analysis of pollution control policies within the EC and with the economics of educational policy. Recent publications include articles in the *Scottish Journal of Political Economy* (1985) and *Land Economics* (1987) as well as contributions to edited volumes.

Duncan Reekie is E. P. Bradlow Professor of Business Economics at the University of the Witwatersrand, Johannesburg. He was previously Lecturer and subsequently Reader in Business Economics at the University of Edinburgh. He is a specialist in the economics of industrial organization and has written several books on the pharmaceutical industry and on advertising. He has also written numerous articles for a wide range of academic journals. He is the founder and editor of *Managerial and Decision Economics*. He was a member of the UK Government National Economic Development Committee for Pharmaceuticals and more recently was Research Associate at the Technical Change Centre, London.

Garel Rhys holds the Society of Motor Manufacturers and Traders (SMMT) Chair in Motor Industry Economics in the Department of Economics, University College, Cardiff. This post reflects his main research interest, which began with a postgraduate study of the British Commercial Vehicle industry undertaken at the University of Birmingham. His initial academic appointment was at the University of Hull. He has acted as economic adviser to various Select Committees of both Houses of the UK Parliament, but mainly to the Trade and Industry Committee of the House of Commons. He has been consultant and adviser to other official bodies, including some concerned with aspects of the Welsh economy. He has written widely on the economics of the motor industry.

Colin Robinson worked for 11 years as an economist in industry, most of the time in one of the major oil companies. Since 1968, he has been Professor of Economics and Head of the Department of Economics at the University of Surrey. He has written a book and several papers about business forecasting, but most of his writings have been about energy economics, with an emphasis on policy issues. Recent books and long articles (sole or jointly-authored) deal with North Sea oil, oil self-sufficiency, the economics of energy self-sufficiency, gas privatization and policy towards the British coal industry; he has given evidence to Commons and Lords committees on a variety of energy policy matters; and he acts as consultant to a number of companies in the energy and other natural resource industries. He is a member of the Electricity Supply Research Council and the Secretary of State for Energy's Advisory Council on Research and Development in fuel and power (ACCORD).

Richard Shaw is Principal of Paisley College of Technology. His previous appointments include Professor of Economics and Management at the College, Senior Lecturer and Head of Department of Economics at Stirling University, and Lecturer at Leeds University. His main research interests are the economics of competition policy and the processes of competition. Publications include *Industry and Competition* (1976), with C. J. Sutton, as well as numerous articles in professional journals.

Paul Simpson is a Lecturer in Economics and Management in the Department of Textiles, UMIST. He was previously Research Fellow at the University of Stirling. His main research interest is in the area of industrial/managerial economics and he is particularly concerned with public policy towards industry. His publications include *World Textile Trade and Production Trends* (1987).

Paul Stoneman is currently Reader in Economics at Warwick University. His previous appointments include a period spent as a Visiting Professor at

Stanford University. His main research interests are in the area of the economics of technological change and technology policy. He has acted as a consultant to the OECD, has worked with the Advisory Council on Science and Technology on policy issues and has been a member of the Economic Affairs Committee of the ESRC. He is also currently an ESRC Research Fellow acting as Co-ordinator of an ESRC Initiative on New Technologies and the Firm. Recent publications include *The Economic Analysis of Technological Change* (1983) and *The Economic Analysis of Technology Policy* (1987).

Barry Thomas is a Senior Lecturer in the Department of Economics, Durham University. His previous appointments were at the University of Salford and the University of Warwick. His main research interests are in labour economics and the economics of education, and he has recently completed a study of redundancies in the European Coal and Steel Community. He has acted as an academic consultant to the Manpower Services Commission and the European Commission. Recent publications include articles on the Coal and Steel industries, and on performance in education.

Nicholas Wells has been with the Office of Health Economics since 1974, initially as an Economist, then as Senior Economist and currently as Associate Director. He has written a large number of the OHE booklets on contemporary health care issues and regularly contributes papers to non-OHE meetings and publications. His current research interests include the economics of preventive medicine, the problems in forecasting the impact of the AIDS virus, the challenge posed by Britain's ageing population as well as the economics of pharmaceutical innovation.

Index

capacity 287, 288
operating 287–90
regulations 302
traffic 287, 288
Dan Air 283, 291 (Table 13.3), 293, 297
   (Table 13.4)
delays 285
demand 285–7, 298
discount, 'frequent flier' 294
discounts 294
East Midlands 283, 296
economies of scale 289
Edinburgh 283, 287, 293
   – Aberdeen 293
   – Heathrow 284, 286
elasticities 286–7, 295
embarkation fees 287
employment 282
fares 285
fuel 288
Gatwick 283–5 *passim*, 289, 292, 293,
   299–302 *passim*
Genair 290, 292, 298
Glasgow 283, 286, 287, 292, 293
   – Heathrow 284, 295
Guernsey Airlines 291 (Table 13.3) 297
   (Table 13.4)
Heathrow 283, 284, 289, 292, 293,
   297–303 *passim*
inputs 286, 289, 303
interline traffic 284, 294
Inverness 283
Isle of Man 283, 291
licences 293, 296, 300
Liverpool 293, 297
Loganair 291, 296, 297 (Table 13.4)
London-Channel Islands 283
London-Norwich 284
maintenance 289
Manchester 283, 293
Manx Airlines 291, 292, 297 (Table 13.4)
   298
meals/catering 285, 287, 294
mergers 291, 292
Metropolitan Airways 292, 298
Newcastle 293
Norwich 296
output 286, 298
overheads 288
performance 297–8
Plymouth 296
pricing policy 285, 295–6, 298, 301
productivity 286
profitability 298
profits, small airlines 296
provincial routes 283
radar 287

regulation 298–302
runway (slot) allocation 299, 301, 302
safety 286, 298, 300
Scottish internal services 284
Servisair 289
shuttle service 283, 293
Stansted 283, 296
structure, industry 290–4
Teesside 293
training, crew 287
trunk routes 283, 292, 293, 297
UK airlines 282
Air Transport Licensing Authority 300
Allied Farm Foods 194
Amalgamated Society of Locomotive
   Engineers and Firemen (ASLEF) 262
ANIC 133
Asda 240, 242, 246
Associated British Foods (ABF) 194, 196,
   199
Association of British Insurers 317, 371
Association of British Travel Agents
   (ABTA) 367, 374
Association of the British Pharmaceutical
   Industry 97, 103
Audit Commission 274
Australia and coal conversion 63

B & Q 243
Barclays Bank 320
Barratt Developments 217
Baxters 195
Bayer 123
Beeching, Dr Richard 266
Belgium 123 (Table 6.3) 137, 370
Berisford, S & W 207–8
Best Western Hotels 368–9
Bibby Group 194
Bird & Sons, Alfred 197
Birds Eye 196, 200, 207
Boots 240
Bovril 192, 198
Bowyers 195
Brand & Co. 193–4
Brazil 71
Britannia Airways 367, 370
British Airports Authority (BAA) 303,
   304
British Airways (BA) *see* Air Transport,
   Domestic
British American Tobacco Co (BAT) 194
British Celanese 119
British & Commonwealth Shipping Co 291
British Coach Council 367–8
British Constructional Steelwork
   Association 232
British Enkalon 122, 124, 130, 131